READINGS IN ST JOHN'S GOSPEL

READINGS IN
ST JOHN'S GOSPEL

FIRST AND SECOND SERIES

WILLIAM TEMPLE

First published in two volumes 1939, 1940
First issued in St. Martin's Library 1961
Reprinted 1961, 1963
Reprinted in Pocket Papermacs 1968
Reprinted 1970, 1974, 1976, 1978, 1982

Published by
THE MACMILLAN PRESS LTD
London and Basingstoke
Associated companies in Delhi Dublin
Hong Kong Johannesburg Lagos Melbourne
New York Singapore and Tokyo

ISBN 0 333 03148 2

Printed and Bound in Hong Kong

TO
THE MEMORY OF
JOHN LEOFRIC STOCKS

PREFACE TO FIRST SERIES

THE purpose of this book is explained in the Introduction. Here it is only necessary to say that for as long as I can remember I have had more love for St. John's Gospel than for any other book. Bishop Gore once said to me that he paid visits to St. John as to a fascinating foreign country, but he came home to St. Paul. With me the precise opposite is true. St. Paul is the exciting, and also rather bewildering, adventure; with St. John I am at home.

Among commentators my main debt is to Bishop Westcott and Archbishop Bernard; I also owe much to E. F. Scott's *The Fourth Gospel, its Purpose and Theology*; to Bishop Lloyd's *The Life according to St. John*, to Scott Holland's *The Philosophy of Faith and the Fourth Gospel*, and to Canon Raven's *Jesus and the Gospel of Love*. Also at several points I am conscious of expressing thoughts first implanted in my mind by Bishop Palmer when he was Chaplain at Balliol and I was an undergraduate; but I must not put upon him responsibility for what the seeds sown by him have grown to be.

I wish to thank Canon A. E. Baker who has read the proofs and made many valuable suggestions, Miss Joan Hughes, who typed a great part of the manuscript, and especially my wife, who has read most of the typescript and enabled me to make numerous improvements.

WILLIAM EBOR:

BISHOPTHORPE, YORK
December 1938

PREFACE TO SECOND SERIES

THIS Second Series of *Readings in St. John's Gospel* includes all the chapters after that with which the First Series closed. I need not here repeat my expression of indebtedness to commentators and other writers. The same authors have been my chief guides.

For the convenience of those who read this Series without having read the First Series, the Introduction to the whole is reprinted in this volume.

But I must renew my thanks to Canon Baker who has once more read all the proofs, and to my wife who has read the whole in typescript and has helped me with many suggestions for making clearer the movement of thought. I also want to thank Miss Howell-Thomas who typed almost the whole of the manuscript.

WILLIAM EBOR:

BISHOPTHORPE, YORK

October 1939

CONTENTS

ACT V

EPILOGUE

INTRODUCTION

THIS book is not a systematic commentary or exposition; nor is it intended for scholars or theologians — though whatever value it has for souls on pilgrimage may be as real for them as for others. Again, it is not a series of devotional meditations, though it contains some of these. It has no distinctive and consistent character. But it is an attempt to share with any who read it what I find to be my own thoughts as I read the profoundest of all writings.

Consequently it is not chiefly concerned with the question what the writer consciously intended, though of course that question frequently arises; nor again with the question how much of what is here set down has its origin in the deeds and words of the Lord Jesus when on earth, though of that something is said later in this Introduction. I am chiefly concerned with what arises in my mind and spirit as I read; and I hope this is not totally different from saying that I am concerned with what the Holy Spirit says to me through the Gospel.

This is always a legitimate way to read the Bible, and religiously the most important. For the Word of God does not consist of printed propositions; it is living; it is personal; it is Jesus Christ. That living Word of God speaks to us through the printed words of Scripture; and all our study of those printed words helps us to receive it. But the point of vital importance is the utterance of the Divine Word to the soul, the self-communication of the Father to His children. The Fourth Gospel is written with full consciousness of that truth, and so a method, always legitimate and always spiritually valuable, is here almost obligatory. Why this should be so will become clear as we consider the question of authorship and historical reliability so far as it is relevant to these 'readings' to do so.

AUTHORSHIP

It would be quite out of place to discuss in this Introduction the vexed question of the authorship of the Fourth Gospel. The literature of the subject is immense. But it is relevant to set down without argument what my own limited study of the question has led me to believe.

First, I regard as self-condemned any theory which fails to find a very close connexion between the Gospel and John the son of Zebedee. The combination of external and internal evidence is overwhelming on this point. For the external evidence reference may be made to Westcott's classical commentary, and, for the internal evidence, to that and to Scott Holland's brilliant lectures.[1] Scott Holland conclusively proves (as I think) the Apostolic authority of the Gospel. Until recently I held that the balance of evidence was in favour of Westcott's view that John the Apostle actually dictated the book. But the references to John the Elder, as some one distinct from the Apostle, cannot be set aside, and the view which now seems to me to do fullest justice to the evidence is that the writer — the Evangelist — is John the Elder, who was an intimate disciple of John the Apostle; that he records the teaching of that Apostle with great fidelity; that the Apostle is the 'Witness', to whom reference is sometimes made, and is also the 'disciple whom Jesus loved'.

It may be that the Apostle actually dictated to the Elder parts of what now constitutes the Gospel; I incline to think so; but parts are the Elder's own recollection of the Apostle's teaching and parts are his own comment. By adopting this view we can recognise that the author of the First Epistle is also the actual writer of the Fourth Gospel, while also admitting the differences to which Professor Dodd and others have called attention. The Epistles are the work of John the Elder in every sense of the words. They exhibit a smaller vocabulary,

[1] *The Fourth Gospel.*

and in some respects a more crystallised outlook and greater tendency to definition, than the Gospel of which the Elder is the writer but the Apostle is the true author.

It is not possible to say which sections of the Gospel come direct from the Apostle; but I am sure that we are nearer the truth in maximising than in minimising these.

HISTORICAL RELIABILITY

(1) *As regards the Course of Events*

There is a marked contrast between the outline of the Gospel story as recorded by the Synoptists and the outline presented by St. John. The events of the Synoptic narrative, until the Triumphal Entry, take place mainly in Galilee or on the journey from Galilee to Jerusalem; the events of the Johannine narrative take place mainly in Jerusalem. The Synoptic narrative appears to occupy one year only; the Johannine covers three Passovers (ii, 13; v, 1; xii, 1). The dates given for the Last Supper and the Crucifixion are apparently different. These and other such considerations have led many in the past to throw doubt on the reliability of the Fourth Gospel. But closer study leads to a different conclusion. For the fact is that the Synoptists provide no chronology of the ministry at all until the last week; we do not have to choose between two incompatible chronologies, for the Johannine chronology is the only one that we have. Further, the Synoptic narrative is unintelligible unless something like the Johannine story is accepted. How was it possible for the Lord to plan the preparations for the Triumphal Entry and for the Last Supper if He had never been to Jerusalem since boyhood, or had had no opportunity of gaining adherents there? What is meant by the bitter cry over the city 'How often would I have gathered thy children!' (*St. Matthew* xxiii, 37; *St. Luke* xiii, 34) unless there had been missionary enterprises in it on more occasions than one?

Modern commentators mostly accept the Johannine dates for the Last Supper and Crucifixion, on general grounds of probability. The Synoptists retain a recollection of this date in the saying attributed to the Chief Priests, 'Not on the feast day, lest there be an uproar among the people', which harmonises ill with their record of an arrest apparently carried out on the feast day itself.[1] St. John put the arrest earlier, so that the Lord was condemned and crucified on the Day of Preparation, the day on which the Paschal Lamb was killed; and then, of course, the Last Supper was not the actual Passover, but rather a fellowship meal with evident paschal associations.

Moreover it is well to remember that where there is a divergence between the Synoptists and St. John, it is not a case of three witnesses against one; for in this respect St. Mark governs the Synoptic tradition; the first and third Gospels rely on the second for such a framework of order as they display. The divergence then is between the Second Gospel and the Fourth. Now St. Mark wrote his recollection of the teaching and preaching of St. Peter, and the scheme of his Gospel may be represented by saying that it is a narrative of the Passion with an introduction. If we accept this, and also recognise that St. Mark does not even purport to provide a chronological scheme, we must agree that the evidence to be set against the very clear and full chronological scheme provided by St. John is negligible.

We have thus disposed of the main ground for questioning the historical reliability of the Fourth Gospel as a record of events.[2] But it may still be asked how far the author is really concerned with historical facts. He plainly avows his motive in xx, 31. He does not profess to give a complete record; he selects from among abundant material; and he does this with a deliberate purpose: 'these are written that ye may believe

---

[1] But the Synoptists are not explicit as regards the date, and it is possible to interpret them as agreeing with St. John.
[2] About the special problem presented by the Raising of Lazarus something will be said when that point of the narrative is reached. See p. 170.

that Jesus is the Christ, the Son of God, and that believing ye may have life in his name'.

It is no doubt true that St. John selects his chosen events for record because of their significance; but it is essential for his purpose that the significant occasion should also be an event. If the whole story is a myth its quality as revelation is destroyed. The Gospel is that 'the Word was made flesh', and being incarnate so spoke, so acted, so died and so rose from death. It is not the mere occurrence of its several episodes that constitutes the Gospel; it is their spiritual and eternal significance; but part of their spiritual and eternal significance is their physical and temporal occurrence. For it is the whole world, inclusive of matter — of flesh and blood — which God so loved that he gave his only begotten Son.

It is then vital to St. John's purpose that the events which he records should be actual events. We can be quite sure that he never consciously wrote what he did not believe to be fact; he is not a constructor of allegories. And we have already seen reason for thinking that the very points which have led some to doubt his reliability as a witness are in fact grounds for confidence in it. We shall read the Gospel as valid history so far as its record of events is concerned.

(2) *As regards the Discourses*

Can the same confidence be placed in the record of our Lord's discourses, which fills so large a part of the whole Gospel? The answer to that question calls for some preliminary reflections.

(*a*) The discourses recorded in the Synoptic Gospels are mostly such as were delivered to 'the multitudes' or to the local religious leaders in Galilee. Those recorded in the Fourth Gospel are mostly such as were delivered in controversy with the religious leaders in Jerusalem, or in intimate converse with the inner group of the disciples. It is natural that there should be a broad difference alike of subject-matter and of manner.

(*b*) The consideration just mentioned goes far to account for the note of sharper division and even of harshness in the Johannine account — as for example in Chapter VIII. But much depends on the way in which the crucial passages are read. For example, the stern words about the spiritual paternity of 'the Jews' in viii, 31–47 can be, and should be, read in the tone of sad recognition of a fact, not of personal irritation. I see no reason here to doubt that the Lord really spoke very much as is recorded.

(*c*) It is in the light of these considerations that we may meet the complaint that in this Gospel the Lord is presented as self-assertive. Certainly we must admit that if the claims which He here makes are not true they are intolerably arrogant. If He is a very good man completely surrendered to the Spirit of God, He cannot, without offence, speak as the Johannine Christ speaks. But if He is God come in the flesh He not only may, He must proclaim Himself as the fount of salvation. Love, not self-concern, demands that He should call men to Himself as alone the revelation of the Father. At the same time it is appropriate that He should do this either when He is expressly challenged, as the religious leaders at Jerusalem challenged Him, or in conversation with His intimate disciples; and it is precisely in these circumstances that the Fourth Gospel presents Him as making these claims. They are not altogether absent from the Synoptic narrative, but they are naturally less prominent in that record of ministry among the Galilean fisher-folk and peasants.

If, when all is said, any still feel a trace of self-assertion in the sense which involves moral defect, it may be held that the Evangelist has imported into his record of what the Lord said some of his own devoted eagerness. But I find no reason for recourse to such a plea. Those who admit, and wish to proclaim, all that the Lord is here represented as saying about Himself, will feel gratitude, not resentment, that the words are recorded; those who do not admit their truth are bound to resent, or at least to regret, their presence in this profoundly sympathetic presentation of the Lord.

(*d*) What is meant by the question 'Did the Lord say this?' The word 'say' is not so simple as it looks. It may mean the utterance of certain sounds; it may mean the conveyance of certain meanings. If we take it in the former sense no doubt the Synoptists are the more accurate recorders of what they narrate; if we take it in the latter sense I should claim that St. John is the more accurate recorder.

It is commonly found that those sermons which most profoundly stir their hearers are comparatively insipid when read 'in cold print'; and those which are most moving to read were comparatively ineffectual in delivery. The atmosphere of conviction generated by the great preacher is due to his whole personality rather than to the words used, and the sermons for which we are most grateful are those which help us to believe vitally what we knew quite well before the sermon started. My father, who was described by one who knew him as 'granite on fire' and was certainly never regarded as sentimental, could not speak of the love of God without tears. His Good Friday sermons are still stirring to read; but they are not what they were to those who felt, as they listened, the impact of his passionate conviction. The exact record of the words spoken cannot carry that; but a great artist might do much to convey it, and, by re-writing the sermon, give a truer record of it.

Let us take another illustration. A good photograph is vastly preferable to a bad portrait. But the great portrait painter may give a representation of a man which no photographer can emulate. And he does it by drawing what is not at any moment altogether actual. The Synoptists may give us something more like the perfect photograph; St. John gives us the more perfect portrait.

And he does this, as every artist must, by letting his mind and his subject interpenetrate one another and then expressing the result. We are not likely of ourselves to come closer to the

Lord by exercising our coarse faculties upon the more exact
record of words spoken and deeds done than by entering into
communion of thought and feeling with the mind of that
disciple who lay 'breast to breast with God'.

There is a truth of general import which is relevant here.
Christ wrote no book; he left in the world as His witness a
'body' of men and women upon whom His Spirit came. There
was to be nothing stereotyped. The living society — the Church
— was to be the primary witness. The Gospels were written by
members of the Church for their fellow-members, and each is
'The Gospel according to' somebody. What reaches us is never
a certified record but always a personal impression. Thus our
concern is always with the Christ of faith, not with some
supposed different Jesus of history. It is by the faith of others
that our faith is kindled, even when that other is a Synoptic
Evangelist. And this is true to the whole purpose and method
of Christ in His mission. Had it been otherwise, the movement
of the Spirit might have been fettered; but now it is free. Yet
in the wisdom of God there come to us two kinds of personal
impression — both that which is more akin to the photograph
and that which is more akin to the portrait. And each illumi-
nates the other.

(*e*) Because St. John is the portrait-painter, consciously sub-
mitting his mind to be interpenetrated by his subject, and then
giving forth what his mind contains, he is not careful to distinguish between what the Lord historically 'said' and what
that saying has come to mean for him in his lifelong meditation.

> What first were guessed as points, I now knew stars,
>   And named them in the Gospel I have writ.

So speaks St. John in Browning's poem *A Death in the Desert*,
which remains the most penetrating interpretation of St. John
that exists in the English language.

Thus a historical conversation may be coloured by a later
experience, as in iv, 38 where the words 'I sent you to reap that
whereon ye have not laboured' refer rather to later experience

than to a mission already launched at the time of the conversation with the Woman of Samaria. It is important to remember that the convention of historical writing in the ancient
world approved the attribution to leading personages of
speeches expressing what was known to be their view in a
form which is due to the historian. In such compositions
key-phrases actually spoken would naturally be recorded.

We may sometimes feel sure that this saying or that was
uttered by the Lord as it is recorded; but it would be, I think,
a mistake to look for original and authentic utterances as each
the nucleus of a discourse. It is Jesus who speaks — Jesus who
is 'the same yesterday and to-day and for ever' — whether in
the flesh or in the experience of His Beloved Disciple. And
we have to remember that when St. John records a promise
made by our Lord he does so not only because the promise
was made but because it is fulfilled. When St. John records
the words 'I will not leave you desolate; I come to you'
(xiv, 18) their value is not only that this, or something fairly
represented by this, was uttered, but that the thing described
has happened.

This fusion of the purely historical with the spiritual is part
of the character and meaning of this Gospel, which is not
purely historical, nor in the proper sense mystical, but in the
completest possible degree sacramental. Each conversation or
discourse contained in the Gospel actually took place. But it
is so reported as to convey, not only the sounds uttered or the
meaning then apprehended, but the meaning which, always
there, has been disclosed by lifelong meditation. Thus I am
convinced that conversations with Nicodemus and with a
Samaritan woman at Jacob's Well actually occurred, and
followed substantially the course of our record. But the record,
while obviously condensing the original by reducing it to its
own analysis or synopsis, yet presents it in the literary style of
the Evangelist rather than of the Lord. It is worthy of notice,
incidentally, that the conversation with Nicodemus, having
been heard by the Beloved Disciple, has become part of his

own experience, and therefore passes over into comment at a quite uncertain point, whereas the conversation with the Woman of Samaria, of which the Lord Himself must (one supposes) have given the digest to the disciples on their return, appears without any appended comment.

So, to take another illustration, I am sure that the Lord said, as they crossed the Temple Court with the Golden Vine full in view, 'I am the true Vine' (xv, 1). This carries within it, by implication, all that follows. But when later He is recorded as also saying 'Apart from me ye can do nothing' (xv, 5) this is a record as much of the disciples' experience as of the Lord's utterance: but it is the record not only of an empirical impotence, but of a divine assurance, like that which came to St. Paul — 'My grace is sufficient for thee; for my power is made perfect in weakness' (*II Corinthians* xii, 9).

Thus, by the passage of the old remembered words and deeds through the experience, thought and adoring love of the disciple, we are helped to a knowledge of Christ which is not 'after the flesh' but 'after the spirit' (*II Corinthians* v, 16). In the historical life we behold the eternal glory.

We shall read the Gospel, then, in order to enter into the Evangelist's and the Beloved Disciple's communion with the Lord, not asking at each point precisely what was spoken or done, but knowing that as we share the experience, historical and spiritual, from which the Gospel flows we shall come nearer to the heart and mind of Jesus our Lord than ever our own minds could bring us by meditation upon the precise words that He uttered.

(*f*) The same reason which leads St. John to record the words of the Lord in the form expressive of their significance, as that has become clear to him, permits him also, as we have noticed, to pass from the record to his own comment upon it without any indication of the transition. There is a clear instance of this in Chapter III after the conversation with Nicodemus. I do not think this calls for any further discussion here, but consonantly with what has already been said, I think we are wise to regard all that we can as utterance of the Lord in the sense described, and to put the point of transition to comment on the part of either the Beloved Disciple (the Witness) or the Evangelist as late in the text as possible.

SOME GENERAL CONSIDERATIONS

(1) The Gospel is through and through Palestinian. The notion that it is in any sense Hellenistic is contrary to its whole tenour. It is set in all the vivid concrete scenery of the actual Ministry in Palestine. What Hellenist could, or would, have written Chapter IX? And this is no more than a specially clear instance of an all-pervasive character. The whole idea of a Hellenistic quality comes from the Prologue. But this, too, is essentially Jewish, though the term 'Logos' is used in its Hellenistic as well as its Jewish sense, as a medium of interpretation to the Greek-speaking people of Ephesus. The Prologue bears evident traces of a mind accustomed to think in Aramaic, even if we consider that Dr. Burney failed to establish the case for an Aramaic original afterwards translated into Greek. After the close of the Prologue the term Logos does not recur. The thought which it was used to introduce — that the historical life and death and resurrection of Jesus Christ is a self-utterance of the Eternal God, so that in the temporal event we behold the eternal reality — governs the whole Gospel. But this is neither Jewish nor Greek; it is specifically Christian. A partly Greek term was used to introduce this truth to minds formed by Greek culture, and was then used no more. With St. John as truly as with St. Mark we accompany the Lord in Galilee and in Jerusalem, and breathe the air of Palestine.

(2) In the proper sense of the word 'mystical', as signifying a direct apprehension of God by the human mind, St. John is strongly anti-mystical. But he is even more strongly sacramental. He is emphatic that 'no man hath beheld God at any

time' (i, 18);[1] that saying repudiates the essentially mystical
experience; but he is equally emphatic that 'God only begotten
hath declared him'. In the great affirmation that 'the Word
became flesh and we beheld his glory' (i, 14) is implicit a whole
theory of the relation between spirit and matter. Christianity
is the most materialistic of all great religions. The others hope
to achieve spiritual reality by ignoring matter — calling it
illusion (*maya*) or saying that it does not exist; the result is a
failure to control the physical side of life, a lofty religious
philosophy side by side with sensual indulgence, not indeed in
the same persons but in the same religious tradition. Christianity, based as it is on the Incarnation, regards matter as
destined to be the vehicle and instrument of spirit, and spirit
as fully actual so far as it controls and directs matter.

Thus the appointed Sacraments of the Church are not something unrelated to all other human experience; some have
wished to treat them so, with a view to a greater reverence for
them; but the result is an inclination towards magic, and an
evisceration of the Sacraments by elimination of their ethical
content. The Sacraments of the Church are appointed means
of grace wherein the Lord of the Church makes use, for His
central purpose, of the character implanted by Him in the
constitution of the universe as a whole. They represent and
focus a principle at work far beyond themselves. It is no
accident that the discourses in the Fourth Gospel which contain references to Baptism and the Eucharist are recorded
in complete detachment from the practice or institution of
either.

(3) One marked characteristic of the mind of the Evangelist,
or of the Beloved Disciple, is worth mention. He often records
argument in debate, but he does not argue from premises to
conclusions as a method of apprehending truth. Rather he
puts together the various constituent parts of truth and con-
templates them in their relations to one another. Thus he seems

---

[1] The possibility that these words only mean that God is invisible is ruled out by vi,
46, where there cannot be any reference to physical vision.

to say 'look at A; now look at B; now at AB ; now at C; now at BC; now at AC; now at D and E; now at ABE; now at CE', and so on in any variety of combination that facilitates new insight. It is the method of artistic, as distinct from scientific, apprehension, and is appropriate to truth which is in no way dependent on, or derived from, other truth, but makes its own direct appeal to reason, heart and conscience.

THE JOHANNINE AND SYNOPTIST PICTURE
OF CHRIST

A Gospel is essentially a proclamation of the good news concerning God and His Kingdom which is offered to men in Christ, in whom 'God hath visited and redeemed his people'. The question of greatest importance that can be asked concerning it is this: Is it the true picture of Christ?

It has been said that the picture in the Synoptic Gospels and the picture in the Fourth Gospel are incompatible, and that we have to choose between them. So far as this contention is based on difference in the record of facts, or on the matter or manner of the Lord's speech, we have dealt with it already. Broadly speaking, there is no incompatibility in the record of facts, though there are some points at which adjustment is difficult — e.g. the Cleansing of the Temple — and one, the Raising of Lazarus, where it is supremely difficult. Something will be said of these in their own place. But, speaking generally, the truth is that the Synoptic narrative is unintelligible without the narrative of St. John. Far from being incompatible with the former the latter is necessary to it.

As regards the 'style' of the discourses, the character of the Johannine record has been discussed. No one suggests that a phonographic record would have retained from the utterance of the Lord the sounds which we make as we read the Fourth Gospel aloud, or even their Aramaic counterpart. What is maintained is that the themes were actually handled by the

Lord, and that this Gospel gives to us what His utterance was afterwards known to have contained.

This gives rise to one special source of complexity. The relation of the Beloved Disciple or of the Evangelist to the Lord was at the date of dictation or of writing that of a worshipper to his God. This, too, is read back into the old story. It depicts the disciples as conscious of His Messiahship and His Deity, because they are now conscious of it, and the spiritual meaning of what was said in Jerusalem or Galilee is partly derived from the divine status of the Speaker. And this has probably coloured, as later experience has throughout coloured, the form given to the utterance. Our generation, with its eagerness to get back to 'what actually happened' should begin with the Synoptic narrative, and there watch the dawn and growth of apprehension. But 'what actually happened' is not — was not — the real occurrence, for it did not of itself disclose the supremely important fact that the words were spoken and the deeds done by God Incarnate. So the Fourth Gospel brings us nearer to the reality — the 'substance' — of what happened.

History is always involved in ambiguity at this point, because fact and interpretation cannot be disentangled. If I say 'Charles Stuart was executed', that is true, but not the whole truth. I add something if I say 'King Charles I was executed'. I add a good deal more if I say 'King Charles I was martyred'. This new term is interpretative; but if the interpretation is true the statement is historically true. Yet it requires other than historical categories to justify it.

So if it had been said to the shepherds 'A baby is born in Bethlehem' it would have been true, but only part of the truth. If it had been said 'A baby is born who will be called Jesus by divine command' that also would have been true, and evidence for what was understood to be a divine command would have been available. Such evidence could never amount to historical proof that God gave that command; but if He did, that, too, is historical fact. The statement 'To you is born a Saviour which is Christ the Lord' uses categories of which History knows nothing; yet if it is true at all, it is historically true.

It is in an analogous manner that the Fourth Gospel leads us to the heart of facts whose merely 'actual' aspect did not fully exhibit this full reality.

But the question is raised on deeper grounds. When all is allowed for, is the Johannine Christ the same person as the Synoptic Christ? Has He the same outlook on the world? Has He the same conception of His own relation to God? and of His mission in the world?

Two prejudices have in the past obscured this question. In the later nineteenth century there was a tendency to suppose that 'the Jesus of History' must have been a purely human and non-supernatural person; and this was believed in spite of the fact that, admittedly, the earliest of the four Gospels, St. Mark's, is crowded with miracles. It was held that the simple preacher of love towards God and man could be discerned behind the Marcan, Lucan and Matthaean narratives. (Why anyone should have troubled to crucify the Christ of Liberal Protestantism has always been a mystery.) But this view is now almost everywhere abandoned. It is now recognised that the only Christ for whose existence there is any evidence at all is a miraculous Figure making stupendous claims. These would naturally be less prominent in narratives of the Galilean ministry than in a narrative of controversy with the ecclesiastical leaders in Jerusalem. But they are there, and from the earliest and best of our strands of evidence — the document or tradition on which the First and Third Gospels draw, commonly called Q — comes a saying purely 'Johannine' in quality: 'All things have been delivered unto me of my Father; and no one knoweth the Son save the Father, neither doth any know the Father save the Son, and he to whomsoever the Son willeth to reveal him' (*St. Matthew* xi, 27; cf. *St. Luke* x, 22).

The other prejudice dies harder. It is to the effect that the Lord was deeply affected by an 'apocalyptic' outlook, and

anticipated His own return in glory at an early though unknown date. This, it is urged, is the Synoptic picture; and the
situation disclosed in the early chapters of the *Acts of the
Apostles* corresponds to this. On the other hand, St. John,
writing when the great transition in thought had been effected
and there was no longer expectation of an early 'return', sub-
stitutes the discourse on the coming of the Paraclete for the
apocalypse of *St. Mark* xiii and the corresponding passages
in *St. Matthew* and *St. Luke*. It is recognised that St. John
has an outlook peculiar among writers of the New Testament,
though the later Pauline Epistles approach it. This finds its
focus in the conviction that the divine glory, which we behold
throughout the life of Christ, is most fully expressed in His
Passion. But this is commonly regarded as part of a profound
readjustment of thought in the light of the fuller experience of
the Church.

We must candidly admit that the view thus traced to the
Synoptists is certainly that at which the Apostles had arrived
at the time of the speeches recorded in the *Acts of the Apostles*
as having been made by St. Peter on the feast of Pentecost and
in the immediately following period. It represents what the
first disciples at that date supposed the Lord to have said and
meant. None the less I maintain that the Synoptic record itself
discloses as the real mind of the Lord what St. John first makes
clear. St. Peter and St. Mark probably held the outlook which
these critics attribute both to them and to the Lord Himself;
yet their reproduction of His own teaching shows that they
had not fully understood Him, and that He was in historical
fact what St. John for the first time set forth.

Every great man is greater than his followers at first appreciate; it is posterity by which he is truly understood. And
every original genius is hampered by the terms which contemporary language offers as the necessary and sole medium
of his self-expression. He must take the best terms available,
and trust that his special use of them will gradually correct
the suggestions attaching to them, which are alien from his

thought, until at last he has imposed his own meaning on them. So the Lord used the language of apocalyptic for certain of His purposes; so He accepted the title of Messiah, though He never took the initiative in using it of Himself. It was full of suggestions bearing no relation to what He had to do; yet it was the best term available, and it was far more true to say that He was the promised Messiah than to deny it; for to Him was entrusted the essential task of the Messiah — to inaugurate the Kingdom of God.

My contention is that there is no incompatibility between the Synoptic and the Johannine portraits, because the Synoptic portrait is substantially Johannine. In support of this contention I offer an outline-sketch of the Synoptic portrait. Many of the points included in it will also be recalled in their appropriate places in the Johannine story.

The Lord, at His Baptism, is conscious of the call to begin now the work of Messiah: the voice from heaven — ' This is ' (*or* 'Thou art') 'my beloved Son in whom I am well pleased' — undoubtedly carries this meaning. At once, therefore, He goes into solitude to consider what manner of Messiah He shall be. The story of the Temptations is, of course, a parable of His spiritual wrestlings, told by Himself to His disciples. It represents the rejection, under three typical forms, of all existing conceptions of the Messianic task, which was to inaugurate the Kingdom of God. Should He use the power with which, as Messiah, He is endowed to satisfy the creature wants of Himself and His human brethren, so fulfilling the hope of a 'good time coming' which prophets had presented in the picture of the Messianic Banquet — (cf. e.g. *Isaiah* xxv, 6)? Should He be a Caesar-Christ, winning the Kingdoms of the world and the glory of them by establishing an earthly monarchy and ruling from the throne of David in perfect righteousness — (cf. e.g. *Isaiah* ix, 6, 7)? Should He provide irresistible evidence of His divine mission, appearing in the Temple courts upborne by angels, so that doubt would be impossible — (cf. e.g. *Daniel* vii, 13, 14, and *Enoch*)? Every one of these conceptions contained truth. When men are obedient to the Kingdom of God and His justice, everyone will have what he needs for food and clothing (*St. Matthew* vi, 33). The Kingdom of God is the realm of perfect justice where God's righteous will is done (*St. Matthew* vi, 10). The authority of Christ is absolute and can claim the support of the hosts of heaven (*St. Matthew* xxviii, 18; xxvi, 53). Yet if any or all of these are taken as fully representative of the Kingdom and its inauguration they have one fatal defect. They all represent ways of securing the outward obedience of men apart from inward loyalty; they are ways of controlling conduct, but not ways of controlling hearts and wills. He might bribe men to obey Him by the promise of good things, and so encourage man's evil tendency to care more for creature comforts than for the Word of God. He might coerce men to obey by threat of penalty, as earthly rulers do, and so Himself worship, and encourage men to worship, the Prince of this world. He might offer irresistible proof so that men would have to think the Gospel true even if they wished that it were not, putting to the proof the God who claims men's trust. In other words, all the rejected methods are essentially appeals to self-interest; and the Kingdom of God, who is Love, cannot be established in that way.

He has stripped Messiahship bare, repudiating all existing conceptions of it. Only the essential task remains — to inaugurate the Kingdom of God. He starts His Ministry, leading the life of perfect love, and teaching the precepts of perfect love. He is endowed with supernatural power, and uses it for the works of love. But His miracles are a hindrance to His main purpose rather than a help, because they lead men to think of Him as a wonder-worker and excite in them a quite unspiritual interest and curiosity. So He commonly bids those whom He heals to be quiet about it; yet He still heals; for Love confronted with need must meet the need if it can.

The enquiry of John the Baptist is full of interest. He had

once recognised the Lord for what He was. But he has begun to doubt because he hears what the Lord is doing. There are some blind folk who can see, some dumb folk who can speak, some deaf folk who can hear, even some dead folk raised to life and some devils vanquished; but where is the throwing down of strongholds and the uplifting of the meek, that should be the evidence of Messiah's presence in the world? So he sends to ask 'Art thou he that should come or do we look for another?' The answer directs his attention to the causes of his doubt; let John consider it all again — with the addition 'that the poor have the good news proclaimed to them; and blessed is he who is not scandalised at me' (*St. Matthew* xi, 1–6; *St. Luke* vii, 18–23). If we follow this advice what do we find? Power — yes, but the marvel is not in the power. What we find is power in complete subordination to love; and that is something like a definition of the Kingdom of God.

At first the Ministry was public. Then came a change, and the Lord began to concentrate attention on the Twelve whom He chose 'that they might be with him' (*St. Mark* iii, 14). At about the same time He spoke the Parable of the Sower. To us it seems so beautiful in its simplicity that we are puzzled at the association with it of the dark words of Isaiah — about seeing and not perceiving (*St. Mark* iv, 11, 12). But we must ask what was the Word which this Sower had been scattering; it was not exhortation to virtue; it was the proclamation of the Kingdom of God. And it was very hard for men trained in the Jewish tradition to believe that the Kingdom of God is something scattered broadcast, which here meets with failure, there with brief success which gives place to failure, and only occasionally reaches full success. So in His explanation He says to the chosen few 'Unto you is given the mystery — (the secret disclosed to initiates) — of the Kingdom of God, but unto those that are without all things are done in parables that seeing they may see and not perceive', etc. (*St. Mark* iv, 10, 12).

But if the method of the Kingdom is to be that of Love winning answering love what the Parable of the Sower sets forth is inevitably true concerning it.

Having chosen the Twelve 'that they might be with him', he takes them on two long journeys on foot, outside the areas of Jewish controversy, so that they may come to an intimate knowledge of Him. First they go to Tyre and Sidon, and, after return from there, to Caesarea Philippi; and now He feels that they are ready, and He asks whom men suppose Him to be. They mention the various guesses. Then — 'Who say ye that I am?' — and Peter with a leap of inspired insight answers 'Thou art the Messiah'. The Lord recognises that this is not something that he has been told, though John the Baptist long before had pointed to it; it is a revelation from heaven in answer to his loyalty.

Then the Lord, having been freely recognised, begins two new things: first a new teaching — 'The Son of Man must suffer'. This is the new conception which takes the place of all those rejected at the outset in the wilderness; and St. Peter is not ready for it; but it is necessary. The Son of Man *must* suffer. For the manifestation of love, by which it wins its response, is always sacrifice. The principle of sacrifice is that we choose to do or to suffer what apart from our love we should not choose to do or to suffer. When love is returned this sacrifice is the most joyful thing in the world, and heaven is the life of joyful sacrifice. But in a selfish world it must be painful, and the pain is the source of triumph.

As He begins to give the new teaching, and now reiterates it frequently, so He starts at once on that journey, near the beginning of which He ascends the Mount of Transfiguration, and at the end of which He ascends the Hill of Calvary. In the ecstasy of the Transfiguration the theme of discourse between the Head of the Law, the Head of the Prophets and the Head of the New Order is the Exodus which He will accomplish at Jerusalem; the word Exodus carries a double meaning — for Him decease, for His people deliverance. On the journey to Jerusalem, as the Messiah marches on His capital, two disciples ask if they may be specially near Him in His glory. His answer is 'Can you share my sacrifice?' — for the sacrifice *is* the glory. On reaching Jerusalem He challenges the High Priests by deliberately fulfilling Zechariah's prophecy in the Triumphal Entry. They must either accept Him or condemn Him to death for blasphemy, and He knows which they will do. He speaks repeatedly of His Coming as imminent; there is nothing said about a Second Coming, though there is truth in the expectation so expressed. But the Lord speaks only of the Coming of the Son of Man. Before the High Priest He declares that this is now a present fact. 'From henceforth there shall be the Son of Man seated on the right hand of God and coming in the clouds of heaven' (*St. Luke* xxii, 69; cf. *St. Matthew* xxvi, 64). In each case the translation 'hereafter' is a mere mistake. It is ἀπ' ἄρτι in *St. Matthew* and ἀπὸ τοῦ νῦν in *St. Luke* — the different expression for the same substance makes strong evidence). Daniel's prophecy, He claims, is then and there fulfilled.

In power the Kingdom was established when Christ was lifted up upon the Cross. From that moment it is true that 'He cometh with clouds'; that is present fact. He reigns from the Tree. But not all have eyes to perceive; and the time when 'every eye shall see him' is still future, and this is the truth in the expectation of a Return or Second Coming.

The progress of the Kingdom consists in the uprising within the hearts of men of a love and trust which answer to the Love which shines from the Cross and is, for this world, the glory of God — the shining forth of His very self; and that newly experienced power of love and trust is the activity of the Holy Spirit, the Paraclete, who could not be given till Jesus was glorified (*St. John* vii, 39).

There remains a final consummation which involves a change in our mortal state and a removal of our present limitations. The Kingdom cannot come in all its perfection in this world for at least two reasons. First, it is a fellowship of all generations; secondly, every child that is born, being a nucleus of that Original Sin which is self-centredness, disturbs such degree of approximation as has been reached. Consequently here the figure of the Kingdom is the Cross, for in this world it is always winning its triumph by sacrifice; but the Cross is the symbol, not of failure but of triumph — a triumph to be made perfect in God's chosen time.

This is a purely Johannine picture of the Person and Work of Christ. My contention is that it is in fact the picture presented by the Synoptists, though they themselves had not fully grasped its meaning, which the Beloved Disciple first apprehended and declared.

As a confirmation of this view we may recall the fact that the 'Sayings' of Christ recorded in the papyri discovered at Oxyrhynchus give us teaching which is strongly Johannine in substance without any of the distinctively Johannine phraseology. This evidence, the value of which is still a matter of some dispute, supports the view here taken, that the mind of Jesus Himself was what the Fourth Gospel disclosed, but that the disciples were at first unable to enter into this, partly because of its novelty, and partly because of the associations attaching to the terminology in which it was necessary that the Lord should express Himself. Let the Synoptists repeat for us as closely as they can the very words He spoke; but let St. John tune our ears to hear them.

NOTES

(a) *On the Following Translation*

I have set out from the Revised Version as Westcott would have wished it to be. No doubt he exaggerated the importance for Hellenistic Greek of some distinctions that are of great importance for classical Greek — e.g. between the aorist and the perfect tenses. But it was a good fault on the whole for an expositor. I have in a similar way sometimes gone to excess in retaining the order of the Greek words (for this sometimes suggests a valuable emphasis), and also in choosing words and phrases which exaggerate the shade of meaning conveyed by the original. For the purpose in view this is preferable to a better English which misses or obscures these *nuances*. But at all times my translation is intended for private reading with a view to personal meditation. It is not intended as a translation of the original into the most adequate English for reading aloud; for such a purpose it would be (so far as it is distinctive) a very bad translation. Its aim is to supply for those who cannot refer to the Greek original some of the additional illumination which is obtainable from that source. It is hoped that readers will have at hand a copy of the Revised Version in which references may be looked up.

(b) *On Dislocations of the Text*

I have a strong initial prejudice against any suggestion of dislocation in the text. But the arguments for supposing that Chapter VI should precede Chapter V, and that in Chapter VII verses 15-24 should be placed at the beginning of the chapter, are extremely strong. They are set out by Archbishop Bernard on pages xvi to xxx and following in the Introduction to his commentary. Here it is enough to say that the rearrangement proposed not only makes many particular phrases, and the narrative as a whole, far more easily intelligible, but has some objective support in the order followed by Tatian (*c.* A.D. 170).

The other rearrangements proposed by Bernard seem to me far less probable; in particular, though the insertion of Chapters XV and XVI in the course of our Chapter XIII has some advantages, it also involves some disadvantages. In any case, the grounds for these rearrangements are remote from

the purpose of these 'readings'; as it is for the convenience of
readers to follow the familiar arrangement unless there is very
strong reason to vary it, I make no transpositions except in
V, VI and VII; and I believe that this course is not only
convenient but correct.

PROLOGUE

CHAPTER I

(1–18)

1–2. In the beginning was the Word. And the Word was with God. And the Word was God. The same was in the beginning with God.

'In the beginning.' Of course the words take up the opening of *Genesis*. But they do this so as to suggest at once the transition from temporal event to eternal reality which is the essence of this Gospel. For the Greek words can also be translated 'In principle'. It is a great mistake to suppose that, when a word in one language is represented by two or more in another, it is always necessary to choose one or other of these; very often a word covers several meanings because the meanings really are connected together, and the mind easily passes from one to the other without consciousness of movement. So the word really means both things; and here the expression used means both 'in the beginning of history' and 'at the root of the universe'.

What is said so to exist is 'the Word'. This term again combines two meanings. It is the Word of the Lord by which the heavens were made, and which came to the Prophets. It is also the Rational Principle which gives unity and significance to all existing things. In this sense it had been used by Heraclitus of Ephesus in the sixth century before Christ. 'The sun', he says, 'will not transgress his measures; were he to do so, the aiders of Justice would overtake him. He who speaks with understanding must take his foothold on what is common to all, even more firmly than the city stands on the foothold of law; for all human laws are nourished by the divine law. Though this Word (Logos) — this fundamental law — existeth from all time, yet mankind are unaware of it, both ere they hear it and in the moment that they hear it.' This conception of the Logos, the principle of Law or Reason, was taken up by

3

the Stoics and handed on from them to Philo, the Platonising
Jew of Alexandria. Nothing can be more misleading than to
enquire whether the Johannine Logos is the Word of the Lord
familiar in the Old Testament, or the Philonic Logos, who is
spoken of as a 'second God'; for Philo had himself effected
the combination of the Old Testament 'Word' with the Stoic
'Logos'.

I have no doubt that in a general sense St. John is here
following the thought of Philo; but this does not mean that he
was a student of Philo's writings. The term 'Logos' was in
general use in the Hellenistic world; among Hellenised Jews
the intellectual currents represented by Philo inevitably exerted
an influence. The Evangelist is not here proclaiming unfamiliar
truth; rather he is seeking common ground with his readers.
It is of no use to tell the Hellenistic Ephesians that the Messiah
is come; they are not expecting any Messiah and would not
be interested; it would be like trying to excite an English
audience by proclaiming the arrival of the Mahdi. Moreover
he wants a term that carries thought nearer to the heart of
all reality. He finds it in this word 'Logos', which alike for
Jew and Gentile represents the ruling fact of the universe,
and represents that fact as the self-expression of God. The
Jew will remember that 'by the Word of the Lord were the
heavens made'; the Greek will think of the rational principle
of which all natural laws are particular expressions. Both will
agree that this Logos is the starting-point of all things. It exists
as it always did ἐν ἀρχῇ — in the beginning, at the root of the
universe.

Moreover its very essence is a relationship to God such that
it is truly divine. The term 'God' is fully substantival in the
first clause — πρὸς τὸν Θεόν: it is predicative and not far from
adjectival in the second — Θεὸς ἦν ὁ λόγος. Thus from the
outset we are to understand that the Word has its whole
being within Deity, but that it does not exhaust the being of
Deity. Or, to put it from the other side, God is essentially self-
revealing; but He is first of all a Self capable of being revealed.

This same Word, or Self-revelation, is then again said to exist in essential relationship to God.

St. John has thus established common ground with all his readers. If they are Jews they will recognise and assent to the familiar doctrine of the Old Testament concerning the Word of God. If they are Greeks they will recognise and assent to the declaration that the ultimate reality is Mind expressing itself. To both alike he has announced in language easily received that the subject for which he is claiming their attention is the ultimate and supreme principle of the universe.

*

3. Through its agency all things came to be, and apart from it hath not one thing come to be.

The Greek pronoun may be either masculine or neuter. In the mind of the Evangelist, no doubt, it is masculine but not in that of a contemporary reader; ground has not yet been given for attributing personality to the Logos, so it seems better for languages which must choose one or the other to choose the neuter. The supreme principle of the universe is not only its bond of unity, but its ground of existence. In other words, only because it is God's Nature to reveal or communicate Himself is there a world at all; everything in it, every single occurrence in time and space, is subject to this controlling fact, that the world exists as the arena of God's self-revelation. Of course St. John knows that he is stating the religious principle of God's supremacy, the philosophical principle of ultimate unity, in the way that most of any throws the problem of evil into relief. The reference to 'darkness' about to follow shows his awareness of this. But he makes no comment now. The story which he is about to tell contains his comment and even his solution of the problem (xii, 31–32). But as there is no real solution except in the light of that story he will not comment now. He will only assert, in the strongest terms that he can find, his assurance that all things exist or come to be as a result of God's activity by self-expression, knowing that he thus provokes in its acutest form the gravest of all religious difficulties. Just so the hymn of the Elders in the *Apocalypse*, 'Worthy art thou, our Lord and our God, to receive the glory and the honour and the power, for thou didst create all things, and because of thy will they were, and were created', introduces the interpretation of that Book of Destiny in which the chapters are Conquest, War, Famine and Death. And there, too, the interpretation is the same (*Revelation* iv, 11; v, 9; vi, 1–8).

*

4–5. What came to be in it was Life, and the Life was the light of men, and the light shineth in the darkness, and the darkness did not absorb it.

Here the interpretation for Christian and non-Christian begins to diverge.

(*a*) For non-Christians the words would mean that within that supreme principle is, and always has been, Life. Life is not said to be a product of its agency as the world is, but rather to be one of its own inherent characteristics. When we pass from the inert thing to the living creature we reach a stage where there is something in common between the creature and creative principle besides bare existence. And in this vital energy — for it is Life in that sense that the word implies[1] — is the beacon by which men are guided. The impulse to move is also the guide of our movement. Its direction is not yet disclosed; but in the fact that the vital impulse is an element in the divine manifestation we have the assurance that correspondence with the mind of God will be the true satisfaction of that impulse.

(*b*) But for a Christian reader a new suggestion is already present. He would notice the difference in the prepositions used. 'Through its agency all things came to pass'; but they are not said to be all of them Life. 'What came to pass *in* it was Life.' But only of one occurrence is it true to say that it

---

[1] I propose everywhere to translate ζωή by 'Life', and ψυχή by 'life.'

took place not only through but *in* the Logos; that is the nativity of Jesus. All other existing things, though owing their existence to the Logos, and never escaping its final control, yet show some deviation from it. The Cosmos lieth in evil, not in the Logos. Only Jesus is wholly in the Logos. And only Jesus is truly Life — so that all true Life in us is drawn from Him. As He alone is truly Life (xi, 25; xiv, 6), so He alone is truly Light (viii, 12). In all periods, but supremely in the period of Christ's earthly ministry, *the light shineth in the darkness, and the darkness did not absorb it.*

Imagine yourself standing alone on some headland in a dark night. At the foot of the headland is a lighthouse or beacon, not casting rays on every side, but throwing one bar of light through the darkness. It is some such image that St. John had before his mind. The divine light shines through the darkness of the world, cleaving it, but neither dispelling it nor quenched by it. The word translated in the Authorised Version 'comprehended', in the text of the Revised Version 'apprehended', and in its margin 'overcame', is a word of two meanings; literally it is 'to take down or under', and may thus mean 'to take right into the mind' (apprehend) or 'to take under control' (overcome). In this context the two meanings are direct opposites, for to apprehend light is to be enlightened by it, and to overcome light is to put it out. Yet the word truly means both of these. The darkness in no sense at all received the light; yet the light shone still undimmed. So strange is the relation of the light of God's revelation to the world which exists to be the medium of that revelation.

St. John is not yet, as I read him, thinking only of the Life of the Word Incarnate, though what he says is true also of that Life. He is thinking of the period covered by the Old Testament, with the light of the revelation to Israel piercing the darkness of the heathenism by which Israel was surrounded; and this is to him an illustration of a universal principle. It is always so. Take any moment of history and you find light piercing unillumined darkness — now with reference to one

phase of the purpose of God, now another. The company of
those who stand in the beam of the light by which the path
of true progress for that time is discerned is always small.
Remember Wilberforce and the early Abolitionists; remember
the twelve Apostles and the company gathered about them.
What is seen conspicuously in those two examples is always
true; and as we think of the spiritual progress of the race this
truth finds a fresh illustration. As we look forwards, we peer
into darkness, and none can say with certainty what course the
true progress of the future should follow. But as we look back,
the truth is marked by beacon-lights, which are the lives of
saints and pioneers; and these in their turn are not origin-
ators of light, but rather reflectors which give light to us
because themselves they are turned towards the source of
light.

This darkness in which the light shines unabsorbed is
cosmic. St. John is most modern here. The evil which for
him presents the problem is not only in men's hearts; it is in
the whole ordered system of nature. That ordered system is
infected; it 'lieth in the evil one' (*I John* v, 19). St. John might
have had all the modern problem of the callousness and cruelty
of nature before his mind. Anyhow, his approach is the
modern approach. He does not conceive of Nature as
characterised by a Wordsworthian perfection, which is only
spoilt by fallen mankind. To his deep spiritual insight it is
apparent that the redemption of man is part, even if the crown-
ing part, of a greater thing — the redemption, or conquest
(xvi, 33), of the universe. Till that be accomplished the darkness abides, pierced but unillumined by the beam of divine
light. And the one great question for everyone is whether he
will 'walk in darkness' or 'walk in light' (*I John* i, 7; ii, 10, 11).

*

6–8. There came a man sent from God — the name of him John. This
man came with a view to witness, in order that he might give witness
concerning the light, that all might believe through him. That one was
not the light, but was to bear witness concerning the light.

Here is one of those who act as beacons for pilgrims by
reflecting the divine light. But he did more than reflect it;
he pointed to it and bade men follow, not him, but it. His
whole function was witness or testimony. He was a voice.
He would direct attention away from his personality to his
message. He pointed to one whose message directed attention
to Himself; for He, to whom John pointed, was the light itself.

*

9–13. There was the light, the true light, which enlighteneth every man,
— coming into the world. In the world he was; and the world through
his agency came into being; and the world did not recognise him. To
his own home he came, and his own people did not receive him. But
as many as received him, to them gave he the right to become children
of God — to those that believe on the name of him who was born, not
of blood, nor of the will of the flesh, nor of the will of a man, but of God.

We now approach the new revelation. From the beginning
the divine light has shone. Always it was coming into the
world; always it enlightened every man alive in his reason and
conscience. Every check on animal lust felt by the primitive
savage, every stimulation to a nobler life, is God self-revealed
within his soul. But God in self-revelation is the Divine Word,
for precisely this is what that term means. What is constituted
within that divine self-communication, as one element com-
posing it, is the energy of Life; this is what urges all kinds of
living things forward in their evolution; and this is what is
fully and perfectly expressed in Christ. So it may be truly
said that the conscience of the heathen man is the voice of
Christ within him — though muffled by his ignorance. All
that is noble in the non-christian systems of thought, or
conduct, or worship is the work of Christ upon them and
within them. By the Word of God — that is to say, by Jesus
Christ — Isaiah, and Plato, and Zoroaster, and Buddha, and
Confucius conceived and uttered such truths as they declared.
There is only one divine light; and every man in his measure is
enlightened by it.

Yet this light is not recognised for what it is. If it were, its fuller shining would always be welcomed. But it is attributed by each tribe or group to some historic or legendary founder or pioneer of their own, so that each claims to have a monopoly of the light itself, when in fact each has only a few rays of that light, which needs all the wisdom of all the human traditions to manifest the entire compass of its spectrum. Moreover it has to shine through veils of prejudice and obsession, so that even the rays received by each group among mankind are not clear and pure in the illumination which they give.

So the light itself is unrecognised; and when it blazes out more fully, men refuse it, even though it is that by which they already walk. For these reasons it is true both that Christ is indeed the Desire of all Nations, and yet that He is always more and other than men desire until they learn of Him.[1] To come to Him is always an act of self-surrender as well as of self-fulfilment, and must be first experienced as self-surrender.

But there was one nation specially prepared for the reception of the light in its fulness. Israel had received the light in a measure so full as to be called its own home, its own people. But when He came — (and here for the first time a pronoun unmistakably personal in its reference is used) — His own people were as completely unable to receive Him as any others had been to receive light fuller than that to which they were accustomed.

With this direct reference to the coming of the Christ to Israel the drama of the Gospel opens. It is throughout its course the picture of His rejection by His own people generally, and His reception by the few. Over and over again the Evangelist will draw this moral with reference to the various episodes that he relates (cf. vii, 40–44; viii, 30, 59; x, 19–21; xi, 45, 46. These are perhaps the most conspicuous instances, but similar comments are frequent). This is in one aspect a Gospel of Judgement. By their reaction to the impact of Christ men are

---

[1] Cf. Reports of the International Missionary Council(Jerusalem, 1928), *The Christian Message.*

judged, and take their position as children of darkness or children of light (xii, 35, 36).

None can take rank among the children of light by any right, power or merit of his own, but only by becoming (like John the Baptist) beacons who reflect a light of which they are not the source. But to those who so receive the Light when it comes, it (or He, for the Light is Jesus) gives *the right to become sons of God.*

Are we not all children of God? Yes, in one most true sense — by creation. 'It is He that hath made us and not we ourselves.' But the writers of the New Testament all observe a certain use of language which has deep significance. They often imply that God is the Father of all men; but they do not speak of all men as His children; that expression is reserved for those who, by the grace of God, are enabled in some measure to reproduce His character. So the Lord Himself commands us to imitate the universal and undiscriminating Love of God 'that ye may be sons of your Father which is in heaven' (*St. Matthew* v, 45). The phrase is used in the sense in which we sometimes say of a man 'He is the son of his father'; that is, in him we see his father again. In that sense there is only one 'Son of the Father'; but He makes it possible for us to share His Sonship; the Spirit whom He sends from the Father is 'the spirit of adoption whereby we cry Abba, Father' (*Romans* viii, 15).

He gives the right to become sons of God to those who receive Him, that is to those who 'believe on His Name'. The Name is the manifested nature; to baptise into the Name of the Father, the Son, and the Holy Ghost is to plunge or bathe the person in the manifested love of God. To believe on, or put trust in, the love of God made manifest in Christ is the condition of becoming a son of God who reproduces the divine character. But we do not thereby acquire an equality with Christ. It remains true that only through Christ are we enabled to acquire a relationship to God which was, and is, Christ's apart from any mediation. (And even then how

half-hearted is our faith! How defective our reflection of the
divine love!)

Who was (or *were*) *born.* I have adopted above the text
which Tertullian accepted; but I did so rather to challenge
attention than because it is probably correct. The plural verb
has far the greater weight of authority in the manuscripts.
Yet the sense is the same. Nothing can explain the quite
peculiar phrasing of this passage except the supposition that it
refers to the Virgin Birth of our Lord. With the singular verb
this is explicit; and the significance which it gives to that event
is an insistence that the coming of our Lord into the world
is not due to any human impulse or volition but is an act of
God alone.

The reference in the language to the mode of our Lord's
nativity secures that this meaning is still present even if the
verb be plural — *who were born.* For the point is that the
process whereby those who receive Him become sons of God
— are re-born or re-generate as sons of God — is as much
due to the sole activity of God as was the birth into the world
of Him who alone is in His own right Son of God.

And now the great declaration is made. This Word, this
Logos, which Greeks and Hebrews unite in recognising as the
controlling power of the whole universe, is no longer unknown
or dimly apprehended. The Light which in some measure
lightens every man has shone in its full splendour.

*

14. And the Word became flesh and tabernacled among us — (and we
beheld his glory, glory as of an only begotten from a father) — full of
grace and truth.

The Word became flesh. The Word did not merely indwell
a human being. Absolute identity is asserted. The Word is
Jesus; Jesus is the Word. And it is said that the Word became
flesh because 'flesh' is that part of human nature commonly
associated with frailty and evil; commonly, but not necessarily.
In Jesus the flesh is the completely responsive vehicle of the

spirit. The whole of Him, flesh included, is the Word, the self-utterance, of God.

He tabernacled among us; He pitched His fleshly tent among us. The suggestion is of a brief sojourn, but all thought of a momentary apparition is excluded.

Full of grace and truth. He not only disclosed the divine reality, but therein also displayed its beauty. Truth is august, often austere, sometimes repellent. But here it is gracious and winning. John the Baptist, who is also in mind here (6 and 15), was full of truth, but there was not much grace about him!

We beheld his glory. Not all who set eyes on Him did that. 'We' does not mean all who ever met Him. Caiaphas and Herod and Pilate did not behold His glory. But His true disciples did. His glory was not something left behind to which one day He would return — as St. Paul had sometimes suggested (*Philippians* ii, 6–10; *II Corinthians* viii, 9). Of course the Pauline doctrine is true. The Incarnation was an act of sacrifice and of humiliation — real however voluntary. But that is not the last word. For the sacrifice and the humiliation *are* the divine glory. If God is Love, His glory most of all shines forth in whatever most fully expresses love. The Cross of shame *is* the throne of glory. St. John will take his own way of saying that with emphasis as the story goes forward. Now at the outset He makes the proclamation — *We beheld his glory, glory as of an only begotten from a father*. There are no definite articles; the statement is not a piece of technical Trinitarian theology, though it supplies the basis for such a theology. It is a record of experience. The glory which appeared seemed not to have its source in Him, but to stream through Him from beyond. To be with Him was — as it still is — to be with 'Him that sent Him'. He is the only Son (the word μονογενής has no reference to the *process* of begetting and expresses uniqueness rather than mode of origin) who alone perfectly reproduces the Father's character. The glory is, in the phrase that He will use, *not mine but his that sent me*. The glory that

the Word displays to us is the glory of God, whose is that
Word. We are very close to the great utterance *He that hath
seen me hath seen the Father* (xiv, 9). Yet the reference is not
yet quite explicit to the divine Father; the absence of the
definite article excludes that. Only in verse 18 will that reference become quite explicit. Here all the emphasis is laid upon
the fact apparent to the spiritual awareness of those who
beheld his glory that this glory shone from a source beyond
through the Figure with whom the disciples held converse.

That source beyond is the Eternal Father. Consequently,
as we read the story, though it all happened long ago, we
apprehend present fact. It is not only the record of a historical
episode that we read; it is the self-expression of that God 'in
whom we live and move and have our being'; so that whatever
finds expression there is true now, and the living Jesus who
is 'the same yesterday and to-day and for ever' still deals with
our souls as He dealt with those who had fellowship with Him
when He *tabernacled among us*. Our reading of the Gospel
story can be and should be an act of personal communion
with the living Lord.   *

15. John beareth witness concerning him and hath cried saying This is he
   whom I mentioned; he that cometh after me is come to be before me;
   because he was first in respect of me.

This is the second parenthetical introduction of John the
Baptist. For appreciation of the Word made flesh it is important to recognise the witness of this last and greatest (*St.
Matthew* xi, 9–10) of the prophets to whom the Word of the
Lord came. That witness is constant. Though in a certain
sense John was the pioneer and Jesus took up his message of
repentance because the Kingdom was at hand, yet John the
Forerunner always spoke of Him who should follow as greater
than himself. A forerunner goes first; yet the cause of his
activity is the follower for whom he prepares; therefore the
follower, though later in time, is prior in the order of thought.
In this case that relationship does no more than express the

essential relation of the two persons. 'He was — always and in nature — first in respect of me.'[1]

*

16–18. Because out of his fulness we all received, and grace for grace. Because the law was given through Moses; grace and truth came through Jesus Christ.
    God hath no man ever yet seen; God only begotten, who is in the bosom of the Father — he declared him.

The parenthetical reference to the Baptist is finished, and we come to the justification of the stupendous claim made in 14; we can say that the Word *tabernacled among us full of grace and truth* because in our own experience we have drawn upon that treasure store, and have found that the more we drew the more remained that we might also draw from that; for every grace received there was more grace offered. So we learnt the difference between the old dispensation and the new. That was law — commands and prohibitions enforced by rewards and punishments; in fact it was what St. Paul calls 'the spirit of slavery' (*Romans* viii, 15); for the slave has his orders and is rewarded if he obeys them faithfully and punished if he disobeys. But what we have received is 'the spirit of adoption', for if our hearts are open to the love of God made known in Jesus Christ we no longer ask chiefly what has God commanded or what has He forbidden, but rather what — apart from any known command or prohibition — will please our Father; and we do this not to gain reward or to avoid punishment but because our desire and joy is to please our Father.

We are won to that new disposition by the grace and truth in Jesus Christ. The appeal is not to our self-interest, though He uses that also in its place, but to the free assent of heart and mind. And this is made by the disclosure of the Divine Nature.

[1] Does this curious construction πρῶτός μου give the solution of the celebrated problem about the census in *St. Luke* ii, 2 — 'this census took place first in respect of — i.e. before — Quirinius' Syrian governorship'.

God hath no man ever yet seen. St. John is no mystic in the strict sense of that word; indeed he is the most strongly anti-mystical of all writers. Anything resembling a direct vision of God is absolutely ruled out. He is intensely and profoundly sacra-mental; he sees the spiritual in the material, the divine nature in the human nature, which it uses as its vehicle. The central declaration, *The Word became flesh*, is the affirmation of this sacramental principle. But of direct vision of God he shows no trace, nor any admission of its possibility.

God only begotten. This is the reading of the best manu-scripts, and it is easy to see how easily it would be changed — a very small change in the Greek — to 'the only begotten Son'. The meaning is substantially the same, but the phrase 'God only begotten' is by far the more arresting.

It was not a wholly novel phrase, though it is unlikely that it was generally familiar. Its first appearance, so far as my knowledge goes, is in the great sentence with which, in the *Timaeus*, Plato closes his myth of creation: 'And now let us say that our account of the universe reaches its conclusion. For, receiving living creatures mortal and immortal and being fulfilled, this universe, a visible living creature, containing what things are visible, an image of the intelligible, God made perceptible, greatest and best, fairest and most perfect, hath come to be one heaven, as we see, being only begotten' (*Timaeus*, 92 c 4–9).

But there it is the universe which is so described, because of the perfect satisfaction which it affords to aesthetic and intellectual contemplation. The contrast is greater than the resemblance when St. John, with the living God in mind whom no man hath ever seen, speaks of the Word as *God only begotten*, and of His Incarnation as the disclosure of the in-visible God. This can be so only because eternally the Word is *in the bosom of the Father*, and is thus Himself designated as the Son.

The phrase expresses the love of the Son for the Father and at the same time His dependence on the Father. Real and complete knowledge in persons of other persons is not distinguishable from love; it is not so much that the two go together as that the two words express two aspects of one thing. To understand a person means rather to sympathise with him than to have a scientific apprehension of his motives, temperament and character. When understanding is perfected in knowledge properly so called, sympathy is perfected in love. This phrase, therefore, which is suggestive of the child in its mother's arms, points to the fact which enables Christ to bring, or rather to be, the revelation of the Father. Because this is His relationship to the Father He can reveal or declare the Father.

He does not reveal all that is meant by the word God. There ever remains the unsearchable abyss of Deity. But He reveals what it vitally concerns us to know; He reveals God as Father.

ACT I

The Lord introduced to various types of men:

1. The Baptist, i, 19–34
2. John, Andrew and Peter, i, 35–42
3. Philip and Nathanael, i, 43–51
4. The Churchman, iii, 1–17
5. The Simple Woman, iv, 1–42
6. The Seeking Multitude, vi

Certain episodes are inserted in the course of these introductions which will be considered in their place.

CHAPTER I

(19–34)

19–28. And this is the witness of John when the Jews sent unto him from Jerusalem priests and Levites that they might ask him 'Thou, who art thou?' And he confessed and denied not; and he confessed '*I* am not the Christ'. And they asked him 'What then? Art thou Elijah?' And he saith 'I am not'. 'Art thou the prophet?' And he answered 'No'. They said therefore to him 'Who art thou? That we may give an answer to them that sent us. What sayest thou of thyself?' He said 'I am a voice of one crying in the wilderness "Make straight the way of the Lord" as said Isaiah the prophet'. And they had been sent from the Pharisees. And they asked him and said to him 'Why then baptisest thou if thou art not the Christ nor Elijah nor the prophet?' John answered them saying '*I* baptise with water. In the midst of you standeth one whom *ye* know not, who cometh after me, of whom I am not worthy to loose the shoe-latchet.' This happened in Bethany beyond Jordan where John was, baptising.

Now we come to the witness which John gave (7). For that witness he existed; it was his *raison d'être*. Consequently he is impatient at these enquiries concerning his personality. We see his growing irritation in the increasing abruptness of his replies. 'I am not the Christ'; 'I am not'; 'No'. It is not who he is, but what he says, that matters. He is a voice.

Herein already is the great contrast between him and the Lord. John says 'Never mind who I am; listen to what I say'. Jesus says *I am the way, the truth and the life*; in Him the teaching is our introduction to the person, and our aim is not only conformity to His teaching but fellowship with Himself. 'Come unto me, and I will give you rest.'

John is here the type of all Christian witness. 'We preach not ourselves but Christ Jesus as Lord, and ourselves as your servants for Jesus' sake' (*II Corinthians* iv, 5). If ever our witness begins to be to ourselves or to make ourselves very prominent something is going wrong with it. We may mention

our own experience — 'O come hither and hearken all ye that
fear God, and I will tell you what he hath done for my soul' —
but only as a means of pointing men to Christ. It is not ourselves but our witness to Him for which we want to claim
attention. Never mind who or what I am; but do listen when
I speak to you of Christ.

I baptise with water. The pronoun is emphatic. John can
offer the cleansing that comes with confession and the determination to make a fresh start. But the greater One to whom
he bears witness is already there. In this record the full contrast
is not drawn out — only the immeasurable distance that
separates the witness from the Light. But of course the
Evangelist knows that he has recorded enough to bring to
mind the contrast which the Baptist actually drew. 'I baptise
with water; he shall baptise with holy spirit and fire.' The one
is a mere cleansing from past contamination with the possibility of a new beginning; the latter is a positive energy of
righteousness, a consuming flame of purity. (The Synoptists
do not commit the absurdity of attributing to John the Baptist
a Trinitarian theology. There is no definite article with the
term 'holy spirit'. Wherever in the New Testament this term
occurs without the article, it denotes a human experience, not a
divine Person, though that human experience is the work of
the Third Person of the Godhead in man's soul.)

*

29–34. The next day he seeth Jesus coming to him and saith 'Behold, the
Lamb of God which beareth away the sin of the world. This is he of
whom I said "After me cometh a man who is come to be before me
because he always was first in respect of me". And I did not know him;
but that he might be made manifest to Israel, on this account am I come
baptising in water.' And John bare witness saying 'I have beheld the
Spirit descending out of heaven as a dove, and it abode upon him. And
I did not know him; but he that sent me to baptise in water, he said to
me "Upon whomsoever thou shalt see the Spirit descending and abiding
on him, this is he who baptiseth with holy spirit". And I have seen and
have borne witness that this is the Son of God.'

He seeth Jesus coming to him. What follows makes it plain that the Baptism of Jesus has taken place. Probably then He is returning from the forty days in the wilderness and the temptations concerning the manner of His Messiahship.[1] In the Temptation He has rejected all existent forms of the Messianic hope — the 'good time coming' symbolised by the Messianic Banquet, the Davidic King, the apocalyptic Son of Man. There was a truth in each, and He will use them all. But they are not fundamental. If treated as ultimate, each of them reveals the vital fault of making the final appeal to self-interest. He might bribe men into the Kingdom by hope of enjoyment; He might compel their obedience by force exercised in righteousness; He might overwhelm them with evidence — the 'sign from heaven' — so that doubt would be impossible. But in none of these ways would He win their hearts. He has stripped bare the essential function of the Messiah — to inaugurate the Kingdom of God. And He goes forth from His Temptation to live the life of perfect love, to die the death of perfect love, as the way of doing this. So soon as He was fully recognised — at Caesarea Philippi (*St. Mark* viii, 27–31) — He began to declare the mode of His Messiahship: 'The Son of Man must suffer'.

So He comes from the Temptation wherein the Spirit that descended on Him at His Baptism (as we shall see) had been triumphant. The Baptist does not speak of Him clearly as Messiah; the function to which the Spirit points had not yet been associated with the Messiah. That association would only come when the Lord Himself interpreted *Isaiah* liii as Messianic. But the Baptist certainly here applies to Him the figure of the Lamb in *Isaiah* liii, though the reference is also wider than that, for the Lamb was the familiar type of an offering to God. But this is more than a victim for sacrificial offering; for first, *The Lamb of God* is the victim whom God provides, as He provided the ram in place of Isaac (*Genesis* xxii, 8); and secondly, this Lamb Himself *beareth away the sin*

[1] See Introduction, pp. xxix-xxxiii.

of the world. In the coming of Christ, God Himself is active;
He not only accepts an offering made by man, but He provides
(for indeed He Himself is) the offering, and He Himself makes
it. All that man has to do is to participate in this divine action.
And that action is a *bearing* which has the effect of *taking away*
the sin of the world. The word αἴρων means both, and there
is no need to choose. By bearing it He removes it.

The sin of the world. How utterly modern is this conception!
It is not 'sins', as by a natural early corruption of the text men
were led to suppose, but 'sin'. For there is only one sin, and it
is characteristic of the whole world. It is the self-will which
prefers 'my' way to God's — which puts 'me' in the centre
where only God is in place. It pervades the universe. It
accounts for the cruelty of the jungle, where each animal follows
its own appetite, unheeding and unable to heed any general
good. It becomes conscious, and thereby tenfold more viru-
lent, in man — a veritable Fall indeed. And no individual is
responsible for it. It is an 'infection of nature' (Article IX
among the Thirty-Nine Articles of Religion), and we cannot
cure it. We are not 'responsible' for it; but it sets us at enmity
against God; it is the 'sin of the world'.

A few generations ago it was customary to think of Nature
as perfect, and the perfection marred by the Fall of Man.
Such an outlook allows for no 'sin of the world'. To us that
outlook is become impossible; 'Nature red in tooth and claw'
is no fit representative of the God of Love at the infra-human
level. 'Nature' presents to the Theist problems as great as
those arising from human history.[1] The world is one, and its
evil is one. There is a 'sin of the world'. It is this which the
Lamb of God accepts as a burden and thereby, in principle,
destroys. For us that sin, though still active, is a broken
power. We know its conqueror.

This is he of whom I said, etc. The Baptist had known the
Lord in boyhood. No doubt he had in some measure learnt to

[1] Once when taking some children to the Zoo I met Bishop Gore. When, in answer to
his enquiry, I told him where we were going, he said: ' Oh, I do hate the Zoo. It makes
me an atheist in twenty minutes.'

appreciate Him. But he had not known Him for what He was.
The word used is that which stands for knowledge of a truth —
εἰδέναι — not knowledge of a person — γνῶναι. (Contrast
xiv, 9). The Baptist had known Jesus of Nazareth, but had not
known this about Him. It was what happened at the Baptism
which disclosed the truth that Jesus was Messiah, and incidentally what manner of Messiah He would be. Now he knows
that the whole purpose of his mission of repentance was, not
to launch a movement having its end in its own success, but to
prepare hearts to which the Messiah could be manifest — so
that there should be some in Israel who would 'behold his
glory'. *I have beheld the Spirit descending out of heaven as a
dove and it abode upon him.* In St. Mark's account it is only
to the Lord Himself that the vision came; here it is insisted
that the Baptist beheld it also.

Out of heaven. The vision of the descending and abiding
Spirit—and the voice which said 'This is my beloved Son in
whom I am well pleased' (*St. Mark* i, 11) — are the commission from God to enter on the Messianic work, the work of
inaugurating the Kingdom of God. The commission is from
God; the Lord's character as man may qualify Him to receive
it but does not constitute it.

As a dove. Why a dove? No doubt there was a traditional
connexion between the Spirit of God and the dove. Jewish
Doctors had added to *Genesis* i, 2 the gloss 'like a dove'.
The phrase 'the voice of the turtle' (*Canticle* ii, 12) had been
interpreted as 'the voice of the Spirit'. But there is more in it
than this. The dove was the poor man's sacrifice (*St. Luke* ii,
24), and was commonly reputed to be the only sacrificial victim
that offered its own neck to the sacrificial knife. *That* is the
Spirit that descends upon Him; *that* is His Kingly anointing;
that is what marks Him as Son of God.

And so the Baptist is led past all current conceptions of the
Messiah to that of the Priest-Victim in redemptive sacrifice.
He will not maintain the fulness of that illumination. Its
implications are beyond his grasp. Consequently when later, in

his prison, he heard of the works of Christ, he began to doubt (*St. Matthew* xi, 2, 3; *St. Luke* vii, 18, 19).[1] These cures and healings — could they be the fruit of Messiah's presence in the world? Very wonderful, no doubt, but not signs of the present or imminent Kingdom of God. Not in this way will the strongholds of evil be cast down or the universal reign of righteousness be established. And the Lord's answer is to invite John to consider again the very evidence that made him doubt.

For what is the great characteristic of those 'works of the Christ'? Not power, though that is present, but that in each and all of them we see power subordinate to love. And that is very near to being a definition of the principle of the Kingdom of God as Christ disclosed it. Power in subordination to love — that is the Spirit of the whole life of Christ, and it is the Spirit which descends out of heaven *as a dove*.

We do not know how far the Baptist in his prison could rise to the meaning of the answer to his question. But now, with the vision fresh in mind, he is carried to so profound an appreciation of the Person and Work of Christ that he leaves behind the current ideas of Messiahship and speaks in terms of voluntary sacrifice for the redemption of the world. And the result is that his disciples do not know that he has designated Jesus as Messiah in any sense at all. They have heard words of bewildering import, which will lead to their following Jesus rather than John himself. But they do not follow Him — yet — as Messiah. The confession of Simon Peter at Caesarea Philippi was the expression of a new intuition due to divine illumination (*St. Matthew* xvi, 17).

He who baptiseth with holy spirit. The contrasting words omitted in 26 are now supplied. And in the narrative which immediately follows, the process so described begins to be manifest in the first 'disciples'.

This is the Son of God. To let this appear is the purpose of

[1] See Introduction, p. xxxi.

the Evangelist in writing his Gospel (xx, 31). No doubt this is a Messianic title; but it is not necessarily so. If the centurion by the Cross used the phrase (*St. Matthew* xxvii, 54; contrast *St. Luke* xxiii, 47) he would probably not do so with a Messianic sense. The Baptist has made his confession; but the Lord's secret though penetrated is not fully disclosed.

*

(35–42)

35–42. The next day again John was standing and two of his disciples. And looking upon Jesus as he walked he saith 'Behold, the Lamb of God'. And the two disciples heard him as he spoke, and they followed Jesus. But Jesus, turning and beholding them following, saith to them 'What seek ye?' They said to him 'Rabbi (which being interpreted means Master), where abidest thou?' He saith to them 'Come and ye shall see'. They came therefore and saw where he abode, and they abode with him that day. It was about the tenth hour. Andrew the brother of Simon Peter was one of the two who had heard from John and had followed him. He findeth first his own brother Simon and saith to him 'We have found the Messiah (which is, being interpreted, the Christ)'. He brought him to Jesus. Jesus looking on him said 'Thou art Simon son of John; thou shalt be called Kephas, which is interpreted as Peter'.

They followed Jesus. The first in the long roll of followers. And they follow, as do most of us, because of what they have heard another say. We are Christians because we have been taught; and those who taught us were taught themselves; so the line runs back to Christ and those about Him. Even of these first it is true that He did not in the first instance call them to follow; later (*St. Mark* i, 16–20) He would call them Himself to a more dedicated following. Now they follow because of what is said by one whom they already trust, as we began to follow because of what our parents said. And He welcomes them and gives them opportunity to come to know Him and form their own impressions.

One of the two. The other, no doubt, was John, the Beloved Disciple.

He findeth first his own brother and so became the first missionary. We do not know very much about Andrew; but we know a great deal about his brother, and he was Andrew's convert. Who shall say that Peter himself did more for His Lord than Andrew who brought Peter to Him? It is ever so. We never know who is doing the greatest work for God. Here is a man who holds great office in the Church and preaches to multitudes; yet at the end, all he has done is to keep things from falling back. And there is a girl, poor and uneducated, of whom no one ever thinks; but because she is loving and devout she sows the seed of life in a child entrusted to her care who grows up to be a missionary pioneer, or Christian statesman, or profound theologian — shaping the history of nations or the thought of generations. Andrew *findeth his own brother*; perhaps it is as great a service to the Church as ever any man did.

We have found the Messiah. So the half-disclosure of the secret, backed by the impression of an evening in the Lord's company, had taken hold of their minds. Yet, at this stage, this was rather an outburst of exalted hope than a rooted conviction of faith.

He brought him to Jesus — the greatest service that one man can do another.

Thou art Simon. You are the man we know well; and what we know is that you are eager, impulsive, generous, loyal and essentially unreliable. But that is going to be altered. One day you shall be called by a name that no one would give you now — Rock-man.

It is not only through our qualities of native strength that God can work. Quite equally and more conspicuously He can make our weakness the opportunity of His grace. 'My grace is sufficient for thee; for my power is made perfect in weakness' (*II Corinthians* xii, 9). Perhaps to the end of his life the process of making Simon into Peter was not quite complete — as witness the *Quo Vadis* legend. We must consider later the story of the work of grace in St. Peter's life as St. John sketches it. But this promise at the outset of the Gospel is significant. When a man is brought to Jesus, Jesus can make him strong at the very point of his most apparent weakness.

*

(43–51)

43–51. The next day he was minded to go forth into Galilee, and findeth Philip and saith to him 'Follow me'. Now Philip was from Bethsaida, of the city of Andrew and Peter. Philip findeth Nathanael and saith to him 'We have found him of whom Moses in the Law and the Prophets did write, Jesus the son of Joseph, from Nazareth'. And Nathanael said to him 'Out of Nazareth can any good thing come?' Philip saith to him 'Come and see'. Jesus saw Nathanael coming to Him and saith of him 'Behold, truly an Israelite in whom there is no Jacob!' Nathanael saith to Him 'Whence knowest thou me?' Jesus answered and said to him 'Before Philip called thee, while thou wast under the fig-tree, I saw thee'. Nathanael answered Him 'Rabbi, thou art the Son of God, thou art King of Israel'. Jesus answered and said to him 'Because I said to thee "I saw thee under the fig-tree" believest thou? Greater things than these thou shalt see.' And he saith to him 'Amen, Amen, I say to you, ye shall see the heaven opened and the angels of God ascending and descending upon the Son of Man'.

He findeth Philip. Only one of all this group who become disciples is called by the Lord Himself. There is such a thing as a direct call without human intermediary; but it is rare.

Philip findeth Nathanael. As soon as he becomes a disciple he also becomes a missionary; that is the only true discipleship.

We have found. He carries on the exalted hope that breaks out in all this little band; and Nathanael will soon share it. But it is rather a flash than a steady glow of conviction.

Out of Nazareth. Though there is no guile, yet there is some pride of tradition in this true Israelite. There is no answer to that but the challenge of experience: *Come and see.*

c

Behold, truly an Israelite. The Lord's greeting presupposes that Nathanael had (like St. Augustine) gone under the fig-tree to meditate. While there he had been wrestling with God. This new movement, this new teacher — are they to be welcomed as from God? They are so unlike what men had learnt to expect. Above all, the place of origin. The contemptuous wonder of the reply to Philip — *Out of Nazareth?* — expresses the stumbling-block in his own mind. So under the fig-tree he wrestled; and so long ago Jacob the supplanter had wrestled with God and had won the new name Israel (*Genesis* xxxii, 24–29). The Lord hails this son of Israel as one in whom the Jacob-element of guile is not to be found.

Whence knowest thou me? How can you so intimately enter into my secret thoughts?

Before Philip called thee. My sympathy had reached you before your friend broke in with the news that so strangely chimed in with your thoughts.

Thou art the Son of God, thou art King of Israel. The fullest Messianic title yet used. Note the strongly Hebraic mentality for which it is in the order of climax to pass from *Son of God* to *King of Israel.* So our Lord is hailed at the outset with the title that will be used in mockery as He hangs on the Cross (*St. Mark* xv, 32) and will in its less theocratic form be set up over the Cross itself (xix, 19).

Because I said unto thee, I saw thee under the fig-tree, believest thou? Here, as where the parallel construction is used in the words to St. Thomas (xx, 29), the emphasis is on the contrast between the faith expressed and the inadequacy of its alleged ground. 'Do you mean to say it is because I said "I saw you" that you believe? No; of course it is not. It is because of that honest wrestling with doubt in which you showed yourself a true son of Israel. And now I will promise you greater things, still figured by the experience of the same Patriarch.' He had seen a ladder set up to heaven and 'the angels of God ascending and descending on it'. They bore the needs and prayers of men to the Lord 'who stood above it' and brought back His blessing and judgement (*Genesis* xxviii, 12, 13). God was far off, and messengers went to and fro. But now *Ye shall see the heaven opened and the angels of God ascending and descending upon the Son of Man.* No ladder now; the Messiah Himself is the meeting point of human need and divine blessing or judgement. But it is at once the Messiah in glory — for the apocalyptic association of the title Son of Man is inescapable, and also the Messiah in His utter humanity — for the phrase also retains this significance. And when we have fully learnt what is the glory of our God and of His Christ we shall see that no reconciliation of these two is called for; they are the same.

He has not refused the Messianic title; and He has spoken of a Messianic revelation. But He has not claimed the title; and He does not affirm that the Son of Man is Himself.

Amen, Amen I say to you. This is the first use of a phrase characteristic of the Johannine Christ; with the single 'Amen' it is familiar also in the Synoptists. The actual term that He used is retained in the Greek version, as is the term 'Abba' (*Romans* viii, 15; *Galatians* iv, 6) because it so vividly recalled Him and had gained from His use of it a special value. It is a term of strong asseveration. If attached to a petition it means 'So be it'; if attached to a statement it means 'Verily'. Being a familiar word, and the very word uttered by the Lord, it is kept in this translation.

In what precedes I have tried to interpret this first chapter in a manner compatible with the Synoptist narrative, in which the Confession made by Simon Peter at Caesarea Philippi is both a novelty and a turning point. So much of this chapter has the 'feel' of exact memory that I am uneasy about an interpretation which involves a view of it as pervasively influenced by an imagination stimulated by later beliefs; and I am convinced that the Marcan framework is substantially reliable. So I am led to regard the striking confessions here as what I have called them — outbursts of an exalted hope rather than formulations of settled conviction. As such they strike the keynote of the Gospel. For though in the process of the historical event the disciples passed from one stage of apprehension to another, yet we are now to read the story as Christians who at every stage 'behold his glory'.

CHAPTER II

(1) THE FIRST OF THE SEVEN SIGNS

IN the body of this Gospel — apart from the Epilogue — seven signs or miracles are recorded. 'Sign' is the word chosen by St. John to describe them, and he thus warns us that their meaning is something beyond themselves. Moreover the fact that he selects seven is a way of telling his readers that they are not to be read as mere episodes but as conveying a special truth which finds expression only in the whole series taken together. We may set out the signs and their significance in parallel columns thus (for this purpose we may assume the familiar order of the chapters):

1. The turning of water into wine: ii, 1–11	The difference that Christ makes
2. The healing of the nobleman's son: iv, 46–54	Faith the only requisite
3. The healing of the impotent man: v, 2–9	Christ the restorer of lost powers
4. The feeding of the five thousand: vi, 4–13	Christ the Food by which we live
5. The walking on the water: vi, 16–21	Christ our Guide
6. The healing of the man born blind: ix, 1–7	Christ our Light
7. The raising of Lazarus: xi, 1–44	Christ our Life

1. Our first intercourse with Christ — such as we have watched in the typical instances recorded in Chapter I — brings about a change like that from water to wine. Christ is not a grim task-master in obedience to whom life becomes gloomy. He compared himself to children playing at weddings in contrast with John the Baptist whom He compared to children

playing at funerals (*St. Luke* vii, 31–35; *St. Matthew* xi, 16–19). Joy is one of the fruits of His Spirit. We wholly fail to represent Him to men if we fail to make men see this in our lives.

2. But if we are to receive Him with His joy and His peace, we must ourselves put trust in Him. And it must not be a coerced belief (iv, 48) but a free acceptance of Him as Lord because of what we see Him to be.

3. When we first come to Him we are not fresh and unspoilt. Some quality of excellence — of strength or influence or natural charm — which was part of God's endowment of our nature, has already been damaged by our worldliness, selfishness or sensuality. And we cannot ourselves restore what is so lost. We cannot make real that 'face of our birth' — the man God made us to be — which we see sometimes in the mirror of the divine 'Law of liberty' (*St. James* i, 23–25). But Christ can do this for us.

4. When the consecrating touch has changed our life as from water to wine; when we have begun, at least, to fulfil the condition of loyal trust; we have to appreciate our continual dependence upon Him for all the strength with which to serve Him. He offers Himself to be our daily food, that we may 'feed upon Him in our hearts by faith with thanksgiving'.

5. So built up by His life, given that it may be ours, we find that He is our constant guide; and if, when we are battling with the storms of life, we welcome Him to be our companion, immediately we are at the haven where we would be.

6. But He is more than our Guide; the term suggests an external presence, pointing out the way. He is the very Light of Life whereby we see the way.

7. And even more than this: not only our strength, our guide, our light — He is to us Life itself. 'I live, yet no longer I, but Christ liveth in me' (*Galatians* ii, 20).

*

1–11. And the third day a marriage took place in Cana of Galilee, and the mother of Jesus was there, and Jesus also was called, and his disciples, to the marriage. And, the wine failing, the mother of Jesus saith to him 'They have no wine'. And Jesus saith to her 'Woman, leave me to myself; mine hour is not yet come'. His mother saith to the servants 'Whatsoever he saith to you, do it'. Now there were six water pots of stone, set after the manner of the purifying of the Jews, containing two or three firkins apiece. Jesus saith to them 'Fill the water pots with water'. And they filled them up to the brim. And he saith to them 'Draw now and bear unto the ruler of the feast'. And they bare it. And when the ruler of the feast tasted the water which had become wine and knew not whence it was (but the servants who had drawn the water knew) the ruler calleth the bridegroom and saith to him 'Every man first setteth on the good wine, and when men have well drunk, the less good; but thou hast kept the good wine until now'. This as a beginning of his signs Jesus wrought in Cana of Galilee and manifested his glory; and his disciples believed on him.

The third day. In i, 43 we were told of the Lord's intention to go to Galilee. It was a three days' journey. The party arrives to find the marriage feast in full course. Already *the mother of Jesus was there,* and was apparently in some position of responsibility as her concern about the wine and her instructions to the servants show. When the Lord and His disciples appear, they are at once called in. But this involves the addition of unexpected guests — seven of them if all mentioned in the last chapter are there. This puts a strain on the provision that had been made, which would account for Mary's concern, though not for her direction to the servants. When, as a result of the addition to the party, the wine had failed, she calls her Son's attention to this consequence of His presence and that of His disciples. But He has noticed it, and knows what He means to do.

Woman, leave me to myself. No English phrase will represent the original, unless we depart very far from it. For us the word 'Woman' is unfamiliar as a mode of address, and has about it a repellent tone. In the Greek it is perfectly respectful and can even be tender — as in xix, 27, *Woman, behold thy son.* We have no corresponding term; 'Lady' is precious, and

'Madam' is formal. So we must translate simply, and let the context give the tone. But unhappily the next words are as difficult. Here too there is no harshness in the original. The phrase 'What to me and to thee?' is a Greek translation of a Hebrew idiom; it is quite colourless emotionally. Jephthah uses it to the Ammonites when he is ready to fight them (*Judges* xi, 12). Something like 'leave me alone' best represents it; but imports a touch of petulance which is out of place. Perhaps the sense would be carried by 'It is all right. It is not time for me yet'.

Mine hour here immediately refers to His action in face of the emergency; but it means more; it means the hour for manifesting His glory (11); and so it carries the suggestion that this coming manifestation is very partial and, as it were, preliminary. Contrast xvii, 1, *Father, the hour is come; glorify thy Son* — spoken on the threshold of the Passion.

His mother, now satisfied that He will do what is needed, tells the servants to obey whatever He commands. He bids them fill with water the huge waterpots (1 firkin = 8½ gallons), now nearly or quite empty because the feast is near its end and the water has been freely drawn for the washing both of hands and of vessels used in the feast.

The water that had become wine. There is no possibility of doubt that the Evangelist means to record a 'miracle'. And it makes little difference whether we take him to mean that all the water in the stone pots had become wine, or only that which was drawn by the servants to supply what was needed. In any case the Creator of matter is exercising His lordship over it; 'the modest water saw its God and blushed'.

Every man at the beginning. There is a trace of emphasis on *man*; the word is introduced, as, in the Greek, it need not have been; and for us, though not for the ruler, a contrast is implicit. For here we come to a secondary meaning of this sign. The first is the change effected by the touch of Christ upon our life; the second is the reminder that there is always more and better to come. *Every man* puts forward first what is best about him. When people first meet us, they find us civil, friendly, considerate; but as they come to know us, especially if they have to live with us, they have to put up with *the less good — that which is worse.* But in our communion with God it is not so; as we deepen our fellowship with Him, made known in Christ, at every stage we may say *Thou hast kept the good wine until now.*

Manifested his glory. To whom? Not to all men. The ruler of the feast did not know the origin of the wine which he praised. The servants knew, and, doubtless, wondered. But only to *His disciples* (*we* beheld His glory) was the glory manifest; and they believed on Him.

They are first called 'disciples' at the beginning of this narrative; and by that name they are designated throughout this Gospel. It is as learners that we are to think of them, and to take our place among them.

His disciples believed on him. It is the phrase expressive of personal trust. They are not here said to believe Him, in the sense of believing that what He said was true, but to commit themselves to Him in personal trust.

This is the faith which justifies. To believe true doctrine concerning Christ may help us to believe *on* Him; but for our spiritual welfare this latter is alone vital. For the Church, commissioned to transmit to all generations the true doctrine which may elicit saving faith, heresy is more deadly than hypocrisy or even than conscious sin; but for the individual the one vital matter is personal trust, and accepted heresy in its effect upon his soul may be quite unimportant. There have been saintly heretics and orthodox worldlings. Vast confusion has arisen because men have not distinguished between the functions of the Church and of the individual believer in the economy of the divine purpose. To the Church heresy is more destructive than conscious sin; to the individual conscious sin is more destructive than heresy; to both, idolatry — worship of

God falsely conceived — is deadlier than either heresy or sin,
for it is the prolific source of each.

*

12. After this he went down to Capernaum, he and his mother and his
brethren and his disciples; and there they remained not many days.

It is not quite easy to see why this visit to Capernaum is
recorded. Perhaps St. John's motive is to supply the background
of the demand which the Lord is recorded to have anticipated
at Nazareth at the end of His first sermon there after the
beginning of His ministry (*St. Luke* iv, 23).

*

(2) THE CLEANSING OF THE TEMPLE

13-17. And the Passover of the Jews was near, and Jesus went up to
Jerusalem. And He found in the temple the sellers of oxen and sheep
and doves, and the changers of money sitting. And having made a
scourge of small cords he drove them all out of the temple, both the
sheep and the oxen; and he poured out the changers' money and over-
threw the tables; and to the dove-sellers he said 'Take these things
hence; make not my Father's house a house of merchandise'. His
disciples remembered that it is written: 'The zeal of thine house will
devour me'.

The first visit to Jerusalem since the ministry began. His
coming means a purge. So it is always, not less with the shrine
of our hearts than with the Jewish Temple. The place which
should be ordered with the reverence appropriate to the
dwelling-place of God is cluttered up with worldly ambitions,
anxieties about our possessions, designs to get the better of our
neighbours. This traffic of the Temple courts was more than a
profanity against the holy place; it was an exploitation of the
people. The High Priests insisted that the Temple dues should
be paid in Jewish coins — not Roman coins stamped with the
image of a heathen emperor. And they provided an exchange

— at which a large percentage was deducted. Also they arranged for the convenience of worshippers, and incidentally their own large profit, to sell the animals needed for sacrifice. These 'booths of Annas' were an object of detestation. But none had dared to attack them forcibly. They had the sanction of custom; they were not illegal. But it does not appear that the Lord proposed any 'compensation' for their 'eviction'.

It is a tremendous scene. The Lord dominates the multitude by the righteousness of His energy and the energy of His righteousness!

And at once there is that division among those who witness the scene, which St. John records as being the almost invariable result of the words and actions of the Lord. We shall bring all these together in connexion with a key-saying in the next chapter (iii, 19). The disciples remembered a prophecy (*Psalm* lxix, 9) and realised that they had witnessed its fulfilment. The Jews were (very naturally) outraged and demanded some justification.

*

18–22. The Jews therefore answered and said to him, 'What sign showest thou unto us, seeing that thou doest these things?' Jesus answered and said to them 'Destroy this temple, and in three days I will raise it up'. The Jews therefore said 'Forty and six years was this temple in building, and thou — wilt thou raise it up in three days?' But *he* was speaking of the temple of his body. When therefore he was raised from the dead, his disciples remembered that he spake this; and they believed the scripture and the word which Jesus had said.

The Lord had exercised authority, but also He had made a claim which demanded vindication. He had called the Temple *my Father's house*. It was not a new thought to Him. Long ago when His mother and St. Joseph had sought Him sorrowing, He had said 'Did you not know that I was bound to be in my Father's house?' (*St. Luke* ii, 49). In His indignation He has used it now — not (we may suppose) with any intention of making a peculiar claim, but because in the moment of tension His relationship to the Father whose house is profaned forces

its way to spontaneous utterance. But the words have been
spoken and the deeds done. What are His credentials? What
evidence can He give that He really holds the divine commission which He has apparently executed?

Vain enquiry! When God speaks to either the heart or the
conscience He does not first prove His right to do so. The
divine command is its own evidence, and the heart or conscience
that is not utterly numbed by complacent sin recognises its inherent authority.

Yet He offers a sign; it is a sign which only those whose
hearts are already His will be able to accept (xx, 29); but that is
essential to His whole purpose, which positively forbids the
winning by irresistible proof of unwilling adherents to His
cause.

The Temple — the habitation of God among men — is the
subject as well as the scene of the controversy. Very well; let it
furnish the sign demanded. *Destroy this Temple* — not an
empty challenge, but a judgement on their mentality and policy
which will involve the destruction of the Temple (*St. Luke* xix,
41–44). *And in three days I will raise up* what shall thereafter be
the habitation of God among men, that Risen Body which
after the Ascension and Pentecost finds its earthly manifestation in that 'holy temple in the Lord, in whom ye also are
builded together for a habitation of God in the Spirit'
(*Ephesians* ii, 21–22).

Of course the Jews cannot understand, and it was only later
that the disciples understood. The Jews would remember the
saying to another purpose. They would put up false witnesses
who would accuse Him of saying 'I will destroy this temple
made with hands and in three days I will build another made
without hands' (*St. Mark* xiv, 58). That was not what He said.
He did not say He would destroy the Temple, but put forward
the supposition that the Jews would. To that He answered that
this would make no difference to the dwelling of God among
men. He Himself would, in a period so short as to be negligible,
supply that dwelling-place of God.

In three days. The phrase is taken from *Hosea* vi, 2, 'After two days will he revive us, on the third day he will raise us up'. Its meaning has been expressed above.

He was speaking. Of course this does not mean that the words 'Destroy this Temple' referred to His body. Obviously those words refer to Herod's structure. But what gives meaning to His words is the fact that spiritually His body fulfils the function which the Temple was built to fulfil.

It is true that in mere chronology the destruction of the Temple as a physical structure took place after its substitute was already provided. But it had lost its meaning. It was no longer in any true sense the Temple. At the date of the controversy which we are studying it was still *my Father's house*. Before the ministry ends it is 'your house' — 'Your house is left unto you desolate' (*St. Luke* xiii, 35).

*

23–25. Now when he was in Jerusalem at the feast, many trusted on his name, beholding his signs which he was doing. But on his part Jesus did not trust himself to them owing to the fact that he knew all men and because he had no need that any should bear witness concerning any man; for he himself knew what was in the man.

His activity at this first Passover of the ministry wins some disciples in Jerusalem. But their faith at present rests on His signs — outward works — which is later marked as no more than a second best (xiv, 11). Consequently the Lord does not commit Himself to them; for He always knew what anyone — friend or foe — had in him. He never needed to ask concerning any who came to Him, for He knew what was in the man, as He had known all about Nathanael (i, 47–48). It is not only the Fourth Gospel that so represents Him. In the Synoptic record also He appears as always acting towards all men with complete sureness of touch.

He did not trust himself to them because he knew. Yet now that He is ascended, He calls us into His Church to be members of His Body — that Temple of God which He raised up when, breaking the bands of death, He revived the ancient Church of God which two days earlier had found in Him its only representative as He went forth alone to die; and having revived it, He incorporated into it those whom His Gospel reached, so that we are now His limbs through which He speaks and acts.

He knows us; and He does trust Himself to us!

NOTE

The difference between St. John and St. Mark with regard to the date of the Cleansing of the Temple will be discussed when we reach Chapter XI. St. John is right about it.

CHAPTER III

(1) The Conversation with Nicodemus (1–17)

1–17. Now there was a man of the Pharisees, Nicodemus was his name, a ruler of the Jews. This man came to him by night and said to him, 'Rabbi, we know that thou art come from God as a teacher; for no one can do these signs that thou doest unless God be with him'. Jesus answered and said unto him 'Amen, Amen I say to thee, unless a man be born again, he cannot see the Kingdom of God'. Nicodemus saith unto him, 'How can a man be born when he is old? Can he enter a second time into his mother's womb and be born?' Jesus answered 'Amen, Amen I say to thee, unless a man be born of water and spirit, he cannot enter into the Kingdom of God. That which is born of the flesh is flesh; and that which is born of the spirit is spirit. Marvel not that I said to thee "Ye must be born again". The wind bloweth where it listeth, and thou hearest its voice, but thou knowest not whence it cometh and whither it goeth; so is every one that is born of the spirit.' Nicodemus answered and said to him, 'How can these things come to pass?' Jesus answered and said to him, 'Art *thou* the teacher of Israel, and dost thou not recognise these things? Amen, Amen I say to thee that what we know we speak and what we have seen we testify; and ye receive not our testimony. If I told you earthly things and ye believe not, how, if I tell you heavenly things, shall ye believe? And no one hath gone up to heaven but he that came down out of heaven, the Son of Man. And as Moses lifted up the serpent in the wilderness, so must the Son of Man be lifted up, that everyone that believeth on him may have eternal Life. For God so loved the world that he gave his only begotten Son, that every one that believeth on him may not perish but have eternal Life. For God sent not the Son into the world to judge the world, but that the world may be saved through him.'

HERE we see the Lord in conversation with the highly placed ecclesiastic, who, after the manner of his kind, is cautious and diplomatic. He is genuinely impressed. He recognises that the new movement is from God, or at any rate is to some extent approved by God. But he does not want to commit himself irrecoverably. If he comes out into the open, he will lose influence in the exalted quarters in which he moves, and incidentally forfeit the power to help the new movement which a friend in those quarters could exert. So he comes *by night* to where the Lord is seated with His disciples among the olives on the hill-side — perhaps in that garden where *Jesus oft-times resorted* (xviii, 2).

He begins with compliments; we need not doubt their sincerity though we taste their diplomatic flavour. *We know that thou art come from God to teach us; for no one can do these signs that thou doest unless God be with him.* We notice that it is not the quality of the teaching but the evidence of the signs that has won this measure of recognition and approval; at the most then, it is the second-best kind of recognition (xiv, 11). Still, it is recognition of a sort.

But compliments are swept aside. Diplomatic approaches are out of place; sympathetic interest is no good. A new start — that is what is needed. The burden of the Lord's teaching has been the imminence of the Kingdom of God. It is as a teacher that Nicodemus has greeted him — a teacher divinely authenticated. Well — the theme of His discourse is the Kingdom; and it is something that Nicodemus cannot so much as look upon unless he makes that new start. *Unless a man be born again he cannot see the kingdom of God. See* — look upon; he cannot even know what it is that we are talking about.

Born again or *born from above?* The Greek words carry both meanings, and it is not necessary to choose. The element 'again' is here primary; but that new birth has only one source. A man cannot accomplish it for himself — as Nicodemus knows and is quick to point out; '*How can a man be born when* [*like me*] *he is old?*' This Church-leader has inherited a great tradition, for he was a Pharisee; he has tested it in the experience of life; he has conformed to it his habits of conduct, speech, thought and feeling. How can he break away from all this and begin again? It is as hard as it would be literally to return to *his mother's womb and be born*.

All the same, that is what is wanted. And there is a power that can accomplish it, though no man, truly, could do it for himself. *Unless a man be born of water and spirit he cannot enter into the kingdom of God.* There could be no doubt in the mind of Nicodemus what is meant by being *born of water.* The baptism of John was an institution known to all. The first step needed is openly to become an adherent of John's revival, the mission of repentance, in which has sounded after so long a silence the authentic voice of prophecy. That first; but that is not enough. John was greater than all before him, yet not so great as the lesser in the Kingdom of Heaven (*St. Luke* vii, 28; *St. Matthew* xi, 11). To enter that Kingdom something more is needed than open adherence to John the Baptist. The Baptist himself contrasted what he could do for men through baptism with water with what his Successor would do through baptism with holy spirit and fire. That too is needed — for which the condition is discipleship to Christ. In other words — You must do what these disciples of mine have done; first openly seek John's baptism, and then openly join this company, among whom the power of the new birth, the new life, is moving. For life cannot any more than water rise above its source. If its source is flesh, at that level it remains; if its source is spirit, that quality will be apparent in it. *That which is born of the flesh is flesh; and that which is born of the spirit is spirit.*

But now that the Lord has spoken of the manner of the new birth, He no longer connects with this the ability only to *see* or to *look upon the Kingdom of God* as an objective fact; He connects with it the power to *enter into the Kingdom* — to know it from within by personal experience of it. And this is possible for all, because the power is at work. There should be no occasion to *marvel* at this thought of the fresh start. An illustration is to hand. The rustling of the olive trees speaks of the movement of the wind. The Greek word for spirit has the suggestion of breath or wind; the Hebrew word — *Ruach* — actually means the desert-wind, that powerful unseen force that sweeps across the face of the earth, none knows whence or whither. *The wind* — the Spirit — *it bloweth where it listeth,*

*and thou hearest its voice, but thou knowest not whence it cometh
and whither it goeth.* But you can feel its breath on your face if,
hearing it pass, you go out and stand in its course. *So is everyone that is born of the Spirit.* Don't ask for credentials. Don't
wait till you know the source of the wind before you let it
refresh you, or its destination before you spread sail to it. It
offers what you need; trust yourself to it.

But for Nicodemus this only makes matters worse. God has
given the Law, and by devout labour trusted leaders have
worked out its application. He has made a covenant with His
people and they know their part in response to it. This talk
of the freely blowing wind is destructive of the sacred fabric of
institutional religion. *How can these things come to pass?*

And now the Lord turns upon him in sheer amazement. Do
you mean to say that *you* are an accredited *teacher of Israel*
and cannot recognise the experience of which I speak? Why,
with us it is the barest commonplace of intercourse with God.
What we know, we speak; and what we have seen, we testify.
Our witness is drawn from undeniable experience; *and yet ye
receive not our testimony.* And if you cannot believe what to us
is an everyday experience of our earthly life, how can you
become receptive to those higher truths which belong to the
life of heaven and which I am come to make known. *If I told
you earthly things and ye believe not, how, if I tell you heavenly
things, shall ye believe?*

For of those truths there is only one messenger. You cannot
go to heaven and find them; they can be declared only by
one who comes from heaven, the representative of God in
whom human nature finds its true expression. *No one hath
gone up to heaven but he that came down out of heaven, the Son
of Man.*

The Son of Man — that title which represents at once the
Messiah in His glory and the fulfilment of all that humanity
can be and is meant to be. The revelation of divine truth in
human nature and the manifestation of all that human nature
is meant by God to be, are not two things but one. For man

was created in the image of God, and when he corresponds to the divine intention, he is the image of God. But only in one instance has that conformity been complete, so that He alone is the 'image of the invisible God' (*Colossians* i, 15); and He *came down out of heaven*.

Some ancient student has added here the words *which is in heaven*. Whatever their origin, they represent a most important truth. The Second Person of the Blessed Trinity was no less *in heaven* during the period of the earthly ministry than either before or after it. What we see as we watch the life of Jesus is the very life of heaven — indeed of God — in human expression.

And now comes a first hint of the *heavenly things*. It is not enough that the Son of Man should *come down out of heaven*; He *must be lifted up*. The necessity — *must* — is grounded in the nature of God. Because God is what He is, this 'lifting up' is inevitable. But as yet its meaning is undisclosed. In itself the word suggests triumph; and that is part of the meaning. But the reference to *the serpent in the wilderness* makes it clear that something more specific is in view. What that is becomes plain when He says, '*I, if I be lifted up from the earth, will draw all men unto me*' (xii, 32, 33). But here that reference to the Cross is not yet so clear as to obscure in any degree the thought of triumph: so we are prepared to have the thought of triumph in our minds as we approach the Cross, and to enter into the great Johannine apprehension that the Passion is the divine Glory.

The Passion could not be this if it were barren of results; but its purpose is known — *that every one that believeth on him may have eternal Life*.

So we come to the central declaration, more central for Christian faith than even *The Word became flesh;* for that depends for its inexhaustible wealth of meaning on the actual mode of the Incarnate Life. But here is the whole great truth. *God so loved the world that he gave his only begotten Son, that everyone that believeth on him may not perish, but have eternal*

Life. This is the heart of the Gospel. Not 'God is Love' — a precious truth, but affirming no divine act for our redemption. *God so loved that he gave*; of course the words indicate the cost to the Father's heart. *He gave*; it was an act, not only a continuing mood of generosity; it was an act at a particular time and place. 'Blessed be the Lord God of Israel' — it is not a universally diffused divine essence of which we speak, but the Living God — 'for he *hath visited and redeemed* his people'.

No object is sufficient for the love of God short of *the world* itself. Christianity is not one more religion of individual salvation, differing from its fellows only in offering a different road to that goal. It is the one and only religion of world-redemption. Of course it includes a way of individual salvation as the words before and after this great saying show. But its scope is wider than that — as wide as the love of God. It is a *sin of the world* that Christ takes away (i, 29).

Thus is opened up a new conception of the Son of Man and the Day of the Lord. Devout Jews looked forward to the Coming of the Son of Man as meaning redemption for themselves but judgement for the world. It is not so. Judgement may be, must be, an incidental consequence of the Coming; but its purpose is salvation for all the world. *God sent not his Son into the world to judge the world, but that the world may be saved through him.*

Here, as I read it, St. John's version of the Lord's discourse to Nicodemus ends, and his own comment begins. We have been led a long way from the opening. And yet the great saying *God so loved the world* is in no way alien from the opening words about the Lord as a teacher and that Kingdom which was the burden of His teaching. For this great saying states the mode of His sovereignty, and therefore also the quality of His Kingdom. The throne of that Kingdom in this world is a Cross and its crown is made of thorns. It is this revolutionary disclosure which gives ground for the sharp dismissal of diplomatic compliments. The whole conception of the Kingdom is so novel that only those who are ready to make a new start can even *see* it, let alone *enter into* it.

It is a familiar experience to know and accept the verbal statement of the great truths with minds that continue to find them novel; still the new start is necessary if the heirs of a partially Christian civilisation are to see or to enter the Kingdom of God. Always the breath — the wind — of the Spirit is moving. We know it by its effect. We have no need to ask for its authentication — Is it Protestant? Is it Catholic? Where the fruit of the Spirit (*Galatians* v, 22, 23) is apparent, there the Spirit is at work. We should place ourselves in its course that we may be carried by its impulse, even though this leads us to association with strange comrades — as, no doubt, the Galilean fishermen seemed to Nicodemus. For whatever promotes among men love and joy and peace has its source in that divine love which sent the Son into the world, not to judge the world, but *that the world may be saved through him.*

*

(2) SALVATION AND JUDGEMENT

18-21. He that believeth on him is not under judgement. He that believeth not hath been judged already, because he hath not believed on the name of the only begotten Son of God. And this is the judgement, that the light is come into the world, and men loved rather the darkness than the light; for evil were their works. For every one that doeth ill hateth the light, and cometh not to the light, that his works may not be put to the test. But he that doeth the truth cometh to the light, that his works may be made manifest that in God they have been wrought.

The belief in question is more than opinion, or even conviction. It is personal trust. This includes a conviction, explicit or implicit. If it remains implicit there will be little harm done through its being erroneous in some particular; and therefore we need not disturb the naïve convictions of simple people. But if it becomes explicit it is important that it be rightly

balanced; otherwise at some time or other it will occasion
loss of trust to others if not to the man who holds the distorted or heretical view.

One who so trusts in the *name* — the manifested nature — *of
the only begotten Son of God* is not *under judgement*. In St.
Paul's language he is 'in Christ'. And assuredly 'there is no
condemnation to them that are in Christ Jesus' (*Romans* viii,
1). But that implies a completeness of trust to which very few
of us have attained. Most of us do not either believe in this full
sense or disbelieve. We believe enough to wish that we believed more; 'I believe; help thou mine unbelief' (*St. Mark* ix,
24); and even this is enough to earn the longed-for boon.

We can hardly remain in an equipoise between belief and
unbelief. We are inclining to one side or the other. As a wise
man once said, 'There's God and there's yourself; and you
are settling down on one or the other'. If a man refuses belie
— trust — in the manifested nature of the Son of God, *he hath
been judged already*. There is no further verdict needed; his
conduct finds him guilty. His failure to accept the revelation
when it comes is itself the judgement on the character he has
been forming.

For the essence of judgement is not the sentence but the
verdict, the discrimination between the approved and the condemned. The Cross itself, the very means of redemption, is an
agent of that discrimination, that judgement. 'For the word
of the Cross is to them that are perishing foolishness, but to
us who are being saved it is the power of God' (*I Corinthians*
i, 18). The offer of salvation involves judgement, and (for
those who refuse the offer) condemnation. *For this is the
[process of] judgement, that the light is come into the world, and
men loved rather the darkness than the light.* We recall the
words of the Prologue: *There was the light, that lighteth every
man, coming into the world* (i, 9). No greater gift can be offered
to men; yet many refuse it. They *loved the darkness rather than
the light*. That is their choice; there is nothing worse that can
be done to them after that.

So the presence in the world of Christ who is the light of the world issues, automatically so to speak, in the judgement of the world. To make this clear is one purpose of the Evangelist. The Fourth Gospel is in a special sense the Gospel of Judgement. It shows the Lord moving among men and sifting them. Judgement is not the purpose of His coming (iii, 17; cf. *I judge no man*, viii, 15; *I came not to judge the world but to save the world*, xii, 47, 48); yet His coming issues in judgement (cf. *Neither doth the Father judge any man, but he hath given all judgement unto the Son*, v, 22; *He gave him authority to execute judgement*, v, 27; *For judgement came I into this world*, ix, 39). The reconciling thought is here — that the judgement consists in the coming of the light and men's refusal of it.

Accordingly at the close of very many episodes we are shown the discrimination in process. The healing of the impotent man leads the Jews to persecute Jesus (v, 16); the discourse on the Bread of Life leads to a great defection of adherents (vi, 66); later the division among His hearers becomes more marked (vii, 12; 30, 31, 43; viii, 30; x, 19–21; xi, 45, 46; xii, 37, 42). The Lord speaks and acts; by their reaction men are judged.

For everyone that doeth ill hateth the light and cometh not to the light, lest his works may be put to the test. It is not only fear of discovery and punishment that keeps him away. He shrinks from the appearance that he will present in that illumination and in that contrast. Edward Caird once said, 'Poetry is the criticism of life in the sense in which a good man is the criticism of a bad man'. And the bad man resents that form of criticism!

But he that doeth the truth cometh to the light, that his works may be made manifest that in God they have been wrought. A right act is, as Westcott says, 'so much of truth made visible'. So to do good and to *do the truth* are identical. But the phrase is specially appropriate in the context of the light that brings judgement; it suggests the openness and straightforwardness

of right doing, in contrast with the concealment which is a part
of all falsehood. Such right action is always *wrought in God*.
We 'cannot do anything that is good without', that is apart
from, God. And when a doer of the truth is set beside the true
light it becomes evident that he has been guided by that
illumination.

*

22–24. After these things came Jesus and his disciples into the land of
Judaea; and there he tarried with them and baptised. And John also
was baptising at Fountains near to Peace, because water was abundant
there. And men continued to come and were baptised. For not yet had
John been cast into prison.

The Lord left Judaea at the end of Chapter I; the ministry
was then only beginning and He had not preached in public.
In ii, 1–12 we find Him in Cana of Galilee and Capernaum. In
ii, 13 He returns and the Judaean ministry begins. He preaches
first in the Temple itself (ii, 16); then in Jerusalem (ii, 23–iii,
21); then in Judaea (iii, 22–24). As He is rejected in each He
moves further from the centre, until (iv, 3) He goes back to
Galilee, which becomes the chief sphere of His activity, though
He goes to Jerusalem for various feasts, and when there continues His teaching. Rejection by the headquarters of the
Jewish Church is already in process; the judgement has begun.

And now for a while the Lord and His Forerunner are working side by side. There is a symbolism in the name of the place
which John had chosen — Fountains near to Peace. For John
called men to repentance, and he who truly repents has found
the peace of God.

This proximity gives rise to questions, which call forth the
Baptist's last testimony to the Lord.

*

25–30. There arose therefore a questioning on the part of John's disciples
with a Jew about purifying. And they came to John and said to him
'Rabbi, he that was with thee beyond Jordan, to whom thou hast borne
witness, behold he baptiseth and all are coming to him'. John answered
and said 'A man cannot take to himself anything, unless it have been

given to him out of heaven. Ye yourselves bear me witness that I said
"I am not the Christ", but that I have been sent before him. He that
hath the bride is the bridegroom. But the friend of the bridegroom,
which standeth and heareth him, with joy rejoiceth because of the voice
of the bridegroom. This joy, therefore, which is mine, hath been
fulfilled. He must increase, but I must decrease.'

While they worked close together it became apparent that
more were going to the Lord than to John (cf. iv, 1). A Jew,
apparently, brought this information to some of John's company. These are naturally jealous for their master's honour.
First they discuss the relative value of the two ministrations.
Then they turn to their master with the news that has disturbed
them. But it does not disturb him. He knows that if any man
exercises power it is because God has given him that power; he
cannot take it to himself, but receives from God whatever he
has. Moreover, the Baptist had always said that his was a
secondary part; he was a forerunner, not the Christ; he was a
'best man', not the bridegroom. But he is the bridegroom's
friend, and *with joy rejoiceth because of the voice of the bridegroom.*

In the growing influence of Jesus John finds his own joy
fulfilled. Is not this near to the perfection of humility and self-
abnegation? It is hard to lead multitudes and find that another
is leading greater multitudes. It is harder still to rejoice
at it. Yet that is the very quality of the Baptist's joy. *The
joy that is mine hath been fulfilled. He must increase, but I must
decrease.*

The Evangelist adds his comment. It was truly necessary
that the Lord should increase and the Baptist decrease, *for he
that cometh from above is above all.*

*

31–36. He that cometh from above is above all. He that is from the earth
is from the earth and speaketh from the earth. He that cometh from
heaven beareth witness of what he hath seen and heard; and his witness no one receiveth. He that did receive his witness affixed his seal

that God is true. For he whom God sent — the words of God he
speaketh. For he giveth not the spirit by measure. The Father loveth
the Son and hath given all things into his hand. He that believeth on
the Son hath Life; but he that disobeyeth the Son shall not see Life,
but the wrath of God abideth on him.

Every man must speak according to the spring and source
of his moral being. If this is the earth *he speaketh from the
earth.* This has no suggestion of evil; the Lord's teaching
about the free movement of the Spirit was an 'earthly thing'
(12); and in that sense John's preaching was from the earth.
It was indeed in another sense from heaven, for he was
assuredly moved by the Spirit of God. Yet his material,
so to speak, was such experience, religious and other, as is
possible to ordinary men. *He that cometh from heaven
beareth witness of what he hath seen and heard.* Out of that
union with the Father which is His alone the Lord draws
heavenly knowledge which none can have but Himself and
any who learn from Him. We recall the great saying in the
Synoptists: 'All things have been delivered unto me of my
Father; and no one knoweth who the Son is, save the
Father; and who the Father is, save the Son and he to whomsoever the Son willeth to reveal him' (*St. Luke* x, 22; *St.
Matthew* xi, 27).

No one receiveth. For a moment the Evangelist transports
us into his own period, when for a while the Church seemed
to make no progress. But it was not always so. There had
been those who *did receive his witness* and have in most
solemn manner committed themselves to the truth then
revealed.

He whom God hath sent — the words of God he speaketh. It
is stated as a general truth; but it is stated on the basis of an
actual memory — the memory of the days of discipleship
when experience drew from Peter the exclamation *Thou hast
words of eternal Life* (vi, 68). And the power to do this comes
from the completeness of the spiritual endowment of the Christ.
He (sc. *God*) *giveth not the spirit by measure.* The gift of God

is always perfect and complete as He offers it. But we cannot receive it in its perfection because of our defect of faith. But in the Lord was no such defect, and He received the Spirit in all the fulness of the divine gift.

The Father loveth the Son and hath given all things into his hand. We recall again the great saying quoted above, and also the all-embracing claim 'All authority hath been given unto me in heaven and on earth' (*St. Matthew* xxviii, 18).

So we come to the conclusion of the contrast between the Baptist and the Lord, and are carried back to what had been said concerning judgement. *He that believeth on the Son hath eternal Life.* We have already reminded ourselves that this 'belief' is the personal trust of complete self-committal. That committal of ourselves does not earn eternal life; rather it is eternal life; cf. xvii, 3.

He that disobeyeth the Son shall not see Life. It is not only that he cannot enter into it or possess it; he can never know what it is so long as his disobedience lasts. The presentation of the Gospel to the worldly minded always suffers under this disability, that the world confidently believes it to be something quite different from what it is. It cannot 'see' it. So the deepest truths, such as the predestinating grace of God, are perverted and become the source of inferences contradictory to their real meaning.[1] So men think of eternal life as the everlasting happiness of a still self-centred soul. But it is nothing of the kind. It is fellowship with God in which our souls, so far as they are self-centred, can find no happiness.

The wrath of God abideth on him. Terrible words. A sentimental and hedonist generation tries to eliminate 'wrath' from its conception of God. Of course, if 'anger' and 'wrath' are taken to mean the emotional reaction of an irritated self-concern, there is no such thing in God. But if God is holy love, and I am in any degree given to uncleanness or selfishness, then

---

[1] For an elaboration of this theme see my *Nature, Man and God*, pp. 378–381.

there is, in that degree, stark antagonism in God against me. And so long as I am disobedient that *wrath of God* continues. 'O terrible voice of most just judgement. . . .' But let us, *while we have the light, believe in the light, that we may become sons of light.*

CHAPTER IV

1–4. When therefore the Lord knew that the Pharisees had heard that 'Jesus is making and baptising more disciples than John' (and yet Jesus himself was not baptising but his disciples) he left Judaea and departed again into Galilee. And he must needs go through Samaria.

THE Pharisees were already hostile. They were hostile to John, and here is one who continues John's work with greater effectiveness. They were already hostile to Jesus, and His success is bound to quicken their hostility. So He *left Judaea*, and the word used suggests leaving it to its fate. He has been pressed back from the Temple to the city, from the city to the country-side. Now He leaves it altogether; and His way lies through Samaria.

*

5–26. He cometh therefore to a city of Samaria called Sychar, near the portion of ground that Jacob gave to Joseph his son. And there was there Jacob's spring. Jesus therefore being wearied from his journey sat, as he was, by the spring. It was about the sixth hour. There cometh a woman out of Samaria to draw water. Jesus saith to her 'Give me to drink'. (For his disciples were gone away into the city to buy food.) The Samaritan woman therefore saith to him 'How is it that thou, being a Jew, askest drink of me, who am a woman and a Samaritan?' (For Jews have no dealings with Samaritans.) Jesus answered and said to her 'If thou hadst known the gift of God, and who it is that said to thee "Give me to drink", it would be thou that wouldst be asking him, and he would have given thee living water'. The woman saith to him 'Sir, thou hast nothing to draw with and the well is deep; from whence then hast thou the living water? Am I to believe that thou art greater than our father Jacob, who gave us the well, and himself drank of it and his sons and his cattle?' Jesus answered and said to her 'Every one that drinketh of this water shall thirst again; but whosoever drinketh of the water that I shall give him shall not thirst unto eternity; but the water which I shall give him shall become in him a spring of water springing into eternal Life'. The woman saith unto him 'Sir, give me this water, that I thirst not neither come hither to draw'. Jesus saith to her 'Go, call thy husband and come hither'. The woman answered and said to him 'I have no husband'. Jesus saith to her 'Thou saidst well "I have

no husband"; for five didst thou have as husbands and he whom now
thou hast is not thy husband. This thou hast said truly.' The woman
saith to him 'Sir, I perceive that thou art a prophet. Our fathers worshipped in this mountain, and ye say that in Jerusalem is the place
where men must worship.' Jesus saith to her 'Believe me, woman, that
the hour cometh when neither in this mountain nor in Jerusalem shall
ye worship the Father. Ye worship what ye know not; we worship
what we know; for salvation is from the Jews. But the hour cometh and
now is when the true worshippers shall worship the Father in spirit and
truth; indeed the Father seeketh such for his worshippers. God is Spirit,
and they that worship him, in spirit and truth must worship.' The
woman saith to him 'I know that Messiah cometh' (which is called
Christ): 'when he is come, he will announce all things to us'. Jesus
saith to her 'I am he, I that am speaking to thee'.

The course of the conversation is easily followed. The Lord
is alone by the well and has no means of drawing water; so
when the woman comes He asks her to draw and give Him to
drink. She is surprised, for He is manifestly a Jew, and she is a
Samaritan and a woman, both reasons why He should not
address her. This gives Him the opportunity to go further;
it is true that He is a Jew, but if she knew more, and perceived
the opportunity offered to her by His presence, she would be
asking Him for a greater boon — a truly living water. Of course
she is puzzled; Jacob gave this well, and in the ordinary sense it
contains living, that is, running, water; is He greater than
Jacob, the father of all Israel? Yes; His gift at any rate is
greater, for it is inexhaustible. Then, says the woman, give it
me, and save me all this trouble. He does not refuse, but bids
her call her husband to share the gift. She is becoming mysti-
fied and impressed; and, no doubt fearing exposure of her
manner of life, denies that she has a husband. The Lord reads
her thought and says that this denial — intended as a lie in
self-defence — is strictly true. She sees the sign of a prophet's
insight and at once asks the prophet to decide the vexed question which kept Jews and Samaritans apart — Jerusalem or
Mount Gerizim? He, as usual when confronted with a question
which arises from the superficiality and unspiritual quality of
men's thought, deals with the question by penetrating to the

principle governing the sphere of life which it concerns. But
this baffles her. The prophet's answer does not satisfy. She
must wait for the Messiah, who, no doubt, will clear up this
and all other difficulties. *I am he — I that am talking to thee.*

Having thus sketched the outline of the conversation let us
first go through it in more detail, and then consider its symbolic
significance. The Lord is travelling on foot, and is weary from
His journey. He sits down just as He is near the spring which
Jacob has made available by sinking his well. Anyone who is
tired from walking is likely also to be thirsty. It is to satisfy a
perfectly genuine need that He says to the woman who comes
down from Samaria *Give me to drink.* None the less He is
ignoring convention in making the request. It was a precept
of the moralists of the time that 'a man should not salute a
woman in a public place, not even his own wife'. There was a
great contempt for women. 'One of the thanksgivings in the
daily service of the Synagogue is "Blessed art thou, O Lord
... who hast not made me a woman".'[1] The answer made by
the women from their gallery or other separate place was
'Blessed art thou, O Lord, who hast fashioned me according to
thy will'. If we now feel that the women had the best of the
exchange, that is a Christian and not an ancient Jewish sentiment! The prejudice was very strong. But here is someone
that ignores it, and ignores at the same time the equally strong
and far more bitter prejudice of Jews against Samaritans. *How
is it that thou, being a Jew, askest drink of me, who am a woman
and a Samaritan?* (9). The answer begins that undercutting
of the prejudices which is made complete in 21–24. The real
marvel of this conversation is not that a Jewish Rabbi is con-
versing with a Samaritan woman, but that this woman is face
to face with *the Saviour of the world* (42); *If thou hadst known
the gift of God, and who it is that saith to thee 'Give me to drink',
it would be thou that wouldst be asking him, and he would have
given thee living water* (10). The last phrase does not of necessity mean any other water than such as was bubbling up in the

spring at the base of the well. Yet (she thinks) He can hardly
mean that; He seems to be pointing to some contrast; and
anyhow He has no means of drawing water from the well.
*Thou hast nothing to draw with and the well is deep; from whence
then hast thou the living water?* (11). This spring was found by
Jacob himself and given by him to his heirs and descendants,
among whom (as the woman is, no doubt, glad of the chance
to hint) Samaritans claim to rank no less than Jews. *Art thou
greater than our father Jacob?* (12).

Already the conversation is turning, on the woman's side
also, to the Person of her interlocutor. The Lord had given an
impulse towards this (10), but waits to let that take fuller
effect. At present He fastens on the difference between Jacob's
gift and His own. The water in Jacob's well quenches thirst
for the time; this other living water quenches for ever the thirst
which it assuages, and is indeed an inward spring, bubbling
up into eternal life. *Everyone that drinketh of this water shall
thirst again, but whosoever drinketh of the water that I shall give
him shall not thirst unto eternity; but the water that I shall give
him shall become in him a spring of water, springing into eternal
Life* (13, 14).

(*Water*. In ii, 1–11 the water that is drawn at the command
of Christ is wine for him who drinks it. Here is promise of an
inward spring which is an elixir of life eternal for him who
receives it. In vii, 37–39 the water that Christ gives is a source
of refreshment not only to him who receives it but to others, as
the living water flows forth from him. For this living water
is the Holy Spirit, who could only be given in fulness to men
when Jesus was glorified. That was accomplished on the Cross,
and from His crucified Body flowed Blood and Water — xix,
34.)

The woman does not understand; how could she? The Lord
is leading her on towards understanding by words to which
she will attach some real meaning, but not the full meaning
which is in His mind and which she may grasp later. At least
she has reached the stage of asking for the offered boon, though

mainly because it seems as if it will save trouble: *Give me this water that I thirst not neither come hither to draw* (15).

But the *gift of God* (10) cannot be received to be merely enjoyed. It must always be shared. Its very nature involves that; for it is Himself, His own Spirit, the Spirit of Love. To receive that does not mean to enjoy the knowledge that God loves us. It means that His active love is present in our hearts; and if so, it must go out to others. If we are not sharing with others the gift of God, that is proof that we have not received it. So the Lord tells this woman to call the person with whom she would naturally share first. *Call thy husband and come hither* (16). Unknown to herself, her conscience has been quickened. She shrinks from the exposure that may be before her: *I have no husband*. And that is true. By the standard of God's law, before Moses allowed exemptions for the hardness of men's hearts, the intercourse of marriage effects an irrefragable union; 'they are no more twain, but one flesh' (*St. Mark* x, 5, 8). (How far St. Paul regarded this principle as carrying us is clear from *I Corinthians* vi, 16. Any premarital intercourse therefore makes true marriage with any other than the partner of that intercourse permanently impossible. This I have no doubt is the explanation of the 'exceptive clause' in *St. Matthew*. At that point the Church, like Moses, has made allowance for the hardness of men's hearts. How far it should go is open to question. But there is no doubt about the principle upheld in the whole New Testament.)

This woman was probably within the requirements of the Mosaic law. But she has taken a liberal advantage of its exemptions from the truly divine law! By that only true standard the lie with which she hoped to save herself from exposure is itself true: *Thou saidst well, I have no husband; for five didst thou have as husbands, and he whom now thou hast is not thy husband; this thou hast said truly* (18) — more truly than she knew! But now the woman is sure that her interlocutor is a prophet; He interprets the divine law in independence not only of the scribes, but of Moses himself; and He knows the secrets of her heart. So she forgets her request for the living water, and eagerly asks for a ruling from this seer of divine truth on the great question which separates Samaritans from Jews, and is at once the ground and the form of their mutual excommunication. *I perceive that thou art a prophet. Our fathers worshipped in this mountain; and ye say that in Jerusalem is the place where men must worship* (19, 20). But now the divine truth which inspired and justified that neglect of convention, which the whole conversation illustrates, can be stated. As so often with our Lord's replies to enquirers, it does not answer the question, but leads to ground where the question does not arise at all. It is often so. There is no Christian solution of the problems presented by human self-will; but there is a Christian cure for the self-will, and if that is effective, the problem is (not solved but) abolished. So when a man wanted the Lord to divide an inheritance, that is to arbitrate between two self-centred claims, He refuses to take that position. He will not settle the dispute; but He will tell them how to avoid having a dispute — 'Take heed and keep yourselves from all covetousness' (*St. Luke* xii, 13–16). For, of course, if there had been no covetousness, there would have been no dispute to settle.

So here, the dispute between Jews and Samaritans arose from an unworthy conception of God, and the fuller knowledge which the Lord brings will not solve the problem but abolish it: *the hour cometh, when neither in this mountain nor in Jerusalem shall ye worship the Father* (21). Yet the Jew has a certain priority; for the revelation recorded in the Scriptures of the Old Testament is more directly his by inheritance. The Samaritans had had a chequered religious history. Some see in the 'five husbands' a reference to the five gods whom the Samaritans had once served — cf. *II Kings* xvii, 29–31; later, when the priest sent by the King of Assyria arrived (*ibid.* 27, 28), there was a mixed cult — 'they feared the Lord and worshipped their own gods' (*ibid.* 33). The Samaritan tradition was far from pure: *Ye worship what ye know not* — a deity adopted, so to speak, because He was the deity of the place; *we worship what we know; for salvation is from the Jews* (22).

That last phrase is of supreme importance. The difference between East and West, which we so easily regard as geographical and racial, is really, as Mr. Edwyn Bevan has pointed out, a difference between those who have and those who have not come under the influence of the Bible. The world around the Mediterranean Sea — the spring of our modern 'western' culture — was in many ways very like the Eastern countries of to-day. There was a lofty philosophy for those to whom it appealed; but they were few. There was great moral degradation, which the prevalent religions were powerless to remedy; some of them even intensified the degradation. There was one exception. Among the Jews was a living faith in a living God, to whom no honour could be paid without righteousness of life. The distinctive Jewish doctrine that God is a living God, a God of purpose and judgement, who is perfectly righteous, effected the union of religion and morality which was otherwise foreign to the prevalent cults. That is why the Old Testament revelation is the unique source of salvation. *Salvation is from the Jews.* It proceeds from them; but is not confined to them. For the God whom they know and worship is the universal Father.

The hour cometh and now is (because with the coming of Christ the full truth is declared and all exclusions are ended) *when the true worshippers shall worship the Father in spirit and truth; indeed the Father seeketh such for his worshippers. God is Spirit, and they that worship him must worship in spirit and truth* (23, 24). It is impossible to exhaust the wealth of this great declaration. *God is Spirit.* That is the most fundamental proposition in theology. God is not the totality of things — the All; nor is He an immanent principle to which all things conform; He is Spirit — active energy, alive and purposive, but free from the temporal and spatial limitations which are characteristic of matter. Consequently there is no need to seek Him in a local habitation. The kind of persons whom He *seeks for His worshippers* are those who will worship *in spirit and truth*. Both of these words combine two meanings. *In spirit* means (*a*) with that highest element in our nature which is the meeting-point of the divine and the human, and should be the controlling factor in the whole economy of our being; (*b*) in contrast with any literalistic legalism, it means a worship of heart and will, not tied to strict obedience to a code, but expressing a self-dedication more pervasive than the requirement of any code. *In truth* means (*a*) in sincerity — without hypocrisy or self-deception, but also (*b*) according to the real nature of God, so as to be free from all worship of God under a false image, which is idolatry. 'We are in him that is true, in his Son Jesus Christ. This is the true God and eternal life. Little children, keep yourselves from idols' (*I John* v, 21).

But though what the Lord has said is so full of meaning, it has none for the woman. He may be a prophet; doubtless He is; but it is nothing new for the utterances of prophets to be obscure. Some day the Messiah will come and make all plain; we must wait for that. *I know that Messiah cometh; when he comes he will announce all things to us* (25). To that simple, waiting spirit the Lord discloses Himself as hitherto to no other. *I am he, I that am talking to thee* (26).

Stupendous affirmation! And with a strong suggestion, not for the woman, but for the reader, of something more stupendous still. The Greek idiom permits the omission of the pronoun 'he'; and it is omitted. So that the translation very literally is this — *I that am talking to thee, I AM*.

What St. John records, apart from graphic details, is set before us in illustration of the way in which eternal life is actually offered in Jesus Christ, and therefore how we, believing, may find it. Once more, then, we go back to the beginning of the conversation, and consider it as an example of the Lord's pastoral dealing — of His dealing with my soul. Here are the key-sayings, followed by a paraphrase of these:

1.	*Christ*	Give me to drink
	The woman	How is it that thou askest of me?
2.	*Christ*	If thou hadst known the gift of God —
	The woman	Give me this water
3.	*Christ*	Call thy husband
	The woman	Thou art a prophet: solve our problems
4.	*Christ*	Worship in spirit and in truth
	The woman	We must wait for Messiah to come
5.	*Christ*	I am he.

In such a way the Lord leads us on to the knowledge which we chiefly need:

1.	*The Lord*	Do me a service
	The soul	How is it that *thou* askest anything of *me*?
2.	*The Lord*	If thou hadst known what gift from God is offered *thee*
	The soul	Give me this gift
3.	*The Lord*	(*a*) With whom will you share it?
		(*b*) Lay bare your sin
	The soul	Solve my perplexity
4.	*The Lord*	Worship in spirit and truth
	The soul	Ah! no solution yet. We must wait
5.	*The Lord*	I AM

1. The way to call anyone into fellowship with us is, not to offer them service, which is liable to arouse the resistance of their pride, but to ask service from them. Of course the request must be prompted by a real need. The Lord was actually tired and thirsty when He said *Give me to drink*, and drew the woman into conversation by asking for her help. So social workers have found that they cannot bridge the gulf digged by education so long as they live in a style different from their neighbours and offer service. But all is changed when they adopt the manner of life familiar in the neighbourhood and share its needs. One has told of the difference for him when he left a well-appointed settlement in Bermondsey, where he

needed nothing which his neighbours could supply, and went
to live in a workman's flat. The first evening he wanted a
hammer to hang pictures, and went to borrow one from the
people in the flat below. At once the relationship was different.
There was something that they could do for him.

So the Almighty God seeks to win us to fellowship with
Himself by putting some part of His purpose into our hands.
'The kingdom of heaven is as when a man, going into another
country, called his own servants, and delivered unto them his
goods' (*St. Matthew* xxv, 14). That is the way in which God is
King; and He takes that way because it is the way of fellowship.
He who might be all-sufficient to Himself, entrusts His purpose
to us. He makes Himself dependent upon us, as the Lord
was dependent on the woman for the quenching of His thirst.
He asks for our service.

But how can that be? *How is it that* thou *askest of me?* Thou
canst do all things. I have nothing. I am not fit to offer the
meanest service. Surely God will first require, and help me to
form, a character worthy to serve Him, and then appoint me
my task. No; in point of fact it is only through service that
such a character could be formed. Canon Peter Green has
often pointed out that Christ did not first make His disciples
saints and then give them work to do; He gave them work to
do, and as they did it other people (though not themselves)
perceived that they were becoming saints. The service that He
asks of me is a real service, not fictitious; yet it is for my sake,
and out of love for me, that He so orders His world as to need
my service. That is how it is that *He* asketh of *me*. Also
because He loves us, He rejoices that we should be 'fellow-
workers' with Him (*I Corinthians* iii, 9). If He were not Love
He would have no need of us; it is His love that needs us. And
behind His request is the love that prompts it — the love which
He is ready to give me, the gift of God.

2. As I begin to understand this, I begin also to hear His
voice saying that if I really appreciated what is offered in
His request for service, the whole situation would be reversed,

and the request would come from me — the utterance of my
soul's thirst for its only satisfaction. And thereupon the plea
rises in me — Give me this gift of God.

3. But then, like a lightning flash, comes the demand which
means at once 'With whom will you share it?' and 'Lay bare
your sin'. For I cannot receive the gift however truly it is
offered if either I mean selfishly to keep it, or there is some sin
to which, conscious of it and concealing it, I cling. But from
that demand I shrink, and, recognising the voice of divine
authority, quiet my conscience by recourse to intellectual
riddles, which I ask that authority to resolve. How often does
the weak will obscure the clear call of conscience by resort to
intellectual 'difficulties'! Some of these are real enough; but
some are sheer self-protection against the exacting claim of
the holy love of God.

4. Both for perplexity and for dulled conscience the remedy
is the same; sincere and spiritual worship. For worship is the
submission of all our nature to God. It is the quickening of
conscience by His holiness; the nourishment of mind with
His truth; the purifying of imagination by His beauty; the
opening of the heart to His love; the surrender of will to His
purpose — and all of this gathered up in adoration, the most
selfless emotion of which our nature is capable and therefore
the chief remedy for that self-centredness which is our original
sin and the source of all actual sin. Yes — worship in spirit
and truth is the way to the solution of perplexity and to the
liberation from sin.

But to our superficial souls the divine answer seems to evade
the problem precisely because it penetrates to the heart of it.
We must wait till there is offered to us in fellowship and communion the eternal God Himself.

5. 'I that am talking to thee, I AM.' That is the assurance
that we need: that He with whom we know that we have
dealings is none other than the eternal God. If my soul can
hear that word, then it can rest. But it is not enough that I
should believe on grounds satisfactory to myself. I need the

divine assurance of the divine love. 'Say unto my soul "I
am thy salvation"' (*Psalm* xxxv, 3); 'He that believeth on the
Son of God hath the witness in *him*' (*I John* v, 10). *I that am
speaking to thee, I AM.*

*

27. And upon this came his disciples and marvelled that he was talking
with a woman; yet no one said 'What seekest thou?' or 'Why talkest
thou with her?'

We are still in the early days of the ministry and the Lord's
freedom from convention causes astonishment; a little later
the disciples would have become accustomed to the new position
accorded to women by their Master. But already there is that
about Him which forbids the enquiries that curiosity so strongly
prompts.

*

28-30. So the woman left her water-pot and went away into the city and
saith to the men 'Come, see a man who told me all my doings. Can
this be the Christ?' They went out of the city and made their way towards
him.

She left her water-pot, so she meant to come back. It is one
of the graphic touches which strongly suggest the eye-witness.
The Evangelist records what the disciples saw. The water-pot
is a little bit of sheer realism. As Scott Holland used to say,
'You cannot allegorise that water-pot. It is a perfectly empty
water-pot. No one ever found the old Law at the bottom of it.'
She leaves it there and goes to her city to tell people (*men*
here represents the general or neutral Greek word) of her
strange experience. And they start back with her. Meanwhile
the Lord draws a moral from what has happened.

*

31-38. In the meantime the disciples asked him, saying 'Rabbi, eat'.
But he said to them 'I have meat to eat that ye know not'. The disciples,
therefore, said one to another 'Hath any man brought him aught to
eat?' Jesus saith unto them 'My meat is to accomplish the will of him
that sent me, and to finish his work. Say not ye "There are yet four

months and harvest cometh"'? Behold, I say unto you, Lift up your
eyes and look on the fields, that they are white to harvest. Already the
reaper is receiving wages and gathering fruit unto Life eternal, that both
sower and reaper may rejoice together. For herein is the saying true
"One is the sower and another the reaper". I sent you to reap that
whereon ye have not laboured; other men laboured and ye are entered
into their labour.'

The disciples bring back the food which they had gone to
buy (8). They had left the Lord weary beside the spring, and
now they urge Him to refresh Himself with what they have
purchased. But His mood is changed. He has a refreshment of
which they do not know. They wonder among themselves, but
do not venture to ask Him whether someone else has supplied
His needs. But His refreshment comes from another source.
In the soul of the woman and in the influence that she is gone
to exert, a work of God is manifest; the doing of that is His
refreshment. And how rapid is the response! — as though
sowing and reaping were telescoped together. The disciples
have only to garner the fruit of the labour of others. In the
case of the spiritual harvest the *four months* have dropped away.

*

39–42. And from that city many of the Samaritans believed on him because of the word of the woman as she testified 'He told me all my
doings'. When therefore the Samaritans were come to him they asked
him to abide with them; and he abode there two days. And far more
believed because of his word and said to the woman 'No longer because
of thy speech do we believe, for we have heard ourselves, and know
that this is truly the Saviour of the world'.

This illustrates the wholesome development of faith from
a state of dependence on authority to an assurance arising out
of experience. We notice that these 'outsiders', these 'dis-
senters', ask the Lord to remain with them, whereas the Jews
of Jerusalem, the heirs of the great tradition, had pushed Him
further and further away. They do not, here at any rate, use
the traditional expectation of the Messiah to interpret Him
with whom they have now had intercourse; they simply are

convinced that in Him the world has received its Deliverer.
With all of us faith in God begins because of our faith in those
who tell us of Him. This may be fully real, and have strength
to 'save' the soul. But it is less than the faith which rests on a
personal experience, which has already in some measure
supplied to faith its vindication and verification. We must
constantly ask ourselves whether, and how far, our faith is
still based on what we have been told by others, and how far
we have heard ourselves and know.

*

43-54. And after the two days he went forth thence into Galilee. For
Jesus himself testified that a prophet in his own country has no honour.
So when he came into Galilee, the Galileans welcomed him, having
seen all that he did in Jerusalem; for they also went to the feast. He
came therefore again to Cana of Galilee where he made the water wine.
And there was an officer of the King, whose son was sick at Capernaum.
This man, having heard that Jesus was come out of Judaea into Galilee,
went to him, and asked that he would come down and heal his son; for
he was at the point of death. Jesus therefore said 'Unless ye see signs
and portents, will you in no wise believe?' The officer saith unto him
'Sir, come down ere my child die'. Jesus saith to him 'Go thy way; thy
son liveth'. The man believed the word which Jesus spake to him and
went his way. And already, as he was going down, his servants met
him saying that his boy liveth. He enquired of them therefore the hour
when he began to amend. So they said to him 'Yesterday, in the seventh
hour, the fever left him'. The father therefore knew that it was in that
hour in which Jesus said to him 'Thy son liveth'. And he believed
himself and his whole house. This again as a second sign did Jesus after
coming from Judaea into Galilee.

It is suggested that the Lord deliberately sought a place
where He would have *no honour*; if so, it marks the beginning,
though as yet no more than that, of His withdrawal from
public ministry and concentration upon His chosen followers,
which reaches its climax in the Syro-Phoenician journey (*St.
Mark* vii, 24). The Galileans *welcomed* Him as a friend who
had won some distinction for His home in the capital — a very
different thing from the *honour* accorded to a *prophet*.

So we come to the Second Sign — the healing of the nobleman's son — or, rather, the son of the royal officer. It bears resemblance to the healing of the centurion's servant, and some have thought it a doublet of that. But the differences are too great, considering how circumstantial each story is. The Lord's answer is surprising. The fact that the nobleman comes at all is a sign of faith; but the answer to his request is *Unless ye see signs and portents, will ye in no wise believe?* or *ye will in no wise believe.* Perhaps the answer lies in the plural verb. The nobleman has faith, but not these Galileans among whom Jesus lived as a boy. The Samaritans had believed without quite such startling evidence, though the woman's testimony was startling enough. The Galileans were interested by the *signs* which He wrought at Jerusalem, but these came short of the *signs and portents* here referred to. He will for once, and because love towards the 'nobleman' in his distress so urgently prompts it, supply the *portent* of healing from a distance without any personal intercourse with the sufferer. The 'nobleman' is puzzled by this apparently detached observation about readiness to believe; he knows his need, and believes in the power of the Lord to meet it. *Sir, come down ere my child die.* The answer is the healing word: *Go thy way, thy son liveth.* The result is a fuller faith, at least in the nobleman and his household.

Faith is the one requisite — first, enough faith to believe and hope that Christ can satisfy our needs, leading to ever stronger and deeper faith as each measure of trust is vindicated in experience. For though faith is always met with blessing from God, that blessing does not always take the desired or expected form, as in this case it did.

CHAPTER VI

[For reasons mentioned in the Introduction (p. xxxv *supra*) and fully set out by Archbishop Bernard in his Commentary, to which reference is there made, I am persuaded that Chapters V and VI have become misplaced, and that Chapter VI should be read between Chapters IV and V.]

*

1-14. After this Jesus went away over the sea of Galilee (the sea of Tiberias), and a great crowd was following him because they were watching the signs which he did on the sick. And Jesus went up into the mountain, and was sitting there with his disciples. Now the Passover was nigh, the feast of the Jews. Jesus therefore, having lifted up his eyes and seen that a great crowd is coming to him, saith unto Philip 'Whence are we to buy bread that these may eat?' And this he said testing him, for he himself knew what he was about to do. Philip answered him 'Six pounds worth of bread is not sufficient for them, that each may take a little'. Then saith to him one of his disciples, Andrew the brother of Simon Peter, 'There is a lad here who has five barley loaves and two pickled fishes; but what are these among so many?' Jesus said 'Make the men sit down'. Now there was much grass in the place. So the men sat down in number about five thousand. Jesus therefore took the loaves and having given thanks he gave to them that were set down; likewise also of the fishes as much as they would. And when they were filled, he saith to his disciples 'Gather up the broken pieces that remain over, that nothing be wasted'. So they gathered; and they filled twelve baskets with the pieces of the five barley loaves which remained over unto them that had eaten. The people therefore, when they had seen the sign which he did, said that This is truly the prophet who cometh into the world.

The Lord has been at Cana. The healing of the son of a royal officer might easily excite Herod's interest, so it is expedient to leave Herod's territory. He crosses to the eastern side of the Lake near its northern end, as we learn from St. Luke's reference here to Bethsaida (*St. Luke* ix, 10). Probably the actual place was a little plain about a mile south of

Bethsaida and about nine miles from Capernaum, from which
many would have come. For those who had followed all the
way from Cana the distance was, of course, far greater. The
Lord goes up *into the mountain* and sits there with His disciples.
They have come for peace (*St. Mark* vi, 31) in preparation for
the Passover which *was nigh*. But the crowd has marked the
point for which their boat was making, and has come round
the Lake on foot — for many of them a long journey. Jesus
sees them coming and asks Philip how this number can be fed.
Philip estimates what is required and offers this with the evident
implication that nothing is possible. Andrew calls attention to
the only resources which are in fact available, with the same
implication. Then the Lord takes control. Receiving the
ludicrously meagre resources, He gives thanks — (the word is
Eucharistēsas) — and distributes; what was ludicrously in-
adequate is now ample and an abundance is left over. The
people in their excitement regard the Lord as The Coming
One — 'he that should come'.

This is the only incident in the Ministry of the Lord prior
to the triumphal entry which is recorded by all the four evangelists. This does not give it any additional credibility on grounds
of evidence, for the First and Third Gospels here rest on the
Second. But it strongly suggests that a special importance was
attached to it. I have told the story above so as to bring out
part of its symbolism. Then, as now, the Lord and His disciples
were confronting a mass of human need. He asks Philip, who
belonged to the neighbouring town of Bethsaida, what can be
done about it. Philip, like most of us, is daunted by the sheer
magnitude of the task and gives it up. Andrew at least points
to what is available — a lad's luncheon for his day out, five barley
loaves (barley bread was the food of the poor) and a couple
of pickled fish as a relish — but he knows that this is a futile
suggestion. Then the Lord gives thanks and distributes, and
the need is met. It is unnecessary to draw the moral. The
need of the world is not too great for our resources if it is the
Lord who directs the use of those resources.

What actually happened? It is clear that every Evangelist supposed our Lord to have wrought a creative act; and for myself I have no doubt that this is what occurred. This, however, is credible only if St. John is right in his doctrine of our Lord's Person. If the Lord was indeed God incarnate, the story presents no insuperable difficulties. But of course such a creative act is quite incredible if He is other or less than God incarnate.

St. John's narrative has some peculiarities which can hardly be accidental. In view of the connexion between this 'sign' and the discourse which follows, it is significant that the features associating the miracle with the Last Supper are minimised. Thus it is not said that Jesus broke the loaves; nor that He 'looked up to heaven' — which is mentioned by all the Synoptists and is a very ancient feature of the Eucharistic rite. The fact that according to the best text there is no mention of the twelve as intermediaries in the distribution also tends to separate this from the familiar administrations of Holy Communion; if it were thought that the Lord personally distributed to all the five thousand, that would be a point of resemblance to the Last Supper; but evidently this is not intended. And though the word for the thanksgiving includes the very name of Eucharist, it is elsewhere used by St. John with no sacramental suggestion. I cannot doubt that the Evangelist is deliberately eliminating a sacramental reference. The reason for this we shall see later.

Meanwhile the greatness of this sign leads the crowd to the thought that Jesus is the Coming Prophet of *Deuteronomy* xviii, 15: 'The Lord thy God will raise up unto thee a prophet from the midst of thee, of thy brethren, like unto me; unto him ye shall hearken'. But the expectation is become a little confused, and they are also wanting to treat Him as the Coming One, the Messianic King.   *

15. When Jesus therefore perceived that they were about to come and take him by force that they might make him king, he withdrew again into the mountain himself alone.

Here we see 'natural religion' — the religion to which we are impelled by our natural impulses, and which tries to make use of God for our purposes. That popular sin ultimately found its focus and final expression in Judas, who will very soon now stand apart as a 'cell' of disloyalty within the Twelve (70, 71). But the same sin was in Simon Peter, who could not endure that the Lord should suffer (*St. Mark* viii, 32, 33). How close together in common sinfulness are the disciple whose faith is the foundation of the Church and the disciple whose treachery has made his name the worst insult that one man can fling at another! — 'that no flesh should glory before God' (*I Corinthians*, i, 29). Of course the selfishness of this arrogance masks itself as a generous desire to give honour to our leader. But we make ourselves the judges of what is to His honour. If we are not careful, much of our prayer is like that. We batter at the doors of heaven, demanding audience for our proposals whereby God may save His world, or promote His purpose. But faith consists in leaving Him to take His own way.

This excitement of the crowd is no material for the Lord to use. All the Evangelists tell us that after this miracle the Lord withdrew in solitude, but only St. John gives the special reason for this. He cannot use the crowd in the state which is their response to His own action; and He needs the peace and refreshment of solitary communion with the Father.

This third sign is interpreted in the discourse which follows: Christ is the Bread of Life, the sustenance of the soul, Himself the source of the strength whereby we may serve God. But before the interpretation of that sign is given, another is wrought, appropriate to the excitement to which this one had led.

*

16–21. And when even was come, his disciples went down to the sea, and entering into a ship set out across the sea to Capernaum. And darkness had already come on, and Jesus was not yet come to them. And the sea — a great wind blowing — arose. So when they had rowed about twenty or thirty furlongs, they behold Jesus walking on the sea and

drawing nigh to the ship; and they were afraid. But he saith to them
'It is I; be not afraid'. So they were willing to receive him into the ship;
and immediately the ship was at the land whither they went.

St. John tells the familiar story in such a way as to minimise,
if not eliminate, the miraculous element in the sign, and to let
the significance stand out. For his version does not necessarily
imply a miracle at all; the phrase for 'on the sea' is also used
for 'on the sea shore' (xxi, 1). So his narrative can be read as
meaning that the Lord was on the shore to welcome the
disciples as, after much toil, they approached it. Certainly the
story is vivid, and bears all the marks of an eye-witness who,
as a fisherman, was familiar with that Lake, its distances and
its squalls. But for St. John the meaning is to be found in the
peace of attainment which immediately supervenes when,
tossed with trouble, we willingly receive Jesus to be our companion. Christ is the Guide of Life, whom we may follow in
the strength that He supplies into the way of peace.

*

THE BREAD OF LIFE

As there are seven 'signs' in the Gospel as first planned, that
is without the Epilogue, so there are seven parables of the
Lord's Person introduced by the words 'I am'. These are:

1. I am the Bread of Life (vi, 35)
2. I am the Light of the World (viii, 12)
3. I am the Door of the Sheep (x, 7)
4. I am the Good Shepherd (x, 11)
5. I am the Resurrection and the Life (xi, 25)
6. I am the True Vine (xv, 1)
7. I am the Way, the Truth, and the Life (xiv, 6)

There does not seem to be any marked progression of thought
running right through the series. But the first four parables represent a comparatively external relationship and the last three an

inward vitalisation. It is true that bread only gives nourishment
so far as it is taken into the body; but it is first of all outside;
and this first parable thus gives the clue to the series, which
represents the appropriation of what is offered by God
objectively and externally so that it becomes subjective and
inward power; that is the sacramental principle. (1) Christ
nourishes us and gives us strength; (2) He gives us Light to
show the way we should follow in that strength; (3) He is Himself the entrance into the fellowship of Life; (4) He is the
guardian of that fellowship, who by His sacrifice wins for it
new members; (5) He is Himself the life of that fellowship,
which lives by Him alone; (6) He is even the fellowship itself,
for its members are incorporated into Him, and it is His Life
that vitalises them; (7) comprehensively, He is Himself the way
to be followed in action, the truth to be believed, the life to be
lived.

What is set out in the remaining verses of Chapter VI is not
so much one discourse as the summary of a series of conversations on different occasions and perhaps on different days,
though shortly after the miracle of feeding. It is expressly
stated (59) that the closing section represents teaching given in
the Synagogue (though it must surely incorporate similar
teaching given later to the disciples in the Upper Room), and
it is hardly conceivable that the opening conversation took
place there (25 ff.). In fact we have here a double conflation.
First, a series of conversations and discourses has been brought
together in one continuous summary; secondly, as *St. Matthew*
collects ethical teaching from many occasions to constitute its
version of the Sermon on the Mount, and gathers together
parables spoken on many occasions in its thirteenth chapter,
so St. John introduces into the record of what followed the
miracle of feeding some parts of the Lord's later teaching
which carries further the principle of what He taught at that
time. This may make the *hard saying* (60) seem even harder
than it was, especially if words spoken at the Last Supper have
been transposed to this place. But the course of the narrative

requires a saying hard enough to account for the defection of
many disciples.

This discourse includes words nearer than any other that
St. John gives us to those spoken at the Institution of the
Eucharist: *the Bread which I will give is my flesh for the Life of
the world* (51). The record of the Words of Institution as they
appear in the older texts, before the beginning of that assimila-
tion which resulted in the text translated in the Authorised
Version, is as follows:

> 'Take; this is my Body' (*St. Mark*).
> 'Take, eat; this is my Body' (*St. Matthew*).
> 'This is my Body' (*St. Luke*, Western text).
> 'This is my Body which is given for you; this do in remem-
> brance of me' (*St. Luke*, longer text).
> 'This is my Body which is for you; this do in remembrance of
> me' (*St. Paul*).
> 'The Bread which I will give is my Flesh for the Life of the
> world' (*St. John*).

The word translated 'for' is the same in each of the last three,
where alone it occurs — ὑπέρ. It is to be noticed that the
thought of a memorial is expressed only in St. Paul's record,
and in that version of the Lucan text which has been assimi-
lated to the Pauline. That thought could not in fact be absent
from the mind of any one who took part in the Holy Communion. It obviously is a memorial, 'a perpetual memory', of
the Lord and of what He did at the Last Supper, and so of His
Death. But for St. John as for St. Mark all emphasis is laid
upon the thought of 'feeding upon Christ' — so receiving and
assimilating Him that He becomes our very life.

But it is important that St. John separates this teaching from
the moment of the Institution, which indeed he does not any-
where specifically mention, and attaches it to the miracles of
feeding, in the story of which he omits those details which make
any special connexion with the Holy Communion. So far as
any discourse in this Gospel is directly associated with the

Holy Communion or its Institution, it is not that on the Bread of Life, but that on the True Vine, which was spoken by the Lord either in the Upper Room or very soon after He and His disciples had left it. And in view of St. John's treatment of the symbolism of the two 'elements' it is characteristic of his whole attitude to the Eucharist that he should associate the Eucharist more closely with the Wine than with the Bread.

He associates the Bread chiefly with our own reception of Christ; the discourse in Chapter VI begins and ends with that, and has no other theme. But he associates the Wine — 'the Fruit of the Vine' (*St. Mark* xiv, 25) — the Life of Christ coursing in our veins — with that mutual love which is to be the mark of our discipleship (xiii, 34, 35; xv, 12). In the writings of Ignatius, the most Johannine of the Fathers, this association becomes identification; e.g. *Ad Trallianos*, viii: 'Renew yourselves in faith, which is the flesh of the Lord, and in love, which is the blood of Jesus Christ'; on which Bishop Lightfoot comments, 'Faith is the flesh, the substance of Christian life; love is the blood, the energy coursing through its veins and arteries' (cited by Bernard, p. clxxv).

St. John, it would seem, is concerned with two dangers. One is Docetism, which holds that the humanity of the Lord is apparent only — a means of His manifestation to us, but not a substantive part of His Person; as against this he insists that the *Word was made* or *became flesh* (cf. *I John* iv, 2). Hence he gives emphasis to teaching which requires actual participation in the Sacrament, and prefers the realistic term Flesh to the more frequent Body. Yet he sets this teaching in a context which guards against the other danger — that of attributing to physical reception of the Sacrament any magical efficacy. He will not have the Sacrament isolated either from God's general activity in the world or from the fulness of Christian life. The 'Real Presence' in the Eucharist is a fact, but it is not unique. The Word of God is everywhere present and active. The Bread and Wine have a symbolic meaning before they are consecrated — they are the gift of God rendered serviceable by the

labour of man: and that is what we 'offer' at the 'offertory'.
It is this which the Lord takes to make the special vehicle of
His universal Presence and Activity. No words can exaggerate
the reverence due to that divinely appointed means of grace;
but it is very easy to confine our reverence when we ought to
extend it, and to concentrate it only on this focal manifestation
of the divine Presence, instead of seeking that Presence and
Activity also in the Church, which itself is called the Body of
Christ, and in all the world which came to be through Him
(i, 3).

So soon as the Sacrament is isolated it becomes in greater or
less degree magical. It is for avoidance of that danger that St.
John (*a*) keeps the teaching about the Bread and our reception
of it detached from the rite itself, (*b*) expounds the rite rather in
connexion with the Wine interpreted as brotherly love, and (*c*)
closes the teaching of this sixth chapter with the insistence that
Flesh and Blood mean Spirit and Life (vi, 63).

The discourse, or summary of conversations, falls into three
main sections: 26–40, the search for Life and the Bread of
Life; 41–51, the relation of the Son who is that Bread to men;
52–58, the reception of that Bread which is the Son by men.
But first come a few verses of narrative introduction.

*

22–25. The day following, the multitude which stood on the other side of
the sea saw that there was no other boat there save one, and that Jesus
went not with his disciples into the boat, but that his disciples went
away alone. But there came boats from Tiberias nigh unto the place
where they ate the bread after the Lord had given thanks. When
therefore the multitude saw that Jesus was not there nor his disciples,
they themselves entered into boats and came to Capernaum seeking
Jesus. And when they found him beyond the sea they said to him
'Rabbi, when camest thou hither?'

We notice the vivid and crowded recollection of the eye-
witness. Such writing is the expression of personal memory.
The question of the people when they find the Lord is one of

friendly but futile curiosity. It could not matter when He came. But they have been looking for Him, and wonder if He had already started across the Lake when their search began. The Lord passes at once beyond their curiosity to the motive of their search.

*

26–40. Jesus answered them and said 'Amen, Amen, I say to you: ye seek me, not because ye saw signs, but because ye ate of the loaves and were filled. Work not for the food which perisheth, but for the food which abides unto eternal Life, which the Son of Man shall give you; for him the Father sealed, God himself.' They said therefore unto him 'What are we to do that we may work the works of God?' Jesus answered and said to them 'This is the work of God, that ye believe on him whom he hath sent'. They said therefore to him 'What sign then showest *thou*, that we may see and believe thee? What dost thou work? Our fathers ate the manna in the wilderness, as it is written, Bread out of heaven he gave them to eat.' Jesus therefore said to them 'Moses gave you not the bread out of heaven, but my Father giveth you the bread out of heaven, the true bread. For the bread of God is that which cometh down out of heaven and giveth Life to the world.' They said therefore unto him 'Lord, evermore give us this bread'. Jesus said to them 'I am the bread of Life. He that cometh to me shall never hunger and he that believeth on me shall never thirst. But I said to you that ye have even seen me and do not believe. All that the Father giveth me shall come to me; and him that cometh to me I will in no wise cast out. Because I am come down from heaven, not that I may do the will that is mine, but the will of him that sent me. And this is the will of him that sent me that of all which he hath given me I should not lose aught, but should raise it up at the last day. For this is the will of my Father that every one who beholdeth the Son and believeth on him may have eternal Life; and I — I will raise him up at the last day.'

The crowd is excited, and, as is usual with excited people, has not considered the grounds of its own excitement. There were two possible grounds: one was that here was a wonder-worker who could supply their bodily needs; the other was that in doing so He had given proof of the presence with them of One in whom the Kingdom of God — love endowed with power, power subordinate to love — is already actualised. The Lord knows that their excitement about Him really rests on the former ground. *Ye seek me, not because ye saw signs* — not because you knew that what happened was significant of something beyond itself — *but because ye ate of the loaves and were filled.* Whenever we try to use our religion as a solution of our temporal problems, caring more for that than for God and His glory, we fall under the same condemnation. I have heard speakers commend the cause of Christian Missions on the ground that to spread the Gospel, at any rate under Anglican forms, is a way of consolidating the British Empire; but, short of that sort of vulgarity, we are all under the temptation to call in Christian faith as a means of delivering us from the agony of war, caring more for our own escape from that torture than for God's glory. It is very natural; it is a state of mind with which we must all sympathise; but it is at best sub-Christian. If what is eternal is valued chiefly as a means to any temporal result, the true order is inverted, and it is likely that the eternal and the temporal goods will be missed alike.

This lesson is now pressed home under the special instance of food or bread. *Work not for the food which perisheth but for the food which abides unto eternal life.* There is an interplay of words here which cannot be reproduced. The exact translation is 'Work not the food' (i.e. effect or earn, by working), and is paralleled in the phrase 'work the works of God'. But though a certain pointedness is lost in English, it is no more than this. The goal of all our labour is to be an eternal, not a temporal and transitory, satisfaction. And even then what we receive is not a reward but a gift — *which the Son of Man shall give you; for him hath the Father sealed, even God himself.* It is from Him in whom our human nature is perfectly fulfilled that we receive the satisfaction of our souls; for this function His perfect humanity qualifies Him, as also for Judgement, of which this is one possible form — cf. v, 27. And what He offers is His free gift. Our work for it establishes no claim. The creature can have no claim against his Creator; still less can the sinner have any claim against his Redeemer. Eternal life is, to man, a free gift from God Himself; but the Father has *sealed* the Son as the donor of it, as He has *committed all judgement to the Son, because he is Son of Man* (v, 22, 27).

But if we are to *work for the food which abideth unto eternal Life,* how are we to set about it? In one way or another it must mean the doing of what God appoints as our task; He is the donor of life, and the work that makes us fit for it must consist in the *works of God.* But what are these? and how do we set about them? *What are we to do that we may work the works of God?* It is a most natural question. Everyone on the verge of discipleship wants to ask it. We are told that both Fascism and Communism have more appeal to the young people of today than the Christian Church, because each is ready to tell them exactly what to do tomorrow and next week; and the Church has no such practical guidance to offer. How can it have? *This is the work of God that ye believe on him whom he hath sent.* There we have as sharp a statement as can be found of the doctrine of Faith and Works. We all want to *do* things, partly out of a just eagerness that evils should be remedied, partly out of a desire to justify ourselves. But 'by the works of the law' — the God-given law, so that these are the *works of God* — 'shall no flesh be justified in his sight' (*Romans* iii, 20). It is impossible that we should justify ourselves. And it would be very bad for us if we could; for it would tend to make us forgetful of God. The first necessity is to *believe on* Him. This is different from believing things about Him, though that may be one preliminary. It means trusting Him as a man trusts his friend — rather as a child trusts his father. But we are not left to form what conception we can of the God whom we are to trust. He has made Himself apparent to us in the Son *whom he hath sent.*

This is a stupendous claim. For the Jews knew and we know to whom He refers. 'The work of God' — the one thing He requires as the condition for His gift of eternal life — 'is that you put your trust in me'. We must have some evidence first before we admit that claim, so paradoxical in itself and so decisive for our whole conduct of life. *What sign shewest* thou

that we may see and believe thee? They do not grasp the idea of
believing *on* Him, putting all their trust in Him; they get no
further than the thought of believing Him, that is — believing
what He says. And this goes with another failure. They cannot see that He is Himself the evidence for His claim. Men
constantly want external support — such as that He fulfils
prophecies, or that He was miraculously born, statements
which are both quite true, but are perceptible in the one case
and acceptable in the other only because of faith independently
generated. This whole Gospel is an insistence that true faith is
based on the intrinsic quality of the revelation — as it is said
elsewhere 'He that believeth on the Son of God hath the
evidence in him' (*I John* v, 10). But it is only those whose
hearts are ready who can receive, or even perceive, that
evidence. So we want signs. *What dost* thou *work* more than
others that claims so far greater can be advanced? There was
the miracle of feeding, but Moses did something like it. *Our
fathers ate the manna in the wilderness, as it is written 'He gave
them bread out of heaven to eat'.*

This plea contains two errors; first, Moses was not the
donor of that bread, nor was it in truth the heavenly bread. It
was God who gave it; and that same God continually gives the
genuine bread out of heaven. *Moses gave you not the bread out
of heaven; but my Father giveth you the bread out of heaven, the
true bread.* 'My Father' — here the Lord uses this phrase
for the first time in its absolute form. In ii, 16 He had called
the Temple 'my Father's house' — cf. *St. Luke* ii, 49. But
though the suggestion there was present, it was not emphatic.
My Father here is an expression which prepares the way for *I
am the bread of Life* (35). But that claim is not made yet. *The
bread of God is that which cometh down out of heaven and
giveth life to the world.* It is something more than manna.
That kept men alive — for a time (cf. 49); it did not *give Life.*
This true bread, then, is what we need: *Lord, evermore give
us this bread.* That is the universal cry of the human heart.
The Jews do not protest as yet. Rather, they are impressed.

They use a title of respect, and ask to be given this bread at all times. We can all get as far as that. The trouble begins when we are told what *this bread* is.

I am the Bread of Life. Now first the personal claim is made; and it is the first of the seven parables of the Lord's Person. The phrase *Bread of Life* has a double meaning — *the living bread* (51) and the bread which gives Life. It is this Bread — which He Himself is — which gives to the soul a satisfaction that endures eternally. *He that cometh to me shall never hunger and he that believeth on me shall never thirst.* The negatives are the strongest in the Greek language; they rule out not only a fact but the bare possibility of the fact. Hunger and thirst become simply impossible to him that *cometh.* 'Come unto me all ye that labour and are heavy laden, and I will give you rest' (*St. Matthew* xi, 28). The passage before us is itself a reason for linking that invitation with the Bread of Life, as is done by the first of the Comfortable Words in the Anglican Eucharist.

He that cometh; 'Come unto me'. We cannot know whether the promise is fulfilled unless we fulfil the condition. But what is this *coming*? It is the opening of heart and mind to the Good News which He brings, and which concerns Himself. All that is needed is the will to do this; our coming to Him is a movement of desire and will. And if we have no such desire and will, what then? Why then we are in our natural state, and have only to wait for Him; for *no man can come to me except the Father draw him* (44). This must not be made an excuse for spiritual sloth in those who have any sense whatever of the claim of Christ upon their allegiance. Yet dangerous as is the lure of sloth to our half-formed faith, still more dangerous is the effort to develop that faith by any exercise of self-will. The hopeful attitude is not expressed by the words 'I *will* believe' but by the words 'Help thou mine unbelief'. The one fatal thing is to struggle and strive. If we do not trust, it is because we cannot trust; any effort to have faith will convert faith itself into a 'work of the law', and destroy its real character. For my salvation must be altogether His gift, and in no sense at all

my achievement. And there are some who are not — at
present, anyhow — able to receive it. *I said unto you that ye
have even seen me and do not believe*; the miracle of feeding was
to them a convenience rather than a revelation. Yet this is not a
reason for despair, but only for that self-distrust which is the
complement of hope in God.

All that the Father giveth me shall come to me. It is as He
wills. My coming or not coming is in His hands; and where
could I choose by preference that it should be? To realise
that my not 'coming' is itself due to the will of the Father, who
has yet drawn me, and to accept this, is one beginning of trust
in Him, one sign that in fact He is really drawing me to come.
And then there is safety. *Him that cometh to me I will in no wise
cast out*; again that strong negative: 'There is no possibility
that I shall cast him out'. How should He cast away those
whom the Father draws? *For I am come down from heaven* —
those solemn words are enshrined in the Church's confession
of faith: 'Who for us men and for our salvation came down
from heaven'. Here they are a kind of refrain; the phrase
about 'coming down from heaven' recurs in 33, 38, 41, 42, 51
and 58. It is the key-phrase of the passage. *The food that
abideth unto eternal Life*, which is the Lord Jesus Himself,
comes down from heaven. It is a gift from beyond the natural
order, or the normal historical sequence. The Incarnation is
not only an episode related to past and future as are other
episodes; it is the appearance, in the midst of Time, of that
Eternal Being in whom Time itself is grounded. *I am come
down from heaven — not to do the will that is mine but the will of
him that sent me.* Perfect obedience is the characteristic of the
human life of the Son of God. 'Lo, I am come to do thy will,
O God — by which will we have been sanctified' (*Hebrews*
x, 9, quoting *Psalm* xl, 7, 8: P.B. 9, 10). And this is that will,
that of all whom He gives to His Son, none should be lost, but
that I should raise it up again at the last day. Here is another
refrain; see 39, 40, 44, 54. This final achievement balances the
descent from heaven which makes it possible; the two refrains

express the initiation and the consummation of the divine
enterprise of redemption.

The thought of our 'coming' to the Son is now deepened.
*And this is the will of him that sent me, that every one who
beholdeth the Son and believeth on him may have eternal Life.*
For 'we know that if he be manifested we shall be like him for
we shall see him as he is' (*I John* iii, 2) — on which Thomas
Arnold commented 'the contemplation of Christ shall transform us into His likeness'. To be so transformed is to enter into
eternal life. All that we have to do is to look, to contemplate,
to open our minds towards Him that He may fill them. And
then the result is His achievement, His gift; *I will raise him up
at the last day.*   *

The first stage, so to speak, of the great discourse is ended.
It leads to 'murmuring'. The Lord's hearers are more bewildered than antagonised; they talk among themselves —
(43) — until the Lord challenges them by the use of even
stranger words.

41–51. The Jews therefore began to murmur concerning him, because
he said 'I am the bread which came down out of heaven'. And they
said 'Is not this Jesus the Son of Joseph, whose father and mother we
know? How doth he now say "Out of heaven am I come down"?'
Jesus answered and said to them 'Murmur not among yourselves. No
man can come to me except the Father which sent me draw him; and
I will raise him up at the last day. It is written in the prophets "And
they shall be all taught of God". Every one that heareth from the
Father and learneth, cometh unto me. Not that any man hath seen the
Father save he which is from God; he hath seen the Father. Amen,
Amen, I say to you, he that believeth on me hath eternal life. I am the
bread of life. Your fathers ate the manna in the wilderness and died;
this is the bread which cometh down out of heaven, that a man may eat
of it and not die. I am the bread, the living bread, which came down
out of heaven; if any man eat of this bread he shall live for ever; yea, and
the bread which I will give is my flesh for the Life of the world.'

The Jews very naturally *murmured*. No less naturally they
telescoped various expressions and in so doing missed an

important distinction. The phrases which they telescope are these: *the bread of God is that which cometh down out of heaven* (33); *I am the bread of Life* (35); *I am come down from heaven* (38). The *bread of God* comes down continually — in creation, in the word of prophecy, in all that shows the activity of God; but He who is the Bread of Life, in whom this life-giving and nourishing activity is focussed, came once, at the Incarnation. The language is parallel to that in the Prologue concerning *the Light which lighteth every man*, yet at the Incarnation was *coming into the world*. The balance is of great importance. For only if Christ is the consummation of the divine activity in all creation, and therefore no alien from the world, no 'absolutely-other', can He be the self-manifestation of the Creator. The distinction which the murmuring Jews confuse is clearly drawn again in the words of the Lord which follow (50, 51).

The claim to a heavenly origin puzzles those who supposed that they knew all about the Lord's parentage. *Is not this Jesus?* — Yes. *The son of Joseph?* — No. *Whose father and mother we know?* — Yes; you know of them, but not their true relationship to Him; for Mary would not have told the story of the Annunciation to any outside her nearest friends. But as the Jews suppose that they know all about this, they are bound to ask in perplexity, How doth He now say '*Out of heaven am I come down*'? The reply does not ease the difficulty but rather increases it. There are many superficial problems which can be resolved only by making them profound problems. But the Lord's first words convey excuse, if not comfort. *No man can come to me except the Father which sent me draw him.* The initiative is always with God. Even the sternest implications of this truth will be faced and accepted (xii, 39, 40). But when the Father initiates the work of grace, the Son completes it: *I will raise him up at the last day.* The point may be illustrated from the prophetic promise which is in fact fulfilled in the coming of Christ: *They shall be all taught of God.* But teaching involves a double process; the lesson must be spoken so as to be heard, and when heard it must be heeded. The 'drawing' of the Father is not a mechanical impulsion in which our wills play no part; the 'drawing' is effected by the influence of the word spoken on our hearts and minds. We cannot hear unless the Father speaks; all initiative lies with Him; but when we hear it lies with us (sustained by His grace) to learn or not to learn. *Every one that heareth from the Father — and learneth — cometh unto me.* This suggests an error that must be at once repelled, the alluring peril of mysticism, according to which a man may have direct experience of unmediated communion with the infinite and eternal God. That is not so; and any experience taken to be this is wrongly interpreted. Only the Son has that direct communion with the Father. *Not that any man hath seen the Father, save he which is from God; he hath seen the Father* (cf. i, 18).

It is easy to make confusion here. Nothing is more precious in the spiritual life than that communion with God which is enjoyed when the soul reposes upon God in utter self-abandonment, and God exercises His moulding power upon the soul thus resting, plastic, in His hands. That moulding influence comes rather through our sub-conscious than through our conscious nature. The whole experience often seems to be a direct experience of unmediated communion with God. But in fact it never is unmediated. It is mediated by all our thought of God, as this has come to us through our home-life, through natural beauty, through conscience (itself a focus of our moral tradition), through acts of worship, through Jesus the Word of God. The experience of the mystics, Pagan and Moslem, Catholic and Protestant, is infinitely precious; our own most mystical moments have something of the same high value, and we do well to cultivate them. But the strictly mystical interpretation of them, as unmediated communion with God, is illusory and renders them perilous.

Because man is made in the image of God, the attempt to find God through penetrating to the inmost recesses of the self leads in men of all times and races to a similar experience. God truly is the spring of life in our souls; so to seek that spring is to seek Him; and to find it would be to find Him. But this can never quite happen. The image of God in man is defaced by sin, that is by self-will. The mind which seeks to reach that image is distorted by sin, and moulded both for good and for evil by tradition. The *via negativa* of the mystics cannot be perfectly followed. To rely on a supposedly direct communion with God in detachment from all external aids is to expose the soul to suggestions arising from its distortion as well as to those arising from the God whom it would apprehend. Mediation there must be; imagery there must be. If we do not deliberately avail ourselves of the true Mediator, the 'express image' (*Hebrews* i, 3), we shall be at the mercy of some unworthy medium and of a distorted image. If we are learning to see God in Christ, let us by all means steep our minds in that revelation, and repose in God so made known to us with complete immediacy of surrender and trust. But let us be sure that the knowledge of God on which we rely is that which reaches us through Jesus, the Word of God made flesh.

The mediator of the Father's gift of life is the Son, and to believe on Him, to live by trust in Him, is to possess eternal Life. *He that believeth on me hath eternal Life.* The life of faith does not earn eternal Life; it is eternal Life. And Christ is its vehicle. *I am the bread of Life. Your fathers ate the manna in the wilderness and died. This is the bread which cometh down out of heaven. If any man eat of this bread he shall live for ever.* The Jews had appealed to the gift of manna as the equivalent of what the Lord did in the miracle of feeding; and so far as that is understood as a mere event and not as a 'sign', they were right. But as a sign it pointed to something more — to a spiritual nourishment abiding unto eternal Life. Those who ate the manna satisfied present hunger; but that was all. It was a physical refreshment, and could not ward off physical death. But there is a spiritual nourishment continually offered by God, by taking which eternal Life is secured. It is supremely and uniquely offered in Christ, who is Himself *the bread, the living bread,* and is now in unique manner *come down out of heaven.* To *eat of this bread,* in other words — to receive the living Lord into the soul so that He becomes its Life — is to *live for ever.*

But now the Lord will carry us still further. We are to receive His Life to be our Life. And this is offered through the Incarnation. *The Word became flesh*; the term flesh was chosen there to stand for fulness of humanity down to its lowest element. It is by His humanity that He offers us life: if we receive that humanity and it becomes our own, it is found to bring with it eternal Life. *The bread which I will give is my flesh for the Life of the world.*

*

Of course the Jews knew that this was in some way figurative; they would not suppose that He was commanding a form of cannibalism. But of what is this strange expression a figure? A division arises among them, accompanied by strong feeling.

*

52–58. The Jews therefore began to strive one with another saying 'How can this man give us his flesh to eat?' Then said Jesus unto them 'Amen, Amen, I say to you, Except ye eat the flesh of the Son of Man and drink his blood, ye have not Life in yourselves. He that eateth my flesh and drinketh my blood hath eternal Life; and I will raise him up at the last day. For my flesh is true food and my blood is true drink. He that eateth my flesh and drinketh my blood, abideth in me and I in him. As the living Father sent me, and I live because of the Father, so he that eateth me he also shall live because of me. This is the bread which came down out of heaven; not as the fathers ate and died — he that eateth this bread shall live for ever.'

The figure is pressed home and developed. Not only must we eat and so receive the 'flesh', the full humanity, of Him in whom humanity is perfected — the Son of Man; but we must *drink his blood.* The phrase would have been quite as startling, even horrifying, to the Jews as to ourselves. The blood of animals might not be received as food: 'Be sure thou shalt not eat the blood; for the blood is the life; and thou shalt not eat the life with the flesh' (*Deuteronomy* xii, 23; cf. *Leviticus* xvii,

14, 15, and many similar passages). But the reason why the Jews were forbidden to eat the blood of their sacrifices is itself the reason why we must drink the blood of the Son of Man. The blood is the life; especially is it the life released by death that it may be offered to God.

It is clear that the 'Flesh' and the 'Blood' are thought of as separated and separately received. But flesh from which the blood is separated is dead. We receive the Broken Body; we make our own the 'dying of Jesus' (*II Corinthians* iv, 10). Blood, on the other hand, when poured out, is the life released by death and given to God. As we make our own the 'dying of Jesus', so we make our own the risen life of Jesus, so that in Him we may be 'dead unto sin but alive unto God' (*Romans* vi, 11).

To 'eat the flesh' and to 'drink the blood' of the Son of Man are not the same. The former is to receive the power of self-giving and self-sacrifice to the uttermost. The latter is to receive, in and through that self-giving and self-sacrifice, the life that is triumphant over death and united to God. Both 'elements' are needed for the full act of 'communion' — which suggests that to receive the Holy Communion in one kind only is grievously detrimental to the full reality of the sacrament. The life that gives itself even to death; the life that rises from death into union with God: these are the divine gifts without which *ye have not Life in yourselves*. But he who receives and makes his own those gifts *hath eternal Life*. For those gifts are true food and drink of men; he who receives them and makes them his own *abideth in me and I in him*.

Those words express in completeness the substance and the goal of the Christian life. They recur in the discourse on the True Vine (xv, 4) — the other and still more distinctively Eucharistic discourse. It is not the momentary eating but the permanent abiding that is of primary importance; the sacramental communion is an end in itself so far as it is communion, but a means to an end so far as it is sacramental. The sacrament is normally necessary; but it is the communion alone that is vital. That is why St. John keeps all this teaching, which so obviously bears upon the Eucharist, carefully separated from the Last Supper and the Eucharist itself. That we should 'take' and 'eat' is an indispensable aid which the sincere Christian cannot omit; but the one thing that matters is that we should 'feed upon him in our hearts'.

Our dependence for life upon the Son corresponds to the dependence of the Son upon the Father. He is truly the Mediator (cf. xv, 9; xvii, 18; xx, 21). Only the Father is source of His own life; even the divine Son, though co-eternal, is yet 'begotten', and lives *because of the Father*, of whom He is 'begotten before all worlds'. And we too, creatures who owe all to our Creator, have no life in ourselves; but if we make our own the living, dying and rising of the Son, we shall live because of Him.

So the whole can be summarised: *This* (the Son in the Flesh and Blood which He gives as food and drink) *is the bread* that we spoke of *which came down from heaven* in all its quickening power at the Incarnation. It is like the manna in that God gave it, but it is a better gift. *The fathers ate and died; he that eateth this bread shall live for ever.*

*

This difficult language was used publicly and many who had become disciples were bewildered. He offers a clue to the understanding of what He has said; but He lets the hard saying sift those who can discern something of its spiritual truth from those who cannot. After all, the prelude to the discourse was that false excitement which had led the multitude to try to *take him by force to make him a king* (15), and it was imperatively necessary to bring that to an end before His real message could be received. The discourse by which He sifts and tests them alienates some; so He lets them go.

59–65. These things he said in synagogue, teaching in Capernaum. Many therefore of his disciples, having heard, said 'Hard is this saying; who

can hear it?' But Jesus, knowing in himself that his disciples were murmuring concerning this, said to them, 'Doth this offend you? — If then
ye behold the Son of Man going up where he was before? The Spirit is
the Life-giver; the flesh doth not profit at all; the words which I have
spoken to you are spirit and are Life. But there are some of you who
do not believe.' For Jesus knew from the beginning who they were who
did not believe and who it was who would betray him. And he said
'For this reason have I said to you that no one can come to me except
it have been given to him of the Father'.

The teaching was given *in synagogue* (as we say 'in Church').
This may have been on a sabbath subsequent to the miracle
of feeding, or at one of the mid-week gatherings for instruction.
The latter is more likely, as on any of these occasions the
congregation would consist of those who desired to hear the
particular Rabbi who would be giving instruction; when that
was Jesus they would mostly be 'disciples' or those who were
considering whether or not to become 'disciples'. And it is
many of his disciples who are said to have been disturbed. The
point that specially disturbs them would seem to be, not only
the claim that to feed on Him is to have eternal life, but equally
the claim that He is *come down out of heaven*; for what is
offered in response is the prospect of beholding Him *going
up into heaven*.

It is part of the Lord's method to confront those who are
shaken by some marvel with a marvel greater yet; cf. i, 50, 51.
This is appropriate to His theme. For the one important
question is whether or not in Jesus Christ *the Word became
flesh*. If that occurred, nothing else is marvellous; and stupe-
faction at lesser marvels may hinder the soul from facing that
question. Do we in Him behold *glory as of an only begotten
from a Father*? If so, there is the all-comprehensive marvel,
and nothing else, in comparison, is marvellous at all.

As for the demand that men should feed on His flesh and
drink His blood, of course this is figurative. There is no magical
sacrament to be appointed any more than there is a reversion
to primitive savagery. 'The Spirit is the Life-giver' as we
confess in the Nicene Creed; *the flesh* — even the flesh of the

Son of Man, literally understood — *doth not profit at all; the words that I have spoken to you are spirit and are Life.*

The reference is not to this discourse as a whole; still less is it to the Lord's teaching as a whole.[1] *The words that I have spoken to you* are the words *Flesh* and *Blood*; for these we are, so to speak, to read *Spirit* and *Life.* This, again, does not mean that Flesh=Spirit and Blood=Life; it means that Flesh-and-Blood=Spirit-and-Life.

But, if so, why not say Spirit and Life to start with and so avoid very great perplexity? A number of reasons can be given, and all, no doubt, had some part in fixing the choice of words which presented to would-be disciples a *hard saying* and alienated many.

(1) To talk about receiving a Spirit or even Life is ineffective as a challenge. It easily coheres with a vague religiosity which has no definite and critical moments, no fixed religious practice, no cutting edge. We all know the people who seek to absorb the Spirit of the Creator by contemplation of the beauties of creation — an admirable exercise in itself — instead of anything that could by any stretch of language be called eating the flesh and drinking the blood of the Son of Man. It is vital for our spiritual well-being that we be brought to the point of specific worship, wherein we seek to receive Christ into our souls.

(2) But we must not only receive Him in some general way, or by recollection of such scenes from His life as we prefer to contemplate. We must receive Him in the fulness of His self-sacrifice, that we may be united with Him in the self-emptying of His *obedience unto death, even the death of the Cross* (*Philippians* ii, 8). The Gospel finds its focus, not in the happy scenes of Galilee, but in the Cross and Resurrection. It is the Body broken and the Blood outpoured that we must receive as our own life.

(3) Therefore our worship finds its focus in our repetition of the action of the Lord and His disciples at the Last Supper.

---

[1] Cf. Gore, *The Body of Christ*, pp. 21, 22, 290, 291.

But then there is a danger lest we think that the outward acts
have efficacy by themselves. No doubt it is true that the Bread
and Wine are after Consecration the Flesh and Blood of the
Son of Man.[1] But there is danger that we may turn that objective truth into a subjective delusion by supposing that to receive
by the mouth the consecrated species is to receive eternal life.
Therefore we must be reminded that the flesh doth not profit
at all, if it be only flesh, and even though it be the flesh of the
Son of Man. Hence the appropriateness of the reference to the
Ascension. For the Flesh and Blood of the Ascended Son of
Man are plainly not mere matter; if they were, the resultant
astronomical problems would be overwhelming — for where
in the universe are they? But the 'right hand of the Father'
where the Ascended Son is seated is not a far-off place; it is
here; wherever a man be, for him it is here. (See xx, 17 and
comment there.) The Flesh and Blood of the Ascended Son
of Man are Spirit and Life.

So the purpose of this strange language is at least threefold:
(1) to give point and effectiveness to a purely 'spiritual'
dependence on Christ; (2) to guard against materialism or
magic in the use of the Eucharist, which is itself the chief
means of effecting (1); (3) to secure that our sense of dependence on Christ is inseparably associated with His redeeming
sacrifice. And if any still wonder that the Lord should so
bewilder His disciples, let them reflect that the Eucharist,
understood in the light of this discourse upon the Bread of
Life, has in fact through all the centuries achieved this threefold purpose. Perhaps it was worth while that a score or so
of people should be momentarily puzzled or even alienated
to secure that end for all generations of Christian worshippers.[2]

But there were some who could not be described as 'would-
be disciples'. *There are some of you who believe not.* A sifting

[1] Or if we are so materialistic as to hold that an object *is* its physical constituents rather
than its spiritual meaning, let us say that they signify that Flesh and Blood. This is very
bad philosophy, but the religious value is the same.
[2] It is not intended to suggest that these considerations were present in this form to
the human consciousness of the Lord. These comments are my reflections on the Evangelist's interpretative version of the Lord's actual words. But that He envisaged and
prepared for a long history of His Church, I have no doubt whatever.

is beginning. Some are waverers and will return; some are
spiritual aliens — one in particular; for the Lord had already
felt the hardening hostility of Judas. *From the beginning.* Did
He then choose Judas so as to equip the Twelve with a traitor?
That is incompatible with His whole method. No doubt He
knew that the nature of Judas supplied very intractable
material; but He chose him 'that he might be with Him',
and at the last made a final appeal to his loyalty and shame.
But all through He had known the difficulty. If His victory
and kingdom were to be all-embracing they must include such
as Judas; the world must be welcomed into the Church if the
Church is to convert and direct the world. But the issue is
in the Father's hands: *For this reason havè I said to you that
no one can come to me except it have been given to him of the
Father.*

*

66–71. Upon this many of the disciples went back and walked no more
with him. Jesus therefore said to the Twelve 'Do ye also want to go?'
Simon Peter answered him 'Lord, to whom shall we go? Words of Life
eternal hast thou. And we at least have believed and recognised that
thou art the Holy One of God.' Jesus answered them 'Did not I choose
you the Twelve? and of you one is a devil'. Now he was speaking of
Judas the son of Simon Iscariot; for it was he that was about to betray
him, being one of the Twelve.

So the division is complete. *Many* even *of the disciples went
back*; the phrase is due to the spiritual reality which their
departure indicated. They not only went away, retaining what
they had learnt in their discipleship; they *went back*, positively
losing ground. For when we depart from Christ, even for a
time, we do not retain the level of spiritual life to which He
had raised us; we begin at once to slip down. And if after
even 'tasting the good word of God and the powers of the
age to come' men then 'fall away', our plight is so grievous
that one says 'it is impossible to renew them again unto
repentance' (*Hebrews* vi, 4–6). They *went back and walked
no more with him*; and He let them go. As He will not coerce

us into His companionship, so He will not hold us there against
our will. Our coming to Him and our abiding with Him must
be our own free acts.

Even the Twelve it seems are shaken. *Do ye also want to
go?* The words must have been spoken with a wistful smile.
And one day they will go. 'They all left him and fled' (*St.
Mark* xiv, 50). But that time is not yet. For the present Simon
Peter rallies them by his own loyalty and confidence. '*Lord,
to whom shall we go? Words of Life eternal hast thou.*' He at
least has learnt enough to know that the hunger of his soul
could be satisfied here and nowhere else. This chosen group
has reached the stage of understanding their Lord and His
relation to the Father. *We (at least) have believed and recognised
that thou art the Holy One of God.* As having *words of eternal
Life* the Lord is recognised as Prophet; as *Holy One of God* He
is recognised as Priest. Perhaps here as elsewhere St. John
reads back into the earlier time a knowledge that was actually
reached later. But the title is not necessarily Messianic, for it
is used of Aaron in *Psalm* cvi, 16. The note of Kingship is
still lacking (though Nathanael is recorded as striking it at
once — i, 49). This title — the Holy One of God — is that
by which the demons greeted the Lord. It points to the spiritual
character rather than the official status of the Messiah. That
will be affirmed at Caesarea Philippi (*St. Mark* viii, 29; *St.
Matthew* xvi, 16).

(It is not suggested that the Evangelist is conscious of these
distinctions. For him, Jesus is Messiah from the first, and his
object is to persuade his readers of this fact. He is not concerned with the progress of the disciples in appreciation of it.
This makes it all the more noticeable that, according to the
best text, the full affirmation is not made here.)

With Simon Peter's eager affirmation all are in evident
agreement save one: and the detachment of that one stands
out against the background of the others' faith. Probably
Judas had shared the excitement that followed the miracle of
feeding. A great opportunity was offered and his Master

threw it away . Not only did He miss the psychological moment, but He deliberately dissipated the psychological fervour by talking more and more difficult language about Himself as bread, and about feeding on His flesh. Judas was not among them that *went back*, and separated himself. He did worse; he stayed, as an enemy within the chosen group of friends. *Did not I choose — Was it not I that chose — you the Twelve? and of you one is a devil. A devil?* Yes; for his will is opposed to the purpose of Christ who came *not to do the will that is mine but the will of him that sent me* (38). So he is opposing the will of God.

(Oh, be careful, Peter. Soon you will make a greater confession still; and just afterwards it is you that will be called Satan. How near the saint is to the sinner!)

So the story has proceeded to the first great division — the division between 'the disciples' and 'the Jews'. This division is present even in the innermost circle of disciples. Now we are to trace the development of controversy between the Lord and His opponents — a dark record, lit here and there by gracious utterances — until a final rejection is pronounced. That will be followed by the infinitely sacred intercourse of the Lord with His chosen friends, preparing them for the great crisis and what would follow from it.

ACT II

THE LORD IN CONTROVERSY

1. Chapters V and VII, 15–24 :
   Controversy about the Sabbath
2. Chapters VII and VIII :
   The Feast of Tabernacles — a national festival. 'Before Abraham was, I am'
3. Chapters IX and X :
   The Feast of Dedication — a 'Church' festival. 'I and the Father are one'
4. Chapter XI :
   The Culminating Sign and its Challenge. 'The world is gone after him'
5. Chapter XII :
   The Rejection of the World. 'Now is the crisis of this world'

THE LORD IN CONTROVERSY

Iᴛ is in these controversial chapters that we most of all need to remember the quality of this Gospel as the interpretative expression of a memory. The discourses of the Lord recorded in it follow in general the same line that He followed, and indeed the Rabbinical type of dialectic employed is regarded by eminent Jewish scholars as evidence for the substantial authenticity of the account. But the discourses as reported by St. John represent, as was said earlier, the meaning which they were found to have after a lifetime of meditation. Just as the knowledge that He was the Messiah throughout the Ministry has coloured the record of His dealing with disciples and others in the early days — (for the real fact, though not then ascertained, was the intercourse of the Messiah with His people) — so the relationships which matured into antagonism and rejection are viewed in retrospect as having this quality from the beginning. Perhaps the temperament of the Son of Thunder, who wished to call down fire from heaven (*St. Luke* ix, 54), still survived to some extent in the aged apostle through whose consciousness these controversies have passed before reaching us. St. John records no saying of the Lord which shows sympathy for the difficulty which the Jews had in recognising Him, such as that which very characteristically St. Luke reports, 'No man having drunk old wine desireth new: for he saith, The old is good' (*St. Luke* v, 39). The relationship is, in memory, hardened into antagonism from the outset. And this, no doubt, was the spiritual fact. The outlook of 'the Jews' was irreconcilable with that of Jesus; unless they should undergo personal conversion, they must end in direct opposition, for their spirit was already in opposition. The Lord knew this from the beginning; they found it out by degrees.

But though the relationship is depicted as one of sheer

antagonism, with consequent hardness in the outlines of the
opposing persons, there is not in the picture here given of the
Lord any petulant irritation, such as some have thought that
they found there. Our moral antagonism to the spirit of those
who oppose us is so much mixed up with the emotional
reaction of our offended self-concern that we are almost
incapable of impersonal anger — the dreadful anger of perfect
love at hate or selfishness. So we read the Lord's stern words
as though they were contemptuous or ferocious. But there
is no necessity to do that. The dramatic quality of the narrative
requires that the ferocity should be all on one side, and confronted with unruffled calm on the other. That such calm is
provoking to the irritated cannot be denied; but the fault is
not with the calm. The hardest of all the Lord's sayings,
'Ye are of your father the devil' (viii, 44), is to be read in a
tone, not of hostility, but of sad recognition of a spiritual fact.

CHAPTER V
AND
VII (15–24)

1–9. After these things there was a feast of the Jews; and Jesus went up to Jerusalem. Now there is at Jerusalem by the sheep-gate a pool, which is called in the Hebrew tongue Bethesda, having five porches. In these were lying a multitude of sick folk, of blind, halt, withered. And a certain man was there, which had an infirmity thirty and eight years. When Jesus saw him lying and knew that he had been now a long time in that case, he saith to him 'Is it thy will to become whole?' The sick man answered him 'Sir, I have no man, when the water is troubled, to cast me into the pool; but while I am coming, another steppeth down before me'. Jesus saith to him 'Rise, take up thy pallet, and walk'. And immediately the man was made whole, and took up his pallet and walked. Now on that day was a sabbath.

A feast. The Passover, mentioned in vi, 3 as 'at hand'. If the traditional order of the chapters is retained it would be perhaps Purim or perhaps Pentecost; either is difficult, but on the whole the former is more likely. But it makes no difference to the meaning of the story, which tells of the restoration of lost powers. Our fellowship with Christ not only hallows and intensifies all the powers that we have when we first meet with Him. It restores those which are atrophied by neglect or abuse. It is part of the deadly quality of sin that it hinders us from seeking its cure. It is our will to be cured; but we have lost through past sin the power to submit ourselves to the curative influence. Or else we, half-converted we, are no longer 'dead in our sins'; but still sickly and weak through sin. We need someone to 'cast' us into the cleansing stream; and often there is no one to do this for us. So we linger, discontented but acquiescent. How common that is!

Thirty-eight years. So long Israel wandered, unable to reach the promised land. It is not only individuals but nations that lose strength, but may receive it again from Christ. Not only a nation, but a 'Church'! When we meet with the Lord He uses no intermediate means, for He is Himself the source of strength to obey His commands. *Rise, take up thy pallet, and walk.* The impotence is gone. But the critics are on the watch. It is the sabbath day! That was always the chief occasion of friction. Observance of the sabbath was, for the devout Jew, the first requirement of the law. The Lord never denied its divine origin; but He affirmed that God ordained it for man's sake, and the divine purpose conditions the divine enactment. See *St. Mark* ii, 23–28. In Galilee, also, the bitterness of opposition first appears in connexion with the sabbath.

*

9–18. Now on that day was a sabbath. The Jews therefore said unto him that had been cured 'It is the sabbath, and it is not lawful for thee to carry thy pallet'. But he answered them 'He that made me whole, even he said to me "Take up thy pallet and walk"'. They asked him 'Who is the man that said to thee "Take up and walk"?' But he that had been healed did not know who it was; for Jesus withdrew, a multitude being in the place. After these things Jesus findeth him in the temple and said to him 'Behold, thou art made whole: sin no more, lest a worse thing befall thee'. The man went away and told the Jews that it was Jesus which had made him whole. And for this cause the Jews began to persecute Jesus, because he was doing these things on a sabbath. But Jesus answered 'My Father worketh even until now, and I work'. For this reason the more they sought to kill him, because he not only was breaking the sabbath; but also was calling God his own Father, making himself equal to God.

The Jews were not wrong to challenge the man. He undoubtedly was breaking the letter of the law, and it was reasonable to question him. No doubt this cure was helped and established by the activity of carrying the pallet. The man needed to be convinced that he could do it. Therefore his doing it was part of the work of mercy. But the Jews had not grasped the great principle 'I will have mercy and not sacrifice' (cf. *St. Matthew* xii, 7, where the Lord appeals to this text, also in connexion with the right keeping of the sabbath).

He that had been healed did not know who it was. Of what

countless multitudes this is true! Christianity founds hospitals, and atheists are cured in them, never knowing that they owe their cure to Christ. Prisons are reformed under the influence which flows from the Gospel; and the prisoners never know — sometimes the reformers themselves do not know — that Christ is the Author of the reform.

Sin no more lest a worst thing befall thee. That is the danger of escape from the result of sin. If we are not vigilant, we relapse into a repetition of the sin; and next time the resulting impotence is greater and the process of cure is harder. It can happen as a result of the expulsion of an evil spirit that 'the last state is worse than the first' (*St. Matthew* xii, 45; *St. Luke* xi, 26). But this is because we abuse the divine mercy; the quality of that mercy is undimmed.

But the opposition now reaches the point of definite persecution. Perhaps one offence could be overlooked, but the Lord *was doing* — had an evident habit of doing — works of mercy on the sabbath, which involved technical breaches of the sabbath-law. His defence is radical.

My Father worketh even until now, and I work. What is the ultimate ground of the sabbath-law? It is, as the text of the Fourth Commandment makes clear, that God rested on the seventh day from the activity of Creation; His people are to keep it holy for fellowship with Him; therefore they must rest as He rests. But the Lord repudiates the thought that the divine rest from Creation took the form of idleness: 'My Father worketh even until now'. As for Himself, refreshment was found in doing the Father's will (iv, 34), so for the Father the sabbath rest is an activity of love, and our sabbath must be fellowship with that active rest.

Thus, the Lord is not justifying a breach of the sabbath-law but offering a more profound interpretation of it. He is saying in effect 'It is I who rightly keep the sabbath, rather than you'.

Dialectically this is the same argument in substance as that in *St. Mark* iii, 1–6. There His enemies are watching to see whether He would heal on the sabbath. He prepares to do so, and then asks 'Is it lawful on the sabbath day to do good, *or to do harm*? to save a life, *or to kill*?' (The emphasis is, of course, on the second alternative in each question.) We want to answer 'There is no suggestion of killing; you are only asked to wait till sunset when the sabbath will be over'. But there *was* a suggestion of killing — see verse 6; and of course they knew it, and He knew that they knew it. He was saying to them 'Which of us is keeping the sabbath holy? I am thinking of healing a man, you are thinking of killing one; which of us is keeping the sabbath holy?' 'But they held their peace.' There was not much else for them to do.

So here He asks 'Who is truly keeping the sabbath?' But here, in accordance with His custom of going to the roots of the matter when dealing with the doctors in Jerusalem, He bases Himself on the true conception of God in His sabbath rest. 'My Father worketh even until now; and I work.'

But this creates new difficulties. The opponents shift their line of attack. He is worse than a sabbath-breaker; He is guilty of the supreme blasphemy; He is claiming equality with God. That is a phrase introduced by His enemies. It cannot be either directly accepted or directly repudiated. The implied charge can only be met by a full statement of His relation to the Father.

*

19–27. Jesus therefore answered and said to them: 'Amen, Amen, I say to you, the Son cannot do anything of himself, except he seeth the Father doing something. For what things soever *he* doeth, these also the Son in like manner doeth. For the Father loveth the Son, and showeth him all things that he himself doeth; and greater works than these will he show him, that even you may marvel. For as the Father raiseth the dead and quickeneth them, even so the Son also quickeneth whom he will. For indeed the Father judgeth no man but hath given the judgement wholly to the Son; that all may honour the Son as they honour the Father. He that honoureth not the Son, honoureth not the Father who sent him. Amen, Amen, I say to you that he who heareth my word and believeth him that sent me hath Life eternal, and into judgement he cometh not but is passed over out of death into Life.

> Amen, Amen, I say to you that the hour is coming and now is, when
> the dead shall hear the voice of the Son of God, and they that hear shall
> live. For as the Father hath Life in himself, so gave he also to the Son
> to have Life in himself. And he gave him authority to execute judgement,
> because he is Son of Man.'

The discourse begins in terms of the relationship of the Father
and the Son; yet this is not primarily the relationship as it was
before 'the Word became flesh', for the designation of the
Father as 'he that sent him' shows that it is the Son in His
earthly mission who is in mind. But the relationship is described with the minimum of reference to that mission, so that
it strongly points to an eternal relationship 'before all worlds'.
This part of the discourse continues to the end of verse 23.
Thereafter its concern is with the relation of the Son to men.
Thus the total effect is to set forth the Son as the Mediator.

The Son can do nothing of himself. That is why the ancient
Greek and Hebrew ideas of the Logos could be used to interpret His being and function. A 'word' does not utter itself;
it must be somebody's word; and its importance depends upon
the person whose word it is. The *glory* that we see in Christ
is not His own, but *from a father* (i, 14). The Son is in all
ways derivative and dependent — 'begotten'. But though in
this way He is 'subordinate', the range of His derived activity
is coextensive with the Father's. He can do nothing of Himself, but He does all that the Father does. He is agent, not
principal; but He is universal agent. *All things came to be
through him* (i, 3). Therefore the revelation given in Him,
though mediated, is complete and final.

The root of this perfect coincidence of activity is perfect love.
The Father loveth the Son — (that is the foundation truth of the
whole universe) — and has no secrets from Him. The word
for *loveth* is that which stands for affection between friends:
it is thus in some ways a lesser word than that which stands for
the selfless love which is the very nature of God (*I John* iv, 8),
as appears in Chapter XXI. But here the context ensures the
utmost exaltation, and the greater warmth of the more familiar

word is peculiarly appropriate. There will be *greater works* than this healing of the impotent man, so that even these Jews who are so hardened in self-content that they see ónly the breach of a rule and not the activity of mercy and love, may be startled into some measure of perceptiveness. The raising of Lazarus did at least make them *marvel* and for some this led to more (xi, 45).

And that sign would be an illustration of the intimacy of the Father and the Son. For to raise the dead is clearly a property of God alone; yet the Son exercises that function also. *As the Father raiseth the dead and quickeneth them, so also the Son quickeneth whom he will.* And even this is not the end; for the supreme attribute of Judgement is given by the Father to the Son, so that in honour Father and Son may be coequal and *that all may honour the Son as they honour the Father.*

We are accustomed to reflect with adoring gratitude that the Son *thought not equality with God a thing to clutch at* (*Philippians* ii, 6); here we have the still deeper truth which is the ground of that, namely, that even in His humility the Son was not doing something of Himself but only what He sees the Father doing. For the Father so loves the Son that He retains no prerogative that is not shared, and wills that all should *honour the Son as they honour the Father.* At no point do we reach a limit of that self-giving which is the activity of the divine love.

It follows, of course, and is stated in a single sentence that failure to honour the Son is failure to honour the Father (23).

Now having established the status of the Son as derivative yet (by the Father's will) coequal with that of the Father, we turn to His relation to men.

He that heareth my word and believeth him that sent me hath Life eternal. If when we hear the Son we believe what the Father declares through Him, that is in itself an entry into fellowship with God, and therefore involves eternal life. For this is — it does not earn, but it is — eternal life (xvii, 3). For such a one, judgement is over; the passage *out of death into Life* is accomplished. The evidence to us that this passage is accomplished is that we 'love the brethren' (*I John* iii, 14), for the test of our love to God — true love of the true God — is always found in the question whether we love men (cf. *I John* iv, 20). Love of God is the root, love of our neighbour the fruit, of the Tree of Life. Neither can exist without the other; but the one is cause and the other effect, and the order of the Two Great Commandments must not be inverted.

Death is used throughout in both its senses — physical and spiritual. The Son raised some who were physically dead during His earthly mission. This was a *sign* of the quickening of the multitudes spiritually dead. *The hour is coming and now is*; for the Son was manifest in the world, and they that truly heard received life — Lazarus physical life, Mary Magdalene and countless others spiritual life.

So we are led back to the ground of the Son's relation to men in His relation to the Father. By the will and gift of the Father, the Son has the prerogative to be a spring of life. We have life in Him; He has *Life in himself.* And in the same way the Father has given Him the prerogative of judgement, be-cause — can it be so? Yes —

Because he is Son of Man. The words come in as a thunder-clap, as the same words did in i, 51. We could easily under-stand that He should represent God in the judgement because He is Son of God. Yet that is not the reason given. The Father *gave him authority to execute judgement because he is Son of Man.* There is no definite article, so it is not the Mes-sianic title that is used; though there could not fail to be re-collection of that title, which is especially associated with the Messiah, coming in glory as Judge. And that suggestion eases the way. But that is not the meaning. The Son is Judge in virtue of His humanity. It is not by the standard of remote and awful deity that we are judged, but by the standard of human perfection. More than that. As 'we have not a High Priest', so also we have not a Judge 'that cannot be touched

with the feeling of our infirmities, but one that hath been
tempted in all points like as we are, apart from (the temptations that spring from) sin' (*Hebrews* iv, 15).

> Rex tremendae majestatis,
> Qui salvandos salvas gratis,
> Salva me, fons pietatis.

*

28–29. Marvel not at this; for the hour is coming in which all that are
in the tombs shall hear his voice, and shall come forth, they that wrought
good to a resurrection of life, and they that did evil to a resurrection
of judgement.

There is no call to marvel at what is said, in comparison
with the great event which is to be — the universal resurrection, where life awaits *them that wrought good*, and judgement them *that did evil*. The contrast of phrase is interesting.
Good is something substantive and enduring; evil is an evanes-
cent quality.

*

30. For me — I cannot do anything of myself. As I hear, I judge. And
my judgement is just, because I do not seek the will that is mine but the
will of him that sent me.

A transition from the general teaching, with its reference to
the historic Jesus, to the claim of that historic figure Himself.
As *the Son cannot do anything of himself* (19) so now the Lord
says *I cannot do anything of myself*. Hearing is substituted for
seeing because the special action in question is judgement. *As
I hear, I judge.* Judgement, like glory (i, 14) and activity (v, 19),
proceeds from the Son, but its origin is in the *Father*. Consequently it is perfectly just, for it is God's own judgement.

Judgement introduces the idea of evidence, so we pass on
to the evidence which should lead to belief and how it comes
to be rejected.

*

31–40. If I bear witness concerning myself, my witness is not true. He that beareth witness concerning me is another, and I know that the witness which he beareth concerning me is true. Ye have sent to John and he hath borne witness to the truth. But I receive not witness from a man. But this I say that ye may be saved; he was the lamp that burneth and shineth; and ye were willing to rejoice for a season in his light. But I have witness greater than John's. For the works which the Father hath given to me that I may finish them — the very works which I am doing — bear witness concerning me that the Father hath sent me. And the Father who sent me, he hath borne witness concerning me. Ye have never either heard his voice or seen his form. And ye have not his word abiding in you, because whom he hath sent ye do not believe. Ye search the scriptures, because ye think in them to have eternal Life, and they are what bear witness concerning me; and ye will not come to me that ye may have Life.

To all that had been said the Jews might answer 'We have only your word for it. Why should we believe a man making these claims for himself?' The Lord admits, or rather asserts, that if there were nothing but His word for it, that would not be convincing evidence. Indeed, if His word stood alone, it would not be true at all. For divine revelation did not begin and end in Him, though it reached its crown and finds its criterion in Him. There must be other evidence, not only to support His own, but because the nature of His claim is such that it can only be true if all the work of God — the entire universe so far as it is not vitiated by sin — attests it. But indeed that attestation is forthcoming. *He that beareth witness of me is another* — that is, the Father, who bears witness through *the works* and through *the scriptures*.

The Jews had themselves asked John and *he hath borne witness to the truth*. But it is not from him or from any man that the Lord accepts testimony. Yet He is willing to refer to this in hope that the memory may stir His hearers and so they *may be saved*. And John, though *not the light, but sent to bear witness of the light* (i, 8), was yet a *lamp burning and shining* in whose light they had once rejoiced; so they may heed his witness. But the Lord does not rely on that; He has a *greater witness than John's*; the works that He is doing — like this healing of the impotent man — *which the Father hath given me that I may finish them* — these are the witness for those who can understand them. They are also the means whereby the Son glorifies the Father (xvii, 4); and in reference to them He will one day cry *It is finished* (xix, 30). For we must not isolate the signs; they are but points in the whole activity to which attention is easily drawn. *The works which I am doing* includes the whole activity of the Word made flesh.

And the Father which sent me, he hath borne witness concerning me — through the voice which spoke at the Baptism saying 'Thou art my beloved Son' (*St. Mark*, i, 11). But that voice was not for all to hear. These Jews never heard it. Nor was the vision of the descending Spirit for all to see (*St. Mark* i, 10; *St. John* i, 33): *Ye have never either heard his voice or seen his form.* And as they were incapable of receiving that outwardly given revelation, so they were without the inward word that speaks in the heart and conscience. *Ye have not his word abiding in you.* There is ground for this assertion; for if they had God's word within they would recognise the objective utterance of the word of God without; but they do not: *whom he hath sent ye do not believe.*

We are always clamouring for compelling proof. It is really there. But we are blind to it.

There is one resource left to them. Though they reject the witness of *the works* and cannot hear the witness of the Father Himself, they have the scriptures. But they treat them wrongly. *Ye search the scriptures.* The word for *search* does not suggest spiritual penetration but meticulous analysis — such as led to the tortured interpretations of the Midrash. Such a prying (like that of our contemporaries who suppose that God is such as to hide the chronology of all history in the numbers given by *Daniel* or *The Apocalypse*, or the Great Pyramid! 'Yet He also is wise', as Isaiah remarked) — such a prying proceeds from a supposition that in the scriptures we have eternal life. So we have; but much turns on that little word *in*. It is not prying into the letter of the sacred text that leads to life,

though we cannot study that text too diligently if we are
looking in the right way. For *they are what bear witness concerning me*; but that witness can only be found by those who
read in order to arrive at spiritual communion with the divine
Spirit 'who spake by the Prophets'. The Jews did not so read
them; and therefore cannot recognise the fulfilment of them.
*Ye search the scriptures; and they bear witness concerning me;
and ye will not come to me that ye may have Life.* There is
nothing so pathetic as devotion gone astray. And we are in
that state whenever our devotion does not lead us to Christ
Himself — not the Christ of our fancy but the true Christ.
'And if any man have not the Spirit of Christ, he is none of
his' (*Romans* viii, 9).

*

Now the two passages — the Son and the Father, the Son
and men — are brought together.

41–47. Glory from men I receive not. But I know you, that the love of
God ye have not in yourselves. I am come in the name of my Father,
and ye do not receive me. If another come in his own name, him ye will
receive. How can such as you believe, receiving glory from one another,
and the glory from the only God ye do not seek? Do not think that I
shall accuse you to the Father; there is one that accuseth you — Moses,
on whom ye have set your hope. For if ye believed Moses, ye would
believe me; for concerning me he wrote. But if ye do not believe his
writings, how shall ye believe my sayings?

Glory from men I receive not. No: His is *glory as of an only-
begotten from a Father* (i, 14). And this is His because of that
love which binds together the Father and the Son, and is the
principle of that unity of action described above. In the Jews
this love of God finds no place — as is proved by their rejection of one who is *come in the name of the Father* — that
is as His accredited representative, doing His works and speaking His words. But some false Messiah, who has no divine
commission, but comes *in his own name*, they will receive —
as they did, to their destruction.

What is the root of this spiritual failure? As always, it is
pride. They are loyal to their tradition; but they wish to be
praised for their loyalty. So they are in fact only loyal to that
in it which their comrades value. Each wants to be a good
Pharisee, or a good Sadducee — a good Catholic or a good
Evangelical. Instead of penetrating to the living heart of the
tradition, which was God-given, each eyes his neighbour, and
seeks his applause. So partisans are made, for whom faith itself
is perverted. *How can ye believe receiving (as you do) glory
from one another, and do not (even) seek the glory from the only
God.* I heard a great sermon which Bishop Gore preached on
that text with its terrible refrain. 'To be the inheritors of a
great tradition gives men heroism, and it gives them blindness
of heart.'

The Lord will not accuse us to the Father. There is no need.
All that we trust in accuses us, if it has not taught us to hear
and believe on Him.

*

vii, 15–24. The Jews therefore began to wonder, saying 'How knoweth
this man letters not having been a pupil?' Jesus therefore answered
them and said 'My teaching is not mine but his that sent me. If any
man wills to do his will, he shall know concerning the teaching whether
it is of God or I speak from myself. He that speaketh from himself
seeketh the glory that is his own; but he that seeketh his glory that sent
him, this man is true and unrighteousness is not in him. Did not Moses
give you the law? and none of you keepeth the law. Why do ye seek to
kill me?' The crowd answered 'Thou hast a demon; who is seeking to
kill thee?' Jesus answered and said to them 'One work did I do and ye
are all wondering because of this. Moses hath given you circumcision
(not that it is of Moses but of the fathers) and on a sabbath ye circum-
cise a man. If a man received circumcision on a sabbath that the law
of Moses be not broken, are ye angry at me because I made a whole
man healthy on a sabbath? Do not judge by looks but judge righteous
judgement.'

The manner of the Lord's reply (v, 39–47) had been that of a
Rabbinical disputant. Yet He was not, so far as was known,
the pupil of any well-known Rabbi, as Saul of Tarsus was a

pupil of Gamaliel. From whom had He learnt? The Lord accepts the position assumed in the question. He does not say that He had no need of any teacher; and He expressly denies that He is Himself the source of His teaching. He speaks what He has heard — from the Father (16; ch. v, 19, 30). But the condition of hearing what the Father says is union of will with the Father. The Son was come to do that will (30). But the Jews had not this purpose, and therefore could not 'hear' the Father. *If any man wills — purposeth — to do His will, he shall know concerning the teaching whether it is of God.* It is not necessary for this that a man should have reached the point of perfect obedience; but it is necessary that he should intend perfect obedience.

It is *the pure in heart* who *see God* (*St. Matthew* v, 8) and it is the vision of God that purifies the heart (*I John* iii, 2). The two mystical sayings are both of them true: 'We see what we are'; 'we become what we see'. How then can we make any progress? If we were all, so to speak, of one piece we could not. But we are compact of many elements; we have our better and our worse moments. Spiritual progress depends on the use which we make of our best moments. Much spiritual discipline is rendered futile by its concentration upon what is bad in the soul, that it may be purged away by confession and penance. This is a necessary element in any spiritual discipline. In order to be cleansed of any sin we must first confess the sin, recognise that it is there or, as some psychologists would say, 'accept' it. But this, though necessary, is secondary and derivative. Our conviction of sin springs from our vision of God, and each fresh conviction of sin from a new and clearer vision of God. That vision is the all-important matter; our moments of vision are the vital and vitalising moments. The clarity of the vision will be proportionate to our purity of heart; but the vision itself — clear or blurred — is the only purifier of the heart.

So we must at least intend to do God's will if we are — not indeed to 'see' Him, which is a more advanced stage, but — to 'hear' Him and so know that *the teaching is from God*. That can never be proved to us while we intend disobedience, as a reason for becoming obedient.

The suggestion that the Lord is no 'pupil', which He meets by the claim to be a pupil of the Father, suggests the motive of teaching. One who sets out to be original, who *speaks from himself*, is likely to be seeking his own honour and glory. The modern world with its strange, new and probably transient belief in 'progress', tends to give much credit to 'originality', even to the point of doubting whether anything else is quite sincere. It wants a new contribution to thought; and in its grotesque individualism supposes that every man who truly expresses his own relation to the world will say something different from what anyone else would say. But there must be some great and fundamental truths in comparison with which the peculiar reactions of individual souls are an irrelevance and an impertinence, and of which a man should seek to be no more than an undistorting medium. Where the eternal truths are concerned the search for originality by speaker or hearer is a puerility. One who indulges in it will only falsify his presentation. But if the whole desire is to give glory to Him concerning whom the truth is to be spoken, there will be sincerity and accuracy in the presentation — *this man is true and unrighteousness is not in him*.

All the trouble arose from the question about the sabbath. Moses gave the law of the sabbath, but none of these champions of the law really keep it — as is evidenced by the fact that there had been an attempt to murder (of course by respectable methods) a teacher of whom they disapproved (v, 18). But the crowd had not known about that; they had followed the open discussion, but had not known what was secretly plotted. So they think the Lord is the victim (as we say) of a delusion, or (as they said) of a demon. The Lord, to make His meaning clear, takes up again the relation of His action to that law of Moses by which they would condemn Him. The law said 'Whosoever doeth any work on the sabbath day he shall surely

be put to death' (*Exodus* xxxi, 15; xxxv, 2). The Lord states
in set terms that He has brought Himself under that law, *I did
one work* — *sc.* on the sabbath; and it has thrown them all into
a turmoil of bewilderment. But wait. Moses himself solves the
problem. Moses gave the sabbath law; Moses also gave the
law of circumcision — though the rite and the obligation to
perform it go back to the Patriarchs. These two laws may
clash; and when they do, the law of the sabbath yields to the
law of circumcision which requires the doing of that *work* on
the eighth day, even though it be the sabbath. But if what
concerned only one member of the body might — nay, must —
be done on the sabbath, might not a work which gave health
to the whole body be done on the sabbath?

Their whole temper and method were wrong. They would
search the scriptures and then try to apply texts to life in
meticulous detail. The result was bound to be superficial. Do
not judge by *looks*. Go to the heart of the matter; that is to
say, consider God's purpose expressed in the law and the
relation of any action (act and motive together) to that purpose; *judge righteous judgement*.

So the first controversy, which was started by the healing
of the impotent man at the pool of Bethesda, comes to its end.
The Lord has turned the methods of the Rabbis against them;
He has disclosed to those who have eyes to see a conception
of God, and therefore of obedience to Him, wholly foreign to
them. He has been triumphant in the argument; but has
aroused a hostility that can be satisfied only by His death
(vii, 1).

CHAPTER VII

(1-14) AND (25-52)

1-9. And after these things Jesus walked in Galilee; for he was not willing to walk in Judaea because the Jews were seeking to kill him. But there was at hand the feast of the Jews, the Feast of Tabernacles. His brethren therefore said unto him 'Depart hence and go into Judaea, that thy disciples also may behold thy works that thou doest. For no man acteth in secret and seeketh to be himself in public. If thou doest these things, show thyself to the world.' For not even his brethren believed on him. Jesus therefore saith to them 'My moment is not yet come; but the moment that is yours is always ready. The world cannot hate you, but me it hateth, because I bear witness concerning it that its works are evil. Go ye up to the feast. Not yet do I go up to this feast, because my moment is not yet fully come.' And having said this he remained in Galilee.

IT was natural that after so scathing a rebuke to the leaders in Jerusalem, who had already begun to think how they might kill Him (v, 16 and 18), the Lord should return to the more friendly Galilee, and *walk* there. The peculiar term vividly recalls the manner of His mission, walking from place to place with His own company of disciples, partly instructing them and partly making His proclamation (*St. Mark* i, 14, 38) to the people at large. We do not know how long this sojourn in Galilee lasted; that depends on the amount of time allowed for the controversy which developed, near the time of the Passover (vi, 4, and v, 1), about the healing at the Pool of Bethesda. It is at the close of that controversy that He goes to Galilee; it is at the end of September or beginning of October that He returns to Jerusalem. Anyhow, the time is long enough to make His sceptical brethren impatient.

The Feast of Tabernacles was the great feast of the year. It was at once a Harvest Thanksgiving and a commemoration of the settlement in the Promised Land. It is thus a specially national festival, and the controversy that arose at it appropriately finds its culmination in the relations of Jesus to Abraham, the father of the Chosen People. The story that follows is full of the turmoil of a popular festival. Westcott writes: 'No section of the Gospel is more evidently a transcript from life than this. It reflects a complex and animated variety of characters and feelings. Jerusalem is seen crowded at the most popular feast with men widely different in hope and position: some eager in expectation, some immovable in prejudice. There is nothing of the calm solemnity of the private discourse, or of the full exposition of doctrine before a dignified body, such as has been given before. All is direct, personal encounter. The "brethren" of the Lord (vii, 3 ff.), "the Jews" (vii, 1, 11, 13, 15, 35; viii, 22, 48, 52, 57), "the multitudes" (vii, 12 ff.), "the multitude" (vii, 12, 20, 31 f., 40 f., 43, 49), "the people of Jerusalem" (vii, 25), "the Pharisees" (vii, 32, 47; viii, 13), "the chief-priests (i.e. the Sadducean hierarchy) and Pharisees" (vii, 32, 45, for the first time), "Nicodemus" (vii, 50), "the Jews who believed him" (viii, 31), appear in succession in the narrative, and all with clearly marked individuality. Impatient promptings to action (vii, 3 ff.), vague enquiries (vii, 11), debatings (vii, 12, 40 ff.), fear on this side and that (vii, 13, 30, 44), wonder (vii, 15, 46), perplexity (vii, 25 ff.), belief (vii, 31; viii, 30), open hostility (vii, 32), unfriendly criticism (vii, 23 ff.; viii, 48 ff.), selfish belief in Christ's Messianic dignity (viii, 31 ff.), follow in rapid succession. All is full of movement, of local colour, of vivid traits of conflicting classes and tendencies.'

His brethren were (no doubt) the sons of Joseph by an earlier marriage. They attempt to exercise the authority commonly claimed by elder brothers. They are sceptical, as elder brothers might be expected to be. They are not hostile, but are puzzled by their younger Brother's reputation in Galilee, and would like it and its grounds to be subjected to the test of the more sophisticated minds in Jerusalem. His retirement to the relative seclusion of Galilee is incompatible with His claim to be one sent from God. That involves publicity for Himself; if so, His works also must be as public as possible. The feast gives the opportunity; it will collect vast crowds. *If* (as rumour has it) *thou doest these things, show thyself to the world*.

He answers that *his moment is not yet come*. The phrase is unique, and points, not to the predestined 'hour' (ii, 4), but to a fitting opportunity — what we call 'the psychological moment'. It was always their *moment*; they fitted into the world and shared its outlook; they had no need to watch for the fitting occasion on which to declare themselves. Towards them there was no antagonism; *the world cannot hate you*. But towards Him there was antagonism, because He disclosed the evil of the world. So they should go up with the other pilgrims to the feast; He will not go yet. Thus, in fact, He would avoid the mob of pilgrims; and when He appears at the feast it is not as one of the pilgrim-worshippers but as a Prophet.

This is a not infrequent experience in the life of discipleship. We want Him to accompany us (so to speak) on some enterprise, and to vindicate what is said on His behalf by us or by others through the signal success that He enables us to win. But we are left in fact to toil on with no glad sense of His presence as our companion; and at the end we find Him awaiting us with the Prophet's rebuke for our defect of wisdom or of loyalty; when we have Him again with us it is not as the encouraging fellow-traveller, but as the Judge condemning the faults which unfit us for His service. Yet that judgement too is mercy; for the goal of the 'call upwards of God in Christ Jesus' (*Philippians* iii, 14) is not our service of Him, with which He can very easily dispense, but that we should, like Him, 'be perfect as our heavenly Father is perfect' (*St. Matthew* v, 48).

*

10–14. But when his brethren were gone up to the feast, then he also went up, not openly but, as it were, in secret. The Jews therefore were looking for Him at the feast and saying 'Where is that man?' And murmuring concerning him was rife among the crowds; some were saying that he

was a good man; others were saying 'No, but he misleads the crowd'.
Yet no one was speaking publicly about him for fear of the Jews. But
when the feast was already half over, Jesus went up into the Temple and
began to teach.

The absence of the Lord causes a concern about Him greater
than His presence. (Most of His followers have found that to
be true in their own experience.) We find a contrast drawn
between 'the Jews' and 'the crowds'. The latter also were
Jews; but that name is mostly kept by St. John for the more or
less official representatives of Jewry. It is they who are actively
looking for the Lord — presumably in order to carry out their
now fixed intention of killing Him. But their interest is re-
flected in the interest and doubts of the crowds, who, however,
are hindered by fear of the religious leaders, 'the Jews', from
any open expression of their feelings. Then suddenly the Lord
arrives and begins to teach. There is no ground on which He
could be arrested, and the attention of both 'Jews' and
'crowds' is ensured.

*

(25-52)

25-36. Some therefore of the people of Jerusalem began to say 'Is not
this he whom they seek to kill? And lo, he speaketh publicly and they
say nothing to him. Can it be that the rulers indeed know that this man
is the Christ? But we know whence this man is; but when the Christ
cometh, no one recogniseth whence he is.' So then Jesus cried aloud as
he was teaching in the Temple saying, 'Ye both know me and ye know
whence I am; and yet I am not come of my own motion, but genuine is
he that sent me whom ye know not. But I know him, because from him
I am and he sent me.' They sought therefore to arrest him, and yet no
one laid his hand on him, because his hour was not yet come. But
from the crowd many believed on him and were saying 'When the Christ
cometh, will he do more signs than this man did?' The Pharisees heard
of the crowd murmuring thus concerning him, and the chief priests and
the Pharisees sent officers to arrest him. Jesus therefore said 'Yet a little
while I am with you, and I go to him that sent me. Ye shall seek me

and shall not find me, and where I am, ye cannot come.' The Jews
therefore said among themselves 'Where is this fellow about to go that
even we shall not find him? Will he go to the dispersion among the
Greeks and teach the Greeks? What is this saying which he spake "Ye
shall seek me and shall not find me and where I am ye cannot come"?'

The crowd, impressed, wonder for a moment if He really is
the Christ and if the rulers know this. They put this aside, not
because they think the rulers would not willingly kill the
Christ — they knew too much about 'rulers' to suspect them
of tender consciences, but because the coming of the Christ
was to be a mystery and there was (they thought) no mystery
about the origin of Jesus. He accepts their claim that, in the
obvious sense of the words, they know His origin; but in
another sense they do not; for they know nothing of His
mission, His sending. Yet that is His real significance. Behind
Him is one who *sent* Him, and is a *genuine* sender — that is,
who has full right and authority to send. He does not represent
a sham authority; He is the ambassador of the real King. The
Jews do not know that King, but the Lord knows Him, *and
he sent me.*

Here surely is ground for a charge. But no action follows.
The crowd is inclining towards Him, and the Pharisees bring
the authority of the Sanhedrin into play. (St. John never
mentions 'scribes', which is one reason for declaring viii, 1–11
to be non-Johannine.) The Sanhedrin consisted of three
classes, the Chief Priests, the Elders, and the Pharisees or
Lawyers. The first were mainly concerned with the Temple,
the last with the Synagogues. The Elders were closely associated with the Chief Priests, who were the members of the
families which had held the office of Chief Priest. The Pharisees are the group in touch with the crowds, and become aware
of what is being murmured among them; then the Chief Priests
and Pharisees act together, sending some of the Temple-
police in the hope of an arrest.

It was an 'unholy combination'. It is sad to reflect that
when the extreme wings of ecclesiastical opinion are found

united, it is usually in resistance to some movement which is afterwards seen to be blessed by God. No doubt it sometimes happens under the positive inspiration of a common faith; but more often it happens through fear for the safety of a tradition — which, if true, can be defended by manifestation of its truth but not by a display of ecclesiastical authority. The Saddu-cees or Chief Priests now combine with the Pharisees to check this innovator who threatens the common element in their traditions.

But there was as yet no ground for an arrest, and what the Lord proceeds to say certainly does not provide one. He will be with them *yet a little while* — in fact, about six months. And then *I go to him that sent me, and where I am ye cannot come*. This is the first introduction of a theme to which He will return (xiii, 33). His departure will be misunderstood. It will seem like the end of Him and the ruin of His cause; but it will in fact be His triumphant return to the Father (xvi, 10). Some hint of the mystery is offered in the words *where I am*. It is not merely where He will be that they cannot come, but where He is now, that is, *in the bosom of the Father* (i, 18). When He *came down out of heaven* (vi, 38), He did not leave Heaven, but all the while *is in heaven* (iii, 13). For Heaven is fellowship with the Father; from that fellowship He came down, or forth, into the world, yet He was never without it. That fellowship with the Father is His abode at all times, to which none the less, in a certain sense to be more fully set forth later, He will return; and that is where His enemies *cannot come*.

But, of course, they interpret the words as referring to move-ments on the earth; and ask contemptuously whether He will leave the sacred places of Israel, where there are competent authorities to expose His claim, and go to those who are scattered among the Greeks, or perhaps try to win adherents among the Greeks themselves. And He would indeed do just that after His Resurrection in His Body, the Church; but though that would be present to the minds of all readers of the

Gospel, it is irrelevant to the meaning of the words as first spoken.

*

And now the Lord makes appeal to the people generally.

37–44. Now on the last day, the great day of the feast, Jesus stood and
cried aloud saying 'If any man thirst, let him come to me and drink. He
that believeth on me, as the scripture said, out of his belly shall flow
rivers of living water.' (But this spake he of the Spirit which they who
had believed on him were about to receive; for not yet was there spirit
because Jesus was not yet glorified.) From the crowd, therefore, some
hearing these words began to say 'This man is truly the Prophet'.
Others were saying 'This is the Christ'. Others again were saying 'Doth
the Christ come out of Galilee? Did not the scripture say that from the
seed of David and from Bethlehem, the village where David was,
cometh the Christ?' Division therefore arose in the crowd on account
of him. And some of them were ready to arrest him, but no man laid
hands on him.

Part of the ceremonial at the Feast of Tabernacles was a
libation of water, which was understood as symbolising the
out-pouring of the Holy Spirit. On the last day, when this
thought had been thus emphasised for a week, the Lord made
a proclamation. Like other Rabbis, He was accustomed to sit
as He taught (*St. Matthew* v, 1, 2 and many other passages).
But now He *stood and cried* aloud saying '*If any man thirst,
let him come to me and drink*'. He claims that in Him may be
found the fulfilment of all which this ritual represents. Not
only so, but those who slake their spiritual thirst at that spring
will become themselves fountains for the spiritual refresh-
ments of others. He thus carries further the teaching given to
the woman of Samaria (iv, 14). He who trusts in Christ not
only receives the water of life that springs up to eternal life,
but becomes the source of that gift to others. For no one can
possess (or, rather be indwelt by) the Spirit of God and keep
that Spirit to himself. Where the Spirit is, He flows forth; if
there is no flowing forth, He is not there.

The fulfilment of these words came at Pentecost. The experience which the early Church called holy spirit and attributed to the Holy Spirit was as yet unknown. It could not arise until *Jesus was glorified*. For it was precisely that new power of God over the heart and will which was won by the eliciting of loyalty and love in answer to the divine love manifested in Jesus. Therefore it could only come when Jesus had fully disclosed that love in His Passion, wherein the glory was consummated.

Some, caught by the splendour and authority of the claim, are ready to hail the Lord as *the prophet* who was to come; others, as the Christ. But to this it was replied that He lacked the scriptural qualifications which were that the Christ should be of the seed of David, and from Bethlehem. (Readers of the Gospel would know that in fact He had both.) So there is a division. The judgement is at work. Some are prepared for an arrest, but no one actually moves to effect it.

*

45–49. The officers therefore came to the Chief Priests and Pharisees, and these said to them 'Why did ye not bring him?' The officers answered 'Never man so spake as this man speaketh'. The Pharisees therefore answered them 'Have ye also been led astray? Did a single one of the rulers believe on him or a single one of the Pharisees? But this mob which knows not the law are accursed.'

Even the officers are impressed; they feel that there is a strange power in His words. Their masters are indignant; these fellows have only to obey orders and carry out their duties in a straightforward way; and have they been misled? They might follow the lead of those competent to form a judgement, not this ignorant and accursed crowd.

*

50–52. Nicodemus saith unto them — he that came to him before — being one of their number 'Doth our law judge the man except it first hear his statement and take note what he is doing?' They answered and said to him 'Art thou also from Galilee? Look closely and see that out of Galilee a prophet is not arising.'

Nicodemus still does not come out into the open. The most he can do is to find a legal ground for deferring judgement. This irritates his colleagues. They ask if he too is a Galilean that he sympathises with the Galilean upstart. There had arisen prophets from Galilee, no doubt — Jonah and Hosea, for example; but it was not happening this time; a little close observation would convince him of that!

*

NOTE

The story contained in vii, 53–viii, 11 is out of place here. It is not Johannine in phrasing; it is, in fact, Lucan. It is not found at this point in any of the oldest manuscripts. But one family of manuscripts has it at the end of *St. Luke* xxi. I have no doubt that that is its proper place. Where it occurs in our Bibles it interrupts the movement of thought. It was probably introduced here originally as an illustrative gloss on the words *I judge no man* (viii, 15). I shall reserve comment on it till the end of Chapter VIII.

CHAPTER VIII

(12–59)

WE are still in the Feast of Tabernacles, one phase of the controversy having been recorded. On the first day of that feast the great golden candlesticks in the Court of the Women were lit; and in general this Feast was associated with the thought of light.

12–20. Again therefore Jesus spake to them saying 'I am the Light of the World. He that followeth me shall in no case walk in the darkness, but shall have the light of Life.' The Pharisees therefore said to him 'Concerning thyself thou bearest witness; thy witness is not true'. Jesus answered and said to them 'Even if I bear witness concerning myself, true is my witness, because I know whence I came and whither I go; but ye, ye know not whence I come or whither I go. Ye judge according to the flesh; I do not judge any man. Even if I judge, the judgement that is mine is true, because I am not alone, but I and he that sent me. And in your own law it is written that the witness of two men is true. I am he that beareth witness concerning myself, and the Father which sent me beareth witness concerning me.' They began therefore to say to him 'Where is thy Father?' Jesus answered 'Ye know neither me nor my Father. If ye knew me, ye would know my Father also.' These words spake Jesus in the Treasury as he taught in the Temple; and yet no man took him, because not yet was his hour come.

Light is one of the dominant themes of the Gospel (cf. i, 4, 5). It will be constantly before us till the end of this controversial section (cf. xii, 46). The great controversy is indeed between Light and Darkness. We are familiar with the darkness of this world; we know from experience that the world is walking in darkness, and that Light is our supreme need. *I am the light of the world.* (It is useful to look up Light and Darkness in a concordance and use the passages so brought together in meditation.) To follow that light is to be delivered from *the darkness* which encompasses the world, and to *have the light of Life. The Life was the light* (i, 4); to follow Christ, to walk in His spirit — the spirit of love — is to be in the light (*I John* ii, 9–11). The light both flows from the life, and issues in the life. The cynic, who goes into the world determined to trust men no further than he can see them and to use them as pawns in his own game, will find that experience confirms his prejudice; for to such a man men will not show the finer sides of their nature. The Christian, who goes into the world full of love and trust, will equally find that experience confirms his 'prejudice', for to him men will show the finer and more sensitive sides of their nature, and even where there was no generosity his love and trust will, at least sometimes, create it. But though each finds his view verified, the latter has the truer view, for he sees all that the other sees and more beside.

You groped your way across my room i' the dear dark dead of
     night;
At each fresh step a stumble was; but, once your lamp alight,
Easy and plain you walked again; so soon all wrong grew right.

What lay on floor to trip your foot? Each object, late awry,
Looked fitly placed, nor proved offence to footing free, for why?
The lamp showed all, discordant late, grown simple symmetry.

Be love your light, and trust your guide; with these explore my
     heart!
No obstacle to trip you then — strike hands and souls apart!
Since rooms and hearts are furnished so — light shows you —
     needs love start?[1]

But this can only be known by experience, and at first by experiment. *The Pharisees* had no such experience of following Christ, and saw no reason for making the experiment. After all this was no more than a claim on His own behalf such as any fanatic might make. Yet in such a case testimony is out of place. The evidence for light is that it shines. But it is true that the light which we see is never its own source.

---

[1] BROWNING, Shah Abbas in *Ferishtah's Fancies*.

What qualifies the Lord to *bear witness concerning himself* is that He knows the origin of that light which shines in Him and which He is. The Pharisees do not know His relation to the unseen word (*whence I come*), still less the fact that in Him the Word was made flesh (*whence I came*). And such knowledge is beyond them because they *judge after the flesh*, by appearances and with unspiritual standards; *I do not judge any man*. This was not the purpose of the Lord's coming (iii, 17), nor was it His active practice; but judgement resulted from His presence (v, 22, 27; iii, 19). And so, in a most profound sense, He judges, and His *judgement is true*, because it is not based on His sole testimony, but on the mind of the Father.

The relevance of this theme of judgement arises from the fact that what constitutes the judgement is the relation which men take up towards the Lord. Therefore His testimony concerning Himself and His judgement of men are one and the same thing. Earlier (v, 31) He had Himself asserted the principle to which the Pharisees here make their appeal; self-witness is suspect; but now the Lord justifies self-witness by claiming that only in appearance (*after the flesh*) is it self-witness at all. In reality His witness is like the shining of light; it is its own evidence, and its source is its sustaining principle.

This involves a claim of such relationship to the Father as might well be made a charge of blasphemy. But that had been attempted before (v, 18) without effect. Now they try ridicule. If self-witness is suspect, an absent witness is futile. *Where is thy Father?* Produce Him. But to ask that question is to disclose an incapacity to receive the answer; the light is shining and they cannot see it. *Ye know neither me nor my Father; if ye knew me, ye would know my Father also.* We are very near the declaration to Philip: *He that hath seen me hath seen the Father* (xiv, 9).

Those expressions were used in the colonnade of the Court of the Women where the Treasure-chambers were, close beside the hall of the Sanhedrin. It was the most public place in the

Temple, and within hearing of the chief authorities. *Yet no man took him,* and the real reason for this was not the medley of human motives, but the divine purpose.

*

The rest of this Eighth Chapter contains the crisis of the controversy with the Jews. Let us recall what was said earlier (p. 103) about the hardening process which is so natural in the recollection of what is long past; a relationship which developed into antagonism is felt to have had that quality throughout. Episodes which contribute to the final breach are recalled; those which expressed a more friendly but less permanent relation tend to be forgotten. Yet even so, we find that the section in which the Lord is sternest opens with an indication of the way of hope (31–33). Moreover, much turns on the tone adopted for reading. The Lord uses language which no man such as we are is entitled to use to another; on our lips it could only express, not knowledge of an awful fact, but personal irritation. But with Him it is different. He knew the hearts of those to whom He spoke, and said these words of fearful condemnation, not in the irritation of one who is opposed, but in the sad and solemn quietness of one who recognises a dreadful truth. It is quite possible, and surely right, to read all that He says in the tone appropriate to perfect love as it faces in calm sorrow the self-complacency and self-will of those who choose darkness rather than light.

The first section (21–30) states the Lord's claim to be sent by the Father with unmistakable lucidity, and leads up to the adherence of 'many' (30). The next discloses the false basis of that faith which led the Jews to reject His claim, and leads up to the first violent assault upon Him (59), following His assertion of His priority to Abraham, the father of the faithful (58). So the controversy at this Feast of Israel the Nation leads to His claim to be the fulfilment of that nation's destiny and the repudiation of that destiny by the nation.

21–30. He said therefore again to them 'I go away, and ye will seek me, and in your sin ye will die. Where I go, ye cannot come.' The Jews therefore began to say 'Will he kill himself, because he saith "Where I go, ye cannot come"?' And he was saying to them 'Ye are from below, I am from above; ye are of this world, I am not of this world. I said therefore to you that ye will die in your sins. Unless ye believe that I am, ye will die in your sins.' They began therefore to say to him 'Thou — who art thou?' Jesus said to them 'Why do I speak to you at all? I have many things to say concerning you, and to judge, but he that sent me is true, and I — what I heard from him, this I speak to the world.' (They perceived not that he was speaking to them of the Father.) Jesus therefore said to them 'When ye shall have lifted up the Son of Man, then shall ye recognise that I am, and that from myself I do nothing, but as the Father taught me I speak these things. And he that sent me is with me; he hath not left me alone, because what is pleasing to him I do at all times.' As he was speaking these things many believed on him.

Again, as in vii, 34, the Lord declares that He is going where the Jews cannot follow Him; this goal of His journeying is the *bosom of the Father*, the perfection of love which is perfect unity with God. In one sense He is there all the time (i, 18; iii, 13); yet to be there in the conditions of human life, which passes from infancy through boyhood to manhood and so to death, is to be ever advancing in the completeness with which love finds expression in life. Jesus was always perfect or sinless — the two words mean the same; but the perfection of the boy is not that of the man, so He could 'increase in wisdom and stature and in favour with God and men' (*St. Luke* ii, 52). And as man He could advance in fulness of love's expression till He loved *to the uttermost* (xiii, 1) and in love's perfect manifestation on the Cross attained to the eternal glory (xvii, 1, 5). This is where the Jews cannot come — nor the disciples now, though they shall later (xiii, 36). And everything else is sin, for sin is all that 'falls short of the glory of God' (*Romans* iii, 23). There are only two possible centres for life — God and self. If we are not becoming centred upon God, we are becoming centred upon self; and self-centredness is the essence of sin. The Jews — and we — may seek for the Light of the world, the Light of life. But so far as we remain self-centred we can never find it, and must die in our sin.

The Jews try to escape by mockery; there was a path they could not follow, the suicide's path to the lowest hell! The answer is that while He is *from above*, they are *of this world*, with vision limited to it. Unless they can trust in Him who is *from above*, they will *die in their sins* — the varied manifestation of the essential sin spoken of immediately before.

Unless ye believe that I am. The phrase *I am* occurs here (24) and again in 28 and in 58 (cf. iv, 26; xiii, 19). The fact that it occurs three times in this controversy is a pointer. It cannot be reproduced in English, for it combines three meanings: (*a*) that I am what I say — *sc.* the Light of the World; (*b*) that I am He — the promised Messiah; (*c*) that I am — absolutely, the divine Name. All these are present; none is actually indicated; the hearers must take that (or those) which their own minds suggest.

Let us recall here that the controversy is inevitably conducted at cross-purposes because of the different moral levels on which the parties to it stand. The Lord is obliged to be obscure and allusive, because only so can He lead His hearers to His own standpoint. If He spoke to them in plain terms, they would interpret these according to their own outlook, and so in uttering truth He would convey falsehood. Thus when they ask explicitly *Who art thou?* — the natural enquiry after what He has just said — He cannot reply 'I am the Christ', still less 'I am God incarnate', because they would interpret these words according to their own conceptions of Christ and of God and would therefore entirely misunderstand Him. He is not the conquering Messiah of their hopes; He is not the Sultanic God of their beliefs. He is true Christ and true God; but what these are we see only in Him. Therefore He must go on directing attention to His own Person — to the Light that is come into the world — leaving them to appreciate its brightness. So when they ask *Who art thou?* He answers *Why do I speak to you at all?* Speaking does no good. The only way to answer that question is to live, as He is living, the perfect life.

[The reply in 25 is a famous difficulty. The translation given follows the interpretation of Chrysostom. The words could also mean 'Essentially I am what I say' — My Person is My message. The upshot is the same. The words can hardly bear the translation given by both A.V. and the text of R.V.; but the margin of R.V. should nearly always be preferred to its text.]

He has indeed *many things to say,* not concerning Himself, about whom they ask, but *concerning you, and to judge.* But they are not of His origination. They come from the Father, and what the Lord speaks to the world is what He has heard in the intimacy of union with the Father; and the Father's truth is beyond question. But they do not recognise that it is of the Father that He speaks; so the Lord goes on to foretell the critical moment. *When ye shall have lifted up the Son of Man, then shall ye recognise that I am, and that from myself I do nothing, and as the Father taught me I speak these things.* The supreme revelation of the Cross would do its work, not at once, perhaps, but at last. So in xii, 32, where this phrase is repeated, the Cross, to which the Jews condemn their rejected Messiah, is to be the means of winning them — *all men* — to discipleship. It may happen at Calvary; it may happen through the preaching of the Gospel; it may happen only on that final day when 'every eye shall see him and they which pierced him' (*Revelation* i, 7). But it cannot fail.

He that sent me is with me; he hath not left me alone, because what is pleasing to him I do at all times. It is this simple claim to divine companionship based on obedience which wins *many* to faith. So it always is. When a Christian can say that he has Christ in his heart, and offers a practical obedience as evidence and ground of this, he too wins many for his lord. *As he was speaking these things many believed on him.*

*

Now the tone changes. The Lord turns to those who do not believe on Him, but do believe Him — that is to say, those who do not put their personal trust in Him, but are disposed to think that what He says is true. To go so far and then stop is a sign of very grave spiritual trouble. If a man cannot believe the Gospel at all, it may be that some new presentation of it may carry it past all obstacles to reach his conscience, heart, and mind. But if he does believe it, yet fails to put practical trust in Him whom it presents, there is some fatal influence at work in opposition. And how many of us fall, wholly or in part, under that description! As we read the stern words that follow, let us not ask so much how He the Lord of Love should so speak to the Jews, as whether we have deserved that the Lord of Love should so speak to us. Above all, let us remember, and here observe, how resistance on grounds of self-will to what we recognise as right and noble, has a hardening and embittering effect on those in whom it is found which involves mortal peril to the soul.

31–51. Jesus therefore began to say unto the Jews which had believed him 'If ye abide in the word which is mine ye are truly my disciples, and ye will recognise the truth and the truth will set you free'. They made answer unto him 'Abraham's seed are we, and to no man have we been in bondage at any time; how sayest thou "Ye shall become free men"?' Jesus answered them 'Amen, Amen, I say to you, that everyone who practises sin is the bond-slave of sin. Now the slave doth not abide in the house for ever; the son abideth for ever. If therefore the Son shall set you free, really free shall ye be. I know that ye are seed of Abraham; yet ye seek to kill me, because the word that is mine makes no way in you. I for my part speak what I have seen with my Father; and ye therefore do what ye heard from your father.' They answered and said to him 'Our father is Abraham'. Jesus saith to them 'If ye are the children of Abraham, do the works of Abraham. But as it is, ye are seeking to kill me, a man who has spoken the truth to you, which I heard from God. This Abraham did not. Ye do the works of your father.' They said to him 'We were not born of fornication; one Father we have — God'. Jesus said to them 'If God were your father, ye would love me; for from God I came forth and am here. For I have not come of myself, but he sent me. Why do ye not recognise my manner of speech? — because ye cannot hear the word that is mine. Ye are of your father,

the devil, and the desires of your father it is your will to do. He was a
murderer from the beginning, and stood not in the truth because there
is no truth in him. When he speaketh the false saying, he speaketh
from his own store, because he is a liar and the father of falsehood.
But because I speak the truth ye do not believe me. Who of you convicteth me of sin? If I say the truth, why do ye not believe me? He that is
of God heareth the words of God; for this cause ye do not hear, that
ye are not of God.' The Jews answered and said to him 'Are not we
right in saying that Samaria is thy home and thou hast a demon?'
Jesus answered 'I have not a demon, but I honour my Father and ye
dishonour me. But I do not seek my glory; there is one that seeketh
it — and judgeth. Amen, Amen, I say to you, if a man observe my
word he shall not notice death unto eternity.'

The address to those who believe the Lord yet do not commit themselves in trust to Him, begins with encouragement.
They have His word, which they believe; if they will make that,
as it were, their home, then they are truly disciples, and so
abiding and learning will come to recognise the truth. *If ye
abide in the word which is mine, ye are truly my disciples, and
ye will recognise the truth.* This perception or knowledge of the
truth is more than intellectual and scientific knowledge, for
which there is another word; it is the knowledge of acquaintance. Loyal adherence to what they believe will convert that
belief into trust; they will advance, so to speak, from being
orthodox to being real Christians. And in that trust they will
find freedom. *Ye will perceive the truth, and the truth will set
you free.* Truth is the objective apprehension of things as they
are, as distinguished from a vision distorted by desires and
special interests. The way to spiritual freedom for men is
always by surrender to the object — to the real facts in the life
of science, to the goal or cause in practical conduct, to God as
He reveals Himself in worship. But we do not always recognise our need for emancipation. When a man is both orthodox
and self-assertive, believing the Gospel but not believing in it
— a very familiar spiritual state — he is not recognising and
making acquaintance with the truth. He is probably quite
unconscious that he is in any bondage. He may preach the

Gospel of redemption to others, and never know that he needs it himself. Pharisaism is not an exclusively Jewish phenomenon. The first of our needs is to know what our first need is — to be set free from bondage; but then we must accept and confess the fact that we are in bondage, and the more complete the bondage, the less are we aware of it. So these Jews insist that they are free men by heredity — *Seed of Abraham are we and to no man have we been in bondage at any time* — for they know that the Lord is not speaking of the freedom of political independence. What gift of spiritual freedom is there which the Chosen People have not received?

The answer is a solemn asseveration of a general principle. *Amen, Amen, I say to you that every one who practises sin is the bond-slave of sin.* The phrase excludes reference to the occasional lapse into sin, and refers to habitual or persistent sin. This thought of being enslaved to sin is expressed in the New Testament only here, and in *Romans* vi, 17 and 20, and in *II Peter* ii, 19. It is rather Greek, or at any rate Socratic, than Hebraic. And it coheres with the specifically Christian thought of sin as essentially lack of faith (cf. xvi, 9). These Jews believe with their minds, but have not faith, which is belief active in trust or self-committal. To stop there is in a conspicuous degree to *practise sin.* Sin is the assertion of our own will as opposed to acceptance of God's will; belief which stops short of faith is a conspicuous instance of this. Such a man *cannot hear* the word (43) by abiding in which he might come to perceive or recognise the truth and so find freedom.

The term 'slave' suggests by association a new distinction. No slave has a permanent status; that belongs only to the children of the house. For the slave of sin this is, in one way, good news: for he can be set free, and leave the house of sin; but what if in that house he is not only slave but son, as he must be if his father is the devil? (44). Equally — and this is the line of thought first pursued — a bond-slave of God, who serves Him with the spirit of bondage (*Romans* viii, 15), has no permanent status in the house of God. Now, the spirit of legalistic Judaism was precisely the 'spirit of bondage' — the spirit in which a man does what is commanded and avoids what is forbidden, hoping for reward and fearing punishment. But the spirit of sonship, which can be ours only by adoption (*Romans* viii, 15) is that which prompts us to go far beyond commands and prohibitions and do at all times what is pleasing to our Father (29), not for reward or avoidance of punishment, but for love of Him; and this is the self-committal of faith. One who is thus committed in faith has a permanent status in the home. *The slave doth not abide in the house for ever; the son abideth for ever.*

How can we acquire that status? A slave cannot emancipate himself; the sinful will cannot convert itself — its sinfulness must hinder that. If it could will its own conversion, it would already be converted. St. Augustine has said the last word about this in the *Confessions* (Book VIII, Chapters VIII and IX). The state which occasions the need for conversion renders it impossible actually so to will. Conversion must be wrought in us, indeed; but it cannot be wrought by us; it is something done to us. Expressed in terms of the contrast between the slave and the son, who can effect this? Only one who has in His own being the status of Sonship, and who, having it, can impart it. *If therefore the Son shall set you free, really free shall ye be.*

The physical descent from Abraham is not challenged. But the corresponding conduct is not found. For that physical descent is not the deepest truth of the matter. In quality the Jews are children of another father than Abraham, and they, like the Lord, act in accordance with their spiritual origin. *I know that ye are seed of Abraham; yet ye seek to kill me* (v, 18; vii, 1, 25) *because the word that is mine makes no way in you.* They believed it, and that was the end; it had no free course in them; so their desire to be rid of Him remained. Both were true to their origin. *I speak what I have seen with my Father; and ye therefore do what ye heard from your father.* The utterance of the divine truth calls out in reaction a repudiation which, being in direct antagonism to God, is an impulse from the devil. But this is not yet made explicit. The Jews reiterate their descent from Abraham; *Our father is Abraham.* The Lord had admitted that in its superficial sense (37), but now He presses the inconsistency of conduct. If you are, act accordingly; but you do the opposite. *If ye are children of Abraham, do the works of Abraham. But as it is ye are seeking to kill me, a man who has spoken the truth to you. This Abraham did not; ye do the works of your father.* It is someone else's character, not Abraham's, which is reproduced in their conduct. They see that He is speaking of spiritual paternity, not physical. But the form of their reply is pointless unless it refers to rumours about the Lord's own birth — rumours which were the almost inevitable by-product of the actual fact; the Mother of the Lord did not escape the calumny that she foresaw when she accepted the highest honour ever given to human being (*St. Luke* i, 38). *We* (for our part — the pronoun is emphatic) *were not born of fornication; one Father we have — God.* But if this were the spiritual truth about them, they would love one who comes forth from God. They cannot recognise His way of speaking, because their spiritual ears are not attuned to the utterance which is characteristic of Him. *If God were your father, ye would love me; for from God I came forth and am here. For I have not come of myself but he sent me. Why do ye not recognise my manner of speech? — because ye cannot hear the word that is mine.* No — neither Abraham nor God is their spiritual progenitor. *Ye are of your father the devil —* and there follow characteristics of the devil which explain the condition of his children. Killing and lying are natural to him; his children disbelieve what is said precisely because it is true. *Because I speak the truth ye do not believe me.* They have no case to bring in refutation; they can accuse Him of no sin. *Who of you convicteth me of sin? If I say the truth* (and no one argues to the contrary), *why do ye not believe me?* It is because they are not, as they claimed to be (41), of God.

But this is to abandon the Jewish creed and fall into Samaritan heresy. The Jews were the chosen people of God; for anyone who accepts the Law to deny that is to adopt the Samaritan outlook. He is no better than a Samaritan, and a fanatic, demon-possessed, at that. The Lord does not quarrel with the taunt of Samaritanism. He was indifferent to that (iv, 21–24). The other taunt He quietly denies. *I have not a demon, but I honour my Father, and ye dishonour me.* What seems to them delusion is assurance based on obedience to the Father. *I do not seek my glory*; for the Father's glory is His only concern. But *there is one that seeketh it*; the Father seeks glory for the Son, and as He seeks He judges men according as they give or withhold it. And the glory of the Son is that, by appointment of the Father, He is the giver of eternal life (v, 21–27), which may be so fully received from Him here and now that death becomes an incidental irrelevance. *Amen, Amen, I say to you that if a man observe my word, he shall not notice death unto eternity.*

Some verbal comments are needed here. The familiar translation is 'If a man keep my saying he shall never see death'. And this, no doubt, is correct, and is the best that can be done in English, unless we are to exaggerate suggestions and *nuances*; but it is part of my purpose rather to exaggerate them than to miss them, and while my version is guilty of this exaggeration, it may be useful in calling attention to points otherwise obscured from those who cannot make reference to the Greek.

First, I have substituted 'observe' for 'keep', because the primary thought is not that of preserving, or even obeying, but of watching. (So it is in *Ephesians* iv, 3, where we are not urged to preserve the unity of the Spirit — that is not our responsibility! — but to watch or observe it; we are to 'give diligence to observe the oneness of the Spirit' however diverse His operations.) We are, so to speak, to live in observance of the word of Christ as our constant standard of reference. Secondly, the Greek negative phrase does mean 'never'; but it is not the usual word for 'never'; it is an emphatic and expanded form — 'not unto eternity'. Thirdly, the Greek words so translated are rightly rendered 'see death', and to 'see death' is a recognised Hebraic expression for 'die'; but again it is not the usual word for 'see' which appears in the phrase 'not see death' with reference to Simeon (*St. Luke* ii, 26) and Enoch (*Hebrews* xi, 5). The word chosen here is the word which implies special attention, as when it is used at its height, so to speak, of the contemplation of God (τὸν θεὸν θεραπεύειν καὶ θεωρεῖν Aristotle, *Eudemian Ethics*, 1249 b 20), or, again, of noticing something as matter of interest, as when in vi, 2 the crowd is said to follow Jesus because they were noticing, or taking note of, the signs which He was working.

So here, the Lord does not promise that anyone who keeps His word shall avoid the physical incident called death; but that if his mind is turned towards that word it will not pay any attention to death; death will be to it irrelevant. It may truly be said that such a man will not 'experience' death, because, though it will happen to him, it will matter to him no more than the fall of a leaf from a tree under which he might be reading a book. It happens to him, but he does not in any full sense see or notice it.

R. L. Nettleship, in one of his letters, writes: 'Fear of death, or clinging to life, is fear of or clinging to certain fragments of ourselves. If we could "energise" a great deal more continuously than most of us can, we might experience physical death literally without being aware of it.'[1] There is no mode of energy possible to man so absorbing and stimulating as to *observe the word* of Him who is the Word of God.

*

The Jews realise that a stupendous claim has been made. They do not pause to notice the special expressions used; indeed in their irritation they unconsciously alter these.

---

[1] R. L. Nettleship, *Philosophical Remains*, p. 93.

52–59. The Jews said to him 'Now we are sure that thou hast a demon. Abraham died, and the prophets, and thou sayest "If any man observe my word, he shall not taste of death unto eternity." Art thou greater than our father Abraham who died? — and the prophets died. Whom makest thou thyself?' Jesus answered 'If I shall glorify myself, my glory is nothing; there is my Father that glorifieth me, of whom ye say that he is your God. And ye are not acquainted with him, but I know him. And if I say that I do not know him, I shall be like you — a liar. But I know him and observe his word. Abraham your father exulted in the hope of seeing my day; and he saw and rejoiced.' The Jews therefore said unto him 'Not yet fifty years old art thou, and hath Abraham seen thee?' Jesus said to them 'Amen, Amen, I say to you, before Abraham came into being, I AM'. They took up stones therefore to cast at him. But Jesus hid himself and went out of the Temple.

The claim that if a man observe His word he shall be freed from death is the claim of a fanatic or lunatic — unless it is true! And the indignant Jews make it worse by missing the special *nuance* of the phrase used. They do not deliberately misquote; they have misapprehended, and use a phrase more appropriate to what they suppose to have been His meaning. Anyhow, there is no doubt about the loftiness of the claim. Abraham, who kept God's word, died like other men; so did the prophets, to whom the word of the Lord came. And here is one who claims that *if any man observe my word, he shall never taste of death*. [No; He had not said that. Jesus Himself 'tasted' of death (*Hebrews* ii, 9); and His followers taste of it. Yet His mind was not fixed on death, but on the Father, into whose hands He committed His spirit (*St. Luke* xxiii, 46); and His followers may commit their spirits to Him (*Acts* vii, 59).] What claim is this? *Whom makest thou thyself?*

The Lord answers that He makes no claim for Himself. He seeks not His own glory (50), nor will He glorify Himself. To do so would, as they had rightly said (13), be futile. But there is one who glorifies Him (we learn how more fully later — xvii, 5) — His Father, *of whom ye say that he is your God*. They offer Him worship; but they are not acquainted with Him — they only know about Him. *I know him*; it is the absolute knowledge of perfect understanding. He cannot deny that knowledge; to do so would be to come down to their level of falsehood. *I know him and observe his word.* Here, as always, the Lord is the true mediator. We: Christ:: Christ: the Father.

But as concerns Abraham — he *exulted in the hope of seeing my day.* The Greek does not, so far, say that he saw it; the cause of exultation was the prospect, as opened by the great promises (*Genesis* xii, 3; xxii, 18). But there was fulfilment as well as anticipation; *and he saw and rejoiced.* There was a tradition among the Jews that in the vision recorded in *Genesis* xv, 8–21 Abraham saw the whole history of his descendants. There may be a reference here to this tradition. I am disposed to think the reference is rather to that apprehension of the eternal justice and mercy recorded in *Genesis* xviii, 16–33 — the pleading for the doomed cities. That stands out as a peak in the series of human apprehensions of the uttered mind — the Word — of God; and what follows shows that we are to think of the Lord as both existent and active in that time. But to attach these words to any recorded episode can be no more than a personal speculation.

The Jews are partly puzzled, partly outraged. According to the best manuscripts they again, in the inaccuracy born of irritation, misquote what had been said: *Not yet fifty years old art thou, and hast thou seen Abraham?* But perhaps it is more natural to prefer the other reading, though less well supported — *hath Abraham seen thee?* In either case contempt for a foolish assertion is now added to bewilderment and anger.

Amen, Amen, I say to you, before Abraham came into being, I AM. There is no doubt now about the assertion of an eternal personality; there can be hardly any doubt about the claim to Deity. Yet it is made by allusion and implication. The words *I AM* need not of necessity mean more than an assertion of existence; they need not be the Divine Name revealed to Moses at the Bush (*Exodus* iii, 14). It still cannot be said that He has explicitly affirmed His Deity. That He will never do —

as we shall find again at x, 30–36; the apprehension of that truth must come through the response of men's souls. But He does lead us to the very verge of it. And if it is not true His language is the grossest blasphemy. These Jews, who began by fighting their own knowledge that His words were true, now have their chance to break into open and justified violence against Him. The Temple was still a-building, and there were stones lying about in its courts. *They took up stones therefore to cast at him; but he hid himself and went out of the Temple.*

The breach with the Jews has reached its climax. But the hour for the consequence of that breach was not come, and we watch the now declared hostility maturing through further episodes; and before we come to these we have to consider that interpolation which occupies the opening verses of Chapter VIII.

*

THE WOMAN TAKEN IN ADULTERY

This episode is not Johannine; its language alone shows that. 'It is not found in any of the early Greek uncials with the single exception of Codex Bezae.' It is introduced here in illustration of viii, 15 — *Ye judge according to the flesh; I do not judge any one.* But though not Johannine it is undoubtedly a genuine record; its style is Lucan; and there is little reason to doubt that its proper place is at the end of *St. Luke* xxi, where some manuscripts actually give it.

But the scribe who first wrote it in the margin as an illustrative gloss on viii, 15 had genius, and we are all his debtors.

*

vii, 53–viii, 11. And they went every man to his own home. And Jesus went into the Mount of Olives. And early in the morning he came again into the temple, and all the people came to him, and sitting down he taught them. And the Scribes and the Pharisees bring a woman taken in adultery, and having set her in the midst say to him 'Master, this woman was taken in the very act of committing adultery. Now in the law Moses commanded us to stone such; what then sayest thou?' But they said this tempting him, that they might have opportunity to accuse him. But Jesus stooping down began to write on the ground. But when they went on asking, he lifted himself up and said to them 'He that is without sin among you, let him first cast a stone at her'. And again stooping down he wrote upon the ground. But they, having heard, began to go out, one by one, beginning from the elders, and he was left alone, and the woman who was in the midst. And Jesus, having lifted up himself, said to her 'Woman, where are they? Did no one condemn thee?' And she said 'No one, Lord'. And Jesus said 'Neither do I condemn thee; go; from now on do not sin any more'.

The story carries its own meaning. These odious ecclesiastics are so set upon their barren controversy that they will use a woman's shame as a chance to score a point. They seem to gloat over the loathsome circumstances of the woman's arrest — *in the very act*. Now, will this mercy-loving teacher, who is so lax about the law of the Church, openly express dissent from Moses? If He does, He is trapped.

But the Lord is tortured with the horror of it all. He will not look at them or at her. He stoops down to hide the burning confusion of His face and relieves His agitation by tracing patterns in the dust. Then for a moment He lifts up that face which is 'of purer eyes than to behold iniquity' and shoots out the challenging words. The Law is just, and adultery is horrible. But are any of these men qualified to inflict the sentence which that Law imposes? And the words go home. Something in the Speaker's mien breaks down the concern, the quite real concern, of the controversialists to score their point, and penetrates to the springs of conscience. The scribe who inserted the words 'being convicted by their own conscience' knew what had happened. One by one they slink away. Then two are left — the Lord and the sinner. '*Where are they? Did no one condemn thee?*' '*No one, Lord.*' '*Neither do I condemn thee; go; from now on do not sin any more.*' It is not a formal acquittal; it is a refusal to judge. He who so refuses is the only one who ever was *without sin*; He alone was entitled to condemn; and He did not condemn. But neither did He condone. He said *From now on do not sin any more*. Perhaps that

spiritual power which flashed His challenge into the consciences of the accusers carried this charge to the will of the
sinful woman, so that, not condemned, she was purged.

May it at least be so with us! May the Wrath of the Lamb
against our combination of impurity and complacency quicken
our slow consciences, and may His cleansing glance so pene-
trate us that from now on we do not sin any more!

CHAPTER IX

AFTER the tense atmosphere of the controversy recorded in Chapters VII and VIII the Evangelist passes, with divine art, to a chapter of vivid movement, disclosing the spiritual outlook of those concerned with singular clearness, but not demanding specially close thought or deep meditation. Once more, as at the beginning of Chapter VII (see Westcott quoted *ad loc.*), we notice the qualities which only the narrative of an eyewitness would show.

There is no note of date for the miracle recorded, but the ensuing controversy comes to a head during the Feast of Dedication (x, 22) and the whole story may fall within the period of that feast. As the controversy connected with the Feast of Israel as nation (the Feast of Tabernacles) led up to the Lord's assertion of His priority to Abraham (viii, 58), so this, which is connected with the Feast of Israel as Church (the Feast of Dedication) leads up to His assertion of His unity with the Father (x, 30).

＊

THE SIGN

1–7. And passing by he saw a man blind from birth. And his disciples asked him saying 'Rabbi, who sinned, this man or his parents, that he should be born blind?' Jesus answered 'Neither did this man sin nor his parents; but it was for a manifestation of the works of God in him. I must work the works of him that sent me while it is day; there cometh night when no man can work. Whensoever I am in the world, I am light of the world.' Having said this he spat on the ground and made clay of the spittle, and smeared his clay on the eyes, and said to him 'Go, wash in the pool of Siloam' (which means sent). He went away therefore, and washed, and came seeing.

Blind from birth. It is said that St. John likes to heighten the miraculous element in his narrative. But if he does, it is not from any love of the marvellous. It is not the wonder, but the symbolism, of the acts of the Lord which he would emphasise. The works are for him not primarily miracles but signs. The man *blind from birth* is every man. For it is a part of that *sin of the world* which *the Lamb of God beareth away* (i, 29) that by nature we are blind, until our eyes are opened by Christ the *Light of the world* (viii, 12; ix, 5). It is in bearing away that sin of the world that the Son is glorified, and God is glorified in Him. The vitally important question is not 'Who is responsible?' — *this man or his parents?* — but 'How can this fact be turned to the glory of God?' All things exist for that glory; even sin, and every form of evil, is compelled to minister to that glory; and the opportunity of glorifying God is the ultimate moral factor in every situation.

The primitive and crude conception of divine justice, from which (in spite of *The Book of Job*) the Jews had not freed themselves, regards every calamity as a punishment for some sin. A man born blind thus presents a problem. Perhaps the sin was in his parents; but then we are involved in contradiction of Ezekiel. So the Rabbis invented the possibility of pre-natal sin to account for inherited defects. What will this Rabbi say? As usual He carries the matter to a new level of thought. Calamity and guilt are not thus adjusted in the world. But there is always the opportunity of glorifying God. What matters about this man is not that he illustrates a theory of divine justice, nor even (which is the fact) that he contradicts it; but that a manifestation of the works of God may take place in him.

The Lord must do such works while it is possible. He is come to do the works of God (v, 17, 19, 20); this must continue till His hour is come and His work is accomplished (xvii, 1, 4). For Him as for all men it is true that *there cometh night, when no one can work*. The manner of work now possible is possible only while life lasts. It is true, indeed, that His activity in the world is not limited to that channel. *Whensoever I am in the world*, as agent of creation (i, 3), as coming to prophets,

I am light of the world. There is no emphasis here as in viii, 12 on the personal pronoun, and no definite article. Every manifestation of the divine word is illumination of the world; and that manifestation is all around us; but we are blind from birth and pay no heed, till He anoints our eyes.

It is true that all creation manifests the Creator. 'The heavens declare the glory of God and the firmament sheweth his handiwork' (*Psalm* xix, 1). But we see all this awry until we have first learnt to see God in Jesus Christ. We cannot ascertain the character of God by induction from what He has done and is doing in nature and history. But when we have found it in Jesus Christ we can begin to trace it there also. As we look back we see that the special revelation in Christ is the crown of the general revelation in nature and history; but if we start with this and look forward, we cannot even adumbrate that only true revelation.

So the Lord turns to the blind man to heal him. He follows the current and, doubtless, well-founded belief that saliva has curative properties; and, in order to apply it, mingles it with dust, so making a sort of clay-ointment. There could be no objection to this on any other day; but this was a sabbath, and 'the application of spittle to the eyes, which was considered very salutary, was expressly forbidden by Jewish tradition on the sabbath' (Westcott *ad loc.*). The making of clay would be an additional offence.

He anointed the sightless eyes, and told the man to wash in the Pool of Apostleship; and when he did this, he saw. The Father *sent* the Son; the Son *sent* His disciples. This Apostolic mission is the only source from which the darkness of the world can win light and sight. But of course this suggestion is given by the Evangelist's note, calling attention to the meaning of the name Siloam: that name itself merely indicated the fact that the water was artificially brought to this pool, and had long ago become a proper name with no other meaning than to denote a particular pool.

❈

THE EFFECT ON NEIGHBOURS

8–12. The neighbours therefore, and those who noticed him before, that
he was a beggar, began to say 'Is not this he who sits and begs?' Some
were saying 'This is he'; others were saying 'No, but he is like him'.
He was saying 'I am (the man)'. So they began to say to him 'How
then were thine eyes opened?' He answered 'The man called Jesus
made clay, and anointed my eyes and said to me "Go to Siloam and
wash". So I went, and washed, and received sight.' And they said to
him 'Where is he?' He saith 'I do not know'.

Little here calls for observation, except that the man uses,
to end the discussion, the same words 'I am', which in the
mouth of the Lord must suggest an assertion of Deity, without any sort of claim for himself. Thus we are reminded that
when the Lord used those words they carried no necessary or
overt claim, and it was possible to hear them without any
thought of a further implication.

'*Where is he?*' '*I do not know.*' So natural; and in a sense
so terrible. We who have received sight in some measure are
often asked, sometimes by implication, sometimes by direct
challenge, from what source we gained it; and frequently we
answer 'I do not know' — either from cowardice, or from real
ignorance. Not all men recognise their obligation to trace the
source of the light by which they live. If they are heirs of a
Christian tradition, they often ignore or even repudiate what
is in fact the 'master-light of all their seeing'. And even if, in
their hearts, they know the truth they are ashamed to confess it.
Well for us if direct opposition and threat of persecution
matures our conviction and leads us to explicit confession of
faith, as happened with the blind man whom the Lord had
healed!

•

EXAMINATION OF THE BLIND MAN

13–17. They bring him to the Pharisees — the man who had been blind.
Now it was a sabbath that day on which Jesus made the clay and

opened his eyes. So again the Pharisees also began to ask him how he
received sight. And he said to them 'He put clay upon my eyes, and I
washed myself, and I see'. Some of the Pharisees therefore began to say
'This man is not from God, because he does not observe the sabbath'.
Others were saying 'How can a man that is a sinner do such signs?'
And there was division among them. They say therefore to the blind
man again 'What dost thou say of him, seeing that he opened thine
eyes?' And he said 'A prophet is he'.

Probably *the Pharisees* here are not a casual collection of
them who happened to be available, but one of the two smaller
courts, or Synagogue Councils, that existed in Jerusalem. They
conduct a more or less formal examination, and end with a
dismissal which, though short of formal excommunication, is
more than an expression of personal annoyance. We notice
how the man sticks to bare facts — always the real foundation
of faith. He offers no interpretation till he is challenged.

*

THE EXAMINATION OF THE PARENTS

18–23. The Jews therefore refused to believe concerning him that he had
been blind and had received sight, until they had called the parents of
him that received sight. And they asked them saying 'Is this your son,
of whom ye say that he was born blind? How then does he now see?'
His parents therefore answered and said 'We know that this is our son,
and that he was born blind. But how he now sees we do not know, or
who opened his eyes we do not know; ask him; he is of age; he will tell
his own story.' His parents said this, because they feared the Jews; for
already the Jews had agreed that if any one should confess him as
Christ, he should be excommunicated. For this reason his parents said
'He is of age; ask him'.

The parents have not had the experience that has come to
their son. They are frightened, and have nothing to put up
against their fear. But the man himself has. And when he is
challenged, he stands by his experience and is ready for the
worst that his examiners can do rather than deny it.

*

SECOND EXAMINATION AND EXPULSION OF THE BLIND MAN

24–34. So they called a second time the man who was blind, and said to him 'Give glory to God; we know that this man is a sinner'. He therefore answered 'Whether he is a sinner I know not; one thing I know, that being blind I now see'. So they said to him 'What did he do to thee? How did he open thine eyes?' He answered 'I told you already and ye did not listen; why do ye want to hear again? Surely ye do not wish to become his disciples?' And they reviled him and said 'Thou art a disciple of that fellow, but we are Moses' disciples. We know that God hath spoken to Moses, but this fellow — we do not know whence he is.' The man answered and said to them 'Why, then, herein is the marvel, that ye do not know whence he is, and he hath opened mine eyes. We know that sinners God doth not hear; but if any man be devout and doeth his will, him he heareth. From the beginning of time it was unheard of that any one opened the eyes of one who was born blind. If this man were not from God, he would not be able to do anything.' They answered and said to him 'In sins wast thou born, all of thee; and dost thou teach us?' And they drove him out.

The pious phrase with which the Court now addresses the blind man is a formula of solemn adjuration. It does not mean, 'Give glory to God, and not to Jesus, for your sight' though that would have been appropriate enough. It merely means what may now be meant by the opening words of a solemn announcement — 'In the Name of God, Amen'. The Court, which is a competent authority, has decided the matter, and calls on this former beggar to accept its decision — *We know that this man is a sinner*. That is a matter of opinion; the beggar has a fact — *one thing I know*. And that is the most important thing for any believer to be able to say. It may be this thing; it may be that; but if there is *one thing* let a man hold to that. And whatever threatens, whatever high authority ecclesiastical or civil may have to say, let him for no consideration deny his own experience.

The Pharisees ask to have the story over again. No doubt they hope to find some flaw in it. But he begins to mock at them; do they want to hear again and again till they become disciples? No, they say; *Thou art a disciple of that fellow; we are Moses' disciples . . . (If ye believed Moses, ye would believe me; for concerning me he wrote*; v, 46 — there is no such conflict of discipleships as is implied.) They know whence Moses derived his teaching, but they do not know what may be Jesus' credentials. This goads the man to the conviction that Jesus is *from God*. Divine mission at least he will ascribe to Him. And now the Court falls back on the one thing it knows about him; he was born blind, doubtless because of his own sins or those of his parents (2); anyhow he came into the world bearing the mark of divine judgement and disfavour. Such a man cannot be allowed to instruct the Court, and he is driven out with contumely. This is not excommunication, either that total severance from Israel which only the Sanhedrin could decree, or the suspension from the synagogue, which had been agreed on as the penalty for confessing Jesus as Christ (22); but it is a contemptuous expulsion from the Court, implying recalcitrance and alienation.

*

THE WELCOME OFFERED BY JESUS

35–38. Jesus heard that they drove him out, and found him and said 'Thou — dost thou believe on the Son of Man?' He answered and said 'And who is he, Lord, that I may believe on him?' Jesus said to him 'Both seen him hast thou, and he who is talking with thee is he'. And he answered 'I believe, Lord'; and worshipped him.

The man who is driven out by the Pharisaic Court is not left to wander as an outcast. Jesus *found him*. The man did not find Jesus; Jesus found him. That is the deepest truth of Christian faith; Jesus found me. Our fellowship with Him is rooted in His compassion.

For it is into His fellowship that He welcomes the blind beggar; and to do this, He offers Himself explicitly for the first time as an object of faith. Westcott sees here 'the beginning of the new Society'. That presses the point too far. But

it is true that here for the first time the Lord offers Himself
as an object of faith, and does this as a way of receiving into
His fellowship one who is alienated from another.

The Son of Man is the title of the Messiah both as fulfilling
the divine intention for humanity, and as reigning with divine
glory. This man, who has confessed that Jesus is *from God* —
will he go further and put his whole trust in the Son of Man?
Yes, if he knows where to find Him. In other words, he trusts
Jesus enough to put his trust where Jesus shall point him.
Then Jesus points to Himself. *Seen him hast thou.* This man
has not had time yet to see many people! The Son of Man is
one of the few whom he has already seen; and is now talking
with him. *He said 'I believe, Lord'; and worshipped him.*

*

The Judgement on the Pharisees

39–41. And Jesus said 'Unto judgement into this world did I come, that
they who see not may see, and they who see may become blind'. From
among the Pharisees they who were with him heard, and said to him
'Can it be that we are blind?' Jesus said 'If ye were blind ye would not
have sin; but now ye say "We see"; your sin abideth'.

Judgement was not the purpose of His coming (iii, 17); but
was its inevitable result (iii, 19). It led to an opening of blind
eyes; it led to a blinding of eyes that had seen. Some of the
Court which had driven out the blind man, and doubtless
knew that the Lord had received him, ask ironically whether
they are to be classed among the blind. Of course they expect
to be told that they are — 'blind guides' (*St. Matthew* xxiii,
16). But, on the contrary, they are told that blindness would
be an excuse; their claim to sight is their condemnation; their
sin stands.

It is a crushing, overwhelming retort. Can we escape its
impact? Only in one of two ways. Either we must confess our
blindness and seek the opening of our eyes; or else we must

accept the light and walk by it. What we may not do, yet all strive to do, is to keep our eyes half-open and live by half the light. That kind of sight holds us to our sin and our sin to us. But the only way of avoiding it is to look with eyes wide open upon ourselves and the world as the full light reveals it; but this is the surrender of faith, and pride resists it.

CHAPTER X

We must picture the Pharisees who have received that crushing retort (ix, 41) as reduced to silence, till strange language about the laying down of life in obedience to divine commands stimulates them to further protest (x, 18, 19). A man has been driven from one fold and received into another. After a solemn and awestruck silence the Lord speaks again.

1–6. 'Amen, Amen, I say to you, he that entereth not through the door into the fold of the sheep, but climbs up by some other way, he is a thief and a robber. But he that entereth through the door is shepherd of the sheep. To him the doorkeeper openeth, and the sheep hear his voice, and his own sheep he calleth by name and leadeth them out. When he hath put out all his own, he goeth before them, and the sheep follow him because they know his voice. But a stranger will they not follow, but will flee from him, because they do not know the voice of strangers.' This parable spake Jesus to them, but they perceived not what things they were which he was saying to them.

The fold of the sheep was the courtyard in front of the house, where the sheep were brought for the night. The only alternative to entry by the door was by climbing over the walls. No one will enter that way except one who has no business there, and is therefore presumably come to steal. The man who openly comes by the door is a man entitled to enter — a shepherd. The door-keeper will know him and open to him. There may be sheep from several flocks gathered for the night; each shepherd will call his own sheep by name, and his own will recognise his voice and follow him. They will not follow a stranger, because his voice is unfamiliar. When a shepherd has brought out all his own sheep, he leads them to pasture.

It was a parable, and they did not understand it. He goes on to explain it as giving a double interpretation of His mission. He is both the Door (7–10) and the Shepherd (11–16).

*

7–10. Jesus therefore said to them again 'Amen, Amen, I say to you, I am
the door of the sheep. All that came before me are thieves and robbers.
But the sheep did not hear them. I am the door; through me if any man
enter, he shall be kept safe, and shall go in and go out and shall find
pasture. The thief cometh not but for to steal and to kill and to destroy.
I came that they may have life and may have it abundantly.'

I am the door of the sheep — the door through which both
sheep and shepherd go in and out. The sheep must come into
the fold — the Church — *through the Door.* They must not
come for convention or respectability or for any other reason
than trust in Christ. If they come so they will be *kept safe;*
they will *go in and go out and shall find pasture.* Their pasture
is outside, in the world. Clergy often forget this. Here is the
root of the difference between clerical and lay religion. The
layman finds in religion the strength for doing in a Christian
spirit work which unbelievers also do. The priest's work is
religion; he is being in the special sense 'religious' all the time.
He does not *go out* to *find pasture.* Hence he lays upon devotional observance a stress which seems to many laymen
disproportionate; but also, because for him religion is his
daily work, he sometimes slips into speaking of it in a way
which to the layman seems casual and irreverent. One of
our chief needs is a clear recognition of the proper difference between the religion of the layman and of the cleric.
Then we may reach the point where the priest will stand for
the things of God before the laity — who seek the help
that a religious specialist can give them, while the laity stand
for the things of God before the world — which will pay
more heed to them than to shepherds who are (incidentally)
hirelings (12).

But the Lord is more concerned with the use of the door
by the shepherd than by the sheep. There is no question
of sheep climbing over the walls, so that part of the contrast
concerns only shepherds and thieves. The rightful entrant is,
therefore, the true pastor; the wrongful entrant is the false
pastor.

The pastoral office, like all other offices in the Church, is a focalisation, so to speak, of a function of the whole Church and all its members. We all exercise influence; that is a natural fact. If we are Christians, our influence is qualified by that consideration, and will draw men nearer to Christ or drive them further from Him, according to the balance of attractive or repellent qualities in ourselves. Our first question must be — how can we be sure that it draws men nearer? And the answer is that our entry to the lives of our neighbours must be *through the door*. But not only are we possessed by nature of the power of influence; we are responsible for exercising it to the uttermost. We are called to be Christ's witnesses. But by what right do we dare to attempt the direction of a neighbour's life, or even of a child's? And again the answer is that we approach him *through the door*.

I have no right to call men to adopt *my* traditions or to follow *my* manner of life. But I may call them to accept the Truth and to follow the Way which is Life. The ordinary way of saying this is to insist that we can only be the agents of God's work so far as God is Himself acting through us. But how are we to ensure this? We so easily assume that what seems to us good must be the will of God. We make our plans for the work of God, and ask Him to prosper them. But they may be seriously infected with our prejudice, ignorance and short-sightedness. In particular, we can never see in advance that the way to final success lies through immediate failure; yet God may know that this is so; it is the way of the Cross. How are we to avoid putting self as an obstacle in the way of God's purpose as we offer it to be the agency of that purpose? Again — by coming *through the door*.

The meaning becomes clearer if we consider the alternatives. We may come to our pastoral work, the exercise of influence, through love of power and the satisfaction which we derive from guiding others; or through love of fame and repute (v, 44); or through partisanship, and the desire to win adherents for our own 'school of thought'. But none of these entitles us to exercise deliberate influence over another. A man who attempts it is *a thief and a robber*. He is not merely an intruder; he is usurping functions to which he has no right. Nothing can give me warrant for the sacred responsibility of deliberately influencing a soul except that I approach that soul *through the door*, which is Christ.

All that came before me are thieves and robbers. The word *came* is, of course, technical, as in the phrase 'he that cometh — the coming one' (*St. Matthew* xi, 3; *St. Luke* vii, 19). There had been false Messiahs. To claim Messiahship is the extreme form of the usurpation of which all are guilty who accept the position of pastors otherwise than through Christ.

To come to it *through the door* means at least three things: (1) to come to the task, and every part of it, in prayer; (2) to refer all activities to the standard of the Mind of Christ; (3) to accept what actually happens as nearer to the Will of God than our own success would have been. It means putting Christ in the forefront of thought and self, in all its forms, right out of the picture.

And Christ Himself comes 'not to be ministered unto, but to minister' (*St. Mark* x, 45). He comes, not for His own sake, still less to make profit out of the sheep, but *that they may have life and have it abundantly*; with which we pass from the thought of Him as the Door, to the thought of Him as the Shepherd.

*

11–16. I am the shepherd, the beautiful one. The shepherd, the beautiful one, lays down his life for the sheep. The hireling, not being withal a shepherd, whose own the sheep are not, noticeth the wolf coming and leaveth the sheep and fleeth — and the wolf snatches them and scatters them — because he is an hireling and careth not for the sheep. I am the shepherd, the beautiful one, and I know mine own and mine know me (as the Father knoweth me and I know the Father) and I lay down my life for the sheep. And other sheep I have which are not of this fold; them also I must bring, and they shall hear my voice and there shall come to be one flock, one shepherd.

The shepherd, the beautiful one. Of course this translation exaggerates. But it is important that the word for 'good' here is one that represents, not the moral rectitude of goodness, nor its austerity, but its attractiveness. We must not forget that our vocation is so to practise virtue that men are won to it; it is possible to be morally upright repulsively! In the Lord Jesus we see 'the beauty of holiness' (*Psalm* xcvi, 9). He was 'good' in such manner as to *draw all men to Himself* (xii, 32). And this beauty of goodness is supremely seen in the act by which He would so draw them, wherein He *lays down his life for the sheep.* The function of the shepherd is to care for the sheep, and to do and bear whatever is required by that care; the perfect shepherd faces death itself for the sheep. If the man who holds the office exercises it for the sake of his pay and not for the sake of the sheep, he is *a hireling and not withal a shepherd.* Of course a man may be a shepherd at heart, and also a hireling in the sense that he is paid for his work. Many hired shepherds are true shepherds. The test comes when he has to choose between his own interest and that of the flock. If he then follows his own interest and not that of the sheep, this shows that he is there for what he can earn and not for the service he can give.

Readers of Plato will remember how Socrates, in the First Book of the *Republic,* insists on the difference between the true artist (not only in the fine arts) who practises his art — e.g. medicine — for the sake of its true object (in the case of medicine, health), and one who practises it 'as a money-maker'. That the doctor should in fact earn his fee is right enough; but the earning of the fee must not be the directing motive of his practice (*Republic,* 341 C–346 D).

So the shepherd — the pastor — may rightly be paid for his service. He must be kept alive, or he cannot tend the flock. But his dominant motive must be care of the flock; and nothing must ever take precedence of that.

The true shepherd not only cares for the sheep with a devotion even to the death; but he knows them and is known

by them. This is the secret of all true pastoral work; it is
achieved through personal acquaintance. The shepherd *calleth
his own sheep by name* (3); he knows their qualities; he can
pray for each intelligently; he can offer appropriate guidance.
And *the sheep hear his voice* (3) — something in them responds
to the call which his knowledge of them enables him to utter
so as to reach their souls. The best preaching is a fruit of
constant pastoral visiting; it springs out of the relationship
between pastor and people. But only *his own* will hear and
answer. Some belong to other shepherds — perhaps (as he is
but one among many) they will call and be heard. But when
the Shepherd, the Beautiful one, calls and is not heeded, that is
because of some deep defect in those who are addressed: *Why
do ye not recognise my speech? even because ye cannot hear my
word* (viii, 43).

It is by knowing *us* that men are to be saved! Then of what
sort must we be? It is not by what we say that we are good
pastors, nor by what we do; but by what we *are*. And we *are*
poor sheep like those whom we would tend. The one hope
is that as folk come to know us they find in fact another —
not the sheep turned shepherd, but in truth the Shepherd the
Beautiful one. It will be so if we abide in Him and He in us
(xv, 4) — not otherwise.

But this mediatorial status is that also of the Good Shepherd
Himself. *I know mine own and mine know me as the Father
knoweth me and I know the Father.* Once again the analogy is
introduced; the Father: the Son :: the Son: ourselves. Always
it is in virtue of what is not the self, but acts or speaks through
the self, that any, even the Lord Himself, is a minister of
salvation. We recall again i, 14.

And I lay down my life for the sheep. There is no limit to His
care for the sheep; no sacrifice is too great for them. But the
thought of sacrifice recalls that of the *other sheep*, the Gentile
world, just as in xii, 20–25 the approach of the first fruits of
that world will turn His mind to sacrifice. The two are joined
together; for the universality of His appeal is due to His death

(xii, 32). We saw above that in any one courtyard-fold there might be sheep from several flocks; in like manner, there might be sheep from one flock in several folds. To every fold the Shepherd must go and call His own sheep by name; and they that are His own will hear and follow; so He will reconstitute His *one flock* under the care of the *one Shepherd* (cf. *Ezekiel* xxxiv, 23).

*

17-21. 'For this cause the Father loveth me — that I lay down my life, in order that I again may take it. No one took it away from me, but I lay it down of myself. I have authority to lay it down and I have authority again to take it. This commandment I received from my Father.'
A division again arose among the Jews because of these sayings. Many of them were saying 'He hath a demon and is mad; why do ye listen to him?' Others were saying 'These are not the words of one possessed by a demon; can a demon open the eyes of the blind?'

The love of the Father for the Son is based on the self-giving quality of the Son, while this in turn is grounded in the love of the Father. Love is like that. Each partner loves because the other is lovable, and is lovable because loved by the other. Nothing in these words is incompatible with the great assertions of the priority of the Father in v, 19, 20, 26. For while the self-giving of Christ is a perfectly free act — *I lay it down of myself* — yet this is done under a conferred *authority*. (The translation 'power' here, in i, 12, in *St. Matthew* xxviii, 18 and in *Acts* i, 7 — where it is actually contrasted with 'power' in *Acts* i, 8 — is one of the worst blemishes of the Authorised Version.) His freedom to offer His life is a gift from the Father; and the Father gave a commandment how that gift of freedom was to be used. The sacrifice of the Son is no less free, and is more, not less, meritorious, for being an act of obedience. 'He humbled himself, becoming obedient even unto death, yea, the death of the cross. Wherefore also God highly exalted him' (*Philippians* ii, 8, 9; cf. *Hebrews* x, 8-10).

But He lays down His life that He again may take it. His Death is not a defeat cancelled by the Resurrection triumph. It is itself triumphant, and the passage to a fuller vitality than was compatible with the limitations of the earthly ministry — 'I have a baptism to be baptized with; and how am I straitened till it be accomplished!' (*St. Luke* xii, 50). 'The Resurrection (of Jesus Christ) has made possible for Christians a new interpretation of the facts of death and mortality. . . . Death becomes not a mere gateway to be passed through, nor the mere casting away of a perishable body, but a loss which is turned into gain, a giving up of life which is made the means whereby that life is received back again renewed, transfigured, and fulfilled' (*Doctrine in the Church of England*, p. 85).

No one took it away from me: the reference is not directly to the Crucifixion but to the whole act of Incarnation with all its implications. The self-giving of Christ is an eternal action; to give Himself is His very nature; it is not imposed on Him from without, but springs from His own inner being. This self-giving is the ground of His actual submission to death, when, in a superficial sense, many persons *took away* His life — Caiaphas, Pilate, the soldiers. But His consent was the prior condition of their action (cf. *St. Matthew* xxvi, 53, 54). Those enemies of His were after all the agents of His own purpose.

*

This language about laying down life under a command from the Father divides His hearers. The more hostile think it the expression of a fanatical lunatic, who might suppose that God required His suicide as an act of self-immolation. Others remembered the blind man, out of whose recovery of sight the whole controversy had arisen. There was a crowd in the Temple, assembled for the feast, so they gathered round and demanded a plain answer to a plain question. Crowds are given to that demand!

22–31. At that time took place the Feast of Dedication at Jerusalem; it was winter; and Jesus was walking in the Temple in Solomon's porch. The Jews therefore surrounded him and began to say to him 'How long dost thou hold us in suspense? If thou art the Christ, tell us plainly.' Jesus answered them 'I told you, and ye do not believe. The works which I do in my Father's name these bear witness concerning me. But ye do not believe, because ye are not of the sheep that are mine. The sheep that are mine hear my voice, and I know them, and they follow me. And I give to them eternal life, and they shall not perish unto eternity, and no one shall snatch them out of my hand. My Father who gave them to me is greater than all, and no one can snatch from the hand of the Father. I and the Father are one.' Again the Jews fetched stones that they might stone him.

While the controversy is still raging, the Feast of Dedication came on. It 'was instituted by Judas Maccabaeus to commemorate the purification of the Temple from the pollutions of Antiochus Epiphanes by the dedication of a new altar (*I. Macc.* iv, 36, 59; *II. Macc.* x, 5, 6), and was kept at the winter solstice (Chislev 25)' (Bernard *ad loc.*). The crowd gathers round the Lord, and its leaders demand a plain statement. They introduce it with a play upon words intended to throw contempt on His own expression. He had said that 'no one took away His life, or soul', and they use the same terms; 'How long dost thou take our soul?'— a phrase for holding people in breathless suspense.

If thou art the Christ, tell us plainly. How could He? He was indeed the Christ, and had avowed this to the Woman of Samaria (iv, 26), and in very slightly veiled terms to the man born blind (ix, 37). But if He tells these controversialists that He is the Christ, either they will suppose Him to offer Himself as what they suppose the Christ to be, or else they will start asking Him which of the anticipations He will fulfil. To say either Yes or No is equally misleading. He had abandoned all the extant anticipations in the threefold Messianic Temptations immediately after His Baptism (*St. Luke* iv, 1–13; *St. Matthew* iv, 1–11). And the new type of Messiahship which He has adopted —'the Son of Man must suffer' (*St. Mark* viii, 31)

— could only be spoken with hope of understanding to the chosen disciples, and could not be received even by them; but at least it did not make them scoff or turn away.

And yet the answer to the question had been given many times in terms which could have conveyed it to their minds if they had only been schooled by their own teachers (v, 46). And His works — those signs in which power is subordinate to love — are evidence. But they cannot hear the evidence, however clear it be. They are not *of the sheep that are mine*. They cannot hear His word (viii, 43). To them He is *a stranger*. But as He is the one true Shepherd this is their condemnation. His own sheep hear, and follow and are safe. *They shall not perish unto eternity*. They may suffer loss, tribulation, death in this world; but at the last they will be found still safe. For they are in the hand of the Shepherd.

No one shall snatch them out of my hand. The word 'snatch' is the same that was used of the wolf who attacks the flock. If we are truly committed to Christ, no assault can tear us from Him. 'Shall tribulation, or anguish, or persecution, or famine, or nakedness, or peril, or sword? . . . Neither death, nor life, nor angels, nor principalities, nor things present, nor things to come, nor powers, nor height, nor depth, nor any other creature, shall be able to separate us from the love of God, which is in Christ Jesus our Lord' (*Romans* viii, 35, 38, 39).

This is implicitly, as is the invitation 'Come unto me . . . and I will give you rest' (*St. Matthew* xi, 28), a claim to divine status; and this is now made explicit. The reason why He can confidently say that none can snatch from His hands is that this is certainly true concerning the Father; and what is true of Him is true of the Son; for *I and the Father are one*.

He has not given a plain answer to the plain question. That was impossible. But He has made a very plain statement — not indeed that it necessarily carries all that we tend to read into it in the light of our Christian faith and experience; the justification of it which follows rules that out. But it is a stupendous affirmation of union with the Deity. As at the national feast He asserted His priority to the founder of the nation, so at this Church feast He asserts His union with the God to whom the worship of the Church is offered.

We must not read into such an utterance the solution of theological riddles which only the development of Christian thought and experience prompted men to ask. But it is quite right to note the precise terms used, for these are governed by an instinctive sense of appropriateness which points towards a more developed apprehension. So the famous saying is not wholly illegitimate 'Per *sumus* refutatur Sabellius, per *unum* Arius', though 'refutation' is too definitive a word for what may properly be deduced from the Lord's declaration.

This claim was blasphemy if it was not true. So much the Jews saw, and made ready *again* (cf. viii, 59) to stone the Lord as a blasphemer. But there is another consideration. The claim is ridiculous if it is not true. The fact that no one ever felt an inclination to laugh at it is very strong evidence of its truth.

But it is not an assertion of all that Christians believe concerning their Lord; it is not as though He had said 'I am God'; for see how He justifies it.

*

32–39. Jesus answered them 'Many works I showed you, beautiful works from the Father. For what kind of work among these do ye stone me?' The Jews answered him 'Not in connexion with a beautiful work do we stone thee, but in connexion with blasphemy, and because thou, being man, makest thyself God'. Jesus answered them, 'Is it not written in your law "I said, Ye are gods"? If he called them gods to whom the word of God came, and the scripture cannot be broken, do ye say of him whom the Father hallowed and sent into the world "Thou blasphemest" because I said "I am Son of God"? If I do not the works of my Father, do not believe me; but if I do, even though ye do not believe me, believe the works, that ye may perceive and know that the Father is in me and I in the Father.' They sought therefore again to arrest him, but he went forth out of their hand.

As they prepare to stone Him the Lord diverts their attention from His words to His deeds, of which the giving of sight to the man born blind was the last. They are deeds that display the very goodness of God — power used for love's purpose. But the Jews fasten on the saying. He is plainly a man and He claims to be God; that is undoubted blasphemy. But is it? The Psalmist (*Psalm* lxxxii) had attributed divinity to those who held office as judges by divine appointment. Here is One whom the Father hallowed for His work and sent into the world; the same principle applies. Thus the Lord suggests that His union with the Father is no more than the perfect form of a relationship open to others and in a certain measure achieved by some; what He has claimed in the phrase censured by the Jews is not necessarily anything unique. It is the perfect Sonship. But there is implied an acceptance of, and emphasis upon, an element of teaching present in the Old Testament, but not prominent there, which finds some real divinity in human life and action; and this is now brought to the fore. For the complete contrast between God and Man characteristic of Jewish orthodoxy, affords no basis for a doctrine of Divine Incarnation. Moreover, while the Lord makes it clear that He is not asserting a unique position for Himself, neither is He denying it. For the refutation of the charge it is enough to show that it was not asserted. The Jews are checked; they do not cast their stones; and their attempt to make an arrest is so half-hearted that the Lord can make His departure.

*

40–42. And he went away again beyond Jordan into the place where John was at first baptising, and abode there. And many came to him and began to say 'John worked no sign, but all things that John said of this man were true.' And many believed on him there.

The controversies must have strained the faith of many who had committed themselves to faith in the Lord. Others have been set wondering. He says nothing to reassure or to win. But He goes to a place connected with the beginning of the whole amazing series of events; and the place with its memories and its associations does its work. They go over the story together, and its coherence begins to be apparent, with the Lord as One on whom all the evidence converges. And *there*, under those influences, *many believed on him.*

CHAPTER XI

[WE come now to the seventh, last and greatest of the signs — though it is noticeable that the first had already manifested creative powers. The story of the raising of Lazarus is a notorious problem for critics. The question for them is not 'Could it have happened?' but 'If it happened, how did it come about that St. Mark omitted it?' It is important that this is the form of the question. The narrative framework of the first Gospel is purely Marcan, and the negative evidence of the first two Gospels is no weightier than that of the second alone. St. Luke had an independent source, and may even have made a first draft of his gospel from this and 'Q' before he became acquainted with *Mark*, which he then fitted into his own scheme. So the absence of this story from *Luke* is a more serious consideration than its absence from *Matthew*, because it shows that it was absent from St. Luke's special source as well as from *Mark*. But that special source seems to have been even more a collection of episodes and even less a coherent narrative than *Mark*; for *Mark* has a coherent scheme, though not a chronology. We may therefore say that the difference to be adjusted is between *John* and *Mark* only. But it is a serious difference. For the Marcan scheme, which omits the raising of Lazarus, treats the cleansing of the Temple as the occasion for the intervention of the High Priests and the Sadducees — which is very intelligible, for in that act the Lord had challenged their financial interests. In the Johannine scheme the cleansing of the Temple takes place at the outset of the Ministry, and it is the raising of Lazarus which brings in the High Priests.

It is contrary to the design of this book to argue such points, and I state only my own conclusions. I accept the Johannine narrative as correct, and I account for the Marcan divergence from it as follows. St. Mark was recording his impression of the course of the ministry which he derived from constantly hearing St. Peter preach the Gospel and acting as his interpreter. Such preaching would not provide a chronology of the ministry; but it would concentrate upon the events of the last week, containing the Triumphal Entry, the Last Supper, the Trial, the Crucifixion, the Resurrection. Various stories from the earlier period would be told, including the cleansing of the Temple. These St. Mark arranged in a coherent order — and one which, as Burkitt showed, had far more than guesswork behind it; it has substantial accuracy; but it only had occasion to record one — the last — visit to Jerusalem; so the cleansing of the Temple was inserted there, and the indignation, which it assuredly caused whenever it took place, was treated as the occasion for the intervention of the High Priests, which assuredly took place at that time. If the cleansing had taken place earlier it would still be remembered as a 'count' against the disturber of the peace.

St. Peter may have had no positive reason to dwell in his preaching on the raising of Lazarus; he cared more for episodes connected with his Galilean home, and did (apparently) tell the story of Jairus' daughter. It is noteworthy that as the Marcan narrative omits the ministry in Jerusalem before the last week, so there is no mention of St. Peter in the whole of Part II of this Gospel (V, VII–XII). It is probable that he remained in Galilee, coming up for the last Passover in time to take part in the Triumphal Entry. If so, he said nothing about the raising of Lazarus because he had not himself seen it; he may also have had some reason for omitting the story, for if Lazarus was still alive, to tell his story in public preaching might cause him grave inconvenience, if not ridicule and persecution. Of course all this is mere conjecture, and by no means satisfactory. All I contend is that the origins of *Mark* are such that the omission of this story there is not at all decisive; and to accept, as I do, the Johannine narrative is in no way false to the principles of evidence. The story is singularly vivid and has all the characteristics of the record of an eye-witness. For its undoubtedly miraculous character see pp. *73–74*.]

*

Some period must be supposed to pass while the Lord consolidates the faith of His disciples beyond Jordan, away from the scene of controversy. There the messenger from Martha and Mary reaches Him.

1–6. Now a certain man was sick, Lazarus of Bethany, sprung from the village of Mary and her sister Martha. (Now Mary was she that anointed the Lord with ointment, and wiped his feet with her hair, whose brother Lazarus was sick.) The sisters therefore sent unto him saying 'Lord, behold he whom thou lovest is sick'. But when Jesus heard it he said 'This sickness is not unto death but for the glory of God, that the Son of God may be glorified by its means'. (Now Jesus loved Martha and her sister and Lazarus.) When therefore he heard that he was sick, then he abode in the place where he was for two days.

Of Bethany — sprung from the village of Mary and her sister Martha. Probably that village was in Galilee, for the episode recorded in *St. Luke* x, 38–42 seems there to be placed in Galilee. If so, it is the more possible that Mary is the woman also mentioned in *St. Luke* vii, 36–50, as is certainly here implied. Perhaps that episode was the beginning of the Lord's intimacy with this family. We notice that Mary is here named first, as the better known. Anyhow, they are all now at Bethany, whether they have removed there altogether or had a house there for business in the capital as well as their home in Galilee. And Lazarus is sick. So the sisters send to tell the Lord. It is evident that they expect Him to come at once, partly (no doubt) to see His friend before he dies, partly in hope that His presence may prevent death from occurring (21, 32). But the Lord does not hasten to Bethany; on the contrary He seems deliberately to delay. He says that *this sickness is not unto death, but for the glory of God*; so far it resembles the congenital blindness of the man whose story is given in Chapter IX (see ix, 3). But here the addition is made, *that the Son of*

God may be glorified by its means. In one sense the sickness of Lazarus was *unto death*; it was sickness of that quality, and in fact he died of it. But that was not its final issue. It and the death in which it culminated were both *for the glory of God* as manifested in the restoration of Lazarus to life; and this *glory of God* took the form of the glorifying of the Son, who was disclosed as the Lord and Conqueror of death. But to that end death must first occur. So before recording the apparent in-difference of the Lord, the Evangelist inserts the note assuring us of His love for the two sisters. That, however, is a paren-thesis; in order that the divine purpose in Lazarus' illness might be fully realised, the Lord abode two days where He was. Perhaps if He had started at once He would have arrived just in time to fulfil the sisters' hope; but Lazarus must have died very soon after the message reached the Lord and His disciples, if not before; as it was, He brought them something beyond all their hopes.

*

7–16. Then after this he saith to the disciples 'Let us go into Judaea again'. The disciples say to him 'Rabbi, but now the Jews were seeking to stone thee, and again goest thou there?' Jesus answered 'Are there not twelve hours of the day? If any man walk in the day, he stumbleth not, because he seeth the light of this world; but if any man walk in the night, he stumbleth, because the light is not in him.' This he said, and after this he saith to them 'Lazarus our friend hath fallen asleep; but I go that I may awake him'. The disciples therefore said to him 'Lord, if he hath fallen asleep, he will recover'. But Jesus had spoken of his death; but they thought that he was speaking of taking rest in sleep. At this point therefore Jesus said to them plainly 'Lazarus died; and I rejoice for your sakes that I was not there, that ye may believe; but let us go to him'. Thomas therefore, the one called the Twin, said to his fellow-disciples 'Let us also go, that we may die with him.'

The Lord does not at first say that He is going to Bethany, but names only Judaea. The disciples naturally think of its perils — *But now* (x, 31, 39) *the Jews were seeking to stone thee, and again goest thou there?* The answer is a reply to their fears. His day has not yet run its course. But He so expresses this as to convey a deeper meaning. He refers to daylight as *the light of this world*; but He has already described Himself as *the light of the world* (viii, 12). As he that walks in daylight is secure against stumbling over obstacles, so he that walks by *the light of the world* is secure against spiritual accidents. The disciples need not fear to go into Judaea with their Master because, first, He still has some time before the appointed hour of His death, and, secondly, to be with Him is always to be in the light; and to be away from Him is to be in darkness and stumble — *because the light is not in him*. For Christ the Light of the World shines first upon the soul, and then from within the soul upon the path of life. He does not illumine our way while leaving us unconverted; but by converting us He illumines our way. 'We all, with unveiled face reflecting in a mirror the glory of the Lord, are transformed into the same image.' It is 'in our hearts' that God hath 'shined ... to give the light of the knowledge of the glory of God in the face of Jesus Christ' (*II Corinthians* iii, 18; iv, 6).

Then the Lord begins to explain the motive of His return to Judaea. *Lazarus, our friend, hath fallen asleep*. The disciples later will use this beautiful expression for death as Christians understand it (*Acts* vii, 60; *I Thessalonians* iv, 13, 14). It was not an altogether new use of the word; but it was natural that the disciples should take it literally. Then He speaks quite plainly; *Lazarus died*. And for the disciples' sake He rejoices that He was not there to save him from death; for now He can act in a way that will strengthen their faith: *that ye may believe*.

Did they not believe already? Yes, most truly but also precariously. Their faith is not very firm yet; they will all forsake Him and Peter will deny Him. They have faith; but compared to that which is to be theirs later, it is as though they had not yet entered on the life of faith.

It is hard to know what one's faith is worth till some severe test comes. I believe — in some measure; of that I am quite sure. But in what measure I do not know. I pray God to do for me, or to me, or in me, whatever will have the result that I *may believe*.

But let us go to him. No more talk about it: action now. This calls from Thomas the expression of that faith which was deeply real, yet as deeply needed confirmation (xx, 29). Thomas is literal, prosaic, tending to see the gloomy side of things in his sincere resolve to face realities; and he is utterly loyal: *let us also go that we may die with him*.

*

17–27. So Jesus when he came found that he had been four days already in the tomb. Now Bethany was near Jerusalem, about fifteen furlongs off. And many of the Jews had come to Martha and Mary to comfort them concerning their brother. So Martha, when she heard that 'Jesus cometh', went to meet him; but Mary was sitting in the house. Martha therefore said to Jesus 'Lord, if thou hadst been here, my brother had not died. Even now I know that whatsoever thou shalt ask of God, God will give it thee.' Jesus saith to her 'Thy brother shall rise again'. Martha saith to him 'I know that he shall rise again at the resurrection at the last day'. Jesus saith to her 'I am the resurrection and the life; he that believeth on me, even though he die, shall live, and every one that liveth and believeth on me shall not die to eternity; believest thou this?' She saith to him 'Yea, Lord, I have believed that thou art the Christ, the Son of God, he that cometh into the world.'

When the Lord arrives, the time of bereavement is already running its course. It is more than three days since Lazarus died; friends from Jerusalem are coming out to offer consolation. Then the message is brought to Martha, as elder sister and mistress of the house — *Jesus cometh*. She goes to meet Him, and this takes her beyond the limits of the village (30). When she reaches Him she says the words that have so often been on her lips and her sister's concerning Him: *Lord, if thou hadst been here, my brother had not died*. No doubt they had often said this to one another during those sad three days; and now each says it as almost a greeting to the Lord (21, 32). It is an expression both of affection and of faith — with a touch of sadness that their message had not brought Him sooner. But faith predominates. She has no actual petition, and does not urge the Lord to make one; she only knows that whatever He may ask will be done by God. He does not now

or later offer a spoken prayer; but later He thanks the Father
for hearing Him, so that we know He was all the time praying
in His heart (41). Now He leads her on to a fuller faith in
Himself. He starts with a promise, in words which admit of
fulfilment either at once or in an undefined future: *thy brother
shall rise again.* Martha has already accepted this article of
Pharisaic faith at least so far as it refers to a general resurrection *at the last day.* But that is remote, and she finds little
comfort in it. The answer is startling. *I am* — the words of
Divine self-declaration — *the Resurrection and the life.* How
can He actually be the Resurrection? He might be its cause,
its donor, its controller; how can He *be* a future event? Of
course there is a forcing of language to express an unutterable
thought. But we can put part of what it means in other words.
Fellowship with Christ is participation in the divine life which
finds its fullest expression in triumph over death. Life is a
larger word than Resurrection; but Resurrection is, so to
speak, the crucial quality of Life, and the inclusion of it therefore adds vastly to the effectiveness, though not to the actual
content, of the saying. There is no denial of a general resurrection at the last day; but there is an insistence that for those
who are in fellowship with Jesus the life to which that resurrection leads is already present fact. 'If a man believe in Him,
although his body dies his true self shall live' (25); or, as it may
be put in other words, no believer in Jesus shall ever die,
so far as his spirit is concerned. 'Your friend is alive now;
for in me he touched the life of God which is eternal; in me,
he had already risen before his body perished.' This is the
Johannine doctrine of life; it is also the doctrine of Paul (cf.
Col. iii, 1).[1]

Martha is puzzled. When asked if she can accept this she
falls back on faith in Christ, not saying she accepts what has
been said, but accepting Him and therefore, for His sake, whatever He may say. Her confession is the most complete yet
made by any. But it is not a new faith; it is an old faith come

[1] Bernard *ad loc.*

to fuller consciousness: *I have believed that thou art the Christ, the Son of God, he that cometh into the world.*

*

28–32. Having said this she went away and called Mary her sister secretly, saying, 'The Master is here and calleth thee'. And she, when she heard, arose quickly and began to go to him. Now Jesus was not yet come into the village, but was still in the place where Martha met him. The Jews therefore which were with her in the house and were comforting her, seeing that Mary rose up quickly and went out, followed her supposing that she was going to the tomb to weep there. Mary, therefore, when she came where Jesus was, seeing him fell at his feet saying to him, 'Lord, if thou hadst been here my brother had not died'.

After her confession of faith, Martha returns to give the good news of the Master's coming to Mary. This less practical but more emotionally affectionate sister is still sitting in the house (20) among those friends who have come to offer comfort. Martha gives her news secretly in the hope that Mary may escape from the friends and have, as she has had, a few moments alone with Jesus. Mary hurries out with the same object; and with that object, as we may suppose, the Lord has waited in the quiet place outside the village where the conversation with Martha took place. But in vain; the kindly but now unwittingly intrusive friends have followed. Mary, emotional and impulsive, throws herself down at Jesus' feet, and says what Martha had said and what the two sisters had (we think) often said together: *If thou hadst been here, my brother had not died.* But this time the answer is in act and not in word.

*

33–38. Jesus, then, when he saw her wailing and the Jews which came with her also wailing, groaned in spirit and shuddered and said 'Where have ye laid him?' They say to him 'Lord, come and see'. Jesus wept. But some of them said 'Could not this man who opened the eyes of the blind man bring it about that this man also should not die?' Jesus therefore again groaning in himself cometh to the tomb. It was a cave and a stone lay upon it.

The passage represents the Lord as passing through a time of most severe tension. The word *groaning* does not suggest grief, but tensity of feeling, with an inclination to indignation rather than sorrow. He is full of sympathy — truly feeling with, and not only for, the bereaved sisters: *Jesus wept*. But this giving way to sorrow, however natural the sorrow, is alien from Him, so that some antagonism is mingled with His sympathy, and the tension finds expression through inarticulate sounds and physical tremors. It is not only that His relation to those around Him is a divided one; but He is preparing for a mighty act of power. His 'signs' were not wrought without cost to Him. There was self-giving in them; and when a sufferer drew healing from Him without His knowledge, He was conscious 'that the power proceeding from him had gone forth' (*St. Mark* v, 30). So, deeply moved, He comes to the tomb.

*

39–44. Jesus saith 'Lift the stone'. The sister of the dead man, Martha, saith 'Lord, already he stinketh; for he is four days dead'. Jesus saith to her 'Did I not say to thee that if thou believest thou shalt see the glory of God?' So they lifted the stone. And Jesus lifted his eyes upward and said 'Father, I thank thee that thou heardest me. But I myself knew that at all times thou hearest me; but for the sake of the crowd standing by I spoke, that they may believe that thou sentest me.' And having said this, with a great voice he cried aloud 'Lazarus, come forth'. There came forth the dead man bound — hands and feet — with grave clothes, and his face was bound with a napkin. Jesus saith to them 'Loose him and let him go home'.

Lift the stone — the stone which shuts the soul into its tomb of anxiety, or worry, or resentment. It involves the exposure of habits grown horrible in their rigidity. But it is the condition of response to the quickening voice.

Martha, the practical but loving sister, shrinks from the disclosure of her brother's body now already (as she supposes that it must be) subject to decay. But the Lord reminds her of His words to her, which He now recalls in a summary paraphrase. Her objection is silenced and the command is obeyed.

Before the great word of command the Lord, for the sake of
the by-standers, utters aloud His constant thanksgiving for
the Father's unfailing answer to His prayer. We are not told of
any prayer; there was no one moment of prayer; He lived in
prayer, and doubtless was in prayer from the time when the
message of the sisters reached Him. Now for a moment He
reveals His prayer and His assurance that it is answered.

Lazarus, come forth. The voice of the Lord quickens the
dead. If only that stone be lifted, it will reach and quicken my
dead soul.

There came forth the dead man. The word is obeyed. The
dead man came forth, but now alive.

Loose him and let him go home. The grave clothes hold him
fast. So old habits that are the symptom of sin may cling
about us when the sin itself is eradicated. If we are truly to be
alive we must be freed from these also. And then the task is to
resume ordinary life. The dead man raised, the sinner forgiven, is not to be treated as an exhibit; *let him go home.* It is
Bernard's translation, and imports a little more content than
the original has; but what it further suggests is not out of place.

Let him go home. As spoken the words are an expression of
sympathetic considerateness. As remembered they express the
goal of our destiny, to move towards which is impossible till
we are raised from the 'death of sin', called forth from the
grave of convention, and released from the trappings of habit.
Only the divine Voice can say of the earth-bound mortal *Let
him go home.*   *

The sign, as usual, produces a division. For some it is the
inauguration of faith; this is true of those whose presence was
due to love. Others report what has happened to the authorities, and so bring them into effective action.

45–57. Many then of the Jews — those who came to Mary and were
  spectators of what he did — became believers on him. But some of
  them went away to the Pharisees and told them what Jesus had done.
  The chief priests and the Pharisees therefore brought a council together

and began to say 'What are we doing? For this man is doing many signs. If we let him go thus all will believe on him, and the Romans will come and take away both our place and our nation.' But one of them, Caiaphas, being High Priest that year, said to them 'Ye do not know anything, nor consider that it is expedient for you that one man should die for the people and the nation not perish as a whole'. (But this he did not say of himself, but being High Priest that year he pro- phesied that Jesus should die for the nation, and not for the nation only, but that he should also gather together into one the children of God that were scattered abroad.) From that day therefore they took counsel to kill him. Jesus therefore no longer openly walked about among the Jews, but went away from there into the country near the desert, into a city called Ephraim, and there abode with the disciples. Now the Jews' Passover was nigh, and many went up to Jerusalem from the country before the Passover to purify themselves. So they began looking for Jesus, and were saying among each other as they stood in the temple 'What think ye? That he will not come to the Feast?' Now the chief priests and the Pharisees had given directions that if any man knew where he were, he should show it, that they might arrest him.

Many of the Jews became believers: the evidence convinced them. But it was not the evidence that made them susceptible to its implications. Those on whom it had this effect were people whose presence on the spot was due to a kindly motive. Love of man, even in a very simple form, may often be the precursor of faith in God; for indeed it is already, in its measure, communion with God (*I John* iv, 12).

But others were not so affected and went off to tell the news to the authorities. Now the Chief Priests are united with the Pharisees. So it had been in vii, 32, but then the Pharisees took the lead. In ix, 13, 15, 40 the Pharisees are alone. But now the Chief Priests take the lead, and from now onwards the Phari- sees are mentioned only twice (xii, 19 and 42). This continues. In the *Acts* the Pharisees are inclined to be even friendly, and the Chief Priests are the opponents and persecutors of the Church.

The motive of these Chief Priests is less religious than political. The raising of Lazarus is an event so stupendous that they expect the crowd to put the Lord at the head of a Messi- anic revolt, and expect Him to accept that part to play. They do not know that He has already refused it (vi, 15); what they do know is that imperial Rome has shown no patience towards native governments that cannot suppress revolutionary risings. They stand to lose their Holy Place and their national existence. Better than this, let *one man die for the people*.

When the evangelist wrote, the irony of this situation had become manifest. The Romans had come and had taken away their place and nation. Jerusalem was a heap of ruins, and the Jews have been without a national home to this day. Moreover, the destruction of the city was due to precisely that blindness to its true destiny which led to its rejection of Christ: 'If thou hadst known in this day, even thou, the things which belong unto peace! But now they are hid from thine eyes' (*St. Luke* xix, 42; see also 43 and 44).

Caiaphas was consciously uttering a piece of cynical utilitarianism. Unconsciously he was summarising the Gospel. In one sense what he said was true; but that sense was unkown to him — it is expressed in iii, 16, *God so loved the world that he gave his only begotten Son, that whosoever believeth in him should not perish but have eternal life*. But Caiaphas' unwitting prophecy was accepted as the agreed policy.

So the Lord withdrew for a while, and we see the crowds speculating whether He will come to the Passover (yes, He will, at the head of exultant crowds) and face what has been prepared for Him (yes, He will, quite alone).

CHAPTER XII

(1) THE ANOINTING AT BETHANY

1–11. And so Jesus, six days before the Passover, went into Bethany, where was Lazarus, whom Jesus raised from the dead. So they made for him a supper there, and Martha served, but Lazarus was one of those that reclined with him. Mary therefore, taking a pound of ointment of genuine spikenard, very precious, anointed the feet of Jesus and wiped his feet with her hair, and the house was filled with the odour of the ointment. But Judas Iscariot, one of his disciples — he who was about to betray him — saith 'Why was not this ointment sold for three hundred pence and given to the poor?' But he said this, not because he cared for the poor, but because he was a thief and having the money-box used to steal what was cast into it. Jesus therefore said 'Let her alone that she may keep it for the day of my preparation for burial. For the poor at all times ye have with you, but me ye have not at all times.' A great crowd of the Jews therefore knew that he was there, and came, not on account of Jesus only, but that they might see Lazarus also whom he raised from the dead. But the chief priests took counsel to kill Lazarus also, because on his account many of the Jews began to go away and began to believe in Jesus.

And so. The connexion is logical, not temporal. The Lord has ended his controversy with the Jews, and at the close of this chapter His judgement will be pronounced. Their leaders are set upon killing Him. He has withdrawn for a while to a place of quiet and security. But now His hour is come. *And so* He returns. He comes first to His friends at Bethany. They most naturally arrange a supper for Him. They do this, not in their own home, but in the house of Simon the leper. (*St. Mark* xiv, 3, only St. Mark has a wrong note of time; his chronology of Holy Week, and consequently that of the other two synoptists, is mistaken at several points, specially the date of the Crucifixion itself. St. John is all through this period both referring to the Marcan record and correcting it.) Lazarus was one of

182

the guests who reclined, with the Lord, at the table. Martha, characteristically, was serving.

Then follows a wonderful scene. Mary has some strange instinct that the moment is most solemn. The Lord has returned to a place where His life is in danger; she at least will show her devotion, and she will do this in such a way as to prove that it is based on gratitude. Long ago, when she was still *a woman in the city, a sinner* (*St. Luke* vii, 37), she had crept into the place where One was reclining to whom her affectionate heart was wholly given; she had brought 'an alabaster cruse of ointment, and standing behind, at his feet, she began to wet his feet with her tears, and wiped them with the hair of her head, and kissed his feet, and anointed them with the ointment'. And the Lord had said 'Her sins which are many are forgiven, for she loved much' (*St. Luke* vii, 38, 47). That was the moment of her forgiveness. Since then she has been a devoted friend of her Saviour. And now He is in danger. A great crisis is before Him. She will show her devotion, and the gratitude which was its source. She re-enacts that earlier scene.

It would have been natural to anoint the head of the honoured guest, and St. Mark says that this is what she did (*St. Mark* xiv, 3). Even if St. Peter's recollection was not at fault, it was very easy for his interpreter to miss the point. But St. John knew it, and by his repetition of the words *His feet* shows that he is correcting the current version. Mary does just what she did before, with only one exception. Then there were tears, but now there are none; for there is no remorse or shame in her devotion now; it is sheer gratitude and love.

It is probable that in most of us the spiritual life is impoverished and stunted because we give so little place to gratitude. It is more important to thank God for blessings received than to pray for them beforehand. For that forward-looking prayer, though right as an expression of dependence upon God, is still self-centred in part, at least, of its interest; there is something which we hope to gain by our prayer. But the backward-looking act of thanksgiving is quite free from this. In itself it is quite selfless. Thus it is akin to love. All our love to God is in response to His love for us; it never starts on our side. 'We love, because he first loved us' (*I John* iv, 19). And His love is most of all shown in His treatment of our sin. 'God commendeth his own love toward us in that, while we were yet sinners, Christ died for us' (*Romans* v, 8). That is the fact which constrains our gratitude and so inspires our love.

To the worldly mind the acts of devotion are always foolish. God does not require our costly gifts for His honour; better spend on good works what is lavished on worship; so men often say. And there is a lurking truth. For what men spend on acts of worship is spent on what they share, and the gift may therefore be infected with self-interest. We ought (for example) to offer to God in worship the best music that we can. But our subscription to the organ fund at our Church is likely to be more self-regarding than our support of a mission in a place we shall never see; for we ourselves shall enjoy the music. Yet it is true also that where lavish expenditure expresses the overflowing of a heart's devotion, it is unspeakably precious. For love is the best thing that there is, and what represents its best moments shares that preciousness. *The poor at all times ye have with you, but me ye have not at all times.* The Lord would soon be taken away from Mary; and it is only at moments of vivid insight that any of us perceive His presence. At those times, there is a fervour in our love for the present Lord that will not often be found in our kindly attitude towards the poor. That may be genuine enough; and what we do for them is done to Him (*St. Matthew* xxv, 40); but it lacks the completeness of the love which is adoration. As the best thing is love itself, not the benefits which it confers, there must be no censure of its lavishness as disproportionate.

It is only here that Judas is called a thief. Quite apart from this, a man who *was about to betray him* would be incapable of appreciating Mary's devotion to the Lord. But we know that he had that love of money which is *a root of every kind of evil* (*I Timothy* vi, 10); at any rate, when he thought of delivering his Lord to the Chief Priests, he wanted to know what he would get for it (*St. Matthew* xxvi, 15). It may be that when he left the little group it was found that he had peculated. At that stage the Beloved Disciple had no suspicion of him (xiii, 28, 29).

Let her alone that she may keep it for the day of my preparation for burial. This, which seems to be the meaning of the best text, suggests first, that the real complaint was that so much had ever been spent on the *very precious* ointment, and secondly that only a portion of the whole *pound* had been used now — at any rate before the interruption. The day of death and burial is not far distant. This ointment can be used then. Will Judas think it too costly for that?

The house was filled with the smell of the ointment. So should every Church and every home be filled with the fragrance of devoted love. May this be daily more true.

The story of the supper spread abroad, and a great crowd came to see Jesus, and (no less) to see Lazarus. This only meant that the Chief Priests, who had the much-belauded merit of being realists, decided that he must be put out of the way also.

*

(2) THE TRIUMPHAL ENTRY

12–19. On the next day a great crowd which had come up to the feast, having heard that 'Jesus is coming into Jerusalem', took the branches of the palm trees and went out to meet him, and kept crying aloud 'Hosanna, Blessed is he that cometh in the name of the Lord even the King of Israel'. And Jesus, having found a young ass, took his seat upon it, as it is written 'Fear not, daughter of Sion; behold thy king cometh, seated upon the foal of an ass'. These things his disciples did not understand at first, but when Jesus was glorified, then they remembered that these things were written upon him, and that they did these things to him. So witness was borne by the crowd which was with him when he called Lazarus from the tomb and raised him from the dead.

For this reason also the crowd met him, because they heard that he had
done this sign. The Pharisees therefore said to one another 'Take notice
that ye are gaining nothing. Behold, the world is gone away after him.'

On the next day. Simon's supper took place on what we
should call Saturday evening, but after sunset, so the sabbath
was over. The events now to be recorded took place on Sunday
morning. A crowd which hears the news *Jesus is coming* flocks
out to meet Him. This would consist largely of Galilean pilgrims bivouacking round the city till the day of the feast a
week later. Besides these, a crowd of those who witnessed the
raising of Lazarus took part. They cut off *the branches of the
palm trees* along the road that runs from Bethany along the
slopes of Olivet, and perpetually utter their cry of welcome to
the King of Israel. The Lord is ready for this and this time He
yields Himself to it, for He knows what the sequel will be
(xii, 24). There is no need now to escape from the zeal of
those who would make Him a King, as there had been after
the miracle of feeding (vi, 15). But He will declare the manner
of His Kingship.

The story of the Entry, and of the fetching of the ass, was
well known. The latter can be briefly dismissed with the
words *Jesus, having found a young ass.* The ass was actually
fetched by two disciples; but they were acting under Jesus'
directions, who had evidently warned the owner of the ass to
expect them and had supplied a pass-word which the disciples
were to use (*St. Mark* xi, 1–6). A king or chief rode on a horse
when his purpose was warlike, on an ass when he came peace-
ably. Thus the Lord, by deliberately fulfilling Zechariah's
prophecy, at once claims to be the Messiah and declares in
part the kind of Messiah that He will be. That prophecy in
its complete form emphasises the lowliness of the Coming
King, and describes Him as ending war and establishing universal peace: 'Rejoice greatly, O daughter of Zion; shout, O
daughter of Jerusalem; behold, thy King cometh unto thee;
he is just, and having salvation; lowly, and riding upon an
ass, even upon a colt the foal of an ass. And I will cut off the

chariot from Ephraim and the horse from Jerusalem, and the battle-bow shall be cut off; and he shall speak peace unto the nations; and his dominion shall be from sea to sea, and from the river to the ends of the earth' (*Zechariah* ix, 9, 10). The Lord was coming to found a universal fellowship centred upon Himself (32); and later *when Jesus was glorified* His disciples looked back and understood the meaning of what He had·done and had consented that others should do to Him; they realised that He is the basis of those Scriptures (for this is what the curious Greek phrase means). The end of the Evangelist's note — *they did these things to him* — fits much better with the fuller Synoptist narrative than with the Johannine abbreviation of it; no doubt the Evangelist had it in mind as he wrote.

So two crowds accompany the Lord — those who had seen the raising of Lazarus, and those from within or round about the city who go out to meet Him. The Pharisees are utterly dismayed. Their own folk have gone after Him with the rest.

*

(3) THE FIRST-FRUITS OF THE WORLD-WIDE KINGDOM

As the Lord thus enters His capital as King, to establish a Kingdom 'from sea to sea', there seek Him some who are *not of this fold* (x, 16) and their approach turns His thought at once to the sacrifice by which they will be won and His Kingdom established (23, 24, 32).

20-26. Now there were certain Greeks from among them that were going up to worship at the feast. These therefore came to Philip, who was from Bethsaida of Galilee, and began to ask him saying 'Sir, we would see Jesus'. Philip cometh and telleth Andrew; Andrew cometh, and Philip, and they tell Jesus. But Jesus answereth them saying 'Come is the hour that the Son of Man may be glorified. Amen, Amen I say to you, if the corn of wheat do not fall into the earth and die, it abideth itself alone; but if it die it beareth much fruit. He that loveth his life destroyeth it, and he that hateth his life in this world shall keep it unto

Life eternal. If any man serve me, let him follow me, and where I am,
there also my servant shall be. If any man serve me, him will the Father
honour.'

   The Greeks come to Philip, perhaps only because of his
Greek name; but that name may represent Greek parentage.
He was from Bethsaida, at the north end of the sea of Galilee,
to the east of the Jordan. It was therefore within easy reach
of the Greek cities of Decapolis, from which these Greek
pilgrims may have come. Philip, as usual, is cautious. The
Lord had said with emphasis that He had no mission to the
Gentiles (*St. Matthew* xv, 24; *St. Mark* vii, 27), and had
excluded them from the mission of the Twelve (*St. Matthew*
x, 5). Will He be ready to receive these Greeks? So he consults Andrew. Andrew, also as usual, is ready to put the matter
before Jesus. Whether they were brought we do not know;
the meaning of their approach, and the comment of the Lord
upon it, fills the mind. But that comment would have an
added relevance if they were present, as will be apparent when
we consider verse 25.

Come is the hour that the Son of Man may be glorified. The
long waiting — first intimated at Cana (ii, 4) — is now ending.
Three times this solemn phrase is used — here, at the Last
Supper when Judas is gone out (xiii, 31), and in the High Priestly
prayer (xvii, 1). Each time it is in close association with His
death. For it is from the Cross that the light of God's love
shines forth upon the world in its fullest splendour; that therefore is in a supreme degree the 'effulgence of his glory'
(*Hebrews* i, 3). Even if the Cross had had no results, it would
still be His glory; for His death is the sealing of His victory.
That His body should die was no defeat; defeat for Him must
have taken the form of cursing His enemies or sinking into
self-concern. But through all the anguish love was serenely
unshaken. To die thus was, in and for His own person, to
conquer hate. But it was more than that, it was the means of
winning that great multitude of whom the first-fruits were now

ready to be gathered in. From the Cross He puts forth His
might —

> The Man of Sorrows! And the Cross of Christ
> Is more to us than all His miracles.[1]

So He goes on at once to lay down the law of life through
death — the principle which lies at the heart of the Gospel.
Characteristically He finds it first in nature, which illustrates
God's laws. At a former crisis He had compared Himself to
a Sower, and His proclamation of the Kingdom of God to the
scattering of seed, which here and there fails altogether to take
root, here and there shows promise and then fails, and only
here and there succeeds (*St. Mark* iv, 3–12). Now He speaks of
what happens to the seed that bears fruit. It must first die. It
must lose its own identity, that the new plant may spring up.
If it do not thus die and lose itself, it remains itself and nothing
else; there can be no fruit. Death is the condition of fuller life.

Thus in this reply to the Greeks He takes up a point familiar
in their Mysteries and gives to it an added spiritual depth.
There is in all Greek thought no appreciation of the excellence
of self-sacrifice. It might be necessary, and then those who
were capable of it were praiseworthy, and the law of life
through death was recognised as a natural fact, and was used
in the mysteries as a ground for hope of a future life. But its
moral value was not perceived, and no Greek ever dared to
say that love is the best thing in life, and that accordingly
sacrifice, whereby love at once expresses itself and strengthens
itself, is the best form of action. Sacrifice need not be painful;
its principle is the doing or suffering for love's sake what
(apart from love) one would not choose to do or suffer. If
love is flouted that is painful; and the suffering chosen for
love's sake may be acute; the sacrifice of love in face of selfishness (or sin) is always painful. But the mutual sacrifice which
expresses mutual love is the most joyous thing in the world.
It is the life of Heaven.

[1] From the 'Sermon in a Hospital' in Mrs. Hamilton King's *The Disciples*.

The Greeks never saw this. Plato calls upon his Guardians to leave the contemplation of eternal truth and govern the city in its light, and half apologises for doing so (*Republic*, VII, 519 D–520 E); it is no injury to them, because they owe to the training provided by their city their capacity to behold the truth, and we are only asking them to pay their debts. But that it is real loss to them is not disputed; nor is there any suggestion that to endure loss in a good cause is itself a good. Plato never took the step from Justice to Love in his conception of the Idea of Good. This is the point — the vital point — at which the ethics of the Gospel leave the ethics of Greek philosophy far behind. Consequently to those who told the Lord of the approach of the Greeks, and probably in the hearing of the Greeks themselves, the Gospel paradox is stated in its extremest form.

He that loveth his life destroyeth it; and he that hateth his life in this world shall keep it unto Life eternal. Self-love is self-destruction; self-centredness is sin, and self-love is hell. It is a condition that is bound to be miserable. The soul feeds on itself and so devours itself. But indifference to this earthly life, even to the point of dislike for it, is the counterpart to that absorption in things eternal which is eternal life. There are two Greek words here, and we have to use 'life' for both. The 'life' which we must not love, the *life in this world*, is the animal life with all that goes with it of sentience and its pleasures. The other word, used in the phrase *Life eternal*, is the vitalising energy itself.

The Lord Himself is giving the supreme example of the truth which He proclaims. His *hour is come*, the hour of His death and of His life through death, the life which is perfect fellowship with the Father. Therefore He continues: *If any man serve me, let him follow me.* Thus is struck the keynote of the command to the disciples that will shortly be elaborated. *Follow me*: that is the whole of a Christian's duty. *And where I am there also shall my servant be*: that is the whole of a Christian's reward. But the place to which He goes is perfect fellow-

ship with God, who admits to that fellowship as the highest
honour that man can receive, so that to be where the Lord is
and to receive honour from the Father are one and the same:
If any man serve me, him will the Father honour.

*

So the Lord turns to the journey before Him, the journey
that leads by Gethsemane and Calvary to the right hand of
God.

27–33. 'Now is my soul toubled; and what am I to say? "Father, save me
from this hour?" But for this cause did I come to this hour. Father,
glorify thy name.' There came therefore a voice out of heaven, 'I did
glorify it, and I will glorify it again'. The crowd therefore which stood
and listened began to say that it had thundered, others to say 'An angel
hath spoken to him'. Jesus answered and said 'Not for my sake hath
this voice happened but for yours. Now is judgement of this world;
now the prince of this world shall be cast out. And I, if I be lifted up
from the earth, will draw all men to myself.' This he said signifying by
what manner of death he was about to die.

Life comes through death, but it is real death, and the soul
shrinks from it. In the Greek the word for soul is that translated 'life' in *life in this world*. His whole human nature, His
natural humanity, shrank from what lay before Him. And
what is He to say? Shall He pray *Father, save me from this
hour*? No; that would be to contradict the whole purpose of
His life and to frustrate the great hope of this hour. No; His
prayer now as at all times shall be *Father, glorify thy name*.
For the Father's glory He has lived, and will so live unto death;
His prayer is not to be freed from death, but that, whatever
the cost, the Father's name may be glorified.

St. John does not record the Agony in the Garden, though
he points to it very clearly (xviii, 1, 11). Here we find the
substance of the prayer then offered, though at a less pitch of
tension, as befits the moment. What took place in the Garden
was not an isolated crisis; it was the focus of a lifelong temptation and of a lifelong victory over temptation.

As He spoke a thunder-clap gave the answer. Thunder was, by common consent, the voice of God; the same sound could be interpreted as thunder or as the voice of an angel; to the Lord Himself it was the divine assurance that as God glorified His name in the death and raising of Lazarus (xi,.4), so He will again in the death and raising of the Son. Yet it was not for His sake that the voice came, for He needed no reassurance; it was for those who *stood and listened*.

Now — for the hour is come and the climax is at hand — *is judgement of this world.* 'This world' will set its forces in array — a worldly government and a secularised hierarchy will bring the Lord before their judgement seats. Yet they will not be the judges. They will pronounce sentence upon Him, but it is not He that will be condemned. 'Gentle, and just, and dreadless' — He is the judge, and they are the convicted and sentenced prisoners. So men have read the story of that strange trial through the ages.

Now shall the prince of this world be cast out. They will suppose that they are casting Him out. They will think on that first Good Friday evening which is now so near that they and the world are rid of Him for ever. But through the ages it is He who calls, and judges, and reigns; and we have heard of Caiaphas and Pilate only because they came for a moment into touch with this Galilean.

And I if I be lifted up from the earth will draw all men to myself. Decade by decade, century by century, this prophecy finds fulfilment. From the Cross and to the Cross He draws men of every race and nation. And the prophecy goes on to ever more complete fulfilment in this world and the next. *I will draw all men* — including, then, those who condemn Him and kill Him. Sin sends Christ to the Cross, and by the Cross He conquers sin. My lust and selfishness crucify Him afresh, and by the agony I cause He wins me from the selfishness and lust. Here is the pivot of universal history and the interpretation of it all: 'Thou art worthy to take the book and to open the seals thereof, for thou wast slain' (*Revelation* v, 9).

Here is the meaning of my life and the hope of eternal life for me: 'the Son of God loved *me* and gave himself up for *me*' (*Galatians* ii, 20). He will draw to Himself *all men* — even Caiaphas and Pilate, even Judas; — even me, at last, not only (as already, I trust) to a genuine though intermittent devotion, a deliberate though half-hearted service, but to that fulness of adoring companionship which is foreshadowed in the promise *where I am* in the intimate fellowship of the Father's love, *there also shall my servant be*.

*

34-36. The crowd therefore answered him 'We heard out of the law that the Christ abideth unto eternity, and how sayest thou that the Son of Man must be lifted up? Who is this Son of Man?' Jesus therefore said to them 'Yet a little while the light is among you. Walk while ye have the light lest the darkness absorb you. And he that walketh in the darkness knoweth not whither he goeth. While ye have the light, trust in the light, that ye may become sons of light.'

This language about 'lifting up' begins to fascinate the minds of His hearers; He repeats it, but does not interpret it. He had not on this occasion used the actual phrase quoted; but He had used it before (iii, 14; viii, 28), and here He evidently means the same, though the reference is explicitly to Himself. Usually the phrase *Son of Man* is a title of the Messiah; but surely (they think) it cannot be so intended here; for this 'lifting up' has a suggestion of finality, even of death, and *we have heard out of the law that the Christ abideth unto eternity*. So the Son of Man, as the phrase has been used, can hardly refer to the Christ. To whom then does it refer? *Who is this Son of Man?*

The current expectations concerning the Messiah are thus set in sharpest contrast with the conception of His Messianic office which the Lord has formed: *The Son of Man must suffer* (*St. Mark* viii, 31; *St. Luke* xxiv, 26). The identity of title in that declaration and in this passage gives the clue to the interpretation. The Son of Man is the apocalyptic Christ who

comes with the clouds of Heaven; that apocalypse is actualised
in the moment of crucifixion. Of course the idea is too novel
to find acceptance. It can be received only by the faith that
grows out of habitual companionship with the Lord. So He
does not answer the question of the crowd directly; to do so
would involve an affirmation of the central dogma of the
Church, which could only confuse His hearers. The Lord
urges instead that they should practise that companionship; to
begin that is open to them now. It is only for *a little while*
that the present form of companionship will be possible. Let
them take advantage of it. Light is available now; if they do
not use it to guide their steps they will be swallowed up in the
darkness which everywhere surrounds that light. For *the light
shineth in darkness and the darkness did not absorb it* (i, 5).
But it is ready to absorb, to swallow up, all who stray from
the path of light. While, therefore, they have the light, let
them believe in it, trust it, that they *may become sons of light.*

It is by trusting in and living by whatever light we have that
we become sensitive to fuller light, till at last we are 'full of
light' (*St. Matthew* vi, 22). And 'God is light' (*I John* i, 5).
By trusting in Christ as we see Him, dimly because of our imperfect vision, we are led on to such appropriation of Him,
that at last we are 'filled unto all the fulness of God' (*Ephesians*
iii, 19).

●

This Second Act of the Gospel now closes with the deliverance of two judgements; one is that of the Evangelist (37–43);
one is that of the Lord Himself (44–50). Some have suggested
that they should be transposed; and it is true that the trans-
position gives an easier sequence and a more conclusive *finale.*
But I think the familiar order is right. It is seemly to close
the controversy, not with the comment of the Evangelist, but
with the verdict of Christ. Moreover, the conclusive *finale* is
dramatically wrong. What is wanted is not that Act II should
be effectively wound up, but that expectation of Act III should

be aroused. The close provided by the traditional order secures this.

(4) THE JUDGEMENT OF THE EVANGELIST

36–43. These things spake Jesus, and went away and was hidden from them. But though he had done so many signs before them, they did not believe on him, that the word of Isaiah the prophet might be fulfilled which he spake — 'Lord, who believed what we heard? And the arm of the Lord, to whom was it revealed?' For this cause they could not believe, because again Isaiah said 'He hath blinded their eyes and darkened their heart, lest they should see with their eyes and perceive with their heart and should turn themselves and I should heal them'. These things said Isaiah because he saw his glory and spake concerning him. Nevertheless even of the rulers many believed on him, but because of the Pharisees they were not confessing him, that they might not be put out of the synagogue. For they loved the glory of men more than the glory of God.

The Lord withdraws into secrecy, so that He may have that precious time with His friends on which so much would hang. So in the Synoptist narratives the directions to the two disciples who are bidden to prepare for the paschal meal are given in a kind of cypher; for no one must know, especially Judas must not know, where that Last Supper will be held, lest there be an interruption before its purpose is accomplished (*St. Mark* xiv, 13–16). The Evangelist sums up the situation by reference to *Isaiah* liii. That prophecy was bound to be fulfilled, for it was an expression of the divine will; in a certain sense, therefore, it was, or (more accurately) what it expressed was, the cause of the spiritual failure of the Jews. The attachment of blindness to sin as its consequence is part of the divine order. God does not cause sin, but He does cause its appropriate consequence to result from it by the law of the order of creation. The prophet had apprehended this through a vision of the glory of Christ — who is thus identified with Jehovah; and this is correct, for Jehovah is God revealed; and God revealed is the Logos, Word, self-utterance of God; and the Logos is Jesus Christ.

There were many *even of the rulers* who believed secretly;
only they lacked courage to confess, for they cared more for
glory among men than for glory given by God. The Lord had
said that this was the source of their failure to believe (v, 44).
It is a penetrating test. Do I (I wonder) really care more about
honour that God gives than honour that men give? Of course
I know mentally that it is the more precious; but am I more
eager to receive it?

*

(5) THE LORD'S JUDGEMENT

44–50. But Jesus cried and said 'He that believeth on me, believeth not
on me but on him that sent me. And he that beholdeth me beholdeth
not me but him that sent me. I a light into the world am come, that
every one who believeth on me may not abide in the darkness. And if
any one hear my words and keep them not, I do not judge him. For I
came not to judge the world but to save the world. He that rejecteth me
and my sayings hath one that judgeth him; the word which I spake, that
will judge him at the last day. Because I did not speak of myself, but
the Father who sent me hath himself given me commandment what I
should say and what I should speak. And I know that his commandment is eternal Life. What therefore I speak, as the Father hath said to
me, so I speak.'

There is no note of time attached to the record of this
utterance. It is a summary statement of His own claims and
of the judgement upon those who reject Him. The vital point
is that He is the spokesman and representative of the Father.
To trust Him is to trust the Father; to observe or contemplate
Him is to observe or contemplate the Father. He is come not
to give light to the world, but to be light in the world, so that
those who believe in or trust Him are delivered from its darkness. His purpose is not judgement but redemption. But
judgement follows the offer of redemption. He who has heard
and rejected the Gospel is not in the same position as one who
has never heard it. The message which he heard is his accuser.
And this is so because that message is not original in the sense

of originating in the speaker. It comes through Him, like His glory (i, 14), from the Father. The Father gave commandment what the Son should say, and *his commandment is eternal life.*

It is not said that His commandment leads to eternal life, or that by keeping it we may win that life; but *his commandment is eternal life.* For His commandment is not a stark precept given by supreme authority; it is direction given by almighty love; it is the bidding of a Father given to His children for their true welfare; it is the impact of His holy love upon our consciences and wills.

O Almighty God, who alone canst order the unruly wills and affections of sinful men; grant unto thy people that they may love the thing which thou commandest and desire that which thou dost promise; that so among the sundry and manifold changes of the world our hearts may surely there be fixed where true joys are to be found; through Jesus Christ our Lord.

ACT III

THE LORD AMONG HIS DISCIPLES

CHAPTERS XIII and XIV

THE FEET WASHING (xiii, 1–20)

1–11. Now before the feast of the Passover Jesus, knowing that his hour was come that he should depart out of this world unto the Father, having loved his own, those in the world, to the utmost showed his love to them. And during supper, the devil having already put it into the heart of Judas Iscariot, Simon's son, to betray him, knowing that the Father had given all things into his hands, and that he was come forth from God and went to God, he riseth from the supper and layeth aside his garments, and taking a towel girded himself; then he poureth water into the ewer, and began to wash the disciples' feet and to wipe them with the towel with which he was girded. So he cometh to Simon Peter. He saith to him, 'Lord, dost *thou* wash *my* feet?' Jesus answered and said to him, 'What *I* do *thou* knowest not now, but thou shalt understand hereafter'. Peter saith to him, 'Thou shalt by no means wash *my* feet to eternity'. Jesus answered him, 'If I wash thee not, thou hast no part with me'. Simon Peter saith to him, 'Lord, not my feet only but also my hands and my head'. Jesus saith to him, 'He that is bathed needeth not save to wash his feet, but is clean in his whole person; and ye are clean, but not all'. For he knew the man that was betraying him, wherefore he said, 'Ye are not all clean'.

Before the feast. So the Evangelist emphasises his chronology, which differs from that suggested by the Synoptists.

Knowing that his hour was come that he should depart out of this world unto the Father. The great moment which was still far off at Cana (ii, 4) is now near. The Lord knows this. Though His course is adjusted to the response of men or their lack of it, yet He moves through the drama as always master of circumstances, using each for the fulfilment of His own purpose, which now approaches its goal. That goal had always been that He should go unto the Father; for this means the attainment of the perfection of holiness and love. He was 'perfect' at every stage, as infant, as boy, as youth, as man; but it is evident that there is a height and depth of 'perfection' in the man's obedience to God which has no place in the boy's and no meaning for the infant. 'Perfect' at every stage, He 'yet learned obedience by the things which he suffered, and having been made perfect (*or* full grown) became to all them that obey him the cause of eternal salvation' (*Hebrews* v, 8, 9).

His *hour*, then, *is come* that He should attain to that perfection of holiness and love which is complete union with the Father. Consequently what follows is a manifestation of the meaning of that 'hour'. *Having loved his own, those in the world, to the utmost showed he his love to them.* Love grows by the acts that express it; what the Lord now does is at once the manifestation and attainment of perfect love: *to the utmost* (not 'to the end') — the limit is now reached; it is the *bosom of the Father* (i, 18) in which, in a sense, the Son had always lain, yet to which now He comes in the completion of His self-offering.

During supper — while it was going on, not 'when it was ended' (A.V.). There was a sense of special solemnity about this supper, and this seems to have led to a dispute about precedence (*St. Luke* xxii, 24). St. Luke tells us that the Lord answered this partly in words which He is recorded to have used when the sons of Zebedee had claimed pre-eminence (*St. Mark* x, 42–44), but continuing — 'Whether is greater, he that sitteth at meat or he that serveth? is not he that sitteth at meat? but I am in the midst of you as he that serveth' (*St. Luke* xxii, 27). St. John tells us that He not only spoke, but acted what He said. As a rebuke to their worldly strivings, He, their *Lord and Master* (14), showed them what dignity is in the Kingdom of God by rendering to them the most menial service that could be asked of a slave.

The scene for the consummation is fully set and the actors have their parts. The purpose of Judas is formed. The Lord's supreme opportunity is come.

Knowing that the Father had given all things into his hands and that he was come from God and went to God. The occasion of His action was the dispute among the disciples about precedence; but it had a deeper motive. He is possessed by a special sense of divine commission and authority. How does He express that sense? Does He order a throne to be placed that He may receive the homage of His subjects? No — *he riseth from the supper and layeth aside his garments, and taking a towel girded himself; then he poureth water into the ewer,*[1] *and began to wash the disciples' feet and to wipe them with the towel with which he was girded.* So He will display Divine Majesty.

We rather shrink from this revelation. We are ready, perhaps, to be humble before God; but we do not want Him to be humble in His dealings with us. We should like Him, who has the right, to glory in His goodness and greatness; then we, as we pass from His presence, may be entitled to pride ourselves on such achievements as distinguish us above other men.

But the worship of Jesus Christ makes that impossible to justify. We worship the Infant in the manger, for whom there was no room in the inn. We worship One who meets our obeisance by rendering to us menial service. So far as that worship is genuine and complete, pride is eliminated; for He whom we worship is humility itself incarnate.

The divine humility shows itself in rendering service. He who is entitled to claim the service of all His creatures chooses first to give His service to them. 'The Son of Man came not to receive service but to give it' (*St. Mark* x, 45). But man's humility does not begin with the giving of service; it begins with the readiness to receive it. For there can be much pride and condescension in our giving of service. It is wholesome only when it is offered spontaneously on the impulse of real love; the conscientious offer of it is almost sure to 'have the nature of sin' (Article XIII), as almost all virtue has of which the origin is in our own deliberate wills. For unless the will is perfectly cleansed, its natural or original sin — the sin inherent

---

[1] The 'ewer' is the vessel used for pouring the water over the feet of the guests on their arrival, not a vessel (bason) into which it fell from their feet, or in which their feet might be placed.

in it of acting from the self instead of God as centre — contaminates all its works. So man's humility shows itself first in the readiness to receive service from our fellow-men and supremely from God. To accept service from men is to acknowledge a measure of dependence on them. It is well for us to stand on our own feet; to go through life in parasitic dependence on others, contributing nothing, is contemptible; but those who are doing their share of the world's work should have no hesitation in receiving what the love or generosity or pity of others may offer. The desire 'not to be beholden to anybody' is completely unchristian. Of course, it is equally true that to take all and offer nothing is even more opposed to the Christian spirit.

But it is the service of God which we must above all be ready to accept. We say in the most familiar of the collects, 'O God, forasmuch as without thee we are not able to please thee——' Our first thought must never be, 'What can I do for God?' The answer to that is, Nothing. The first thought must always be 'What would God do for me?' The answer may be put in many ways; one is that He would cleanse me. When I recognise that, I am both admitting that I need to be cleansed, and acknowledging that I cannot cleanse myself. Moreover it is to each singly that the cleansing service is offered, according to his own stains.

So he cometh to Simon Peter. This individual approach leads Him to offer the cleansing service to that loyal, generous, impulsive Simon. His loyalty and generosity rebel. It is not any vice, but the very virtue in him, that is horrified by the Lord's demeanour. *Lord, dost thou wash my feet?* The relationship between them renders such an action incredible. As Simon Peter emphasised the pronouns to display this incompatibility of lordship and service, so the Lord emphasises the pronouns as He points out the incapacity (at present) of the disciple to understand the Master's purpose.

What I do thou knowest not now, but thou shalt understand hereafter. Simon Peter does not question that; he only knows that what is proposed is intolerable and must always remain so: *Thou shalt by no means wash* my *feet to eternity.* Whatever others may allow, he at least will never permit this outrage — no, not to eternity. (Ah, Peter, you have struck the right note there; for it is unto eternity that your Lord would cleanse you.) But none can have fellowship with Jesus save those whom He Himself has washed. *If I wash thee not, thou hast no part with me.* That swings Peter over to demand more than was offered: *Lord, not my feet only, but also my hands and my head.* It is loyalty that speaks, and generosity, but it is not faith; for the one thing Peter cannot do is leave the Lord alone to act as He pleases; the loyalty and the generosity are infected with self-will. So his eager utterance is met by a calm moderation that has the effect of a mild rebuke. *He that is bathed needeth not save to wash his feet, but is clean in his whole person; and ye are clean.*

Guests usually bathed before starting to a feast; but, walking to the appointed place in sandals, they would gather dust on their feet, and there was need for that washing of the feet to which the slaves of the host would attend. So it is said that the disciples are *clean every whit.* They are cleansed by their fellowship with their Lord and by His teaching: *already ye are clean because of the word which I have spoken to you* (xv, 3). But they are come to the feast, the Last Supper or First Eucharist, and to the glorification of the Son of Man. The last traces of stain must be cleansed away from those who are already clean in their whole persons. *Ye are clean, but not all.* Even in that company of friends there was one who had withstood the cleansing influence. He had heard *the word* but was not clean because of it. And the Lord knew.

Every disciple and every company of disciples begin by wanting to give service. No doubt it is wise that the Church should, as far as possible, provide opportunities for this. But every disciple and every company of disciples need to learn that their first duty is to let Christ serve them. We are not now thinking of those outside: the way to win them is often to give them

some job of work to do so that they may feel that they are
wanted and can help, as the Lord began His saving of the
Woman of Samaria by saying, *Give me to drink* (iv, 7). Here
we are thinking of those who are committed to discipleship.
For them the first duty is to let the Lord cleanse them by His
word in their whole persons, and still to let Him cleanse them
day by day from stains that come from life in the world; and
at all times to leave the Lord to do with them as He will, not
demanding either that He should not humble Himself for their
sakes or that He should do them some service that might
correspond to their devotion but would have no usefulness for
His purpose. He knows what is best. It may not be good for
me to be purified at once from some temptation of which I am
ashamed. I must not clamour for that grace which it would
most gratify me to possess. My part is to accept with wondering reverence whatever service He is pleased to offer, even when
service takes the form of judgement: 'It is the Lord; let him
do what seemeth him good' (*I Samuel* iii, 18).

It is exactly the failure of such trust, the absence of such
surrender, that may make us enemies and traitors while we are
still in the company of His friends. We may go to Church
and say our prayers and read our Bibles; the cleansing Word
flows over us; but if our hearts are closed we are not cleansed.
And the Lord knows the man that is betraying Him, perhaps
before that man knows it himself. So of every company of
Christians He may be saying *Ye are not all clean*. Let each of
us ask tremblingly, *Lord, is it I?*

*

12-20. So when he had washed their feet, and taken his garments, and sat
down again, he said to them, 'Do ye understand what I have done to
you? Ye call me The Master and The Lord, and ye say well, for I am.
If then I washed your feet, the Master and the Lord, ye also ought to
wash one another's feet. For I gave you an example that, as I did to you,
ye also may do. Amen, Amen I say to you, a slave is not greater than his
Lord, nor an apostle greater than he that sent him. If ye know these
things, blessed are ye if ye do them. Not concerning you all do I speak;

I know whom I chose; but that the scripture may be fulfilled, He that eateth my bread lifted up his heel against me. From now I tell you before it come to pass, in order that, when it is come to pass, ye may believe that I am. Amen, Amen I say to you, he that receiveth whomsoever I shall send receiveth me, and he that receiveth me receiveth him that sent me.'

The Lord does not leave His acted parable without interpretation. Once He had set a child in the midst of them as an illustration of greatness in the Kingdom of Heaven (*St. Matthew* xviii, 1–4). This time He, the undoubted Great One, has rendered the menial service. He is the Master or Teacher among His pupils; He is the Lord among His slaves: and this is the way in which He disciplines them. Most searching discipline, penetrating to the inward springs of conduct and of character as stripes could never do! But if we are pupils of such a Master, slaves of such a Lord, the consequence is clear. We must act to one another as He acts towards us. We recognise the truth of this: the task is to act upon it — and we shirk that task. We would gladly wash the feet of our Divine Lord; but He disconcertingly insists on washing ours, and bids us wash our neighbour's feet. This is an argument that appears elsewhere in the Johannine writings. 'If God so loved us, we also ought to love one another' (*I John* iv, 11). What gives cogency to the argument is the revealed character of God. It is not cogent argument to say, 'If A loves B, B ought to love C,' unless A loves B and C equally. But the test of my love to God is the question whether I love my neighbour; for I know that God loves him as He loves me, and love of the loving God must show itself in love of all whom God loves. 'If a man say "I love God" and hateth his brother, he is a liar' (*I John* iv, 20).

A slave is not greater than his lord, nor an apostle greater than he that sent him. The word used is actually *apostle*; it means 'one that is sent'; but the choice of it is not an accident. The Apostles are 'set in the Church first' (*I Corinthians* xii, 28), and it is specially needful for them to remember that they are not greater than their Lord, who showed His greatness by washing the disciples' feet.

Not concerning you all do I speak. In that little group of intimate friends one was false. Perhaps he did not know even now how false his own heart was; but the Lord knew, as He had known at the crisis marked by the discourse upon the Bread of Life (vi, 70). He knows the measure of our faith and loyalty better than we do. He may know that it is sound at the core even when our hearts condemn us (*I John* iii, 20). But He may know that it is worthless even when we think it sound. *I know whom I chose,* that is, *what kind of men I chose.* The first pronoun is emphatic. There is no doubt or obscurity in the Lord's understanding of His followers (ii, 24, 25). He, at any rate, knew what manner of men they were whom He chose. And one was this hard nature. The divine love must pit itself against that hardness; if it prevail, a great triumph is won; if it fail in the first impact, that opens the way to a still greater triumph. But love must make its uttermost appeal, as very soon now it will (26). The Lord knows that it must fail; and He knows the terrible strain that this failure and its consequences will put upon the loyalty of the other disciples; they *shall be scattered every man to his own and shall leave me alone* (xvi, 32). He does not hope that while the hour of darkness lasts they will be believing; but He tells them now what is coming so that when it is come and the hour is passed they may recollect that He foretold it. So they will see that all which had dismayed them fell within His plan, and faith in Him would revive: *I tell you before it come to pass, in order that, when it is come to pass, ye may believe that I AM.*

From that assurance would spring the confidence with which they would proclaim the Gospel. They will know that they are sent by the Divine Lord; they will be His ambassadors; to receive them will be to receive Him. *An apostle is not greater than he that sent him;* but he carries the dignity and honour of the King whom he represents. *He that receiveth whomsoever I*

shall send receiveth me. Even more than this is true. For the
Lord Himself is the first Apostle (*Hebrews* iii, 1), and to
receive Him is to receive the Father. So the greatest of all
miracles is accomplished; the gulf between man and God is
bridged, not by man's achievement, but by God's humiliation,
and as a result 'our fellowship is with the Father and with his
Son Jesus Christ' (*I John* i, 3).

*

THE DESIGNATION OF THE TRAITOR

21-30. When Jesus had said this he was troubled in spirit and bare witness
and said, 'Amen, Amen I say to you that one from among you shall
betray me'. The disciples began to look upon one another in bewilderment concerning whom he spake. There was one of his disciples, whom
Jesus loved, reclining in Jesus' bosom. Simon Peter therefore beckons
to him to ask who it might be. He, leaning back as he was upon Jesus'
breast, saith to him, 'Lord, who is it?' So Jesus answers, 'He it is for
whom I shall dip the morsel and shall give it to him'. So having dipped
the morsel, he taketh and giveth it to Judas, the son of Simon Iscariot.
And after the morsel then entered into that man Satan. Jesus therefore
saith to him, 'What thou doest, do more quickly'. But none of them
that sat at meat with him understood with what intent he said this to
him. For some were supposing, because Judas had the money box, that
Jesus was saying to him, 'Buy those things of which we have need for
the feast', or that he should give something to the poor. So, having
received the morsel, that one went out immediately; and it was night.

The thought that one of His chosen friends should betray
Him disturbs that serenity of mind which was unruffled before
the taunts and threats of Pharisees and High Priests. *He was
troubled in spirit.* The hostilities of enemies cannot wound the
soul as does the disloyalty of a friend — 'mine own familiar
friend whom I trusted, who eateth my bread, hath lifted up
his heel against me' (*Psalm* xli, 9). To us He has said, *I have
called you friends* (xv, 15), and our unfaithfulness is the unfaithfulness of friends; our disloyalty is as the sin of Judas;
and the Lord knows our hearts: *One from among you shall
betray me.*

The scene is intensely vivid. The company is at table reclining each on his left elbow at an oblique angle to the table,
so that the right hand is free to take the food. The Lord is in
a central position, and the place to His left would according
to custom be regarded as the place of chief honour. We do
not know who occupied it. Sometimes it is assumed that St.
Peter was placed there as recognised leader of the Apostolic
fellowship. But though his eager and impulsive nature often
made him the spokesman, there is no evidence that he had any
special status; and if he was in this position, his beckoning to
St. John (24) is hard to visualise. On the other hand, Judas was
treasurer, and would very naturally be in this place at the
table; if he were, it was easy for the Lord to give him the choice
morsel, and to speak to him so that the others did not catch
His meaning or, perhaps, His words. St. Matthew records an
interchange — 'Is it I?' 'Thou hast said' — in which the
answer cannot have been generally heard. We assume then
that Judas was occupying the place of honour on the left of
the Lord.

To the right was the Beloved Disciple, John the son of
Zebedee. As he reclined on his left elbow, his head would be
opposite the Lord's bosom, and could be spoken of as resting
in that bosom, that is to say in the folds of His garment. A
slight movement would lead to his leaning against the Lord's
breast, looking up into His face (25).

The Beloved Disciple is the type of complete discipleship.
As the Son is *in the bosom of the Father* (i, 18) so the disciple
is in the bosom of the Incarnate Son.

The other disciples were reclining in a similar position at the
other places round the table.

Into that circle of apparently intimate friendship fall the
words, *Amen, Amen I say to you that one from among you shall
betray me*. What wonder that they *began to look upon one
another in bewilderment concerning whom he spake*. So when
the word that should make us search our own consciences is
spoken we look round to see at whom the shaft was launched.

There are few more moving moments in Bach's *Passion according to St. Matthew* than the moment when, after the Chorus of Disciples — 'Lord, is it I?', the Chorale follows and every soul present confesses, 'My sin it was which bound thee'.

Simon Peter is not content to be bewildered. He beckons to the Beloved Disciple to ask who is the traitor. *He, leaning back as he was upon Jesus' breast, saith to him, 'Lord, who is it?'* So Jesus answers, *'He it is for whom I shall dip the morsel, and shall give it to him.'* The question is asked and answered, but secretly, and only the Beloved Disciple understands what follows.

It was customary for a host to show special honour or favour to one of his guests by dipping a choice morsel in the dish and handing this to him. The Lord shows that special honour and favour to the disciple whom He knows to be planning treachery. He makes a last appeal, and watches to see its effect. St. John, who alone shares the secret, watches also; and what he saw he wrote: *after the morsel then entered into that man Satan.* The traitor's face went dark, and the Lord knew that the appeal had failed. In that moment of tense feeling His one desire is that what must come should come quickly. 'How am I straitened till it be accomplished' (*Luke* xii, 50). *What thou doest, do more quickly.* The rest suppose that this is some command to hasten an ordinary duty or task. But Judas understands; and St. John understands. So, *having received the morsel, that one went out immediately; and it was night.*

Judas moves to the door and opens it; St. John looks through it from the lighted room to the darkness outside. Judas goes of his own free will from that light into that darkness, from the presence of the Light of the World into the outer darkness. There are no more pregnant words in the whole of literature than these — *and it was night.*

The Lord had known what was in Judas' mind. Judas had made his compact with the Chief Priests after the supper at which Mary had anointed the feet of the Lord and brought censure on himself by his reproach of her (*St. Mark* xiv, 1–11).

As a result of this the directions to the two disciples who were to prepare for this *kiddush* or fellowship meal were given in a kind of cypher (*St. Mark* xiv, 13–16). Judas must not hear the description of the place so that he would be able to lead the Temple-guard to it and there carry out the arrest in convenient secrecy. That sacred time in the Upper Room must be kept free from interruption. So all arrangements are made, including the clue which the two disciples are to follow — the man bearing a pitcher of water. The two disciples follow him in silence to the appointed place, where later the Lord joins them with the rest of the Twelve.

Knowing the traitor's intention, what shall He do? Nothing could be easier than to speak a word to loyal and impulsive Simon Peter and the others. We know there were two swords in that room (*St. Luke* xxii, 38); and apart from any such violence as that suggests, Judas could have been left gagged and bound while the Lord escaped. So He would have saved His life; and so He would have lost His Kingdom. He had come to inaugurate the Kingdom of God, who is Love. His method was to live the life of perfect love and die the death of perfect love. He will not now fall back on any other method. So He makes one last appeal to the false disciple's loyalty by singling him out for special honour. The appeal fails. '*What thou doest, do more quickly.*' Judas passes out under the Lord's protecting silence.

In that moment the Lord condemned Himself to death. He can stil lno doubt call for 'more than twelve legions of angels' (*St. Matthew* xxvi, 53). But humanly speaking the Cross is now inevitable; events will lead to it; His doom is sealed; and He has sealed it.

✱

The Glorification of the Son of Man

(xiii, 31–xiv, 31)

In that moment the Lord did certain things. What He did is already familiar to St. John's readers. He took the bread, calling it His Body, and broke it and gave it. He took the cup, calling it His Blood of the New Covenant, and bade the disciples drink of it. For in that moment He was by His own act breaking His Body and pouring out His Blood. Not many hours later He was *lifted up from the earth* upon the Cross. The act of will that led to this — the essential act of self-sacrifice — was the choice of love's way in dealing with the traitor — 'by which will we have been sanctified through the offering of the body of Jesus Christ once for all' (*Hebrews* x, 10).

From the time of His Ascension onwards His followers have met together to unite themselves with Him in His sacrifice by doing again what He did at this, the spiritual crisis of the ministry. They meet in His Name, and He is in the midst of them; they are members of His Body and He acts through them. Still by the hands of the priest He takes the Bread which He calls His Body, breaks it and gives it. But we are that Body — 'very members incorporate' therein. In union with His perfect sacrifice, we offer to God 'ourselves, our souls and bodies, to be a reasonable, holy and lively sacrifice' to Him. Still we drink the Cup, that His Blood, His Life given in sacrifice and triumphant over death, may be in us the spring of eternal life in fellowship with Him. Whether or not He commanded us to use this rite, as I believe that He did, yet its significance and power consists in the fact that we do in remembrance of Him what He did 'in the same night in which He was betrayed', offering ourselves in the power of His self-offering.

As in that moment the Lord did certain things recorded by

the Synoptists and already familiar to all Christians when the Fourth Gospel was written, so in that moment He said certain things which it remained for St. John to record.

31–35. When therefore he was gone out, Jesus saith, 'Now was glorified the Son of Man and God was glorified in him. If God was glorified in him, God shall also glorify him in himself, and straightway shall he glorify him. Little children, yet a little while I am with you; ye shall seek me, and as I said to the Jews, "Whither I go ye cannot come", to you also I say it now. A new commandment I give to you, that ye love one another — as I loved you, that ye also love one another. By this shall all men recognise that ye are my disciples, if ye have love one to another.'

When he was gone out. He went freely; the Lord did not *cast him out* (vi, 37; ix, 34); he went out freely into the night. He goes to fulfil his compact with the Lord's enemies and to effect the Lord's condemnation and death; his going leads to his own unending shame and to the Lord's glory. *Now was glorified the Son of Man.* We picture the Lord watching the door, through which the outer night has been seen for a moment, until it is closed behind the traitor. Then at once He speaks. That going of Judas to hasten his treachery is the moment of the glorification of the Son of Man. For this is the kind of Messiah that He is; 'the Son of Man must suffer' (*St. Mark* viii, 31); that is the way in which He will inaugurate His Kingdom. God is Love; His glory is supremely what most displays His love; the Passion, to which by letting Judas go, the Lord has condemned Himself, is the very focus of the glory of the Son of Man — of man as God meant him to be, of the Messiah who came to restore the divine image in Him.

It is not only Messiah's glory, but *God is glorified in him.* The martyr wins for himself the crown of glory; but also by his death he gives glory to God. So in higher degree the Son of Man wins glory by His obedience unto death (*Philippians* ii, 8–11), but therein also gives glory to God whose love was supremely shown by giving Him for the saving of the world (iii, 16). The Son of Man enters His own glory in the act of self-devotion; but thereby also He gives glory to God to whom He is devoted; and when we confess Him as Lord, we do this 'to the glory of God the Father' (*Philippians* ii, 11).

But if so, *if God was glorified in him* in that devoted act of choice which let the traitor go, God will not leave it there. God will vindicate that self-devotion in the perfected union of the Son with Himself, towards which the words recorded in xvii, 5 are the aspiration and of which the Ascension is the proclamation; *God shall also glorify him in himself.* Nor is this a far-off consummation; it is now at hand; *and straightway shall he glorify him.*

The Lord has spoken of what the great moment — for ever commemorated in the breaking of the Bread and the pouring of the Wine — means for Himself. He goes on to speak of what it means for His friends. It means that there can only be a brief continuance of the form of intercourse that they have known; *yet a little while I am with you.* There is an aspect of the coming separation of which He will speak later (xvi, 7). But separation there will be. He is going where they cannot follow. They will seek Him; it is not said, as it was to the Jews, that they will not find Him (vii, 34), but it is said now to them as it was said earlier to the Jews — *whither I go ye cannot come.*

As we have seen, this phrase does not mean only that the Lord is to die so that those who still live on earth cannot accompany Him; it stands for that union with the Father which has been His without defect from the beginning, but is His in all its plenitude in and through the Passion (*Hebrews* ii, 10; v, 8, 9). That is a goal to which even the disciples cannot attain until a new power is come upon them, though then it will be possible (36).

This unattainable goal is that perfection of love which Christ Himself has shown. This *new commandment*, to love as Christ has loved, is the impossible thing, except so far as we are 'in Christ' (to use St. Paul's great phrase) as the branches are in the Vine (xv, 5, 10, 12). He Himself will make it possible for us, but till then it is not possible.

Does this command supersede the Second Great Commandment 'Thou shalt love thy neighbour as thyself'? No — that
stands as the general rule of our relation to all men, with the
understanding of the word 'neighbour' which it receives from
the Parable of the Good Samaritan; my 'neighbour' is anyone
with whom I have anything at all to do, even by accident, and
even though he is the kind of person that I naturally hate or
despise. I am to care as much for his interest and welfare as
for my own; and I need a most penetrating 'conversion' before
I do that. But here the Lord speaks, not of our relation to
mankind generally, but of the special bond of love that should
unite all fellow-Christians. Within the Christian fellowship
each is to be linked to each by a love like that of Christ for
each. That is the new commandment; and obedience to it is
to be the evidence to the world of true discipleship. If the
Church really were like that, if every communicant had for
every other a love like that of Christ for him, the power of its
witness would be irresistible, and out of that nucleus of self-
giving love — love like that of Christ upon the Cross — would
flow the power making men generally love their neighbours as
themselves. The Old Commandment stands as a universal, and
universally neglected, requirement; the New Commandment
that ye love one another as I loved you has a narrower range and
an intenser quality. When the Church keeps the New Commandment, the world may keep the Old.

*

36–xiv, 3. Simon Peter saith to him, 'Lord, whither goest thou?' Jesus
     answered, 'Whither I go thou canst not follow me now, but thou shalt
     follow me afterwards'. Peter saith to him, 'Lord, why cannot I follow
     thee now? My life for thee I will lay down.' Jesus answered, 'Thy life
     for me wilt thou lay down? Amen, Amen I say to thee, the cock shall by
     no means crow till thou hast denied me thrice. Let not your hearts be
     troubled; believe in God, and believe in me. In my Father's house are
     many resting-places. If it were not so, should I have told you that I go to
     prepare a place for you? And if I go and prepare a place for you, I come
     again and will receive you to myself, that where I am ye also may be.'

St. Peter is puzzled by this language about a journey. To what place does it lead? The answer had been given earlier (vii, 33), but there is reason to think that Peter was not then present (see p. 171). It will be given repeatedly later (xiv, 12, 28; xvi, 5, 10, 28). But the answer must gain its meaning as the discourse proceeds; for it is a spiritual journey on which the Lord is going. He goes to the Father. This involves His death; and His death is involved, not as a physical transition but as a spiritual sacrifice. Therefore, instead of describing His destination, He first insists on the incapacity of Peter and the rest to follow now. They could die; but if they did, that would not bring them where He is going; it would not bring them to perfectly fulfilled union with the Infinite Love. *Whither I go thou canst not follow me now.* But later that will have become possible — *thou shalt follow me afterwards* (cf. xxi, 19). Still Peter cannot understand. He believes that his loyalty is complete; he is ready to lay down life itself for his Lord. *Why cannot I follow thee now? My life for thee I will lay down.* It was no idle boast. A few hours later Peter began to fight when fighting meant certain death. So the Lord does not deny his readiness to die. But He knows that another sort of trial is coming, when the cause of the Lord will seem to be lost, and Peter in utter depression, very cold, will have to face mockery and jeers. Then he will fail. *Thy life for me thou wilt lay down? Amen, Amen I say to thee, the cock shall by no means crow till thou hast denied me thrice.*

We can imagine a little of the shock which those words gave to the hearers. To Peter himself it was such that through all the following scene, though others spoke, he, the readiest of all to speak, was silent. His next appearance is at xviii, 10, where he draws his sword and begins to fight for his Master, and would undoubtedly have then laid down his life if the Lord had not stopped the fighting. But great as was the shock to him, it was little less to his companions, and it is to all of them that the following words are addressed: *Let not your hearts be troubled; believe in God, and believe in me.* They were going to fail, and to fail badly. Peter would deny Him; and of all it is written that they forsook Him and fled (*St. Mark* xiv, 50). The failure must not become a cause of despair or dismay; rather let it teach its lesson. When we fail in our discipleship it is always for one of two reasons: either we are not trying to be loyal, or else we are trying in our own strength and find that it is not enough. The former is known to be sinful, but occasions no bewilderment. If we do not try, our lack of success is explained, though our failure to try may well fill us with dismay. The root of that failure, however, is the feebleness of our faith as a settled direction of mind and will. If our habitual faith were stronger we should always try to be loyal. When we try in our own strength and find it insufficient, this too is evidence of defect in faith. Our faith is strong enough to prompt us to try; but it is not strong enough to claim the power of God for His service. Until our trust is perfect, we need to supplement our habitual reliance upon God with special acts of trust — probably expressed in secret but conscious prayer — at moments of acute difficulty or temptation.

Failure, then, always proves that faith is insufficient. It should drive us back upon God, forgetfulness of whose grace has caused the failure. Then every fall into sin can become the occasion for growth in grace. *Let not your hearts be troubled; trust God, and trust me.*

One who so faces his own failures is steadily advancing on the pilgrim's way; he, like his Master, is going *to the Father*. More than this; if he is thus travelling the right way at all, he is at home with the Father all the time. *In my Father's house are many resting-places. If it were not so, should I have told you that I go to prepare a place for you? And if I go and prepare a place for you, I come again and will receive you to myself.*

The *resting-places* (μοναί) are wayside caravanserais — shelters at stages along the road where travellers may rest on their journey. It was the custom in the East — and still is, where railways and motor cars have not yet penetrated — for travellers to send a dragoman forward to make preparation

in the next of those resting-places along the road, so that
when they came they might find in it comfort as well as
shelter. Here the Lord presents Himself as our spiritual
dragoman, who treads the way of faith before us — the
'captain and perfecter of faith,' τὸν τῆς πίστεως ἀρχηγὸν
καὶ τελειωτήν (*Hebrews* xii, 2) — and makes ready to welcome
us. It may be that we are still far from perfect fellowship
with the Father; like Peter, we are about to deny our Lord,
or, like the rest, we are about to forsake Him in flight. We
have a long journey of many days before us ere our pilgrimage is accomplished. But there are, by God's mercy, *many
resting-places.* Otherwise of what avail would be the promise
of the Lord to *prepare a place* for us? If it were only in
the realm of ultimate attainment, would He mock us with the
promise of a welcome there? *Should I have told you that I go
to prepare a place for you?*

There has not been recorded any promise in those precise
terms. But the whole tenor of His teaching has been such as
to imply the companionship of His disciples with Him as He
goes to the Father. This is not the only instance of reference
to former sayings which are not precisely recorded (cf. vi, 36;
xi, 40). Apart from this, the construction of the words which
has been adopted is preferable to the others which are gram-
matically possible, and it is therefore adopted here.

The Lord calls us to absolute perfection; but He points us
here and now to what is for each one the next stage, the next
resting-place, on the way to it. And as we follow, we find Him
there to welcome us. More than that — He comes to lead
us there. *If I go and prepare a place for you, I come again
and will receive you to myself.* The image of dragoman and
caravanserai is still employed. There is no special reference
to a final Parousia or Return in Glory, though that thought
is in place in reference to the final stage. Our spiritual dragoman, who has gone forward to make preparation, returns to
encourage us and lead us to the resting-place prepared. That
resting-place is fellowship, fuller than before, with the Lord

— *that where I am ye also may be* — until the last stage is reached, towards which we press on, 'the goal of the call upward which God gives in Christ Jesus' (*Philippians* iii, 14).

Every Christian must know something of what is here described. We reach a certain stage of fellowship with Christ, in spiritual apprehension and moral attainment, and find great joy in it. But this seems to fade, until we become conscious that we are called to something higher. The Lord is gone before us to prepare the next resting-place. Then everything depends upon our response. We may stay where we are, becoming more and more torpid in spirit. Or we may, in St. Paul's phrase, 'press on'. If we do this, we find the Lord meeting us and leading us to the next resting-place. Our sense of fellowship with Him revives, and with this our joy in it. Then the process is repeated. So we make progress, 'from glory to glory' (*II Corinthians* iii, 18) till we are 'transformed into the same image'. The new 'call upwards' is sometimes an awareness of something positively wrong, a 'weight' that must be laid aside (*Hebrews* xii, 1), and sometimes an apprehension of service to be rendered which calls for completer self-devotion. If we refuse to start on the new stage of our journey we forfeit the companionship of the Lord; but so soon as we even start, He is at our side again, returning that He may receive us to Himself.

. . . *If I go . . . I come again.* These do not merely follow upon one another. His 'going' is itself a 'coming'. For He goes to the Father, to whom all things are present, so that by His departure He becomes more accessible than ever before: see xx, 17 and comment there.

In this wonderful passage there is another thought, the most wonderful of all. These *many resting-places*, marking the stages of our spiritual growth, are in the *Father's house*. If we are travelling heavenwards, we are already in heaven. And though the perfection of communion with the Father to which the Lord is gone is a place where we cannot follow him now, it is none the less true, not only that we shall follow Him afterwards, but that even now, if our faces are set the right way, 'our fellowship is with the Father and with his Son Jesus Christ' (*I John* i, 3).

Let us hear the amazing words again — we, who are His disciples and would like to think that we could lay down our lives for Him, but also fear lest this night we may deny Him: *Let not your hearts be troubled; trust God; and trust me. In My Father's house are many resting-places. If it were not so, should I have told you that I go to prepare a place for you? And if I go and prepare a place for you, I come again and will receive you to myself, that where I am, ye also may be.*

'"Yea: I come quickly." Amen: come, Lord Jesus' (*Revelation* xxii, 20).

*

OUR ACCESS TO THE FATHER

4–11. 'And whither I go, ye know the way.' Thomas saith to him, 'Lord, we know not whither thou goest; how know we the way?' Jesus saith to him, 'I am the way, and the truth, and the Life. No one cometh to the Father except through me. If ye had recognised me, ye would know my Father also. From now ye are recognising him and have seen him.' Philip saith to him, 'Lord, show us the Father, and it sufficeth us'. Jesus saith to him, 'So long a time have I been with you and hast thou not recognised me, Philip? He that hath seen me hath seen the Father. How dost *thou* say, "Show us the Father"? Dost thou not believe that I am in the Father, and the Father in me? The words that I say to you I speak not from myself, but the Father who abideth in me doeth his works. Believe me that I am in the Father and the Father in me; or else on account of the works themselves believe me.'

The goal of our journey is unknown except in its formal description. It is Heaven; it is perfect fellowship with the Father; but what those phrases really mean it is beyond our faculties to grasp: 'Things which eye saw not and ear heard not, and which entered not into the heart of man, whatsoever things that God prepared for them that love him' (*I Corinthians* ii, 9). But though the goal is thus unknown and unknowable to us, yet the Lord declares that we know the way.

To Thomas, loyal and literal-minded Thomas, this is bewildering. We choose our road with reference to our destination. We do not go to a railway station and ask the officials
to recommend a direction and a train; it is only because we
know where we mean to go that we can reasonably even ask
for advice how to start. '*Whither I go, ye know the way.*'
'*We know not whither thou goest, how know we the way?*' '*I
am the way.*' Though the goal is unknown, the way is well
known, for it is the Lord Himself. We have to pass through
Him if we are to come to the Father; we must be so united with
Him that as He offers Himself to the Father He offers us also.
No one cometh to the Father except through me.

We are to pass 'through the veil, that is to say, his flesh'
(*Hebrews* x, 20). The human nature of Christ conceals the
Deity from us, as it did from the Jews, until we are united with
it and find the Deity indwelling it. We must *eat the flesh of the
Son of Man and drink his blood* (vi, 53) so that His humanity
becomes the substance of our very being; then we find that
'our fellowship is with the Father' (*I John* i, 3).

Only because He is more than an individual man can He
be *the way* for us. Shakespeare is not himself 'the way' for
me to write poetry, nor is even St. Francis 'the way' for me to
be a Christian. These show me how poetry can be written and
how Christianity can be lived; they have a way of doing it,
but neither of them is a way by which others may do it. But
Jesus is not only a man who trod the way to God: He is Himself that supreme Spirit 'in whom we live, and move, and have
our being' (*Acts* xvii, 28). We can become 'very members
incorporate' in His Body as we cannot in the body of any
other. We come to the Father *through* Him, and He is *the way.*

The thought which has been expressed by reference to His
Deity coupled with the Divine Omnipresence is, in the text,
brought forward in another way. *I am the way, and the truth,
and the Life.* It is possible for the Lord to be Himself *the way*
because He is also *the truth and the Life.* He is *the truth.*
Truth is the perfect correlation of mind and reality; and this

is actualised in the Lord's Person. If the Gospel is true and God is, as the Bible declares, a Living God, the ultimate truth is not a system of propositions grasped by a perfect intelligence, but is a Personal Being apprehended in the only way in which persons are ever fully apprehended, that is, by love. The Incarnation is not a condescension to our infirmities, so that 'Truth embodied in a tale' may enter in at the 'lowly door' of human minds. It is the only way in which divine truth can be expressed, not because of our infirmity but because of its own nature. What is personal can be expressed only in a person.

This personal truth is also *the Life*, the vitalising energy of all that lives. Already, even while we recognise Him not, He is the well-spring of what vitality we have. Our task is not laboriously to follow Him, nor in some way to transform our nature; our task is to recognise what is already and always fact, that all progress we make is through Him, all knowledge we gain is of Him, all energy we exercise is from Him. *He is the way and the truth and the Life.*

'*Ye know the way.*' '*I am the way.*' It starts where each one stands. We do not have to find its starting-place. It starts here where we are. For there is no conceivable combination of circumstances in which it is not possible to show love; and 'God is love; and he that abideth in love, abideth in God, and God abideth in him' (*I John* iv, 16).

So close is the union of Christ with the Father that if we know Him for what He is we are thereby brought to knowledge of the Father: *If ye had recognised me, ye would know my Father also.* The disciples are beginning truly to know their Lord, so that they may even be said, in and through that knowledge, to have seen the Father; *From now ye are recognising him and have seen him.* Apart from this understanding of Christ there is no vision of God (i, 18); but through this the vision of God is actual experience. Yet the disciples do not yet grasp the meaning of their fellowship with Christ; they do not appreciate their unique privilege, in that they saw and heard the things which many prophets and kings desired to see and hear, yet saw and heard them not (*St. Luke* x, 24). So Philip, half-consciously perceiving that they stand on the brink of a great fulfilment, utters the deepest yearning of the human heart: '*Lord, show us the Father, and it sufficeth us*'. That is the craving which alone causes all our restlessness; if that be sated, all desire is quiet. It is much to learn that this is our one great need. 'Like as the hart desireth the water-brooks, so longeth my soul after thee, O God. My soul is athirst for God, yea, even for the living God: when shall I come to appear before the presence of God?' (*Psalm* xlii, 1, 2). 'Whom have I in heaven but thee; and there is none upon earth that I desire in comparison of thee. My flesh and my heart faileth: but God is the strength of my heart and my portion for ever' (*Psalm* lxxiii, 25, 26). 'When I wake up after thy likeness, I shall be satisfied with it' (*Psalm* xvii, 15).

But Philip's request is for something more than a manifestation of God as even devout Jews thought of Him. What was novel in the religious language of the Lord was His constant, His almost invariable, use of the word 'Father' as the name of God. It is as though Philip said, 'We have long believed in God, but make Him plainly known to us as Father and we shall be satisfied: *Show us the Father, and it sufficeth us*'.

It is the utterance of the common need of all mankind. But the Christian has no right to make it. For him the satisfaction of that need is already available. Has our discipleship yet taught us that Jesus Himself is the satisfaction of all that hunger expressed, for example, by the Psalmists in the verses which we have quoted? If not, we have not learnt our lesson and our discipleship is incomplete. '*So long time have I been with you and hast* thou *not recognised me, Philip?*' He had been in their company (the word *you* is plural) and here is one of that company who still does not recognise Him for what He is. So too He is in His Body the Church, and here is myself, a member of that Body, who have little more than an intellectual recognition of Him; my heart does not in fact find yet that constant joy in His presence, that 'peace which passeth understanding', which must be the result of communion with the Eternal God. I am assured, with no tremor of doubt, that fellowship with Jesus is fellowship with God; since, then, it has not the effect of fellowship with God, it must be an imperfect fellowship. I have no power to make it perfect; but when I desire that it should be perfect, I can expose myself to the influence which can make it so, and which streams from the Person of Jesus, the Word Incarnate. 'Lord, I believe, help thou mine unbelief.' Lord, I love; help thou my lack of love. *Show us the Father, and it sufficeth us.*

'*He that hath seen me hath seen the Father.*' Those are the words that we long to hear. We cannot fully grasp that supreme truth, as we should if our discipleship were perfect. We need to hear them over and over again, to let the sound of them constantly play upon our ears, the meaning of them perpetually occupy our minds, the call in them unceasingly move our wills. Jesus our Lord is 'the image of the invisible God' (*Colossians* i, 15), 'the effulgence of his glory and the very image of his substance' (*Hebrews* i, 3). In adoration, in supplication, in dedication, let us take care always to address ourselves to God as He is seen in Jesus Christ. Never ask in prayer for any blessing till you are sure your mind is turned to Jesus Christ; then speak to God as you see Him there. 'This is the true God and eternal life. Little children, guard yourselves from idols' (*I John* v, 20, 21).

How are we to hold our minds to this truth? It must be by appreciation of that quality in the Lord which in this Gospel is most frequently emphasised, His constant dependence for all He is and does and says upon the Father. Can we behold that glory which is not His own but streams through Him from the Father (i, 14)? *Dost thou not believe that I am in the Father and the Father in me? The words that I say to you I speak not from myself, but the Father who abideth in me doeth his works.* The *words* of Christ are *works* of God. No man can do God's work; only God can do that. But God can indwell a man and work through him; and this general principle was supremely illustrated by Him in whom Manhood was taken into God.

So there are two levels of faith possible to us. Best of all is that intuitive faith which apprehends Deity when face to face with it and can accept the claim which its very nature must make. *Believe me that I am in the Father and the Father in me.* But if that is beyond us, then it is still possible for us to face the works which He does and, recognising them as divine, acknowledge that He who does them must Himself be God: *or else on account of the works themselves believe me.*

•

THE EFFECTS OF FAITH

12–14. 'Amen, Amen, I say to you, He that believeth on me, the works that I do shall he do also, and greater than these shall he do, because I go to the Father. And whatsoever ye shall ask in my name, this will I do, that the Father may be glorified in the Son. If ye shall ask anything in my name, I will do it.'

The *works* are signs and evidences of the Deity of Christ. But in the days when He was 'straitened' (*St. Luke* xii, 50) they could not be convincing to any except those specially qualified by purity of heart to see God at work. Even the Baptist had been disappointed rather than impressed by them (*St. Matthew* xi, 2). There would be more persuasive evidence when, having accomplished His journey *to the Father*, He empowered His disciples, united with one another in Him as His Body, to act as His representatives in the world. The *greater works* need not be more startling miracles, for the degree of our amazement may be due to the scantiness of our knowledge or the vulgarity of our taste as truly as to the intrinsic marvel of what is accomplished. St. Paul found his converts disposed to give special honour to 'speaking with tongues' as a peculiar manifestation of the Spirit, and had to insist on the superiority of 'charity' as a 'more excellent way'

(*I Corinthians* xii and xiii). That a respectable citizen should love his neighbour as himself is less likely to be announced in double-column headlines than his utterance of ecstatic gibberish in a public place; but it would be quite as unusual, and a far surer sign of the divine presence and activity in him.

In scale, if not in quality, the *works* of Christ wrought through His disciples are greater than those wrought by Him in His earthly ministry. It is a greater thing to have founded hospitals all over Europe and in many parts of Asia and Africa than to have healed some scores or some hundreds of sick folk in Palestine; and it is to the Spirit of Christ at work in the hearts of men that we owe the establishment of hospitals. The accomplishment of the journey *to the Father* means, among other things, that the Lord is no longer 'straitened' by the limitations of our mortal state; He is where God is, and that is everywhere. His *works* are no longer limited to Palestine but are diffused over the world. The transformation of Uganda is one of them; the inspiring record of the Universities' Mission to Central Africa is another; the fellowship of Chinese and Japanese Christians while their nations are at war is a third. The power to do these *greater works* through the agency of His disciples is His because He is gone *to the Father*.

Indeed there is no limit to what He may do through us, or (which is the same thing) to what we may do in His Name. To act in the name of another is to act as His representative. When we pray in the Name of Christ, we pray as His representatives; in other words, we are then praying for what is already His will, but for a part of that will which He waits to fulfil until we recognise Him as the source of blessing by asking it of Him; then immediately His power is released and becomes effective; *whatsoever ye shall ask in my name, this will I do.* But there is a motive behind this. It is not a merely mechanical release of power. There is something more at work than a law of cause and effect; the bestowal of blessing, when that condition is fulfilled on which depends its actual benefit, is for the glory of the Father. This is the supreme motive of every activity of the Son and the supreme object which every created thing exists to promote; our success, or health, or welfare is of very small importance in itself; only because God loves us, unlovely as we are, have we value in ourselves; that value is our value to Him; and what gives importance to our well-being is that it brings glory to God. This is not to say that the Son does not act for love of men; for God is love, and the glory of God is the shining forth and the victory of love. Yet it makes a vast difference whether we suppose that God loves us because we are lovable, or that He loves us, in spite of much in us which deserves His antagonism, because He is overflowing love. So the motive of the Son in granting these prayers which are in His Name or in accordance with His will must be *that the Father may be glorified* in the Son.

Yet this is not to be the last thought on the matter. The last thought, leading us forward to what follows, is the absolute assurance that prayers offered in the Name of Christ will be granted. *If ye shall ask anything in my name, I will do it.*

We can hope to rest in His Name only if and so far as there is complete union of our hearts and wills with His; and that union is love.

●

THE PROMISE OF THE COMFORTER

15–26. 'If ye love me, the commandments that are mine ye will observe. And I will ask the Father and he will send you, besides, a Comforter that he may be with you to eternity, the spirit of truth, whom the world cannot receive, because it observeth him not, neither recogniseth him; but *ye* are recognising him because he abideth with you and shall be in you. I will not leave you bereft; I am coming to you. Yet a little while and the world taketh note of me no more, but ye take note of me, that I live and ye shall live. In that day ye will recognise that I am in my Father and ye in me and I in you. He that hath my commandments and observeth them, he it is that loveth me; and he that loveth me shall be loved by my Father, and I will love him and manifest myself to him.'

There saith to him Judas, not Iscariot, 'Lord, what then has happened that thou art about to manifest thyself to us and not to the world?'

Jesus answered and said to him, 'If any man love me, my word he will
observe, and my Father will love him, and we shall come to him and
make a resting-place with him. He that loveth me not doth not observe
my words; and the word which ye hear is not mine, but the Father's who
sent me. These things have I spoken to you while abiding with you;
but the Comforter, the Spirit, the Holy One, whom the Father will send
in my name, he will teach you all things and will bring to your remembrance all things which I said to you.'

The whole of this passage, though long and packed with
truths, must be considered together. First, love and obedience
are coupled together, and both are associated with the coming
of the Comforter (15, 16); then the meaning of that coming is
partially disclosed (17–24); then the source of the Comforter's power in the historical ministry of Christ is made
clear, and the thought of His coming is thus again linked with
the love and obedience of disciples to their Lord (25, 26).

If ye love me, the commandments that are mine ye will observe.
This is a cumbrous translation, but there is a special emphasis
on the word *mine*, and there is a special suggestion on the word
observe. It is, as in viii, 51, the word which means 'watch'
rather than 'fulfil'. The suggestion is that of a standard of
reference and judgement rather than of a literal obedience to
precepts. The commandments that are Christ's are such as do
not lend themselves to detailed and exact fulfilment, for they
concern the quality of spiritual life and not defined actions.
We are to 'believe on' Him; we are to love our neighbours as
ourselves, and our fellow-Christians as Christ loved us. These
cannot be obeyed with the same precision as commands to go to
Church or to give a tenth of our income for Church work. The
commands of Christ will nearly always carry these and similar
actions as incidental consequences of the obedience claimed,
but they go beyond anything of this kind.

Having thus drawn out the special tone of the words chosen,
we can return to the more familiar version. *If ye love me, ye
will keep my commandments;* and if we don't, we shan't. Let
no one deceive himself about that. There is no possibility of

meeting His claim upon us, unless we truly love Him. So
devotion is prior to obedience itself. I *cannot* obey unless I love;
and if I am to love, I must be with Him whom I desire to love.
Personal companionship with Christ is the first requirement, as
it was for the disciples in Palestine. If we love Christ, and in
whatsoever degree we love Christ, obedience will follow — not
the external obedience of the slave who does what he is told,
but the gladly given obedience of the friend or the son (xv, 15;
Romans viii, 15) whose desire is to give pleasure.

Our love is cold. It is there, but it is feeble. It does not
carry us to real obedience. Is there anything that I can do?
No; there never is, except to hold myself in His presence; the
initiative remains with God. But the Lord, who knows both
the reality and the poverty of our love, will supply our need.
*I will ask the Father and he will send you, besides, a Comforter
that he may be with you to eternity.*

The sending of the Comforter is due to the Son's request.
Here as always He is the mediator between the Father and men.
His love for His disciples, which is itself the manifestation of
the Father's love for the world (iii, 16; v, 19), becomes the
impulse of the Father's action. But the manifestation of
divine love in the Son had to come first (vii, 39) because this
is what calls forth the new response from our hearts, or (to
put it from the other side) breaks through the hard shell of
selfishness and self-complacency so that the Comforter may
enter.

The familiar translation *another Comforter*, though literal,
is misleading. It implies that the Holy Spirit is what Christ
had been; and while this is true and important and is implied
in 18, it is not implied here. We find the same idiom in *St.
Luke* xxiii, 32, though the actual word used is different; the
literal translation there is, 'And there were led also two other
malefactors with him to be put to death'. The English way of
saying this is, 'two malefactors as well' or 'besides'. The point
here is that the Comforter comes, as the Son came, by mission
from the Father. As the Father sent the Son (a truth perpetually

reiterated) so also He will, at the Son's request, send the Comforter.

The Comforter: it seems best to keep the familiar phrase. The only alternative is to transliterate and say 'the Paraclete'. But this is not an English word, and when it occurs in hymns strikes many as exotic. No translation will do it full justice; the Latinisation — Advocate, has to gain its meaning from the actual use of it in this Gospel as much as Paraclete. It represents one who is called in to stand by — it may be as a witness, or as an adviser, or as an advocate in the legal sense. The word 'Comforter' was used by Wyclif and has remained in subsequent versions. Wyclif certainly understood it as meaning 'strengthener' (*confortator*) rather than 'consoler'; the suggestion is of one who makes us brave and strong by being brave and strong beside us. But to strengthen is the best of all ways to console, for it brings a bracing consolation and not a relaxing sympathy.

That he may be with you for ever. Already begins the preparation of the disciples for the separation which is at hand. Their Lord must *go away* (xvi, 7). It is true that He goes *to the Father* (28) and therefore is for ever available for them (*St. Matthew* xxviii, 20). But the old form of intercourse, so familiar and so dear, will have come to an end. There will be no such interruption in the abiding with them of the Comforter.

The Spirit of truth — the Spirit who is Himself the essence of truth and therefore also the Spirit who imparts or produces truth. The phrase carries both these meanings, and each is in itself a double meaning because of the subjective and objective aspects of truth. Truth, when we speak of knowing it, is the objective reality as it actually is, undistorted and completely apprehended; truth as a quality of the mind is sincerity, which includes positively the desire to apprehend reality completely and accurately, and negatively the absence of conflicting interests which may bias or blur the judgement. The Comforter is the source of both kinds of truth.

This title of the divine Spirit is sometimes specially valued by those who have not accepted the Gospel of the unique manifestation of God in Christ. They wish to follow, perhaps to worship, the *Spirit of truth* without first seeing God in Jesus Christ. They are right to pay all possible reverence to *the Spirit of truth* and some Christians can learn from them in this respect. When controversy arises, some theologians seem more concerned to ask concerning any proposition 'Is it orthodox?' than to ask 'Is it true?' Such need the reminder of Coleridge: 'He, who begins by loving Christianity better than truth, will proceed by loving his own sect or church better than Christianity, and end in loving himself better than all'.[1]

Yet those who follow truth without finding it incarnate in the historical Jesus of Nazareth, cannot claim to be led by that Spirit to whom reference is here made. He is one whom *the world cannot receive, for it observeth him not neither recognises him.* The world — that is, the natural order apart from God — pays no attention to the Spirit, and when it sees Him at work cannot recognise what is happening. It must first have the eyes of the mind opened by the touch of Christ. Certainly many who are not professing Christians are more sensitive to the Spirit of truth than many who are; but that profession is not here in question. *The world* is contrasted with those who have both been companions of Christ and have become His disciples in whom response to the revelation and consequently the power of the Spirit are already discernible: *ye are recognising him, because he abideth with you and shall be in you.* The disciples already have some awareness of the Spirit, who is supremely known as a response to the love of God manifested in Christ, because as a company they have been taking note of His glory (ii, 11), though this has not yet shone forth in its fulness, and till that has happened the Spirit will not be active in all His power (vii, 39). At present it is rather in the apostolic company than in the individual disciples severally that the power is at work — *he abideth with you.* He will later indwell each one

---

[1] *Aids to Reflection: Moral and Religious Aphorisms*, xxv.

— *he shall be in you.* That is the necessary order. We are brought to Christ and received by Him into the fellowship of His Church; in that company we find the Spirit at work; as we are shaped and moulded by His influence thus diffused and exercised, we begin to find it within ourselves; this individual experience of the Spirit is normally subsequent to, and consequent upon, our experience of His activity in the Church or Christian fellowship. The two stages are marked ritually by Baptism and Confirmation.

This coming of the spirit is in a sense a coming of Christ Himself; so the Lord can pass in His teaching from one to the other. For St. John, as we shall see more clearly later, the Day of the Lord's Resurrection is the Day of the Advent of the Spirit. It is not true that the Risen Christ and the Spirit are identified; but it is true that the appearance of the one is the occasion for the full bestowal of the other (xx, 22). That is not at all inconsistent with the record of *Acts* that there was a signal manifestation of the power of the Spirit at the ensuing feast of Pentecost; indeed the picture of a period of 'waiting' after the initial bestowal of the gift, while it worked in the apostolic band like yeast in the dough, till at last it broke forth in a vast release of energy, is psychologically most probable.

Having in mind what happened in that closed room on the evening of the first Easter Day (xx, 22) we need have no difficulty in understanding the close connexion here made between the coming of the Spirit and the coming of Christ. He has spoken of the former, and passes to the latter as something not separable from it. *I will not leave you bereft, I am coming to you.*

The translation 'comfortless' with its apparent connexion with 'the Comforter' has no warrant in the original. The Lord is going away; but, because He is going to the Father, His going is itself His return. So the moment of separation is the occasion of re-union. In English, the present tense has often a future reference; though this is not impossible in Greek, it is unusual. The tense here is a genuine present. The going is the

coming; consequently as He begins to speak of going, He also
says *I am coming to you.* The separation which is imminent
will make Him invisible to the world, which will go its way
ignoring the manifestations of His presence; but all the while
the disciples will be aware of these, and will be taking note of
His continued vitality and therein of the promise of their own
eternal life. *Yet a little while, and the world taketh note of me
no more, but ye take note of me that I live and ye shall live.*

When the disciples come to know their Lord as one 'that
liveth, and was dead, and is alive for evermore', they will also
know Him as one that has 'the keys of Death and of Hades'
(*Revelation* i, 18), so that He can release His own from the grip
of death and be to them a source of life. St. John does not
encourage either the Greek doctrine of immortality nor the
Pharisees' hope of a resurrection apart from God's act in and
through Christ; eternal life is a gift of God in Christ who is
Himself *the Resurrection and the Life* (xi, 25). Our hope of
such life is grounded in the knowledge that He lives.

*In that day ye will recognise that I am in my Father, and ye in
me, and I in you. In that day* — the day of illumination which
the Resurrection would inaugurate. By that illumination we
shall recognise the Lord as truly the Mediator. The words
used are the fullest expression yet given to that thought.
Christ is in the Father; the disciples are in Christ; and Christ
is in them. We have already (11) had the declaration that
Christ is in the Father and the Father in Him. He is therefore
in this double relation of 'within-ness' as regards both the
Father and His disciples.

This truth is vitally connected with that of the life which He
has and which by consequence we hope to have (19); for
knowledge of this truth is itself that life (xvii, 3). And it is
vitally connected with the love for Him which issues in observance of His commandments (21); for the 'within-ness'
asserted is the perfection of love.

*He that hath my commandments and observeth them, he it is
that loveth me.* Love was spoken of as the source of obedience

(15); now obedience is spoken of as the test of love. Our love for Christ, won from us by His love for us, wins love from the Father, and loving self-manifestation from Christ. *He that loveth me shall be loved by my Father, and I will love him and manifest myself to him.* The Father loves all His children with an infinite love, such love as could be expressed only by giving His only-begotten Son. Yet there is a special love also in His heart for those who love that Son. The universal love of God is not a featureless uniformity of good-will. Good-will to all there is; but also for each whatever special quality of love is appropriate to him; and there must be a special quality of love for those who love the Son whom the Father loved *before the foundation of the world* (xvii, 24). The Son Himself, who is the 'express image' of the Father's universal love, has a special quality of love (how could it be otherwise?) for those who love Him in return; and to them He will manifest Himself.

As we read these words of the Incarnate Word, we tend to forget that to His disciples He was first and foremost the Messiah, the inaugurator of the Kingdom of God. For them this made His words bewildering. If they had understood the Parable of the Sower it need not have been so; but though the mystery was given to them (*St. Mark* iv, 11) they still could not understand a Kingdom of God which here and there fails to take root, here and there succeeds for a while, and only here and there bears fruit. The manifestation of the Son of Man, when it comes, must surely be to all the world. *There saith to him Judas, not Iscariot* (we picture the Apostle John dictating to John the Elder and Evangelist, and when he comes to the word 'Judas' the Elder looks up to protest that Judas had gone out; — in answer the words are added *not Iscariot*), *'Lord, what then has happened that thou art about to manifest thyself to us and not to the world?'* *To us:* he claims for the whole band of disciples that they love the Lord, for it is to those who love Him that the promise of the manifestation was given (21). But he is bewildered by the thought of a limited manifestation. How can it be *to us and not to the world*? The

Lord gives no direct answer; the question as framed expresses a purely speculative interest, and to such questions the Lord never gives a direct answer, but always points to the moral and spiritual principle involved. Here that principle is the wonder and intimacy of the fellowship with God that results from love of the Lord Jesus. *Jesus answered and said to him, If any man love me, my word he will observe, and my Father will love him, and we shall come to him and make a resting-place' with him.* The answer recapitulates the teaching, bringing together the connexion between love and obedience (15, 21), the Father's love for those that love the Son (21), and the fact that the Father and the Son are so united that the action of either is the action also of the other (20), so that the 'coming' of Christ (18) is a coming also of the Father: *we shall come.* But to all this addition is made; as Christ prepares a resting-place for us, that where He is, we also may be (3), so here the love of Him prepares in our hearts a resting-place for Him, and not for Him alone but for the Father also. There is no emphasis here on the resting-place as a temporary abode; but there is clear expression of the thought that the Father and the Son come to the disciple to be his guests. This is a thought even more wonderful than the other. That I should somewhere find a place, a little place, prepared for me in the Father's house is wonderful, but my memory of God's love makes it not incredible. But it would be incredible in any other connexion than that of this divine discourse, that the Father and the Son should come to lodge with me.

> This sanctuary of my soul
>   Unwitting I keep white and whole,
> Unlatched and lit, if Thou should'st care
>   To enter or to tarry there.
>
> With parted lips and outstretched hands
>   And listening ears Thy servant stands,
> Call Thou early, call Thou late,
>   To Thy great service dedicate.[1]

[1] Charles Sorley, *Expectans Expectavi.*

> My spirit longs for Thee
>   Within my troubled breast,
> Though I unworthy be
>   Of so divine a Guest.
>
> Of so divine a Guest
>   Unworthy though I be,
> Yet has my heart no rest
>   Unless it comes from Thee.[1]

'Unworthy' indeed; and for that reason the warning must be added. Like all words of divine promise, these are words also of judgement. For we may refuse the promise, and turn away the divine Guests. *He that loveth me not, doth not observe my words; and the word which ye hear is not mine but the Father's who sent me.*

He has led them, and us, to the innermost secret (20) and the ultimate hope (19). That is all that can be done now, apart from some elaboration of the same themes as they make their way to the Garden of Agony ('The Son of Man must suffer') and the exaltation on the Cross. For more than this they must wait for the illumination of the Comforter. *These things have I spoken to you while abiding with you; but the Comforter — the Spirit, the Holy One — whom the Father will send in my name, he will teach you all things and will bring to your remembrance all things which I said to you.*

Here first the Comforter is spoken of as the Holy Spirit, and that solemn title is given in its most formal and emphatic form. It was not an unknown title for the divine Being in His intercourse with man (*Psalm* li, 11; *Isaiah* lxiii, 10). But it was not frequent. Thus it was appropriate as the name for this element within the Godhead which became known through the distinctive Christian experience of relationship to God.

The Holy Spirit is not simply the Creator Spirit as He may be understood apart from Christ, though He is the Creator Spirit. It is only through Christ that we are able to recognise Him (17). The Father sends Him in the Name of the Son; He represents

---

[1] *Byrom.*

K

the Son, and His teaching is that of the Son. But it is not
limited, as the teaching of the Lord is, by an approaching
catastrophe which fixes the end of the period available. He
can continue His teaching till all the ground is covered — *He
will teach you all things.* Especially will He make those days in
Galilee and Jerusalem live again and yield up their secret —
and will bring to your remembrance all things which I said to you;
for He is 'the Spirit of Jesus' (*Acts* xvi, 7).

*

The sacred period in the Upper Room has reached its close.
The Last Supper has been shared, the Eucharist instituted, the
innermost secret declared. It is time for the Lord to start on
that last journey of which He has so often spoken. But first He
will say farewell.

27–31. 'Peace I leave to you, the peace that is mine I give to you. Not as
the world gives do I give to you. Let not your hearts be troubled or dismayed. Ye heard that I said to you "I go away and I come to you". If
ye loved me ye would have rejoiced that I go to the Father, because the
Father is greater than I. And now I have told you before it come to pass,
that when it is come to pass ye may believe. No longer shall I speak
many things to you, for there cometh the prince of the world, and in me
he hath not anything. But that the world may recognise that I love the
Father, and that as the Father commanded me thus I do — arise, let
us go hence.'

Peace. It was the ordinary term of greeting or farewell.
But on the lips of Jesus it meant something special. That
special gift is His bequest; *peace I leave to you, the peace that is
mine I give to you.* He is in the toils of a traitor; His enemies
are gathering to destroy Him; and He speaks of *the peace that
is mine.* It is an inward peace, independent of circumstance,
springing from His union with the Father. This it is which He
bequeathes, and which can be ours by His gift if we will
receive it.

Not as the world giveth do I give to you. How does the world
give? The immediate reference is to the words of salutation,

'I give you peace', which can be no more than a good wish. Christ's bequest of peace is effectual, and actually bestows a permanent possession. Moreover the world gives its best at first and *then that which is worse* (ii, 10), but the 'peace of God' is known to those who receive it as deeper and richer and fuller as years pass and the storms of life assail it.

Since our peace is grounded not in circumstance but in the Lord, we should be free from all dismay. So at the close we return to the keynote which had been struck at the outset (1), but here with an added note as well. *Let not your hearts be troubled or dismayed.* The new phrase recalls the charge given to an earlier Jesus, familiar to us as Joshua, on the eve of conquest (*Joshua* i, 9). So, as the later Joshua enters upon the last struggle of His victorious campaign, wherein He will conquer not only a promised land but *the world* itself (xvi, 33, where peace and victory are combined), He bids His followers be free from perturbation or dismay. The ground of their confidence is to be what He has told them of the goal of His journey. *Ye heard that I said to you, 'I go away and I come to you'. If ye loved me ye would have rejoiced that I go to the Father because the Father is greater than I.* His going and His coming are one thing, because the goal of His journey is the Father; to be with the Father is the fulfilment of His being and that He should go to the Father is the ground of their hope and strength (12). What matters is that they, and we, should believe that He is in the Father and we in Him, and that the mode of this reciprocal inherence is the sacrifice wherein is manifested the love which is itself that perfect union. Therefore He expounds the secret in advance so that the event — so strange to human thinking (*St. Mark* viii, 33) — may not destroy their faith but confirm it. *Now I have told you before it come to pass, that when it is come to pass ye may believe...*

There is not much opportunity left for teaching. The world will soon break in upon the companionship of the little band of friends, and there is nothing in common between the worldly principle and the Lord. The force of all that makes *the world* what it is as a kingdom or system not of God will be put forth against Him in sheer antagonism; that will be the opportunity for the supreme proof that He loves the Father and perfectly obeys Him, a proof that must be given in action, not in word. *No longer shall I speak many things to you, for there cometh the prince of the world, and in me he hath not anything. But that the world may recognise that I love the Father, and that, as the Father commanded me, thus I do — arise, let us go hence.*

So they leave the Upper Room and start to walk across the Temple Courts towards Kidron and Gethsemane.

IN THE TEMPLE COURT

Chapters XV, XVI, XVII

In the lighted Upper Room there had been some traces of conversation, and not only continuous discourse. Simon Peter (xiii, 36–38), Thomas (xiv, 5), Philip (xiv, 8), Jude (xiv, 22) are mentioned by name as breaking in with questions or comments. But as the little company moves in the darkness of the night through the city and across the Temple Court no individual disciple intervenes. So far as any speak besides the Lord it is *some of his disciples* (xvi, 17) or *his disciples* (xvi, 29) — a group murmuring their awestruck wonder or assurance.

The first subject of discourse is that union of the disciples with their Lord of which He had spoken earlier (xiv, 20). He now describes it as a living union (xv, 1–10), and goes on to speak of its results, first in the relation of the disciples to their Lord (xv, 11–17), then in the relations of the disciples to the world (xv, 18–xvi, 4). This leads Him to speak more precisely of His departure and the Coming of the Comforter (xvi, 5–7), of the Comforter and the world (xvi, 8–11), of the Comforter and the disciples (xvi, 12–15), of sorrow turned to joy (xvi, 16–22), of prayer and its answer (xvi, 23–27), of divine triumph (xvi, 28–33).

We picture the Lord and His disciples leaving the Upper Room with minds full of what had there been done and said. They walk for a time in silence through the dark street, and enter the Temple Court. There in front of them, glinting in the light of the full moon, was the great Golden Vine that trailed over the Temple porch, the type of the life of Israel entwined about the sanctuary of God. How frequent that image of the the vine or the vineyard had been! It is enough to recall the 'song of my well-beloved touching his vineyard' (*Isaiah* v, 1–7)

or the Psalm about the vine which the Lord brought out of
Egypt (*Psalm* lxxx, 8–16). Here is that vine in symbol; as they
look at it the Lord begins to speak with a gentle smile on His
lips and hand pointing to the golden vine — *I am the vine, the
true vine.*

CHAPTER XV

THE LIVING UNION OF THE LORD AND HIS DISCIPLES

1-10. 'I am the vine, the true vine, and my Father is the husbandman. Every branch in me not bearing fruit — he taketh it away; and every branch bearing its fruit — he cleanseth it, that it may bear more fruit. Already ye are clean because of the word which I have spoken to you. Abide in me and I in you. As the branch cannot bear fruit from itself unless it abide in the vine, so neither can ye unless in me ye abide. I am the vine, ye are the branches. He that abideth in me and I in him, he it is that beareth fruit in abundance, because apart from me ye can do nothing. If a man abide not in me, he was cast outside as the branch and was withered; and they gather them and into the fire they cast them and they are burned. If ye abide in me and my sayings abide in you, ask whatsoever ye will and it shall come to pass for you — (In this was glorified my Father — your bearing fruit in abundance) — and ye shall become my disciples. As the Father loved me, I also loved you; abide in the love that is mine. If ye observe my commandments, ye will abide in my love, as I have observed my Father's commandments and abide in his love.'

I am the Vine, the true Vine. The vine was a recognised symbol of Israel. But it was employed to represent, as it does in the two passages cited above, Israel's failure. The *true vine* stands for what Israel was called to be. Thus the Lord here proclaims that the purpose of God entrusted to Israel is in fact being fulfilled in Himself. He is the true Israel, the faithful Remnant. He is in His own Person the whole People of God. Though the image was familiar, and its implication is startling, yet it has other special suggestions which are here most appropriate; for the vine lives to give its life-blood. Its flower is small, its fruit abundant; and when that fruit is mature and the vine has for a moment become glorious, the treasure of the grapes is torn down and the vine is cut back to the stem. . . .

and next year blooms again,
Not bitter for the torment undergone,
Not barren for the fulness yielded up.

.   .   .   .   .   .

The Living Vine, Christ chose it for Himself:—
God gave to man for use and sustenance
Corn, wine, and oil, and each of these is good:
And Christ is Bread of Life and Light of Life.
But yet He did not choose the summer corn,
That shoots up straight and free in one quick growth,
And has its day, and is done, and springs no more:
Nor yet the olive, all whose boughs are spread
In the soft air, and never lose a leaf,
Flowering and fruitful in perpetual peace;
But only this for Him and His in one —
The everlasting, everquickening Vine,
That gives the heat and passion of the world
Through its own life-blood, still renewed and shed.[1]

Those who heard the Lord speak had lately been in the
Upper Room when He handed to them the Cup of Blessing,
saying it was His Blood of the New Covenant, and that He
would not 'drink of this fruit of the Vine', till the Kingdom
of God should be come (*St. Luke* xxii, 16). Those who transfer
this chapter and the next to the middle of Chapter XIII find
in that Cup the immediate occasion of this saying. We find its
occasion in the Golden Vine on the porch of the Temple; but
the mysterious words so lately spoken must have been vividly
present to the disciples' mind, and they must recognise that
He is here explaining what so lately He did and said in the
Upper Room.

From the dawn of history, even from that twilight where
history, legend and myth are inextricably intermingled, there
had been a Community conscious of divine commission. Its
origin is recorded in the Call of Abraham, in whom all families
of the earth should be blessed (*Genesis* xii, 1–3). If this story
represents rather a tribal migration than an individual adventure, as some scholars think, that sharpens the point of our

[1] Mrs. Hamilton King, *The Disciples*.

contention. When history begins, the commissioned community already exists. We trace God's dealings with it as seen and interpreted by Prophets, with their deepening insight into the divine character and purpose. This shows them that the whole People is incapable of making that perfect response which the divine righteousness demands, and that the divine purpose can find fulfilment only in a Remnant. Then even this hope proves too high, and in the culminating intuition of the Old Testament an unknown Prophet perceives that the perfect response will be given and the divine purpose fulfilled by one individual, in whom the whole significance of Israel will be concentrated (*Isaiah* liii). So it came to pass. The Vine that was brought out of Egypt (*Psalm* lxxx, 8; *St. Matthew* ii, 15) is Jesus Himself, *the true vine*. But because He is not merely one of the sons of Abraham, but Himself *before Abraham* (viii, 58) and *one* with *the Father* (x, 30), He is able to incorporate us into Himself so that we become His branches. The Tree that was planted on Calvary has shoots going out into all the world. By perfectly fulfilling the mission of Israel He released it from national limitations, so that from the Cross and Resurrection onwards the Chosen People is the community of those whose hearts have received the divine Word spoken in Him; from that time the Chosen People is the One Man in Christ Jesus (i, 12; *Galatians* iii, 26–28). For His life is offered that it may flow in our veins, that 'fruit of the vine' which is the Blood of the New Covenant (*St. Mark* xiv, 24, 25), the love which has conquered death. (Let us here recall vi, 52–58, and the thoughts which it suggested — pp. 91–93.)

My Father is the husbandman. As He was sent by the Father, so the Father has care for Him at all times (xi, 42); but the thought passes at once to the activity in which this care is shown, and which concerns not the Lord in His own Person but His disciples.

Every branch in me not bearing fruit — he taketh it away. The construction requires a pause after the word *fruit*. The possibility of a barren branch is real. The fact that we are 'in

Christ' does not make us sinless, as St. Paul recognised with vividness and perplexity. We may have been made 'members of Christ' in Baptism and yet show no 'fruit of the Spirit'. That is not so terrible a thought where Baptism is administered in infancy; for however difficult that practice is to justify, and we ought to recognise that the justification though abundant is not evident, at least it alleviates the problem of post-baptismal faithlessness. But we are not here concerned with questions of ecclesiastical administration, even the most solemn. There is a profound 'mystery of iniquity' here. It is possible to be genuinely drawn to the Lord, to follow His call, to be of His company, and still to bear no fruit. It is possible for a man to betray Him *being one of the Twelve* (vi, 71). When the Lord spoke of Himself as the Bread of Life, Judas was repelled. Before He spoke of Himself as the Vine whose 'fruit' is to become our lifeblood, Judas had been removed. He was in the Vine, 'in Christ', a branch not bearing fruit; and the Father had taken him away.

Did he not go of his own will, when he went out into the night? Yes, certainly; but that action was no more of his own will than is the action of any who comes to the Lord. Yet this is due to the drawing of the Father (vi, 44). For the action of God is through our wills, and does not override them. He draws us by His love; and men are never so free as when they act from the love in their hearts which love shown to them has called forth. If, then, I come by my own will yet because the Father draws me, so also it is the Father who is taking me away if I depart by my own will. He offers me the love divine; it draws me or repels me, according to the condition of my will. It had repelled Judas: *after the sop, then entered into him Satan* (xiii, 27). His going was an act of defiance on his part; it was an act of condemnation and execution on the part of God. This is the thought of judgement everywhere presented in this Gospel.

We are in the Vine. Are we bearing fruit? No amount of ascetic discipline or devotional fervour is a substitute for the practical obedience which alone is 'fruit'. That obedience however is not a matter of 'works', though these will follow from it, and if they are lacking, there is no 'fruit'. Obedience is to God's command; 'and this is his commandment, that we should believe the name of his Son Jesus Christ, and love one another even as he gave us commandment' (*I John* iii, 23). If we really 'believe the name', that is accept as true the divine word spoken in Him, and accept as indeed the revelation of God what we see in Him, and if we truly 'love one another', the works will follow without fail. Are we bearing fruit? Or are we ready for nothing but to be taken away by the husbandman?

Even if we are bearing fruit, there is no ground for contentment; there is still need for the pruning knife of the husbandman: *every branch bearing its fruit — he cleanseth it, that it may bear more fruit*. That cleansing may be painful. It is almost bound to be. But the pain can be the condition of more abundant fruit.

Pain, considered in isolation, is, no doubt, an evil. But we easily misconceive the problem of pain, as it presents itself to a Christian mind. The world, starting from a crude notion of justice as consisting in a correlation of pain and guilt, as though so much pain could be regarded as wiping out so much guilt, is bewildered by the suffering of the innocent. The Christian has no interest in solving the problem as thus stated; he must begin by formulating it afresh. For the evil of sin is so great that no amount of pain could ever be regarded as a counter-weight. Of course it is not meant that it is better virtuously to tell the truth and so facilitate a murder than to prevent a murder by telling a lie; but that is because lying with that object is not sin. Sin is the setting by man of his will against God's — consciously (when guilt is also involved) or unconsciously. This is the essential evil; no pain is comparable to it. Consequently, in a world which sin has once entered, no amount of pain can redress the balance and vindicate the justice of the world's order. The problem as stated above

arises, not from the facts, but from a bad notion of justice.
Pain is in fact evil only in a secondary sense; it is something
which, other things being equal, it is right to avoid. But it
must always be chosen in preference to moral evil, such as
treachery or cruelty; and when it is bravely borne, it has such
an effect that we could not wish it away. From a Christian
standpoint, the suffering of the innocent is not so great a
problem as the suffering of the guilty, or at least very much of
it. It is noticeable in war that the suffering of the trenches
refines still further the finer natures and brutalises still further
the coarser natures. The attachment of mere suffering to
crimes may perhaps deter the potential criminal; it seldom
reforms the actual criminal. It is harder to see the justification
in the eyes of a righteous God of pain which degrades the
sufferer, however guilty he may be, than of pain which en-
nobles the sufferer, however innocent he may be.

It is of ennobling pain that we are thinking here. If we have
any ground to hope that we are numbered among the branches
which bear fruit, we can welcome every kind of pain that comes
to us, knowing that it is capable of rendering us able to *bear
more fruit.*

We can make that claim; for the word of Christ is in our
ears; and this is what makes 'clean' for the bearing of fruit.
*Already ye are clean, because of the word which I have spoken
to you.* When He said to Peter *Ye are clean* (xiii, 10), He had
not given the ground for that assertion. Now it is plainly
stated. The disciples of the Lord are *clean* because they are
disciples, hearing His word — the utterance of Him who is the
self-utterance of God. But this does not mean either that they
are already perfect, or that there is no danger of contamination.
The quality of life which springs from discipleship must be
maintained and deepened by fellowship with the Lord. So we
are led to the words which gather up the whole meaning of
what it is to be a Christian.

Abide in me, and I in you. The whole phrase has an impera-
tive tone: let there be mutual indwelling. Of course the com-

mand is to the disciple, not to the Lord. *Abide in me,* of which
the consequence will be that I shall abide in you; yet the two
are not presented as occasion and consequence, but as a two-
fold condition which we are bidden to bring into existence.

All forms of Christian worship, all forms of Christian discipline, have this as their object. Whatever leads to this is
good; whatever hinders this is bad; whatever does not bear
on this is futile. This is the life of the Christian: *Abide in me
and I in you.* All truth and depth of devotion, all effectiveness
in service spring from this. It is not a theme for words but for
the deeper apprehensions of silence: *Abide in me and I in you.*

*As the branch cannot bear fruit from itself unless it abide in
the vine, so neither can ye unless in me ye abide. From itself* —
as He has used the expression *from myself* (v, 30; vii, 17) in
order to repudiate the thought that He is Himself the origin
of His words and actions, so here He says of the disciple, who
is a branch of the vine, that the source of his fruitfulness is not
in himself the branch, but in the vine of which he is one part.
The disciple makes no claim to originality; his one aim is to
let the life of the Lord, in whom he abides, and who abides in
him, find expression through him. The subtle alteration in the
order of words in the two parallel phrases emphasises the utter
completeness of our dependence, which will be still more
starkly expressed in the next verse.

I am the Vine. Here is the last of the sevenfold declarations
of His Person, beginning with the words of the Divine Name,
I AM; and it sums up all the rest. He is Himself the fellowship in which eternal life is found, and that life is His life.

I am the Vine, ye the branches. He does not say that He is
the stem and we the branches, though He, and none other, is
the stem. So when St. Paul uses the parable of the body, sometimes Christ is the whole Body (*I Corinthians* xii, 12, 27) and
sometimes the Head (*Ephesians* iv, 15). No other is the stem
of the Vine; no other is the Head of the Body. Yet it does
not express the whole relation of the Lord to His disciples to
say that He is the stem and they the branches, or that He is the

Head and they the limbs. He is the whole Vine, the whole
Body, and we, as branches or limbs, are 'very members incorporate' in Him.

This language cannot be used concerning the relation of any
human leader to his followers without such exaggeration as to
be ludicrous. It can only be appropriate if He of whom it is
used is that infinite Spirit 'in whom we live and move and have
our being'. The tone of the discourse is here tender and intimate, not (as in Chapter VIII) severe and judicial; but the
claim made by Christ concerning His own status is as great.
We find the same transition from the claim 'All things have
been delivered unto me of my Father' to the invitation 'Come
unto me . . . and I will give you rest', where the invitation is
justified only if the claim is true (*St. Matthew* xi, 27 and 28).

*He that abideth in me and I in him — he it is that beareth
fruit in abundance.* Here is the answer to our question 'How?'
when we hear the precept 'make the tree good' (*St. Matthew*
xii, 33). Our discipline is not a bracing of our wills to conformity with a law; it is the maintenance of communion with
the Lord to the point of mutual indwelling. This so purifies
the heart that at last there is no need for any deliberate control
of desire, because desire itself is sanctified. But though our
discipline is not conformity with a code, it is obedience to a
commandment; for 'this is his commandment, that we should
believe the name of his Son Jesus Christ and love one another,
even as he gave us commandment' (*I John* iii, 23). The commandment is not primarily to 'do' this or that, but to trust and
to love, as appears very plainly in verses 8 to 12, to which we
are coming.

Apart from me ye can do nothing. 'Works done before the
grace of Christ and the Inspiration of His Spirit are not pleasant
to God, forasmuch as they spring not of faith in Jesus Christ,
neither do they make men meet to receive grace or (as the
School authors say) deserve grace of congruity: yea rather, for
that they are not done as God hath willed and commanded
them to be done, we doubt not but they have the nature of sin.'

Article XIII states the matter in the unsympathetic tone born of theological controversy; but what it says is true. 'The nature of sin' is self-centredness — the putting of self in the centre where God alone should be. We are all born doing this; that is Original Sin. From this condition there may be partial deliverance through devotion to scientific truth or artistic beauty or patriotic loyalty. But such deliverance is only partial. In all my strivings to attain some ideal or perform some service, unless my heart and will are wholly captivated, there will be some self-assertion, and probably a great deal. That is why the consciously virtuous person is disagreeable. It is not virtue that can save the world or any one in it, but love. And love is not at our command. We cannot generate it from within ourselves. We can win it only by surrender to it. The 'strong man armed' of our self-complacency is secure until the 'stronger than he' cometh (*St. Luke* xi, 21 and 22). There will be no full surrender except to the perfect manifestation of perfect love, that is to say to Jesus Christ come in the flesh. But He makes Himself known in fact in other ways besides His incarnate life; so far as it is to the Divine Self-Utterance or Word in truth or beauty or goodness that men open their hearts, their works are done through 'the grace of Jesus Christ and the Inspiration of His Spirit'. That may be a real surrender, but not complete; therefore those works, while not mere sins, yet have some of 'the nature of sin' about them.

We cannot too strongly or harshly drive this truth into our souls, however eager we may be to trace 'the grace of Jesus Christ' in others, even in atheists. Apart from Him, I can do nothing. All fruit that I ever bear or can bear comes wholly from His life within me. No particle of it is mine as distinct from His. There is, no doubt, some part of His whole purpose that He would accomplish through me; that is my work, my fruit, in the sense that I, and not another, am the channel of His life for this end; but in no other sense. Whatever has its ultimate origin in myself is sin: 'O God, forasmuch as without

thee we are not able to please thee, mercifully grant that thy
Holy Spirit may in all things direct and rule our hearts, through
Jesus Christ our Lord'.

*If a man abide not in me, he was cast outside as the branch,
and was withered; and they gather them and into the fire they
cast them and they are burned.* The violent change of tense —
an idiom that cannot be reproduced in good English but which
is repeated in this translation for the challenge which it offers
— indicates the fact that the penalty and the severance from
Christ are simultaneous, for indeed they are identical. It is
not said that if we do not abide in Christ we shall subsequently
or ultimately be cast out of the vineyard on to the fire; what
is said is that our failure to abide in Him is, there and then, that
rejection and destruction. As the labourers gather the branches
that are broken off and dried up, and toss them out to be burnt,
so is already the lot of any disciple who fails to abide in his
Lord. The devout Jews who heard the words were familiar
with the passage which suggested them. Ezekiel had pointed
out that the wood of the vine is useless, and is 'given to the
fire for fuel'. As a channel for the life of the vine, the branch
has use and bears fruit; separated from the vine it is worthless:
'shall wood be taken thereof to make any work? or will men
take a pin of it to hang any vessel thereon?' (*Ezekiel* xv, 2–4).
So useless is the disciple who has become severed from his
Lord.

It need not be so. *If ye abide in me and my sayings abide in
you, ask whatsoever ye will and it shall come to pass for you —
and ye shall become my disciples.* He had already said *If ye
ask anything in my name, I will do it* (xiv, 13 and 14). To ask
in His name is to ask as His representative, or in other words,
according to His will. We acknowledge Him as the source of
the blessing, so that its bestowal will bind us more closely to
Him, not make us forgetful of Him; and as what is asked is
what He already desires to give, the gift follows upon the fulfilment of this condition. Here we are taught how the condition
may be fulfilled. How can I, in practice, ask in Christ's name

or as His representative? Only if I am abiding in Him and His *sayings* abide in me. It is through His sayings that this mutual indwelling is effected. We do well to remember that our Lord is much more than a teacher. But a teacher He is; and it is through His teaching that our minds receive His mind so that we may become one with Him and He with us. In one sense this is itself the culmination and fruit of discipleship; it is so, if the mutual indwelling is complete. That perfection is not reached on earth, and the reward of discipleship is to become more fully disciples, as we receive *of his fulness* and *grace for grace* (i, 16).

Inserted into this sequence of thought is a parenthesis, lest we should for a moment suppose that it is possible to ask in Christ's name for the satisfaction of our own desires; all that we can ask in His name is that we may really do His will and bear fruit for the Lord of the vineyard. We ask whatsoever we will; but being in Christ our will must be for the glory of God and the accomplishment of His purpose. Therefore the coming to pass of what we ask is the glorification of God and the bearing of abundant fruit; *It shall come to pass for you: in this was glorified my Father, your bearing fruit in abundance.* Our fruitfulness is due to God's activity released or called forth by our prayer.

Here we have a searching test of our prayer-life. Is it fruitful — in the effectiveness of our intercessions or our own growth in grace? If not, it is because we are not praying in His name; and that, again, is because we are not abiding in Him nor His sayings in us. If we really so abide, we shall not only desire His will to be done rather than what would have been our own, but we shall know what it is. So often we get far enough to prefer His will to ours in principle; but we are not in communion with Him close enough to avoid insisting upon our judgement of what His will must be — like Peter at Caesarea Philippi or at the feet-washing. We will follow Him. . . . But surely He does not mean to go that way. . . . It leads to certain failure. It leads to a Cross.

There is a most subtle danger of a revival of selfwill in the
very act of surrendering it. The only safeguard is to abide in
Him in still closer communion, still deeper love — love like
His.

As the Father loved me I also loved you. Again we find the
doctrine of mediation, but for the first time in terms of love.
It is a perfect love that has been given to us; it is nothing less
than the love which unites the Father and the Son in the very
Godhead itself, and which is the Holy Spirit. This perfect love
is 'bestowed upon us' through Christ. *Abide in the love that is
mine.* The words mean much more than 'continue in the
shelter of my love for you' (Bernard). The divine love, which
is the Holy Ghost, is much more than a sheltering protection;
rather it is a pervasive atmosphere in which we may dwell,
and which we may breathe, so that it becomes the breath of our
lives (cf. xx, 22). We are to let that love wrap us about, en-
folding us in its embrace. How do we do this? *If ye observe
my commandments, ye will abide in my love, as I have observed
my Father's commandments and abide in his love.* We hold
ourselves in that love by obedience; and the love is the power
in which we obey. He had said *If ye love me, ye will observe my
commandments* (xiv, 15); now He says *If ye observe my commandments, ye will abide in my love.* Love and obedience are
two parts of one relationship — the relationship of creature to
Creator, of child to Father, of sinner to Redeemer. Is my
obedience defective? — let me kindle my love by communion
with the Lord. Is my love feeble? Let me deepen communion
by deliberate obedience. But what kind of obedience is it?
Are we to 'do' this, and avoid 'doing' that? No; that is the
way of the law and its works. Our obedience is to the commandments of the Lord, which are — to trust God and to love
Him (12; cf. vi, 29; xiii, 34; *I John* iii, 23).

The pattern once again is the perfect love within the Being
of God, not this time the love of the Father for the Son, but
the perfect obedience of the Son to the Father and the love
which is in that obedience expressed and actualised. The

divine perfection is our model and standard; and all that falls
short of it is sin (*St. Matthew* v, 45 and 48; *Romans* iii, 23).

*

THE RELATION OF THE DISCIPLES TO THE LORD

11–17. 'These things have I spoken unto you that the joy which is mine
may be in you and that your joy may be fulfilled. This is the commandment which is mine, that ye love one another as I loved you. Greater
love than this hath no man, that a man lay down his life on behalf of his
friends. Ye are my friends, if ye do what I command you. No longer
do I call you slaves; for the slave knoweth not what his lord doeth; but
you I have called friends, because all things which I heard from my
Father, I made known to you. Not you chose me, but I chose you, and
appointed you that ye may go your ways and bear fruit, and that your
fruit may abide, that whatsoever ye ask the Father in my name, he may
give it you. These things I command you, that ye love one another.'

The joy that is mine: the joy of unbroken communion with
the Father; the joy of a world by Him redeemed from selfishness and mutual destruction to love and abundant life; the
'joy that was set before him' (*Hebrews* xii, 2). The promise
and hope is not only that we may be joyful as our Master is
joyful — (my joy) — but that joy of the same substance and
quality as His — *the joy which is mine* — may be in us.

Evidently that joy is no external happiness, nor can it be
produced by any circumstances. It is a state of the soul. It is
the condition of the soul that is filled with love, as joy comes
next to love in the fruitage of the Spirit (*Galatians* v, 22.
N.B.: that catalogue of graces is not a list of 'fruits of the
Spirit' but an articulation of the one and indivisible 'fruit of
the Spirit' which is the surrender of the soul to God under the
impulse of His revealed love). The joy which is Christ's can
only be known by those who, with Him, are obedient to the
divine command and responsive to the divine teaching. So
He gives His command and His teaching in order that the joy
which is His may be in us.

It is no alien gift; it is the completion of our own and our only true joy — *and that your joy may be fulfilled.* For we too were made in the image of God, who is Love. That image in us is distorted and defaced; for we are self-centred and not perfect in love. Yet we can 'reflect as a mirror the glory of the Lord' (*II Corinthians* iii, 18); and He who is the 'express image' of God's substance (*Hebrews* i, 3) is that image which we were created to bear. This call, against which our self-centredness rebels, is the call to be our real selves. The call to the pain of self-sacrifice is also, and more deeply, the call to the fulfilment of our joy.

Corresponding to *the joy which is mine* is *the commandment which is mine.* All His commands are gathered up in this. It had been given before (xiii, 34) in close association with His self-offering to death, when He let the traitor go and thereafter in symbol broke His Body and gave to the disciples His Blood, that is to say His life offered in sacrifice. Now He repeats it with the same reference — *that ye love one another as I loved you.* The words which follow show that His love is to be measured by His death. Love such as that, love to the point of sacrifice even of life, is to be the bond between His disciples. This is not a command to all the world, as will appear very soon (18); nor is it a command concerning the relation of Christians to non-Christians. It is the command to the Christian fellowship. That fellowship owes its existence and quality to the love of Christ. He has drawn us, each one, to Himself; our discipleship is His doing, not ours (16); in the fellowship which we have, each one, with Him we are in fellowship with one another; and this latter fellowship must be the sphere or arena of a love such as created it. The life of the Vine must be in the branches, making of them all a single organism; the Spirit of Christ must be in the members, making them all one body, and that body His.

Do we feel such a bond with our fellow-Christians? Is our fellowship in Christ a reality more profound and effective than our membership of our earthly fellowships — family, school, party, class, nation, race — and able in consequence to unite us in love across all natural divisions and hostilities? Of course not. And the reason is that we do not truly abide in Him. If we did, His life of sacrificial love would flow through us all and unite us in the most intimate bonds. What is called the Oecumenical Movement[1] represents a dawning consciousness of this truth.

That this mutual love of Christians, reproducing their Lord's love for them, is to be measured by His death is now made perfectly clear. *Greater love than this hath no man, that a man lay down his life on behalf of his friends.* Some have said, is it not greater love to die for enemies than for friends? But this overstresses the word *friends*. It does not here represent those who love Him but those whom He loves; the saying declares that love has no more complete expression than death on behalf of those to whom it is directed; the distinction between those who return that love and those who do not does not arise. Love unto death is a complete self-giving; that is what Christ endured for His disciples; that is what Christians must be ready to endure for their fellow-Christians.

Yet that love demands and deserves response. When Christ died, it was for those whom He loved; the supreme wonder is that it was for those who did not (as yet) love Him. 'God commendeth his own love toward us, in that, while we were yet sinners, Christ died for us' (*Romans* v, 8). But though as objects of His love sinners are truly called His friends, yet they are not all that this name should mean while they are content to remain sinners; if they are to be real friends they must obey the commands: *Ye are my friends if ye do what I command you.* So once more love and obedience are brought together as in xiv, 15 and 21 and xv, 10. But now we learn something more about the quality of our obedience.

---

[1] This is the name given to the various enterprises in which the several Churches are invited to co-operate, and for the most part do co-operate, with the one great exception of the Church of Rome. The two chief enterprises of this sort are the Faith and Order Movement and the Life and Work Movement. Both of these held Conferences — at Edinburgh and Oxford respectively — in Great Britain in 1937. One result of these is an attempt to establish a ' World Council of Churches '.

The use of the word *friends* has carried the thought on from the relation of the disciples to one another to their relation with their Lord, in which their relation to one another is grounded. *No longer do I call you slaves, for the slave knoweth not what his lord doeth; but you I have called friends, because all things which I heard from my Father, I made known to you.* To St. Paul this seemed to be the very essence of the transition from the Pharisaic Judaism in which he was brought up to faith in God through Jesus Christ: 'Ye received not the spirit of slavery again unto fear; but ye received the spirit of adoption whereby we cry Abba, Father' (*Romans* viii, 15). What is the spirit of slavery? The slave, who is only a slave, and not also a friend as some slaves were, has his orders and obeys them, perhaps hoping for reward if he does this well, certainly fearing punishment if he does it ill or not at all. He does not care for the feelings of his master. His only concern is what his master may do to him. Such seems to St. Paul, looking back, to have been his state as a Pharisee. (No doubt like all persons who have suffered sudden conversion he exaggerates the remoteness of his former from his latter state; we may be quite sure that Saul of Tarsus had some quite real love of God in his heart.) But the disclosure, in the life and death of Jesus, of what God's love for us really is had won from him a response which makes him feel no longer like a slave before his master but like a child before his father. He no longer thinks — 'this is the command of God which I must obey', but — 'this is God my Father whom I wish to please'. The difference is made by the completeness with which the mind and heart of the Father are disclosed to us in Christ — *all things which I heard from my Father I made known to you.* We are taken into confidence; we are enabled to understand; and what we understand is a wisdom and a love to which we long to trust ourselves in overflowing gratitude and whole-hearted surrender.

Our action is all response; all initiative is with the Lord: *Not ye chose me, but I chose you.* That is fundamental. 'Herein is love, not that we loved God, but that he loved us' (*I John* iv, 10). Those of us who were baptised as infants are without excuse if we forget this. Our being Christians is no doing of ours, any more than our being civilised; it is something done to us and for us, not by us, though we have to make appropriate response in the form of obedience prompted by love.

I chose you and appointed you that ye may go your ways and bear fruit and that your fruit may abide. We were chosen first and foremost for fellowship with Christ — 'that they might be with him' (*St. Mark* iii, 14); that is our first duty, to abide in Him. But He chose us also to send us forth as His witnesses — 'and that he might send them forth to make the proclamation' (*St. Mark, ibid.*). The word which I have translated *go your ways* is that which at the end of the story of the raising of Lazarus I translated (with Bernard) *go home* (xi, 44). It suggests going about one's business, whatever that may be. It is in doing that that we are to *bear fruit*, fruit that will abide. A real Christian, who abides in Christ and Christ in him, exerts an influence among his companions at work or play, in mine or shop or factory or directors' meeting or Parliament, that nothing effaces. But there is more still than this. Such a man becomes a channel through whom the love of God may flow in blessing wheresoever he directs his attention — *and that whatsoever ye ask the Father in my name, he may give it you.* The range of a Christian's fruitful activity is far greater through his prayer, that is the direction of his will, surrendered as it is to God, than through his conduct or direct influence. This is true so far, and only so far, as he prays *in the name* of Christ — that is (as we saw) as His representative; and this we can do only if we abide in Him and His sayings abide in us (7).

Those who do this are a family united in a love which flows through them all, a community of love. So once more the summary is given: *These things I command you, that ye (may) love one another.* To insert that word *may* is to exaggerate the suggestion of purpose and consequence; yet that suggestion is there. Mutual love is the content of the command; it is also the result of obeying it. For the command is also *Abide in me.*

Abide in me; Love one another: these are not two things, but one thing with two aspects, whereof the former is the occasion of the latter. To do this is veritably to participate in the Holy Communion.

*

The Relation of the Disciples to the World

xv, 18–xvi, 4. 'If the world hate you, recognise that it hath hated me before you. If ye were from the world, the world would love its own. But because ye are not from the world, but I chose you out from the world, therefore the world hateth you. Be mindful of the word which I said to you "The slave is not greater than his lord". If they persecuted me, you also will they persecute; if they observed my word, yours also will they observe. But all these things they will do to you for my Name's sake, because they know not him that sent me. If I had not come and spoken to them, they would not have had sin; but as it is they have no excuse for their sin. He that hateth me hateth my Father also. If I had not done among them works which no one else did, they would not have had sin; but as it is they have both seen and hated both me and my Father. But that the word written in their law may be fulfilled — They hated me without cause. When the Comforter cometh, whom I will send to you from the Father, the Spirit of Truth who proceedeth from the Father, he shall bear witness concerning me; and ye also bear witness because from the beginning ye are with me. These things have I spoken to you that ye be not overthrown. They will excommunicate you; indeed there cometh an hour when whosoever killeth you will think he offers worship to God. And these things will they do because they did not recognise the Father nor me. But these things have I spoken to you that, when their hour cometh, ye may be mindful of them, that I myself told you.'

If the world hate you. They would soon know whether it did or not. That heathen world was bound to hate the infant Church which stood for principles so radically opposed to its own. We live in a country where for many generations the Gospel and the faith which it calls forth have influenced the lives and thoughts of men. It is possible that even complete loyalty to Christ would not win its hatred; and certainly we must not suppose that in such a country ecclesiastical persons or assemblies are more sure to be true to the principles of Christ than are secular persons and assemblies discharging their proper responsibilities. Yet that disciple or that Church, which finds that all men speak well of him or of it, has cause for anxiety. 'The kingdom of this world' is not yet become 'the kingdom of our Lord and of his Christ' (*Revelation* xi, 15) even in lands called Christian. The true disciple still offers to the world a challenge, which it will take up if his faithfulness is active. Not all that the world hates is good Christianity; but it does hate good Christianity and always will.

That hatred of the world is hard to face. The world is the most dangerous of the three great enemies. In our conflict with the flesh and the devil the world itself in a civilised country gives us some support. But against the world we must stand alone with our fellow-Christians. If we waver, it must steady us to *recognise* that the world hated our Master before us. It is natural rather than strange that we should stand where He stood, if we *abide in* Him; and that sets us on the other side of a strongly marked dividing line running between us and the world.

If ye were from the world, the world would love its own. It is a question of affinity or the lack of it — not of reasoned attachment or alienation. *From the world;* the phrase suggests a character due to origin (cf. viii, 23). Are we not from the world? Is not that our origin, and do not our characters correspond? Yes — far too largely. But that is not the distinctive and most fundamental fact about us if we are disciples at all. *Because ye are not from the world, but I chose you out from the world:* the phrase *from the world* is repeated, but with a difference. Coupled with the verb *chose out* it no longer represents origin and growth in congruity with that origin, but a place of departure and consequent separation. This is, in part, the occasion of the hate which the world feels. It would not hate angels for being angelic; but it does hate men for being Christians. It grudges them their new character; it is tormented by their peace; it is infuriated by their joy. They belong to it

by nature; and they have found in a place where 'no sane
man'[1] would look for it exactly what the world vainly desires;
they must be impostors and deceivers (vii, 12; cf. *II Corinthians* vi, 8). The world, with its serious work to do, has no
patience with such charlatans. So we must *be mindful* of His
saying (xiii, 16) '*The slave is not greater than his lord*'. When
spoken earlier it had conveyed an exhortation to aim at a
humility corresponding to that of the Lord who washed His
disciples' feet; here it conveys a warning to expect and accept
from the world no better treatment than it gave to their Lord
— *If they persecuted me, you also will they persecute.* But there
is comfort too in the obverse of this — *If they observed my
word, yours also will they observe.* In any case, whatever befalls
the disciple comes upon him because, and in so far as, he is the
representative of his Master: *all these things they will do to you
for my Name's sake, because they know not him that sent me.*
The disciple represents Christ: Christ represents the Father. If
the world could understand that the mission of Christ is divine,
it would not persecute His representatives. The word *know* is
that which stands for scientific knowledge or accurate information, not that which stands for personal acquaintance; *they
know not him that sent me* therefore means 'they know not
that I came forth from the Father' (see xvi, 28). To recognise
this, for almost any reason, is the first stage of Christian faith;
for it leads to reverent attention to the Lord and thus at length
to that recognition of Him (xiv, 9) which culminates in the
vision of the Father in and through Him, and thus again to true
knowledge of the Father Himself which is eternal life (xvii,
3 — where the word for *know* is that signifying personal
acquaintance).

The coming of the Lord, of which the purpose is always and
only to save men from sin, has the inevitable result of revealing
their sin, and even intensifying it if they refuse to be won from
it. *If I had not come and spoken to them, they would not have
had sin, but as it is they have no excuse for their sin.* The teaching

---

[1] See Robert Browning's *Cleon*, the last line.

of the Lord has the same effect as the Law, which also was from God; it revealed to the dormant conscience the sin that was already there, and it provoked the unconverted will to vigorous obstinacy in its sin (*Romans* vii, 7–12). Jews who were loyal to their tradition, the noblest religious tradition in the world, might still be involved in what theologians call 'material sin' so far as that tradition was less than the perfect will of God; but they were not involved in 'formal sin', which is deliberate action in opposition to that will made known. Now that it is made known and they refuse it, the sin becomes inexcusable. For antagonism to Christ is antagonism to God: *he that hateth me hateth my Father also*.

Perhaps it may be said that they were still not guilty of 'formal sin', for that is defiance of conscience. But there is a sin which may not be in that sense 'formal sin' and yet involves guilt as only 'formal sin' is generally supposed to do. This deeper sin is the sin of the darkened conscience (*St. Matthew* vi, 23), which prevents men from seeing goodness when it is before their eyes. *If I had not done among them the works which no one else did, they would not have had sin; but as it is they have both seen and hated both me and my Father*. These works, wherein power is active in manifest subjection to love, are 'signs' of the divine presence and activity in Him. Failure to read those signs argues a profound darkening of the conscience. At one time His enemies had said of such a work — a plainly good work — that it was done by diabolic power; and He had answered that this argued such insensitiveness to the very Spirit of Holiness as to put him who had sunk to it outside the reach of the divine forgiveness (*St. Matthew* xii, 22–32). Pure goodness has been in action before their eyes, and they have repudiated it. There was never a more utterly gross delusion than that 'We needs must love the highest when we see it', unless by 'see it' we understand 'see it for what it is'. *They have both seen and hated both me and my Father*. What more or worse can be said? Yet it is only the extreme form of a spiritual reality common enough and recognised by the

Psalmists (*Psalms* xxxv, 19 and lxix, 4).[1] We shall not, perhaps, ever allow ourselves to hate Christ and His Cross as historically presented; we very easily hate His call to the Cross when it comes to ourselves to-day.

Suddenly, as though this terrible thought of hating the Lord and His Father had recalled the Holy Spirit against whom that hatred is blasphemy, the Person of the Comforter is introduced. The world in its blind sin may persecute and hate; but the Spirit will bear His own witness. *When the Comforter cometh, the Spirit of Truth who proceedeth from the Father, whom I will send to you from the Father, he shall bear witness concerning me.*

The Son sends the Comforter. The coming of the Holy Spirit in power is due to the action of the Son in revealing the love of the Father, and (as we shall see more clearly) one way of summarising the purpose of Christ's coming is to say that He came in order that the Spirit might come. That inward power of God converting desire itself is a result of the disclosure of the love of God and the response which it wins. So the Son is the cause of the Spirit's coming; He sends Him. Yet it is no less true that the Spirit *proceedeth from the Father*; because the Father is infinite love the personal activity of that love ever goes forth. Not only in Jesus Christ does *the Spirit of Truth* touch the hearts of men. He spoke to and through Plato, as the early Christian Fathers fully recognised; and has spoken through many a seer, poet and prophet both within and outside the Canon of Holy Scripture. Wherever there is response in the hearts of men to the manifested glory of God, whether that manifestation be in nature or in history, there the Spirit of Truth is at work. He inspires all Science and all Art, and speaks in the conscience of the heathen child. Yet it is also true that the Son sends Him. For only in the Word made flesh is the glory of God truly displayed. *We beheld his glory* (i, 14); that is the condition of receiving the Holy Spirit

---

[1] ' They that hate me without a cause ' (cf. cix, 3, ' For the love that I had unto them, lo they take now my contrary part ').

in His power. He 'proceedeth from the Father and (or through) the Son'.

The Spirit of Truth — as contrasted with the false prejudice which led the Jews to hate the highest when they saw it. The Gospel is not a call to feed the soul on lofty ideals which may have no counterpart in reality. It is the proclamation of the truth about God and the world. Every sincere seeker after truth is entitled to claim Christ's authority for saying that he is upheld by the Holy Spirit; for that is implied in this title *the Spirit of truth*. But if he is sincere he will also recognise that he cannot claim that authority unless he also acknowledges that the primary concern of *the Spirit of truth* is to *bear witness concerning* Jesus Christ. For He is the very truth of God, the Eternal Word or self-utterance of the Father.

He shall bear witness concerning me; and ye also bear witness. Co-witnesses with the Holy Ghost: that is the calling of Christian disciples; that is our calling. St. Peter would accept that august position: 'We are witnesses of these things; and so is the Holy Ghost whom God hath given to them that obey him' (*Acts* v, 32). The first disciples were qualified for this by their companionship with the Lord from the first days of the ministry: *ye also bear witness, because from the beginning ye are with me.*

We were baptised in infancy; we were (by God's great mercy and election) brought up in Christian homes. Not from the beginning of His ministry, but from the beginning of our lives, we are with Him. What is our witness worth? Does it qualify us to be co-witnesses with the Holy Ghost?

These things have I spoken unto you that ye be not overthrown. The coming persecution would be a very severe trial to faith, not only because it would test courage and men might deny their allegiance to the Lord from weakness and cowardice, but also because it is hard to believe that a cause is truly God's when it seems to meet with no success, and all power is on the other side. *Overthrown:* it is notoriously hard to represent in English the Greek word translated in the Authorised Version 'offended' and in the Revised 'made to stumble'; it stands for a failure due to obstacles put in the way, as contrasted with failure due to disloyalty. If the disciples can remember *these things* — the Lord's prediction of the persecution and, no less, His promise of the Comforter, they will find in them the needed safeguard.

They will excommunicate you: the loyal disciple will be attacked through his religious tradition and association. He will have to maintain his constancy in face of the assurance of his fellows that he is pursuing a course hateful to God. So sure of this will they be that *whosoever killeth you will think he offers worship to God.* They will not only think that in persecuting the disciples they are serving God's purpose in the world, but even that they are therein offering worship; the execution will be carried out in the spirit of a ritual sacrifice. It is this religious conscientiousness of the persecutor which makes him so relentless, and also tests so searchingly the faith of his victim. *And these things will they do because they did not recognise the Father nor me.* The revelation was offered, but they were blind to it. They did not 'behold his glory'. In Christ the Father was manifested, but they could not recognise either the Father so manifested or the Son as manifesting Him.

But these things have I spoken to you that, when their hour cometh, ye may be mindful of them, that I myself told you. Their hour: the hour of their fulfilment. Then the disciples would look back and say, 'This is what He told us to expect; His word is fulfilled'. Thus an experience otherwise calculated to assault faith from without and to undermine it from beneath, will be converted into an evidence and support of faith by the realisation that it is a fulfilment of the Lord's own word.

CHAPTER XVI

(1) THE DEPARTURE OF THE LORD AND THE COMING OF THE COMFORTER

4–7. 'These things I did not tell you from the beginning because I was with you. But now I go my way to him that sent me, and none of you asketh me, Whither goest thou? But because I have said these things to you, sorrow hath filled your heart. But I tell you the truth; it is expedient for you that I go away. For if I go not away, the Comforter will not come to you, but if I depart I will send him to you.'

WHILE the Lord was with them there was no need to speak of *these things* — persecution for His Name's sake, and the coming of the Comforter. For in those days any persecution that arose was directed against Himself, not against them; and while He was with them, the Comforter would not come (7). But now He is leaving them so far as concerns visible presence, and both warning and promise are in place.

I go my way to him that sent me. The words are repeated from vii, 33, but there they follow the saying *Yet a little while I am with you.* Here, for that phrase the word *Now* is substituted. The sacrifice which is at once the separation of death and the perfecting of union with the Father is at hand. It is the supreme moment of His life and ministry; yet the disciples are not thinking of what it means for Him; their thoughts are all of what it means for themselves. *None of you asketh me, 'Whither goest thou?'* St. Peter had asked precisely that, when the Lord had said He was going to a place where they could not follow (xiii, 36); there self-concern prompted the question; here it stifles it. The Lord has now told them the goal of His journey — the Father; but instead of wondering what the joy of that attainment must be, they are brooding over their own imminent loss and the persecutions which they have been warned to expect: *Because I have said these things to you, sorrow hath filled your heart.*

But I tell you the truth; it is expedient for you that I go away.
Even from the standpoint of their own interest they should rejoice rather than feel sorrow: *it is expedient for you that I go away.* How could that possibly be true? We look back and think that there was never any privilege like theirs. They had walked with Him in the corn-fields, and sat with Him in the boat upon the lake; they had supped with Him among His friends. What greater privilege could there ever be? Yes — it was a supreme privilege. But what became of that faith which relied upon the Lord as an external Presence to whom they could turn at every moment of doubt or need? When the crisis came it all went to pieces. 'They all left him and fled' (*St. Mark* xiv, 50). Simon Peter did indeed follow — 'afar off' (*St. Mark* xiv, 54) — to the place where he would stand and warm himself, and say 'I know not this man' (*St. Mark* xiv, 71). Yet a few weeks later these same men are found confronting the rulers of their nation with a calm and unruffled courage, and 'rejoicing that they were counted worthy to suffer dishonour for the Name' (*Acts* v, 41; cf. also (e.g.) *Acts* v, 27–32). What explains the transformation? Of course it is that of which the Lord here speaks; He has withdrawn from them as a visible, external Presence, to return in the Person of the Spirit as the very breath of their lives (see xx, 22).

This hard saying states in its most signal instance the fundamental principle of true education. The task of the teacher is to prepare the pupil for the time of separation, which must come, so that the pupil may find within himself such resources as enable him to follow the direction in which the teacher has started him without any further aid. It is not only that the time of separation must come; it is a good thing that it should come, for otherwise that inward strength, which it is the purpose of education to develop, will never be exercised.

We tend to think of that inward strength as our own, and of our trust in it as self-reliance. But it is not our own. Even apart from religion, the inner quality in which we place our trust is the deposit of the tradition in which we were brought up, of the influence of parents and teachers. We could not civilise ourselves. If we had been carried off in infancy to live among savages, we should be savages now. 'What hast thou that thou didst not receive?' (*I Corinthians* iv, 7). Of all the boons of civilisation the giver is God; and we lose both some of their value, and an added ground for faith, if we forget this.

In the spiritual life it is of urgent importance that we remember from whom our strength comes — the Holy Spirit, the 'Giver of Life'. He is the Spirit of Christ, whom disciples receive through their companionship with Christ. Christ is therefore in that sense the source or sender of the Spirit. He withdraws His visible presence; but He does not *leave us desolate* (xiv, 18); on the contrary, He makes our loss into a blessing. *If I go not away, the Comforter will not come to you, but if I depart I will send him to you.*

*

(2) THE COMFORTER AND THE WORLD

8–11. 'And when he is come he will convict the world in respect of sin and of righteousness and of judgment: of sin, in that they believe not on me; and of righteousness in that to the Father I go my way and no longer do ye take note of me; and of judgment in that the prince of this world hath been judged.'

The Comforter has a relationship to the world as well as to the disciples, and this is mentioned briefly so that the way may be clear for the description of His work among the disciples, upon which most emphasis is to be laid. But though the reference to His task for the world is brief it is almost infinitely pregnant. As we are still in large measure 'of the world' and not yet wholly disciples, it is well for us to draw out the meaning of these close-packed phrases.

He will convict the world. The word translated *convict* means

primarily to cross-examine with a view to refutation or conviction, or to bring forward evidence that proves guilt. (The
corresponding noun is used in *Hebrews* xi, 1, where it is said
that 'faith is the *testing* of things not seen', though there the
suggestion is that the unseen forces will meet the test.) The
Comforter will bring evidence to prove the world wrong in
certain respects. What respects are these? — the three matters
most important to man's life, sin, righteousness and judgement. What then is the evidence that He will bring? In respect
of sin, it is that men do not believe on Christ; in respect of
righteousness, it is that Christ goes to the Father; in respect
of judgement, it is that in the Life and Death of Christ the
Prince of this world is under judgement.

We may interpret this at two levels — the more obvious and
the more profound. Men's failure to believe on Christ is proof
of the world's sin; Christ's going to the Father is proof of His
righteousness; and the judgement upon the Prince of this world
is proof that judgement is operative. All this is true and important; but it does not begin to satisfy the meaning of the
words used; and after all it was not by any means evident that
the Prince of this world was under judgement in the Passion
of Christ.

Let us by all means take to ourselves the lessons of this
more obvious interpretation. Our failure to believe — whether
absolute or partial — is indeed proof of sin in us, and should
stir us to a penitent longing for fuller faith. The Ascension of
Christ is indeed a seal set on His life as a manifestation of
righteousness, and we may learn from Him what righteousness
really is. The judgement of the Prince of this world is indeed
an instance of that divine judgement of whose reality our moral
torpor suggests doubt, and as we reflect upon it we can stimu-
late our own anticipation of that judgement to the quickening
of our sluggish consciences. This would be much; but it is the
lesser part of what the words of the Lord convey.

He will convict the world: He will prove the world wrong —
and us with the world so far as we share the outlook of the

world — *in respect of sin, and of righteousness, and of judgement.* The world has to learn that its very conception of these things is all wrong. If it tries to avoid sin or to seek righteousness, it does not avoid or seek the right things; if it fears or prepares for judgement, it does not fear or prepare for the right thing.

Of sin, in that they believe not on me. Their unbelief is, so to speak, brought into court, not merely as evidence that they are sinful, but as proof that they are wrong in their idea of sin.

We tend to think of sin as consisting of acts which are done in defiance of conscience or are, whether we know it or not, contrary to God's command. Some people even say that so long as a man follows his conscience he cannot be committing sin. (The theologian would say that he is certainly not committing 'formal sin' but he may be committing 'material sin'.) Certainly a man should follow his conscience; but that is not the whole of his duty. Still more important is it to enlighten conscience itself, lest 'the light that is in us be darkness' (*St. Matthew* vi, 23). The greatest crimes in history have been perpetrated at the bidding of conscience — such as the Spanish Inquisition. The disciples were warned to expect a time when *whosoever killeth you will think that he is offering worship to God* (2). A sin committed against the light is more wicked than another; the man who does it is more guilty. But sin is something much wider and deeper than guilt. Everything which is other than God would have it be is sin. 'All have sinned and fall short of the glory of God' (*Romans* iii, 23); that is the definition of sin — to fall short of the glory of God! It is not enough that we should be as good as the people about us; nothing is enough except that we should be as good as God — 'Ye therefore shall be perfect as your heavenly Father is perfect' (*St. Matthew* v, 48). But we shall not set ourselves that standard, to say nothing of attaining it, if we are left to our own resources. And we do not know what the perfection of God is until we have seen it in Christ. Unless we *believe on* Him we are bound to be wrong in our whole idea about sin; for apart from that faith we have neither the stimulus nor the capacity to frame the true standard.

So the world's failure to believe on Christ is the proof that the world is wrong in its conception of what sin is. Here the world is likely to protest. 'A man cannot help his beliefs', they say; 'he is responsible for acting up to them but he is not answerable for what does or does not seem to be true.' Is that so? When a proposition is made to a man, he exercises his judgement to the best of his ability; but is that 'best' as good as it might have been? If it is lacking in some sensitiveness which a more careful discipline of mind would have supplied, he is responsible for his error even though he did his best at the moment. This principle is both clearer and more important in proportion as the matter presented concerns more intimately our moral and spiritual life. A high ideal may be presented to a man and he considers whether or not he shall accept it for the guidance of his life. His answer must depend on his character. He may give the truest and wisest answer of which he is then capable; but if he has allowed himself to settle down to a selfish outlook or to materialist standards, this will affect his judgement. He will reject the ideal in perfect sincerity; but that sincerity is not so much a justification of his conduct as a measure of his sin.

So, supremely, the divine revelation in Christ operates in judgement upon those to whom it is offered (iii, 19). Can men see in the perfect self-sacrifice of Christ the power and wisdom of God? If so, they are in the way of salvation; if not, they are on the way of perdition. 'The word of the Cross is to them that are perishing foolishness; but unto us which are being saved it is the power of God. . . . We proclaim a Messiah on a cross, to Jews a scandal and to Gentiles an absurdity, but to those who are called, a Messiah who is God's power and God's wisdom' (*I Corinthians* i, 18, 23, 24).

If then we fail to commit ourselves in trust to Christ when His revelation is before us, it proves not only that we are sinful, but that we are wrong in our conception of sin. For if only we could realise that, inasmuch as God is Love, the essence of sin is love's opposite, that is to say, self-centredness, our understanding of this would impel us to cast ourselves upon the divine love which alone can win us from our evil state. We are not impelled to that trust, because we wrongly diagnose our disease. We try to cure our symptoms — our habits of lying, or cheating, or resentment, or envy, or contempt, or impurity — but we leave the disease itself alone. But the disease is that we are self-centred, not God-centred; the cure for that is faith; if we do not at least seek after faith, it proves that we have not understood the nature of our trouble: if we knew our sickness, we should know our need of the physician.

Of righteousness, in that to the Father I go my way and no longer do ye take note of me. The world's notion of righteousness is wrong in the same way as its notion of sin. The world admires and approves its honourable and successful men; and that is right enough. But real sacrifice for higher than material or patriotic causes it regards with anxiety and alarm. Even if we can conceive that for ourselves such sacrifice would be righteous, we show how little its claim has gripped us when we recall how we shrink from commending that same claim to our neighbours. We do not believe in any radical self-sacrifice enough to recommend it to our friends, even when we might follow that course ourselves. And when the course in question involves defiance of the State, and the disgrace of imprisonment or a criminal's execution, we regard it as fanatical.

The Lord was about to suffer that disgrace. In the eyes of the wordly-wise He was behaving foolishly; He was cutting short a career of great usefulness, which He could easily have continued; His attitude was quixotic. So an observer by no means cynical might say. But that observer and the world represented by him would be missing the real truth of the situation. The appearance of a criminal's execution and of the untimely collapse of His cause is superficial only: the reality is that *to the Father I go my way and no longer do ye take note of me.*

To the Father I go my way: this is the order of words in the original. Not to the felon's grave, but *to the Father*; not under compulsion of force, but *I go my way.* This complete abandonment to the will of God is the real righteousness, and its issue is not the misery of humiliation but 'the joy that was set before him' (*Hebrews* xii, 2).

No longer do ye take note of me: the word translated *take note of* is that which is used of the people taking note of the miracles (vi, 2) and of the believer taking no note of death (viii, 51). It is used of physical as distinguished from spiritual vision.; in verses 16–19 the contrast is emphatic; and it is used of such physical 'seeing' as involves attention. While the Lord was with them in the flesh, of course the disciples watched and took note of His every word and action. It might easily seem that they depended entirely on His outward presence among them. 'If He be removed', the world might well say, 'His cause will collapse.' But it is part of the proof of righteousness in that Life which the world condemned, that disciples, who can take note of Him no longer, are disciples still. The Spirit, pointing out that what the world thought death and failure is really victory and fulfilment, and that a discipleship which began as external companionship should persist as spiritual agency, exhibits the true nature of righteousness — not the punctual fulfilment of contracts (though that also is righteous) but total self-commitment to the *righteous Father* (xvii, 25).

Of judgement in that the prince of this world hath been judged. If men's conception of sin and of righteousness needs to be deepened, quite equally is this true of their thought of judgement. We tend to think of the Divine Judgement as being the infliction upon us by an irresistible Despot of penalties, not growing out of our characters and deeds, but imposed from without. All through this Gospel we have been learning that this is not the true account of Judgement; see especially iii, 19 and the passages collected in the comment upon it. The Divine Judgement is the verdict upon us which consists in our reaction to *the light* (iii, 19) when it is offered to us; by that reaction we are stamped as *sons of light* (xii, 36) or as children of darkness. If we *love the darkness rather than the light* (iii, 19) there is nothing more or worse to be done to us. With Judas we go out from the Light of the world into the night (xiii, 30).

The world thought that it was judging Christ when Caiaphas rent his clothes, and the people shouted 'He is worthy of death', and Pilate gave sentence as they desired. But we know that it was they, and not He, upon whom sentence was then passed. History has vindicated His claim that in rejecting Him the Prince of this world was already judged. The Spirit points to this reversal and by means of it teaches us how wrong our own idea of judgement is.

How dread a Companion and Guide, then, is this Comforter! We are distressed about some special fault, and ask His aid to overcome it; whereupon He tells us that our real trouble is our self-complacence and self-reliance, and if it is His help that we seek, He will rouse us from these. But we do not want that at all! Indeed our chief reason for wanting to overcome that special fault was that it disturbed our self-complacence, which we hoped, after a little moral effort, to enjoy once more. Or we seek His aid in living according to our standard of righteousness and are told that this standard is hardly worth striving after: only the total committal of 'ourselves, our souls and bodies, to be a reasonable, holy and lively sacrifice' is real righteousness. Or we turn to Him to be our Paraclete, our Advocate, in the judgement; and He tells us that we are judged already by our steady preference of our way to God's.

When we pray 'Come, Holy Ghost, our souls inspire', we had better know what we are about. He will not carry us to easy triumphs and gratifying successes; more probably He will set us to some task for God in the full intention that we shall fail, so that others, learning wisdom by our failure, may carry the good cause forward. He may take us through loneliness, desertion by friends, apparent desertion even by God; that was

the way Christ went to the Father. He may drive us into the
wilderness to be tempted of the devil. He may lead us from the
Mount of Transfiguration (if He ever lets us climb it) to the hill
that is called the Place of a Skull. For if we invoke Him, it
must be to help us in doing God's will, not ours. We cannot call
upon the

> Creator Spirit, by whose aid
> The world's foundations first were laid

in order to use omnipotence for the supply of our futile
pleasures or the success of our futile plans. If we invoke Him,
we must be ready for the glorious pain of being caught by His
power out of our petty orbit into the eternal purposes of the
Almighty, in whose onward sweep our lives are as a speck of
dust. The soul that is filled with the Spirit must have become
purged of all pride or love of ease, all self-complacence and
self-reliance; but that soul has found the only real dignity, the
only lasting joy. Come then, Great Spirit, come. Convict the
world; and convict my timid soul.

*

(3) THE COMFORTER AND THE DISCIPLES

12–15. Yet many things have I to say to you, but ye cannot bear them now.
But when he is come, the Spirit of truth, he will guide you into truth
in its entirety. For he will not speak from himself, but as many things
as he shall hear he will speak, and the things that are coming he will
declare to you. He will glorify me, because from out what is mine he will
take and will declare to you. All things as many as the Father hath are
mine; that is why I said that from out what is mine he will take and will
declare to you.

*Yet many things have I to say to you, but ye cannot bear them
now.* What teaching can be given depends on the pupil's
capacity to receive. Every schoolmaster has had his old pupils
come back, perhaps from the University, and say what a
difference it has made to them that someone has told them this
or that; 'but why' one of them adds 'did no one tell us that

before?' The schoolmaster remembers, but wisely does not say, that he did tell them, many times. But they could not bear it then; they were not ready; and the words passed by them. So the Lord knows that His disciples could not receive much that He would tell them. They have not yet the strength to accept and carry it: *ye cannot bear them now.* Just as they could not *follow Him now* but should *follow afterwards* (xiii, 36) on His spiritual pilgrimage, so their minds cannot yet enter into the full meaning of His ministry and His passion, but shall be led to this later by the Spirit.

It is no true loyalty to the mind of the Lord which confines attention to what He did and said on earth. Then He kept His teaching within the range of His disciples' apprehension. Even so they would not grasp all His meaning; but they would grasp enough to start on the mental pilgrimage or exploration, on which they should be carried further by the Spirit. We are most loyal to the mind of Christ when we are most receptive of all that the Apostles, under the guidance of the Spirit, learnt and taught, and of all that the same Spirit would teach us now.

But when he is come: here, as again in the saying *He will glorify me,* the word *He* is emphatic. To say 'that one' every time is unnatural and intolerably clumsy. But the stress is on the word *He,* not on the word *come.* It is not the future date to which the disciples are pointed so much as to the Agent of their illumination.

The Spirit of truth, he will guide you into truth in its entirety. The title is repeated from xv, 26, where also the function associated with it is witness to Jesus Himself. *The spirit of truth will guide you into truth in its entirety.* If we say 'Spirit of truth' we must say 'into truth'; if we say 'into the truth' or 'into all the truth' we must say 'Spirit of the truth'; for the phrases are identical and balance each other. There is, of course, no reference intended to the discovery of scientific or general historical truth; though, inasmuch as all truth of every kind must ultimately be one, that thought is not at all alien from what is intended. The immediate reference is to the understanding of the Lord Jesus; since He is the word of God, this will supply the clue to the understanding of all else, but that comes by way of corollary. The Holy Spirit is the Spirit of truth because He leads men to an ever fuller understanding of Jesus who is *the truth* (xiv, 6), till at last we apprehend it *in its entirety* or as a whole.

He will not speak from Himself any more than the Lord had done (vii, 17); both the Lord and the Spirit speak what they hear from the Father (xv, 15).

The things that are coming — the Passion, Resurrection and Ascension of the Lord — *he will declare to you*. These were more particularly the things that the Lord could not now expound. The events themselves must take place, and then, in the illumination inaugurated at Pentecost, the Apostles would be able to *bear* their message. So it proved; and the Apostolic teaching, given in the power of the Spirit, mainly concerns the themes which, when the Lord spoke, were *the things that are coming*. Let us consider some of them. 'Him who knew no sin, he made to be sin on our behalf, that we might become the righteousness of God in him' (*II Corinthians* v, 21). 'Being justified freely by his grace through the redemption that is in Christ Jesus, whom God set forth in his blood — a mercy-seat through faith—to show his righteousness' (*Romans* iii, 24, 25).[1] 'We were buried therefore with him through baptism into death; that like as Christ was raised from the dead through the glory of the Father, so we might also walk in newness of life' (*Romans* vi, 4). 'God being rich in mercy, for his great love wherewith he loved us, even when we were dead through our trespasses, quickened us together with Christ (by grace have ye been saved) and raised us up with him and made us

---

[1] I am persuaded that ἱλαστήριον here means Mercy Seat, as it does in the LXX — e.g. *Exodus* xxv, 18. The Mercy Seat was sprinkled with the blood of the victim. So God set forth Christ on the Cross in His Blood to be through faith the true Mercy Seat — the place where God's forgiveness meets man's sin. This it can do freely because in the same place, the Cross, is displayed the cost of sin to God, so that forgiveness is possible without any suggestion that God makes light of sin. Thus if we start from the thought of righteousness, the Cross makes forgiveness morally possible; if we start from the thought of forgiveness, the Cross is found 'to show his righteousness'. It is itself the reconciliation of justice and forgiveness.

to sit with him in the heavenly places in Christ Jesus' (*Ephesians* ii, 4–6). 'Having therefore, brethren, boldness to enter into the holy place by the blood of Jesus, by the way which he dedicated for us, a new and living way, through the veil, that is to say his flesh' (*Hebrews* x, 19, 20). These are some of the declarations made by the Spirit to the Apostles and through them to us concerning the things which, when the Lord spoke, were *coming*. How could the disciples *bear them* then? There must be, first the events themselves; then the new illumination; then the experience of that 'fellowship' in the Spirit which led the disciples to a consciousness of union with one another in the Lord and so made clear what was their true relationship to Him (though He gave its principle in the figure of the Vine) and, by consequence, what His Death, Resurrection and Ascension meant to them.

These *things that are coming* concern the Lord. *He will glorify me* as He makes clear the meaning of what the Lord had spoken and done. Christ is glorified in the Passion (xii, 23, 24; xiii, 31–33; xvii, 1). That glorification is the necessary condition which must be fulfilled before the Spirit can come (vii, 39; xvi, 7). When the Spirit comes He completes that glorification by making its full meaning clear to those who receive Him.

For what the Spirit does is not to impart knowledge of other themes or future events but to interpret Christ. *He from out what is mine will take and will declare to you.* Yet this does not involve any limitation of His activity as revealer. For Christ is the Word *through whose agency all things came to be* (i, 3), so that to declare Him is to declare the principle of all things. Here the same truth is expressed from the other side. *All things as many as the Father hath are mine* so that to say *what is mine* and 'what is the Father's' is to say the same thing. In the same way the Lord said that to snatch His own from His hand or from the Father's hand was the same thing (x, 28, 29). Because He and the Father are One, the relation of the Spirit to Him and to the Father is the same.

Each of the last three clauses ends with the refrain *he will declare to you*. The disciple is not to clamour for the solution of perplexities or for intellectual mastery of divine mysteries. What knowledge he has in this realm is his because the Spirit has declared it to him; and for the Spirit's declaration he must wait.

(4) SORROW TURNED TO JOY

16–22. 'A little while and ye no longer take note of me and again a little while and ye will see me.' Some of his disciples therefore said to one another, 'What is this which he saith to us, "A little while and ye do not take note of me and a little while and ye will see me" and "Because I go my way to the Father"'? So they were saying, 'What is this that he saith, this "little while"? We do not know what he speaketh.' Jesus recognised that they were wishing to ask him, and said to them, 'Concerning this do ye enquire among themselves, that I said "A little while and ye do not take note of me and again a little while and ye will see me"? Amen, Amen, I say to you that weep and lament will ye, but the world will rejoice; ye will be sorrowful, but your sorrow will turn into joy. A woman, when she is in travail, hath sorrow, because her hour is come. But when the child is born, she is no longer mindful of the anguish for the joy that there is born a man into the world. And ye therefore now have sorrow; but I shall see you again and your heart will rejoice, and your joy no man taketh from you.'

The rather elaborately full record of this conversation reflects the concern of the Church for which the Gospel was written. The delay of Christ's 'return' was a cause of serious perplexity. How were devout Christians to answer the 'mockers' who said, 'Where is the promise of his coming? for, from the day that the fathers fell asleep, all things continue as they were from the beginning of the creation'? (*II Peter* iii, 4.) The Lord had spoken of His Coming as imminent; there was no doubt about that. Was He deluded?

No; He was misunderstood. The Coming is the Cross and the ingathering of its triumph through the Resurrection,

Ascension, Pentecost, the Evangelisation of the World, and the final Consummation; its focal moment is the Cross and Resurrection. So He assured the High Priest at His trial that from that moment Daniel's prophecy was fulfilled (*St. Matthew* xxvi, 64; *St. Luke* xxii, 69). Certainly it was imminent. But this transformation of the meaning of the Coming was too great for their apprehension. To explain it in advance was impossible. The event itself was necessary to generate the experience by which alone it could be apprehended. So words were spoken which provided the clue to the mystery though at this stage they could scarcely do more than darken it. Later, remembered in the light of both event and experience, they would be seen to have offered a preparation, and to show that the Lord's own expectation, far from being frustrated, had been precisely fulfilled.[1] He had spoken of a *little while* and at the time it had puzzled the disciples. Now, when the Evangelist is writing, they can look back and realise that all has been as He foresaw.

A little while and ye no longer take note of me. The translation is clumsy; perhaps the Revised Version 'behold me no more' should be retained; but the word used seemed to call for the translation chosen or something very similar on some previous occasions, especially vi, 2 and viii, 51; in any case it is sharply contrasted with 'see' in the following phrase. The Authorised Version makes the passage far more obscure by using 'see' in both places.

While the Lord was with them, the disciples noted all that He said and did. Now the opportunity for that is drawing to an end. From the moment of His death they can 'behold' or take note of Him no longer.

And again a little while and ye will see me. After a short interval of desolation, they will *see* Him with the direct spiritual vision which brings full personal knowledge and communion: this would begin at once after the Resurrection, when the new era of the Son of Man would be inaugurated.

[1] On the subject of our Lord's thought of the Coming, see Introduction, p. xxxiii.

Some of the disciples murmur the phrase to one another, and connect with it another which He has used and which was hard to grasp clearly — *because I go my way to the Father*, which had before been connected with these words *no longer do ye take note of me* (10). They can only confess themselves baffled. The Lord recognises their perplexity; He repeats the mysterious phrases once again; and then He sketches the experience that awaits them in another way.

Weep and lament will ye, but the world shall rejoice. For two days they will mourn a lost Leader and Friend, while the world rejoices that it is rid of a trouble-maker.

Ye will be sorrowful, but your sorrow will turn into joy. It is not only the joy will take the place of sorrow, but the sorrow itself becomes the joy. The Cross is not for Christians a stumbling-block which the Resurrection has removed; it is not a defeat of which the effect has been cancelled by a subsequent victory. It is itself the triumph. What was the devil's worst is become God's best. He has 'Led captivity captive' (*Ephesians* iv, 8 quoting *Psalm* lxviii, 18). Sorrow is become joy. The Christian joy and hope do not arise from an ignoring of the evil in the world, but from facing it at its worst. The light that shines for ever in the Church breaks out of the veriest pit of gloom.

Ye therefore now have sorrow. The Christian is no Stoic. He does not refuse the sorrow occasioned by the mortal lot of man and (still more bitterly) by his sin. He accepts and bears it. But he bears it 'in sure and certain hope'.

But I shall see you again, and your heart will rejoice, and your joy no one taketh from you. The joy of Easter once truly experienced becomes a pervading atmosphere which the soul thenceforth breathes for ever. 'Who shall separate us from the love of Christ? shall tribulation or anguish or persecution or famine or nakedness or peril or sword? Even as it is written, "For thy sake we are killed all the day long; we were accounted as sheep for the slaughter". Nay, in all these things we are more than conquerors through him that loved us. For I am persuaded that neither death, nor life, nor angels, nor principalities, nor things present, nor things to come, nor powers, nor height, nor depth, nor any other creature, shall be able to separate us from the love of God, which is in Christ Jesus our Lord' (*Romans* viii, 35–39). St. Paul's glorious outburst reflecting his own experience is no more than a symphony on the theme propounded before the event by the Lord Himself.

•

(5) PRAYER AND ITS ANSWER

23–27. 'And in that day ye will ask me no question. Amen, Amen, I say to you, if ye pray anything of the Father, he will give it you, in my name. Until now ye did not pray anything in my name; pray, and ye will receive, that your joy may be fulfilled. These things in parables have I spoken to you; an hour cometh when no longer in parables shall I speak to you, but in open speech shall bring you news of the Father. In that day, in my name will ye pray and I say not to you that I will ask the Father concerning you; for the Father himself loveth you because ye have loved me and have believed that I came forth from the presence of God.'

The changes in the word for 'ask' are exaggerated by any English translation which notices them at all; but the feeling tone of the words is not quite the same. Petitions and enquiries overlap in certain ways. The opening phrase in this passage suggests a deference which is absent from the later phrases until the first recurs in a new context. The disciples are not here thought of as making petitions to their Lord, but rather as consulting Him and awaiting His decision. This is our proper attitude in prayer, and it is noteworthy that it recurs in 26 of the attitude of the Son to the Father, so that even in prayer the analogy still holds — We: Christ : : Christ: the Father; though evidently in the latter case there is no absence in the Son of full knowledge concerning the Father's mind.

But a new principle of prayer has been laid down — prayer which is offered and granted *in my name*. This principle was

stated in xiv, 13 and again in xv, 16. Here there is an addition
to the thought then expressed; for the crucial words *in my
name* are, so to speak, held back, so as to be connected with
he will give it you as well as with *if ye pray anything*. Both the
prayer and its answer are in His Name. We have already seen
what is meant for us by prayer in the Name of Christ (xv, 16);
it means that we pray as His representatives, as He would
pray in our place, as He does pray in Heaven. But we are at
first surprised at the thought that the Father gives in His Name
the answer to our prayer; yet we have already been told (xiv,
26) that the Father sends the Spirit in the Name of the Son.
For in fact the Son is the Mediator, through whom our prayers
ascend to the Father and through whom the Father's love
descends in blessings on His children. This does not interpose
a barrier between God and Man, for the Mediator is Himself
both God and Man. Another way of approaching this
thought would be to say that through the union of divine and
human in Jesus Christ, we have both more assured access to
the Father (*Ephesians* ii, 18 and iii, 12) and more abundant
blessing from the Father. It is the same thought which is also
expressed in i, 51, where the Lord speaks of *the angels of God
ascending and descending upon the Son of Man*.

It is a new experience of worship that is offered. *Until now
ye did not pray anything in my name.* They were men of prayer;
but they had prayed as devout Jews, not as disciples checking
each desire as it suggested itself for presentation to the Father
by reference to the Mind of their Master. That is the prayer
that will always be answered, and answered with the consequence of a joy that is complete; *pray* (*sc.* in my name) *and
ye will receive, that your joy may be fulfilled*.

All this will be the experience of the disciples *in that day* —
the day when the Lord sees them again, bestowing the joy that
no one can take from them, the day of His Easter greeting and
His threefold Easter gift of peace, of mission, and of holy
spirit. That day is now very near; its fuller revelation is at
hand. *These things in parables have I spoken to you; an hour*

cometh when no longer in parables shall I speak to you, but in open speech shall bring you news of the Father. The revelation through the Spirit which would follow the Resurrection would be clearer than it was possible to give at the earlier time when *Jesus was not yet glorified* (vii, 39). And this clearer revelation can be ours now, if we are willing to 'abide in Him and His words abide in us' (xv, 7).

In that day (which is now equivalent to saying 'in the power of the Spirit whom I will send'), *in my name ye will pray, and I say not to you that I will ask the Father concerning you:* once again the word for asking questions is substituted for that which stands for making petitions, as though the Son would not presume to ask outright for any boon, but might consult the Father concerning what His loving wisdom would decide; and even that will be unnecessary *for the Father himself loveth you, because ye have loved me and have believed that I came forth from the presence of God.* The word for *loveth* and *loved* is not that which represents the universal and self-giving love of God, but that which represents friendship; perhaps we may translate thus: *the Father himself is friendly to you because ye have been my friends.* Within that holy love of God which goes forth to all men — *So God loved the world* (iii, 16) — there is room for particular relationships to individual men and women, and those whose hearts are won to affection for the Lord Jesus are thereby brought into a special relation of tender intimacy with the Father. An earthly father who loves all his children equally may yet have special ties of intimacy with each one, a peculiar tenderness in every case; this one is so eager, that one so gentle, another so wistfully affectionate; he does not love one more than another, but he loves each differently. It makes the love of God seem less remote in its holiness when we learn that it contains within itself a similar variation of individual attachment. Nor need any be excluded from the 'friendship' of God that is here spoken of, for all may be 'friends' of Jesus.

Yet it is not a mere human friendship that so qualifies the

disciples; it is this in combination with the faith which recognises His mission: *ye have believed that I came forth from the
presence of God* — not only *from* God (30) as a messenger
might come whom God had summoned to receive instructions
and then despatched, but one who dwelt ever with God and
was sent forth from the divine presence which was His home.

*

(6) THE DIVINE TRIUMPH

28–33. 'I came forth from the Father and am come into the world; again,
I leave the world and depart to the Father.' His disciples say, 'Lo, now
in open speech thou speakest and sayest no parable; now we know that
thou knowest all things and hast not need that any one should ask thee.
By this we believe that thou camest forth from God.' Jesus answered
them, 'At this moment ye believe. Behold, there cometh an hour, and
it is come, that ye will be scattered each to his own home, and me ye will
leave alone, and yet I am not alone because the Father is with me. These
things have I spoken to you that in me ye may have peace. In the world
ye have tribulation; but be of good cheer, I have overcome the world.'

The reference to the faith of the disciples (27) leads to this
apparently clear declaration. *I came forth from the Father
and am come into the world; again, I leave the world and depart
to the Father.* The preposition in the phrase *from the Father*
very nearly means *out of the Father;* it would be a mistake to
press it, but the suggestion of an intimate identity with the
Father before the Incarnation is conveyed. The disciples seem
to think that this is the declaration in open speech which had
been promised. But is it really so clear what is meant by 'coming into the world' where the words are used of Him through
whom all things came to be (i, 3), or what is meant by 'departure to the Father' when spoken of Him who is always in the
bosom of the Father (i, 18; see 32). In fact the disciples show,
by a slight but significant misquotation, that, though in one
sense they believe, yet their understanding is very limited.
They welcome the plainness of language: *Now in open speech*

thou speakest and sayest no parable. Now we know that thou knowest all things (even our unspoken thoughts) *and needest not that any man should ask thee.* The Lord had read their longing for a clear declaration, and had given it though they had not asked and the longing was unexpressed. *By this we believe that thou camest forth from God.* A sincere affirmation of a true faith. And yet Nicodemus had said just the same! (iii, 2). For though the Lord had said that He came *from the presence of* or *from beside God* (παρά, 27) and *out of God* (ἐκ, 28), the disciples confess no more than that He came *from God* (ἀπό, 30) as a mere messenger might come. It is something to believe that; but it is very far short of the faith for which the Lord had asked: *Believe me that I am in the Father and the Father in me; In that day ye shall recognise that I am in the Father, and ye in me, and I in you* (xiv, 11, 20).

We should not, then, be surprised that the Lord accepts this profession of faith as no more than a very incomplete instalment. It will not survive the shock that awaits it. *At this moment ye believe:* yes, in the inspiration of what had happened in the Upper Room and of the wonderful awe-creating words, they do for the time and in a measure believe. But it will not last. *Behold, there cometh an hour, and it is come, that ye will be scattered each to his own home.* The prophecy of Zechariah xiii, 7 — 'Smite the shepherd and the sheep shall be scattered' — was prominent in the mind of the Lord that night (*St. Mark* xiv, 27). And it was fulfilled — 'they all left him and fled' (*St. Mark* xiv, 50). *And me ye will leave alone.* He went forth alone bearing His cross, no follower attending on Him. He alone was then the true Israel, the Servant of the Lord, the Vine of God — utterly deserted, utterly alone.

Yet this was not the deepest truth; it would seem so to others; it would seem so to Himself (*St. Mark* xv, 34); but in deepest truth it would not be so; and as He looks forward to what awaits Him He knows the truth: *and yet I am not alone because the Father is with me.* At every stage of His 'departure to the

Father' the Father is with Him, even as at every stage of our pilgrimage to the Father's home we are at home with the Father (xiv, 2).

These things have I spoken to you — the last of the seven iterations of this phrase (xiv, 25; xv, 11; xvi, 1, 6, 25, 33) as the great discourse reaches its conclusion, *that in me ye may have peace.* Peace, *the peace that is mine*, was the promise that accompanied the first mention of the Comforter (xiv, 26, 27); so now it is the last promised gift. Peace — the greatest need of the world and of the soul: *in me ye may have peace.* Only in Him; not in the world, till the world takes Him for its Lord. *In the world ye have tribulation;* that remains true; and the tribulation will become more grievous rather than less (xvi, 1–4). But those who are in Him will not heed it. *Be of good cheer; I have overcome the world.*

That those words should be spoken then is a fact that almost paralyses feeling, even the feelings of awe and adoration. He knew what was before Him; yet He can say *I have overcome the world.* For what the world thought His shame was His glory and what the world thought His defeat was His victory. 'Having put off from himself his body, he made a show of the principalities and powers openly, triumphing over them in the Cross' (*Colossians* ii, 15). Not in gloom or depression, but in solemn triumph, 'for the joy that was set before him' (*Hebrews* xii, 2), He moves forward to His death. Soon the crown of glory and thorns will be upon His brow; soon upon His gallows-throne He will be *lifted up;* already He is the conqueror; *I have overcome the world.*

*

APPENDIX

THE LORD'S TEACHING ON PRAYER

In Chapter XVI we find the culmination of the Lord's teaching on Prayer; in Chapter XVII we have His own prayer of self-consecration offered as Priest-Victim, Victim-Priest.

It is worth while to pause for a moment and consider His teaching on Prayer as a whole.

First must be put the fundamental principle that God is perfect love and wisdom; He has no need that we should tell Him of our wants or desires; He knows what is for our good better than we do ourselves, and it is always His will to give it: 'Your Father knoweth what things ye have need of before ye ask him' (*St. Matthew* vi, 8). Consequently we must not in prayer have any thought of suggesting to God what was not already in His mind — still less of changing His mind or purpose.

But what things are good for us may depend on our spiritual state. Food which is wholesome and nourishing for those who are in good health may be lethal poison to any who are in high fever. The worst of all diseases of the soul is detachment from God, whether by ignorance or by neglect. If all our wants are supplied while we have no thought of God, this may confirm us in our detachment from Him, and so the things that should have been for our wealth are unto us an occasion of falling (*Psalm* lxix, 22). Consequently the question whether what is normally a blessing, such as deliverance from the enticement of some temptation, will be in actual fact a blessing to me may often depend on whether or not I recognise God as the source of all good things. So the first requirement in prayer is that we trust to God for all blessing.

Our Lord, according to His custom, states this in its place without qualification and without reserve. He goes to the greatest possible length in the demand that as we pray we shall believe that God will hear and answer, and in the promise that God will then grant our petitions. Many sayings might be quoted; one is sufficient: 'All things whatsoever ye pray and ask for, believe that ye have received them and ye shall have them' (*St. Mark* xi, 24).

The next requirement is apparently inconsistent with this; for this next requirement is that we should persevere in prayer in spite of disappointment. We are to be sure that God will grant our prayers; and when He does not, we are to go on praying. Our Lord gives His teaching about perseverance in two parables which belong to that well-marked group of parables whose point is that the comparison fails. For in these the Lord illustrates God's dealing with us, or our duty before God, by reference to human actions which are not morally admirable. Such are, evidently, the parable of the Unjust Steward (*St. Luke* xvi, 1–9) and, as I think, the parable of the Labourers in the Vineyard (*St. Matthew* xx, 1–16). The duty of perseverance in prayer is urged upon us in the parables of the Importunate Friend (*St. Luke* xi, 5–10) and of the Unjust Judge (*St. Luke* xviii, 1–8). We know that God does not grant petitions in order to rid Himself of the nuisance which we become by our persistence; His choice of a parallel so completely inapposite is a challenge to us to seek the real reason why God may make long delay and then grant our request.

The first requirement was perfect confidence. Does God wish to test our confidence? Of course not; He knows perfectly well what it is worth. But He may very likely wish to deepen it. The faith which takes the form — almost necessary at first — of confidence that God will do what we ask, is after all faith in our own judgement as much as faith in God. We may not pray for anything except so far as we believe it to be God's will; that belief is very fallible. The purpose of God's delay may well be to detach our faith in Him from all trust in our own judgement. Scarcely anything deepens and purifies faith in God for His own sake as surely as perseverance in prayer despite long disappointment.

So the purification of confidence by perseverance leads us to the third and deepest requirement. The other two were enjoined upon all His hearers; this was urged upon His more intimate disciples in these closing discourses recorded by St. John. Here are the great sayings:

'Whatsoever ye shall ask in my name, this will I do, that the Father may be glorified in the Son. If ye shall ask anything in my name, I will do it' (xiv, 13, 14).

'If ye abide in me and my sayings abide in you, ask whatsoever ye will and it shall come to pass for you' (xv, 7).

'If ye ask anything of the Father, he will give it you, in my name; until now ye did not ask anything in my name; ask, and ye will receive, that your joy may be fulfilled' (xvi, 23, 24).

When the condition mentioned is satisfied, our wills are identified with the will of God; we are then praying for what He desires to give and waits to give until we recognise Him as its source so that our reception of it will strengthen our faith and not encourage our neglect of Him.

This means that the essential act of prayer is not the bending of God's will to ours — of course not — but the bending of our wills to His. The proper outline of a Christian's prayer is not 'Please do for me what I want' but 'Please do in me, with me and through me what You want'. The pattern prayer that our Lord taught us is based on this principle; 'after this manner pray ye' (*St. Matthew* vi, 9). What is the manner?

When we come into our Father's presence, our Lord seems to say, we should be so filled with the thought of Him that we forget all about ourselves, our hopes, our needs, even our sins; what we want most of all and therefore utter first is that all men may know how glorious God is and reverence Him accordingly — 'Hallowed be thy Name'. (How often do we pray that? We say it every day; but do we pray it?) Our next desire is to be that everyone should obey Him, so that He is truly King of His own world — 'Thy kingdom come'; then that His whole purpose of love may be carried out, unspoilt by the selfishness in ourselves and others — 'Thy will be done'. Only after this do we turn to ourselves, and when we do it is to ask for those things which are necessary if we are to serve God with all our hearts: freedom from harassing anxiety — 'daily bread' or 'the morrow's bread'; and restoration to the favour we have forfeited — 'forgive us our trespasses'; and no moral adventures, for there is plenty on the straight path of duty to test character and develop grit without our being 'led' to the lairs of dragons — 'lead us not into temptation';

and some evil has a grip upon us from which we cannot free ourselves — 'deliver us' from that. And why? Is it because then we shall be good and happy? Not at all. It is because we are all the time concerned with God's Kingdom, Power and Glory.

The two sons of Zebedee once approached the Lord with a prayer which perfectly illustrates the wrong way to pray: 'Master, we would that thou shouldst do for us whatsoever we shall ask of thee'. After that, we are not surprised that their request was selfish in the worst sense — it was for something by gaining which they would keep others out of it. To such a prayer for selfish advantage there is and can be only one answer: Can you share My sacrifice? (*St. Mark* x, 35–38).

The essence of prayer is to seek how we may share that sacrifice. It finds its fullest expression in the Eucharist where we offer ourselves to Christ that He may unite us with Himself in His perfect self-offering to the Father — that self-offering to which He dedicated Himself in the great prayer which St. John now calls us to hear with adoring wonder.

CHAPTER XVII

WE now come to what is, perhaps, the most sacred passage even in the four Gospels — the record of the Lord's prayer of self-dedication as it lived in the memory and imagination of His most intimate friend.

It consists of three main sections:

(1) The Son and the Father (1–5).
(2) The Son and the disciples (6–19).
(3) The Son, the disciples and the world (20–26).

*

(1) THE SON AND THE FATHER

1–5. These things spake Jesus, and lifting up his eyes to heaven he said, 'Father, come is the hour; glorify thy Son that the Son may glorify thee, as thou gavest to him authority over all flesh that all which thou hast given him — he may give to them eternal Life. (And this is the eternal Life, to know thee the only true God, and whom thou sendedst — Jesus Christ.) I glorified thee on the earth by finishing the work which thou hast given me to do. And now glorify thou me, Father, in thine own presence with the glory which I had, before the world was, in thy presence.'

These things: the whole discourse from xiii, 31 onwards, but especially its closing words — *I have overcome the world* (xvi, 33). It is in the consciousness of victory and accomplishment (4) that the Lord dedicates Himself to the final sacrifice. So the author of *Hebrews* thinks of Him as going to His death like the victim wearing festal garlands and enduring the Cross in scorn of contempt because He is upheld by 'the joy that was set before him' (*Hebrews* ii, 9 — where see Nairne's commentary[1] — and xii, 2).

[1] *The Epistle of Priesthood*, pp. 308-314, especially 313-314.

These things: the discourse which ended with the declaration *I have overcome the world* or *I have conquered the universe*, had begun with the words *Now was glorified the Son of Man* (xiii, 31) uttered as the door closed behind Judas. Then He had committed Himself to the way of the Cross; now He accepts and welcomes it.

Lifting up his eyes to heaven, he said 'Father'. So it had been before the recalling of Lazarus from death to life (xi, 41). So it is now as He enters on His own passage from life to death. Always His trust is in the Father to whom His obedience is given. So it will be at the very close: 'Father, into thy hands I commend my spirit' (*St. Luke* xxiii, 46).

'Father, come is the hour; glorify thy Son.' When the Greeks came He had greeted their approach with the words: *Come is the hour that the Son of Man may be glorified*, and went on at once to speak of the harvest that can only come through death (xii, 23, 24). When Judas had gone out into the night He said *Now was glorified the Son of Man*. Here is the third use of the solemn phrase: *Come is the hour; glorify thy Son.* It is the hour for the Son of Man to be *lifted up* (xii, 32, 34). His glory is about to reach its full splendour: for it is the glory or shining forth of love, and *greater love than this hath no man, that a man lay down his life on behalf of his friends* (xv, 13).

Glorify thy Son, that the Son may glorify thee. The glory of the Father and that of the Son are inseparable. The Father glorifies the Son by sustaining Him in His perfect obedience even unto death, and the Son glorifies the Father by the perfection of the obedience which He offers. Because God is Love, the Cross is the glory, or, if we will, the 'effulgence of the glory' (*Hebrews* 1, 3) alike of the Father and of the Son.

The Cross is the glory of God because self-sacrifice is the expression of love. That glory would be complete in itself even if it had no consequences. But in fact what is revealed in the Cross is not only the perfection of the divine love, but its triumph. For by its sacrifice the divine love wins those who can appreciate it out of their selfishness which is spiritual death into loving fellowship with itself which is true life: 'we know that we have passed out of death into Life, because we love the brethren' (*I John* iii, 14). But we do not effect that passage in any strength of our own; it is the gift of God through Christ: *as thou gavest to him to have authority over all flesh that all which thou hast given him — he may give to them eternal Life.*

To the Son is given *authority to execute judgment because he is Son of Man* (v. 27). So far this might be displayed in condemnation or in pardon. But if the Father now perfectly glorifies the Son, and the Son perfectly glorifies the Father — if, in other words, that burning love which is the heart of the Godhead be displayed — then the authority of the Son will be exercised in the gift of eternal Life. For the Judge will be Himself the Saviour.

How far this salvation extends is left undefined. It reaches *all which thou has given him,* for if any man responds to the love of God in Christ he does so in virtue of the Father's act; He had said before, *No man can come to me except the Father which sent me draw him* (vi, 44); and those words were at once followed by the promise — *and I will raise him up at the last day.* So here the gift of the Son to those whom the Father has given to Him is *eternal life.* They are thought of as a single company, a single gift — *that which thou hast given him.* For in Him we are one; in so far as we are not one we are not yet in Him; and the prayer for the disciples which follows is primarily *that they may be one* (11). To every member of this fellowship, given by the Father to the Son, the Son will give eternal life, if so be that the Father glorify the Son and the Son the Father.

The condition is indispensable; but if it be fulfilled the consequence is inevitable. For *this is the eternal life, to know thee the only true God, and whom thou sendedst, Jesus Christ.* This knowledge does not earn eternal life; it is eternal life. Do we hesitate to accept that? Does it seem to us that just 'knowing' a theological truth cannot be an adequate occupation for eternity? Certainly it could not be. But the word for *know* here is not that which stands for a grasp of truth; it is that which stands for personal acquaintance. Even in human friendships there is the constant delight of new discoveries by each in the character of the other. Eternity cannot be too long for our finite spirits to advance in knowledge of the infinite God.

We constantly miss the spiritual value of the greatest religious phrases by failing to recall their true meaning. At one time I was much troubled that the climax of the *Veni Creator* should be

> Teach us to know the Father, Son,
> And Thee, of Both, to be but One.

It seemed to suggest that the ultimate purpose of the coming of the Holy Spirit was to persuade us of the truth of an orthodox formula. But that is mere thoughtlessness. If a man once knows the Spirit within him, the source of all his aspiration after holiness, as indeed the Spirit of Jesus Christ, and if he knows this Spirit of Jesus Christ within himself as none other than the Spirit of the Eternal and Almighty God, what more can he want? *This is the eternal life.*

This definition of eternal life can hardly be regarded as a part of the prayer addressed by our Lord to the Father. It is a comment inserted by the Evangelist. But his mind is so identified with its content — in this instance the prayer offered by the Lord — that he so phrases his comment as to make it, in grammatical construction, part of the prayer. It is a signal instance of the extent to which his mind and his theme have interpenetrated one another; this is the cause of modifications in the form of language used, but it is also the condition of the profound apprehension achieved and expressed.

I glorified thee on the earth by finishing the work which thou hast given me to do. His active obedience is the means by which

He gives glory to God; so in *Hebrews* 'Lo, I am come to do thy will, O God' (*Hebrews* x, 7 quoting *Psalm* xl, 7, 8). He has done all that can be done *on the earth*. He has loved *to the uttermost* (xiii, 1) that life in this world permits. One ultimate perfection of love remains to be achieved, and He prays that now this may be His — the perfect expression of love in the perfection of self-sacrifice.

I glorified thee on the earth by finishing the work which thou hast given me to do. What work was that? The revelation of God and, therein, the establishment of His Kingdom; or, in other words, the living of a life of perfect love and thereby the winning of that new control in the hearts of men which is called 'holy spirit'. This He has done so far as it can be done at all *on earth*, that is, under the conditions of human life here. And therein He has glorified the Father. For all that we adore in Him is the Father's glory shining through Him — *glory as of an only-begotten from a Father* (i, 14) — and His showing forth of this is therefore a giving of glory to the Father.

We are all familiar with this double thought in other connexions; a boy is trained by his school to a life of discipline and public service; thereafter the school is proud of him and honours him; but what people admire in him is what his school has given to him, and he, by fidelity to what he has learnt, brings honour to his school. If we sometimes find this thought difficult when applied to the highest levels of spiritual attainment, that is only because of our disastrous tendency to sheer individualism in things of the spirit — (see 10 below); it is never possible to divide up the credit for spiritual achievement and allot portions to different persons.

All that can be done *on earth* — under conditions of earthly life — has been done. But there remains what can be done through death, which is indeed *on earth* so far as it is the close of earthly life, but is already in heaven so far as it is the gateway to fulfilled fellowship with the Father. This it can be, without transition or mediation, only if he who dies is already 'made perfect in love' (*I John* iv, 18). That condition has once, and once only, been fulfilled. Because Jesus had *finished the work* of living the life of love, therefore for Him death is immediate passage to the eternal glory. *And now glorify thou me, Father, in thine own presence with the glory which I had before the world was, in thy presence.*

The love that was always perfect according to the existing reality — perfect in the manger, in the home, in the carpenter's shop, in the works of mercy, in the words of life — now reaches its culmination in the absolute self-abnegation of love undimmed — nay, victoriously intensified — by agony and death. This is the perfect fellowship with the Father manifested under the conditions of a sinful world. In one sense it is true to say that the death on the Cross was the gateway to that eternal fellowship and glory; but more profoundly it is true to say that the death on the Cross is itself the attainment of that fellowship and glory in absolute plenitude.

There is no contradiction between the thought that the Lord Jesus was always, from His Birth, perfectly united with the Father, and saying that He 'advanced in favour with God and men' (*St. Luke* ii, 52) or that He 'learned obedience by the things which he suffered' (*Hebrews* v, 8). If Herod had succeeded in killing Him in His infancy, there would have been an Incarnation, but no effective revelation of the divine love. He grew as boy and man; at every stage He was perfect in that stage; only by all the stages of a life matured to full manhood and then cut short by the self-centredness of a world unable to bear the intolerable glory and judgement of love in its fulness — only so could the whole revelation be given, the whole power of divine love be exercised, the whole triumph of love over selfishness be won. The Cross is the focus of the Eternal glory.

For this perfection of divine love, which had *before the world was* united the Father and the Son, is precisely what sent the Son into the world; *God so loved that he gave* (iii, 16). That love is now to pay the full price and win its longed-for result.

It is not the Cross as an isolated episode which is thus the focus of the eternal glory; it is the Cross as the culmination of the life of love, as the achievement of the purpose of the Incarnation, as the projection of divine light across the spaces of the world's darkness. But in fact the Cross is all of these; therefore as He approaches the Cross, and with direct reference to the Cross, the Son prays to the Father, *Now — now glorify thou me, Fathe , in thine own presence, with the glory which I had, before the world was, in thy presence.*

The Aaronic High Priest entered into the Holiest Place (symbol of the immediate presence of God) to offer the blood of the victim (symbol of the consecrated life of Israel). Our High Priest enters the immediate presence of God in and by the very act of offering His own consecrated life; for to make that offering and to be in that presence are not two things, but one.

In that presence the Lord was *before the world was*; from that presence He has never moved; but, as is necessary in this world of time and change, has *on earth* (4) at once experienced and exhibited its meaning in progressive stages; *now* He will again be in that presence in the uttermost meaning of those words. And He wills that where He is, His disciples also may be with Him (24).

'Having, therefore, brethren, boldness to enter into the holy place, by the blood of Jesus, by the way which he dedicated for us, a new and living way, through the veil, that is to say his flesh; and having a great high priest over the house of God; let us draw near with a true heart in full assurance.' 'For we have not a high priest that cannot be touched with the feeling of our infirmities; but one that hath been in all points tempted like as we are, apart from (temptations due to past) sin'; 'who in the days of his flesh, having offered up prayers and supplications with strong crying and tears unto him that was able to save him out of death, and having been heard for his godly fear, though he was a Son, yet learned obedience by the things which he suffered, and having been made perfect, he

became unto all them that obey him the cause of eternal salvation' (*Hebrews* x, 19–22; iv, 15; v, 7–9).

*

(2) THE SON AND THE DISCIPLES (6–19)

6–8. 'I manifested thy Name to the men whom thou gavest me out of the
world. Thine they were and to me thou gavest them, and thy word they
have observed. Now they recognised that all things which thou hast
given me are from thee, because the sayings which thou gavest me I have
given to them, and they themselves received them, and recognised truly
that from thee I came forth and they believed that thou didst send me.'

I manifested thy Name. Here, as always, the Name is the
revealed Nature. Jesus has manifested the Nature of God.
He has not only described it; He has made it apparent; He has
exhibited it. But this has not been done to all men, but *to the
men whom thou gavest me out of the world*. St. Jude had been
perplexed by the thought that the Lord would manifest Himself
to the disciples and not to the world (xiv, 22). But in fact
nothing else was possible. If God were merely Omnipotence,
that could be manifested to everyone by display of miraculous
power. But Love cannot be so made manifest; the cynical pride
of self-centred men will say that its hope is visionary, its
joy tedium, and its sacrifice weakness. How can love so pen-
etrate the shell of the self-complacent as to be recognised by
them? So the Lord makes known His Father's Nature of love
to those who already belong to the Father as having at least
enough of the 'image of God' still unobliterated to afford the
kinship that makes recognition possible. *Thine they were;*
before ever the Lord called them they were truly among the
People of God. *And to me thou gavest them;* they heard His
call and followed; but this was the Father's doing, for *no man
can come to me except the Father which hath sent me draw him*
(vi, 44 and 65). *And thy word they have observed;* for the word
that the Lord has spoken is what He has heard from His

Father (viii, 26, 40; xiv, 24); in observing the teaching of Jesus they were observing the word of the Father.

Now they recognised that all things which thou hast given me are from thee. This is the crucial recognition — not that Jesus is from God, which is the first stage of Christian faith, but that (since this is so) what we find in Him to love and to worship is in truth not His but the Father's. The religious value of the doctrine of the Incarnation is not found in what it affirms concerning the historical Figure, Jesus of Nazareth, but in what it affirms concerning the eternal God. When we know that all the *grace and truth* (i, 14) which shine in Jesus Christ are shining through Him from the Father, we begin to understand who and what God really is.

All this is made possible through the fidelity with which the Son reproduces the mind and activity of the Father (v, 19) — *because the sayings which thou gavest me I have given to them* — and through the faith with which the disciples received that revelation — *and they themselves received them, and recognised truly that from thee I came forth.* Thus the disciples, and we among them, have been led to that principle and activity of Apostleship which is introduced into this prayer by a fivefold refrain (8, 18, 21, 23, 25) — *and they believed that thou didst send me.*

The Apostolic Mission of the Son is the pivot of human history regarded as an arena wherein the divine purpose is being accomplished. All turns on that. From that flows the Apostleship of Church and Ministry. If God sent the Son, then the witness of the Church and its challenge to the world has divine authority. If God sent the Son, then in that act we see disclosed the heart of the Eternal. There is no cause for wonder that in this prayer, offered as His ministry approaches its climax and its close, the Lord should make this a central theme — *that thou didst send me.*

*

9–11. 'I ask concerning them. Not concerning the world do I ask, but
concerning them whom thou hast given me, because they are thine (and
all mine are thine and thine are mine), and I have been glorified in them.
And no longer am I in the world, and they are in the world, and I to
thee am coming. Holy Father, watch over them in thy Name which
thou hast given to me, that they may be one as we.'

I ask concerning them. Again, as in xvi, 26, the word used
of the Lord's prayer to His Father is that which suggests enquiry
rather than petition, as though, not venturing to make requests
of the Father, He rather consults Him on their behalf. No
doubt the version 'I pray for them' is right in a translation
intended for public or general reading; but the tone of the word
actually used has a suggestion of real beauty and value. Most
of our prayers would be the better if they were completely
free from any element of clamour or demand, and had more of
the quality of a consultation in which we lay the needs of ourselves and of others before our Father that He may supply
them as His loving wisdom suggests.

Not concerning the world do I ask. The world is the whole
system of nature, including human nature, which 'lieth in the
evil one' (*I John* v, 19). It was the object of God's redemptive
love, which prompted the sending of the Son (iii, 16), and the
Lord has overcome it (xvi, 33). It will at last, through the faith
of disciples, be won to that same faith (23). But till the disciples are *perfected into one* (23) the world cannot be penetrated by the Gospel. The Lord yearns to redeem it; but He
will do this through the continuance of His own apostolic
mission in His disciples (18). Therefore His prayer is not
directly for the world, but for the disciples, who, after all, are
part of the world (15), and through whom the world is to be
won.

*But concerning them whom thou hast given me, because they
are thine.* The disciples are a gift of the Father to the Son, for
*No man can come to me except the Father which sent me draw
him; no one can come to me except it have been given to him of
my Father* (vi, 44 and 65). The Father could give them because

they were His. Indeed between the Father and the Son there is complete identity of ownership; *all mine are thine and thine are mine.* And in these who thus belong both to the Father and the Son, the Son has been glorified. The constancy of their loyalty and faith amid all the controversies, even at a time when *many of the disciples went back and walked no more with him* (vi, 66), had brought glory to the Son: *I have been glorified in them.*

And no longer am I in the world. The Lord has been *in the world*, not only locally, but in the sense of sharing all the limitations of human experience alongside His disciples. Now that is ending. Death will at once free Him from the limitations and remove Him from the side of His disciples; but they must remain; *they are in the world*; they will still be subject to all the pressures of the world, including even its hatred (14), without their Master beside them to steady their hearts and minds, because separation from them is involved in the perfecting of His union with the Father — *I to thee am coming.*

What shall be His prayer for them as He leaves them to be His witnesses in the world? Shall it be that they may be courageous? strong? pure in heart? All these are, no doubt, included in what He asks, but these are not foremost. Two things He puts first: that the Father will watch over them with the protection of His Name — His character revealed in Christ; and that they may be united. *Holy Father, watch over them in thy Name which thou hast given to me, that they may be one as we.*

Holy Father. The fundamental element in the concept of holiness is separation from the profane world. In primitive times this separation is conceived locally or ceremonially; as faith becomes more spiritual, the separation is understood as that between righteousness and sin, love and selfishness; but the thought of separateness persists. Here, where the burden of the prayer is deliverance from the evil power of the world (15), the thought of God as wholly separate from that evil is specially appropriate. The Father is asked to grant to the disciples His own immunity from evil.

Watch over them in thy Name which thou hast given to me. The word translated in our versions 'keep' is that which always suggests attentive watching. The Lord prays His Father to watch in loving care these disciples to whom the great task is now committed. This He is besought to do in His own Name, which yet has been given to be the Name of Christ. Thus St. Paul says that the Father gave to Him 'the name which is above every name' (*Philippians* ii, 9) and must therefore be God's own Name; if any Name in the literal sense of that word is in mind, presumably it is Adonai. But the thought is of revealed character, not of any spoken sound. This, which is first the Father's own, the Father has given to the Son. Christ came 'in the Father's name' (v, 43) as representing Him in the world; but this He could do only because He was one in character with the Father, so that seeing Him we see the Father (xiv, 9). In that character of holy love the Father is prayed to watch over the disciples, holding them within the sphere of that love, so that it may possess their hearts — of which the proof will be their unity among themselves.

That they may be one. The Lord is going away. In the whole world His cause will be represented by this little handful of disciples. If they fall apart, the cause is lost. What is most of all essential is that they be united. We see in the *Acts of the Apostles* in how many ways the infant Church was tempted to disunity — as for example in the doctrinal difference concerning the authority of the Law for Gentile Christians (*Acts* xv, 1–29) or the personal difference between Paul and Barnabas concerning John Mark (*Acts* xv, 36–41). Such division at that stage would have been fatal; it has been sufficiently disastrous coming later, as it did. So the Lord's prayer was, and (we cannot doubt) still is, that His disciples may be one.

But the unity of the Church is precious not only for its utility in strengthening the Church as an evangelistic agent. It is itself in principle the consummation to which all history moves. The purpose of God in creation was, and is, to fashion a fellowship of free spirits knit together by a love in all its members which answers to the manifested love of God — or, as St. Paul expresses it, to 'sum up all things in Christ' (*Ephesians* i, 10). The agent of that purpose is the Church, which is therefore called the Body of Christ, through the activity and self-edifying of which Christ Himself is 'fulfilled' (*Ephesians* i, 23) where we should read for 'the fulness of him that filleth all in all' — 'the fulness of him who, taking things all in all, is being fulfilled'. For the fulfilling of Christ to the 'measure of the stature of His completeness' (*Ephesians* iv, 13) is the meaning of universal history. The unity of the Church is something much more than unity of ecclesiastical structure, though it cannot be complete without this. It is the love of God in Christ possessing the hearts of men so as to unite them in itself — as the Father and the Son are united in that love of Each for Each which is the Holy Spirit. The unity which the Lord prays that His disciples may enjoy is that which is eternally characteristic of the Tri-une God. It is therefore something much more than a means to any end — even though that end be the evangelisation of the world; it is itself the one worthy end of all human aspiration; it is the life of Heaven. For His prayer is not only *that they may be one*; it is *that they may be one as we*.

Before the loftiness of that hope and calling our little experience of unity and fellowship is humbled to the dust. Our friendships, our reconciliations, our unity of spirit in Church gatherings or in missionary conferences — beautiful as they are, and sometimes even wonderful in comparison with our habitual life of sectional rivalries and tensions, yet how poor and petty they appear in the light of the Lord's longing. Let all of us who are concerned in Peace Movements or Faith and Order Movements or 'Conversations' with fellow-Christians of other denominations, take note of the judgement under which we stand by virtue of the gulf separating the level of our highest attainment and noblest enterprise, from 'the prize of

the call upwards which God gives in Christ Jesus' (*Philippians*
iii, 14) — *that they may be one as we.*

*

12–13. 'When I was with them, I was watching over them in thy Name
which thou hast given to me, and I guarded them, and none of them was
destroyed except the son of destruction, that the scripture might be
fulfilled. But now to thee I am coming; and these things I speak in the
world that they may have the joy that is mine fulfilled in themselves.'

When the Lord was among His disciples He exercised that
loving care which now He prays the Father to exercise: *When
I was with them, I was watching over them in thy Name which
thou hast given to me.* The divine character of loving wisdom
is at once the motive of His vigilance and the protection in
which He enfolds them. *And I guarded them;* He was, as it
were, their sentry keeping evil influences away from them. And
this was done effectively, for *none of them was destroyed except
the son of destruction, that the scripture might be fulfilled.* The
one exception proves the rule, for he who was destroyed
perished by his own quality from which no external guardian-
ship could protect him; he was a *son of destruction.* It was his
nature to destroy; he sought to destroy Jesus, but he did
destroy himself, when *he went immediately out, and it was night*
(xiii, 30). And even therein was the divine purpose carried
towards its accomplishment, as is shown by the fact that
Judas was fulfilling scripture (see xiii, 18 and the comment
there).

But now to thee I am coming — the first theme of the prayer
and the occasion of all the rest. *And these things I speak that
they may have the joy that is mine fulfilled in themselves.* The
mind and will of the Lord are in their very nature a prayer to
the Father. There is no need for Him to utter any prayer. But
He does utter it, just as He uttered His thanksgiving for answer
to prayer on another occasion (xi, 41, 42), in order that His
disciples may know what His mind and will are, and His
purpose for them, so that there may be brought to full measure

in them the joy which is His — the joy of union with the
Father and, in Him, with all who are united to Him by faith
and love.

*

14–15. 'I have given them thy word, and the world hated them, because
they are not from the world as I myself am not from the world. I do not
ask that thou shouldest take them from the world but that thou shouldest
protect them from the evil one.'

I have given them thy word. This, repeated in substance from
verse 8, is the supreme service of Christ to the disciples. He
has given them the self-utterance, the self-disclosure, of the
Father. They were able to receive it; the world could not
(xiv, 17, 21–24). That is because of the distinctive character
of the world and of the disciples; the world hates anything
which it cannot understand which yet seems to contain a judgement of itself; so *the world hated them, because they are not
from the world as I myself am not from the world.*

The word which I translate *from* throughout this passage
is that which I have elsewhere usually translated *out of.* It
denotes origin, or character due to origin, or (with words of
protection or deliverance) the thought of a hold or grip from
which escape is sought.

Thus when it is said that the disciples, even as their Lord,
are not from the world, it is origin and character due to origin
that are in question. Everything in them which qualified them
to receive the Father's word and to become disciples has its
origin elsewhere than in this world; but in the passage that
follows it is rather separation and protection that are in mind,
though the use of the same preposition makes a connecting
link.

I do not ask that thou shouldest take them from the world.
He is leaving the world, but they must remain in the world,
though they do not belong to the world. They remain there as
witnesses, through whom the world itself will at last believe
(23). For all Christians at all times it is a hard question how
they are to fulfil their vocation to be in, but not of or from,

the world. The hermit seems to err by going out of the world;
the worldly Christian errs by being of or from the world.
Where is the line of true adjustment between the two? This is
the heart of the controversy on Pacifism. All that the Lord
here lays down is the double principle itself — in the world
but not of it.

But that thou shouldest protect them from the evil one. Here
the word translated *protect* is again that which suggests careful
attention, translated in verse 11 *Watch over*; and the word
translated *from* suggests that the Evil One has a hold or grip
upon them. They are not snow-white innocents who only need
to be kept from all contamination by evil. We remember the
desire of the Sons of Thunder to call down fire from Heaven
on the Samaritans who would not receive the Lord (*St. Luke*
ix, 54); or the dispute but a few hours ago *which of them is
accounted to be greatest* (*St. Luke* xxii, 24); or Simon Peter's
imminent denial. The divine watchfulness has not only to keep
them from evil contacts, but to set them free from the hold
which the Evil One has upon them even now.

And we, who are also disciples, know how true this is of
ourselves. Can we even say with confidence that we are not
from the world (which 'lieth in the evil one') as He is not from
the world? Yes — if we have at all received and observed His
word, we can say that. But the Evil One (person or principle
matters little) has a grip upon us: 'deliver us from the Evil
One'.

                                *

16–19. 'From the world they are not, as I myself am not from the world.
   Consecrate them in the truth; "thy word is truth". As me thou didst
   send into the world, I also sent them into the world. And for their sakes
   I consecrate myself, that they also may be consecrated in truth.'

*From the world they are not, as I myself am not from the
world;* the declaration of verse 14 is repeated as an introduction
to the thought of consecration which immediately follows;
for the consecration of the disciples, which is dependent on
that of their Master, is bestowed on the same ground; their

qualification to receive it is the same in kind as His, however far it falls short in degree.

Consecrate them. The Greek word is that used for the consecration of a sacrificial victim or the hallowing of a man for sacred work. It refers more to the external benediction and commission than to the inward character. As contrasted with 'purify' it is positive, not negative. To 'purify' is to cleanse from uncleanness, such as would disqualify a man for consecration; to 'consecrate' is to equip a man already qualified with the commission to work for God. The disciples are already cleansed or purified on account of the word which Christ has spoken to them (xv, 3); their life now has its spring in that word, so that they are not *from the world*. Therefore He prays the Father to *consecrate them* for their work of witness.

Because their work is witness, their consecration is *in the truth*. So St. Paul tells his converts at Thessalonica that God chose them 'as first-fruits unto salvation in consecration of spirit and faith in the truth' (*II Thessalonians* ii, 13). The truth, which is given to them and to which they are to bear witness, is, so to speak, the medium and atmosphere of their consecration. So the word both cleanses and consecrates, and the identity of the cleansing and consecrating word and the truth is then clinched by the citation of *Psalm* cxix, 142 — *Thy word is truth.*

Now follows the purpose and occasion of this consecration: *As me thou didst send into the world, I also sent them into the world.* The Apostolic mission and ministry which originates in the sending of the Son by the Father is continued in the sending of the Apostles by the Son. Once again the Lord appears as true Mediator. The Father : the Son : : the Son : the Apostles. Down the centuries and across the continents and oceans the Apostolate continues, till 'the consummation of the **age**' (*St. Matthew* xxviii, 20). Soon He will repeat this apostolic commission when He breathes upon them the Holy Spirit (xx, 21, 22). But now He turns to Himself, the channel through whom this ministry of salvation flows forth from the Father.

*And for their sakes I consecrate myself, that they also may
be consecrated in truth.* Wonderful words! *For their sakes* He
had come into the world and spoken as *never man spake* (vii,
46): now *for their sakes* — for our sakes — He consecrates
Himself. No other could do that. I cannot consecrate myself;
Aaron could not consecrate himself. But He, who is 'a High
Priest for ever', not by any succession but 'after the order of
Melchizedek' (*Hebrews* vi, 20; vii, 2, 3), consecrates Himself.
But to what end? Is not the Father's mission His consecration?
No; something more is now called for. He has fulfilled that
mission. He has glorified the Father on the earth by finishing
the work which He had given Him to do (4). There remains
the glory which is attained in that departure from earth which
is called death. To this He now commits Himself. But this
death, which to ordinary observers will seem an execution, is
in its true reality a sacrifice. The priest consecrates the victim;
I consecrate myself.

That they also may be consecrated in truth. His mission and
His consecration are alike mediatorial. Their end is not in
themselves, but in their effect, which is the union of those
whom the Father has given Him (6) alike with His mission and
with His consecration. The principle applies to all Christians,
pre-eminently to those who are by office commissioned as
witnesses, but by no means to them alone.

Consecrated in truth: truly consecrated, and commissioned
as an agent of truth. That is our vocation; to most of us it is
still our aspiration rather than our experience; the power to
translate that aspiration into experience flows from the self-
consecration of Christ to that perfect obedience which He
consummated on the Cross.

*

(3) THE SON, THE DISCIPLES AND THE WORLD (20–26)

20–23. 'But not concerning these alone do I ask, but also concerning those
who believe on me through their word, that they all may be one, as thou,
Father, in me and I in thee, that they also may be in us, that the world
may believe that thou didst send me. And the glory which thou hast
given to me I have given to them, that they may be one as we are one — I
in them and thou in me, that they may be perfected into one, that the
world may come to recognise that thou didst send me and didst love
them as thou didst love me.'

Not concerning these alone do I ask. His prayer was for the
disciples for their own sake, but also for the sake of others
whom they would win to discipleship. We are to our Lord
at once ends in ourselves, and means to other ends; it is dangerous for us to forget either. *But also concerning those who
believe on me through their word. Who believe;* present tense;
wherever there is a true disciple, there are others whom he has
won or is winning. The circle of the Church widens for ever
from the moment of the Incarnation till it reaches the limits
of the world. *Through their word* — for 'belief cometh of
hearing, and hearing by the word of Christ' (*Romans* x, 17),
the word which the Father gave to the Son and the Son to His
disciples (8, 14). *That they all may be one* — the spiritual unity
which is perfect mutual love is to include these newer converts
also and bind them into that fellowship which answers to the
perfection of love in the Godhead — *as thou, Father, in me and
I in thee, that they also may be in us.*

Once again we are reminded how transcendent is that theme
which alone deserves the name of Christian unity. We meet in
committees and construct our schemes of union; in face of the
hideous fact of Christian divisions we are driven to this; but
how paltry are our efforts compared with the call of God!
The way to the union of Christendom does not lie through
committee-rooms, though there is a task of formulation to be
done there. It lies through personal union with the Lord so

deep and real as to be comparable with His union with the
Father. For the prayer is not directly that believers may be
'one' in the Father and the Son, though by a natural error an
early scribe introduced that thought. The prayer is *that they
may be in us*. If we are in the Father and the Son, we certainly
shall be one, and our unity will increase our effective influence
in the world. But it is not our unity as such that has converting
power; it is our incorporation into the *true Vine* as branches
in which the divine life is flowing. When all believers are truly
'in Christ', then their witness will have its destined effect —
that the world may believe that thou didst send me.

For the salvation of the world is the goal. *God so loved the
world* (iii, 16). The divine 'election' (*I chose you out of the
world*, xv, 19), whereby some have spiritual opportunities
which are denied to others, does not operate for the sake of the
elect alone; they have those opportunities in order that, by use
of them, they may win others to the divine love. The purpose
of election, as of judgement, is 'that he might have mercy upon
all' (*Romans* xi, 32). The Father sent the Son, the Son sent
the Apostles, the Apostles sent those who should carry on the
message till at last the world should believe — what? That the
Father sent the Son. For in this Mission lies the one hope of
the world; and the world's supreme need is to discover that
its hope lies there.

Now the condition and consequence of this perfect unity are
unfolded. *And the glory which thou hast given to me I have
given to them*. We know now what that glory is — absolute
love in perfect self-expression; this, in face of the selfishness of
the world, is the Cross, but when the divine love has by its
self-sacrifice won its response, it is the perfect happiness of
love given and returned. This, of which the Cross is one aspect
and the New Jerusalem is the other aspect, is what the Father
eternally bestows upon the Son, and the Son historically
bestows upon His disciples.

The purpose and consequence of that gift of *glory* is that the
unity of the Godhead may be reproduced in them — in us —

that they may be one as we are one. The possibility of this,
which seems so unattainable, is grounded in the position and
work of Christ as the perfect Mediator — *I in them and thou
in me* (for the Father : the Son : : the Son : His disciples);
and this unity is, after all, the fulfilment of their own destiny:
that they may be perfected into one. That fellowship of love is
the end for which we were created and for which our nature
as God fashioned it is designed. By His Incarnation the Lord
Jesus not only cancels the consequences of sin and eliminates
sin itself, but carries forward the purpose of God in the
creation of man to its fulfilment. The word translated
perfected does not primarily suggest ethical perfection but
complete realisation of ideal or type; a fair rendering of
the original would be: *that they may become full grown into
one.*

Plainly this purpose of God in creation cannot be complete
in a selection of individuals. So we return to the great hope
that the world may come to recognise that thou didst send me;
only now it is *recognise*, not *believe* as in 21; for now there is
offered something for the world to see, namely *the glory* which
the Father gave to the Son, and the Son to the disciples (22),
the glory which is absolute love in perfect self-expression. So
through the perfecting into one of the disciples and their
converts (23) the world is enabled progressively to *recognise*
the divine activity at work — *that thou didst send me*, but also
that thou didst love them as thou didst love me. It is the manifestation of God's love toward us in our mutual love which
shall at last convert the world.

*

24. 'Father, as for that which thou hast given to me — I will that where
I am they also may be with me, that they may behold the glory that is
mine, which thou hast given to me because thou lovedst me before the
foundation of the world.'

Father: the simple address without epithet (contrast 11 and
25) suggests the intimately personal nature of this prayer. He

does not now *ask*, but states a desire or longing for the eternal companionship of His friends in the Father's presence. He has given to them the glory which He received from the Father (22), and now yearns for fellowship with them in the fruition of it. *As for that which thou hast given to me:* again, as in 2 and vi, 37 and 39, the neuter singular is substituted for the masculine plural to suggest the unity of the fellowship which was the Father's gift to the Son. *I will that where I am they also may be with me.* He came not to do His own will; but He knows that this for which He longs is the Father's will; so at the height of His prayer of self-dedication He can present to the Father His own desire. Indeed it is only at such a moment, when we have no desire which is not His, that we can safely and confidently present in our prayers our own desires.

That they may behold the glory that is mine. The word *behold* is that which we have often rendered by 'notice' or 'take note of'. Here the more exalted tone is essential, but the idea is still that of careful attention, which, in this case, must be adoring contemplation. *The glory that is mine;* for it is not what any had ever dared to call 'glory' before; yet beside it the lustre of all other glory is tarnished and tawdry. This glory is not His own; it shines through Him (i, 14); it is the Father's gift — *which thou hast given to me because thou lovedst me before the foundation of the world.* The perfect love of the Father for the Son and of the Son for the Father — which is the Holy Spirit — is the glory of the Godhead. It is eternal. In the earthly sojourn of the Son it is historically disclosed; but itself it is eternal — *before the world was* (5), *before the foundation of the world* (24).

The prayer of the Lord for His disciples is that they may *behold*, may contemplate with adoration, that glory. Is there an element of hope for His own delight in their full understanding of Him? There is no reason to exclude that thought, for such delight is a fruit of love. But His longing that they may be with Him and behold the glory which the Father eternally bestows on Him is not chiefly for His sake but for theirs; for this is the Vision of God, the Beatific Vision, the infinite joy of the finite soul. *

25-26. 'Righteous Father, the world did not recognise thee, but I recognised thee and these recognised that thou didst send me. And I made known to them thy Name and will make it known, that the love wherewith thou lovedst me may be in them and I in them.'

Righteous Father: the more personal appeal is made and ended. Now He addresses the Father as *righteous* or 'just', because He must needs return from the ultimate hope of a converted and believing world (23) to the immediate need of the present. The world still rejects the light, and only the Lord and His disciples have recognised the Father — He by direct vision, they through the manifestation in the Incarnate Son (vi, 46 and xiv, 9). It is justice which requires a discrimination between the world and the disciples, so that here again as earlier (9) the Lord's concern is for these, that the divine love and the Lord Himself may be in them. *The world did not recognise thee*; the opportunity was given, but the blind world would not take it. *But I recognised thee*; the Lord's unique apprehension of the Father is the basis of all knowledge of God that comes through the revelation in the Son. *And these recognised that thou didst send me*; they have not been blind to the revelation, though as yet their understanding of it is limited to a realisation that their Lord is one sent from God (xvi, 30). The Lord has set the truth before them; but they have not yet fully grasped it; so He will continue to set it before them; indeed His supreme disclosure of it is now imminent. *I made known to them thy Name*; the Name is the manifested character. His whole life and teaching has been making this known; but there remains a still fuller manifestation. *God so loved the world* (iii, 16); the disciples had not yet seen fully how He loved; that was only now about to appear; not yet can the Revealer cry *It is finished* (xix, 30); and so *I made known to them thy Name and will make it known* — upon the Cross.

And what is the purpose of that revelation? Nothing less
than this: *that the love wherewith thou lovedst me* — the very
life of Triune Godhead — *may be in them and I in them.* We
are called to be 'partakers of the divine nature' (*II Peter* i, 4),
of that love which is the essence of Deity. This becomes
possible through the indwelling in us of the Son — *I in them* —
not by any spontaneous or laborious ascent of our own spirits.
How then does the Love of God effect His entrance into our
self-centred and hardened hearts? If we read on we shall see.

*

xviii, 1. When he had said these things Jesus went forth with his disciples
over the brook Kedron, where was a garden, into which he entered,
himself and his disciples.

That garden was Gethsemane.

ACT IV

THE CONFLICT OF LIGHT WITH DARKNESS

Chapters XVIII and XIX

THE CONFLICT OF LIGHT WITH
DARKNESS

HITHERTO the Evangelist has told his story with its spiritual meaning for every reader foremost in his mind. He has recorded acts of the Lord, but always for the sake of a lesson taught by them — a lesson brought out by a discourse contained in the narrative itself, as the discourse on the Bread of Life draws out the meaning of the Feeding of the Five Thousand. The whole section which I have called Act III (Chapters XIII–XVII) consists of discourse, though in Chapter XIII this is connected with the Feet Washing; and in those discourses as thus recorded the living Lord is speaking to our souls, as once He spoke to the disciples and to His Father.

But now, in Act IV (Chapters XVIII and XIX) and in Act V (Chapter XX) we have narrative without any interpreting discourse. It is possible, no doubt, to seek personal application here as elsewhere, to consider how far the sin of Judas or Peter or Caiaphas or Pilate is to be found in our own hearts; and this is profitable in its place. But it seems that St. John would here direct our minds away from ourselves altogether to the Lord; we are now not to meditate, but to contemplate; for the *crisis of this world* (XII) is come, and the conflict between light and darkness is being fought out, until the Victor cries.'*It is finished*' (XIX), even until His victory is made manifest (XX). What most benefits us now is not to seek ' personal applications' but to become wholly concentrated upon the Word of God as He goes forth 'to judge and to make war' (*Revelation* xix, 11).

Consequently we shall follow St. John's own lead and from this point onwards seek only to understand the objective fact itself — the fact which justified the triumphant cry, *It is finished.*

CHAPTER XVIII

(1) THE ARREST (1-11)

1. When he had said these things Jesus went forth with his disciples over the brook Kedron, where was a garden, into which he entered, himself and his disciples.

Jesus went forth from the Temple Court where He had consecrated Himself, to the *garden* where in natural reaction from the mood of exaltation He must face the stark reality of what, by His own choice, awaits Him. We know the prayer that He uttered in that garden, and the stress which accompanied it (*St. Mark* xiv, 32-36; *St. Luke* xxii, 39-44). St. John does not record the prayer, but he alludes to it (1). It is enough to say that He went across the brook Kedron, *where was a garden.*

*

2-11. And Judas also who was betraying him knew the place, because many a time Jesus and his disciples assembled there. So Judas, having received the cohort and officers from the chief priests and from the Pharisees, cometh thither with torches and lanterns and weapons. Jesus, therefore, knowing all the things that were coming upon him, went forth and said to them 'Whom seek ye?' They answered him 'Jesus of Nazareth'. He said to them 'I am he'. (And there stood with them also Judas who was betraying him.) When therefore he said to them 'I am he' they went backwards and fell to the ground. Again therefore he asked them 'Whom seek ye?' And they said 'Jesus of Nazareth'. Jesus answered 'I told you that I am he; if then it is I whom ye seek, let these go their way' (that the word might be fulfilled which he said, 'Those whom thou hast given me, I destroyed of them not one'). Simon Peter, therefore, having a sword drew it and struck the high priest's slave and cut off his right ear; and the name of the slave was Malchus. Jesus therefore said to Peter 'Put the sword into the sheath; the cup which my Father has given me, am I not to drink it?'

Judas who was betraying him; the tense in the original emphasises the fact that Judas was at that moment engaged on his work of treason; it is not a mere description of him as the traitor. The Lord had often used this garden as a place of resort and rendezvous. He does not go there because the traitor will look there first; but neither does He avoid it for that reason. He goes His own way, and lets Judas act as he will.

Judas has been to the Sanhedrin and has received from them not only their own 'officers', that is, the Temple police, but also a contingent of troops from Fort Antonia — *the cohort* — for the loan of which the chief priests must have already made arrangements with Pilate. As they approach, the Lord arouses His sleeping disciples (*St. Mark* xiv, 41–43) and goes forth to meet him. They had come prepared to search for Him in the bushes of the garden; otherwise, with the full moon shining, there would be no use for *torches and lanterns*. But there is no need to search. The Lord knows all that is coming upon Him. He has faced it all, and is assured that it is the Father's will; therefore He accepts it, and makes even His arrest a willing offering: *Jesus, knowing all the things that were coming upon him, went forth and said to them 'Whom seek ye?'* He comes forth, as one disturbed in meditation, to ask what this turmoil means. At first He is not recognised; instead of saying 'We seek you', *they answered him, 'Jesus of Nazareth'.* The name is partly description, partly an expression of contempt; the latter element is emphasised by the actual expression used — *Jesus the Nazarene. He saith to them 'I am he'* or '*I am*'; again we have the phrase which may mean no more than 'I am the man you describe', as in ix, 9, but may also be the sacred Name of God. To the soldiers it meant the former; to us it means also the latter. We are the world to whom our God comes forth in the Person of Jesus the Nazarene saying 'Whom seek ye?' The world is groping after its true leader; He offers Himself; and the world, after yielding for a moment to the impact of His divinity, arrests Him and crucifies Him.

The course chosen by the Lord in thus offering Himself to them has put Judas out of action. He had given the sign that would indicate the Prisoner (*St. Mark* xiv, 44); but there is no need of that. For the moment he can do nothing but stand there with the rest, and the Beloved Disciple saw him: *there stood with them also Judas who was betraying him.*

The effect of the Lord's words, and His dignity as He exposes Himself to His enemies, overpower them for the moment. They drop back, and some even fall down as the crowd shrinks away from the helpless yet dominating Figure: *when therefore he said to them 'I am he' they went backwards and fell to the ground.* The Lord therefore repeats His question — '*Whom seek ye?*' They are able to repeat their answer — '*Jesus of Nazareth*'. *Jesus answered, 'I told you that I am he; if then it is I whom ye seek, let these go their way*'. He alone is able now to bear what is coming; He will not have His disciples involved. Peter's loyal action, about to be recorded, is quite as far from the divine purpose in this scene as are his disloyal words in the court of the High Priest's house. The disciples must be protected, not only from the physical danger but from the insidious spiritual perils that accompanied it. Here was one instance of the care of the Good Shepherd for His flock, justifying the claim '*Those whom thou hast given me, I destroyed of them not one*' (xvii, 12). The Greek means more than *lost*, but hardly so much as *destroyed*; it does, however, represent an action on the part of the Lord, not a deprivation in which He was purely passive. The change of phrase from *not one of them perished* or *was destroyed* to *I destroyed* or *lost not one* is appropriate. If the Lord had at this stage associated the disciples with Himself, He would have been exposing them to trials beyond their strength, and would have become responsible for their failure.

It was, no doubt, at this point that Judas came forward and carried out his promise to the soldiers. His kiss was not only traitorous but futile, for the Lord has not left it to Judas to make known His identity. With Judas come the soldiers and the officers of the Temple police. In the turmoil *Simon Peter having a sword drew it and struck the high priest's slave and cut off his right ear.* He had declared his readiness to give his life for his Master (xiii, 37), and now he shows that this was true; he begins to fight though the odds against him are over-whelming. He draws his sword — there were only two swords among them all (*St. Luke* xxii, 38), but we are not surprised that Simon Peter had one of them — and slashes at one of the newcomers. It is not a soldier at all, but only a slave of the High Priest. The slave swings aside, and the blow aimed at the crown of his head cuts off his ear. *The name of the slave was Malchus*; a realistic touch due to the memory of an eye-witness who knew the High Priest's household (see 15); but perhaps this Malchus was known in the early Church as a convert, so that his name was a matter of general interest; that the action of the Lord in healing his wound at such a moment (*St. Luke* xxii, 51) should begin the process of his conversion is easily intelligible; but of all this we have no evidence.

The words of the Lord are sublime: *Put the sword into the sheath; the cup which my Father has given me, am I not to drink it?* We recall the prayer that this Cup might pass from Him; we recall the Agony and Bloody Sweat; but He knows that the Father Himself is offering the Cup; none shall hinder His drinking it.

*

(2) THE ECCLESIASTICAL TRIALS (12–27)

12–14. The cohort, therefore, and the captain and the officers of the Jews seized Jesus and bound him, and led him to Annas first; for he was father-in-law to Caiaphas, who was high priest that year; and Caiaphas was he who counselled the Jews that it was expedient that one man should die on behalf of the people.

The Roman troops and their commanding officer, with the Temple police, make the arrest and bind their Prisoner accord-ing to their custom; no more need be intended than a binding

of the hands behind the back — the equivalent to our hand-
cuffs. Then *they led him to Annas first.* Only St. John tells this;
it is one of the facts recorded by him alone which makes intelligible the Synoptic narrative where it otherwise would be, at
best, obscure (see Introduction, pp. xv and xvi). St. Mark
records a trial before the High Priest during the night (*St.
Mark* xiv, 53–65) followed by a 'consultation' of the 'chief
priests with the elders and scribes and the whole council' in
the morning (*St. Mark* xv, 1). This is possible, but not easily
intelligible. St. John tells us that the earlier trial was an informal
enquiry at the house of Annas, at which the decision was
reached, though sentence could not there be pronounced. Then,
very early in the morning, the Sanhedrin met in full session
and rapidly confirmed in legal verdict and sentence what had
been informally decided during the night. (St. Luke, who does
not record the informal enquiry, is probably right in saying
the crucial question (*St. Luke* xxii, 67 and 70) was put in the
later and formal trial; but this would be a repetition of what
had happened earlier: cf. *St. Mark* xiv, 61 and 62; and *St.
Matthew* xxvi, 63 and 64. St. Mark and St. Luke give no
name to the High Priest in whose house the earlier enquiry
took place (*St. Mark* xiv, 53); St. Matthew by a natural mistake
inserts the name of Caiaphas (*St. Matthew* xxvi, 57). In fact
this enquiry took place at the house of Annas, as St. John
is careful to make plain.)

*He was father-in-law to Caiaphas, who was high priest that
year*; so St. John accounts for the fact that he presided over
this informal enquiry. He had been High Priest himself, and
was head of the high-priestly family. Moreover, he controlled
from the background his various sons and sons-in-law who
successively held the office. But there may be more involved
than this. Annas was deposed from the office of High Priest
by Valerius Gratus, the predecessor of Pilate as Procurator of
Judaea. It is possible that he himself and a section of Jewish
opinion regarded this act as an unwarrantable intrusion of the
secular State in the affairs of the Church, and consequently

held that he was still *de jure* High Priest. The acts of Rome must needs be accepted for all legal transactions; but it may be that the assent of Annas was thought necessary to give spiritual validity to the acts of the Sanhedrin, even though Caiaphas presided at its formal session. This would account for the very curious expressions in *St. Luke* iii, 2 ('under the high-priest-hood of Annas and Caiaphas'), and *Acts* iv, 6 ('Annas the high priest was there, and Caiaphas and John and Alexander and as many as were of the kindred of the high priest').

The mention of Caiaphas revives the memory of that cynic's counsel which was unwittingly a statement of divine truth (xi, 50): *it is expedient that one man should die on behalf of the people*. Both his cynicism and the divine truth are now to be displayed openly.

*

St. Peter's First Denial

15-18. And there followed Jesus Simon Peter and another disciple. That disciple was known to the high priest and went in with Jesus into the courtyard of the high priest, but Peter was standing at the door outside. So the other disciple, the acquaintance of the high priest, went out and spoke to the door-keeper and brought in Peter. The maid who kept the door saith therefore to Peter 'Thou art not, surely, also one of this man's disciples?' He said 'I am not'. And there were standing there the slaves and the officers, having made a fire of charcoal, because it was cold; and they were warming themselves; and there was also Peter among them, standing and warming himself.

The story is very vivid, though one point in it is notoriously difficult. After the arrest, when all the disciples 'left him and fled' (*St. Mark* xiv, 50), St. Peter 'followed afar off' (*St. Mark* xiv, 54). So much St. Mark knew from St. Peter's narration of his own recollection; also that somehow St. Peter found access to the courtyard of the High Priest. St. John tells us that another disciple followed with Peter; no doubt this is the Beloved Disciple, John the son of Zebedee. But he goes on — *that disciple was known to the high priest*. This phrase has been much discussed, and is the point of notorious difficulty referred

to above. But John the son of Zebedee was, on his mother's
side, of priestly descent; his mother was Salome, the sister of
the Virgin Mary; they were related to Elizabeth, who is described as 'of the daughters of Aaron' (*St. Luke* i, 5). It is
possible at least that John came at times to perform priestly
duties at Jerusalem, and that this is the origin of the statement
of Polycrates that he was a priest and wore the Petalon — a
gold plate attached to the front of the priestly turban or mitre
(*Exodus* xxviii, 36); the same is said of St. James the Just (a
'brother' of the Lord) and of St. Mark; the latter is shown to
be of Levite connexion by the comparison of *Acts* iv, 36 and
Colossians iv, 10. But even if St. John was not himself a priest,
he may have been often in Jerusalem, and had opportunity to
become known to the High Priest; there was much commerce
between the fishermen of Galilee and the capital; some have
suggested that this family, which was sufficiently prosperous
to employ hired servants, had an establishment in Jerusalem
to which St. John was commonly attached.

All of this is speculation, but supplies reason for accepting
without hesitation the simple statement of fact that *that disciple
was known to the high priest*, so that the door-keeper readily
admitted him among those who *followed Jesus* into *the courtyard of the high priest*. It is likely that this was a courtyard
into which different houses opened, one being that of Annas,
another that of Caiaphas. When St. John had made his way
in among the crowd, and was able to take note of what had
happened, he found that the admission allowed to himself had
been refused to the markedly Galilean Peter (*St. Mark* xiv, 70),
so that *Peter was* (still) *standing at the door outside*. So St.
John used the opportunity due to the fact that he was an
acquaintance of the High Priest to speak to the door-keeper
and get leave to bring in Peter. The maid knew, presumably,
that St. John was a disciple and says in effect 'Surely you are
not another of them?' The form of question is that which
'expects the answer No'; but it is satirically spoken; the combination of the form and the tone constitutes a temptation

which finds Peter unprepared; and he slides into the place prepared for him: 'Not another, surely'; 'Oh, no'. So sudden and so easy! But now it will be very hard to go back and give the loyal answer when the direct challenge comes (25–27).

We do not always see how unwitting was Peter's first denial. Of course a perfect loyalty would have avoided it. But we all know with what fatal ease we accept a position prepared for us if it is presented suddenly and offers a refuge from many troubles. And then the harm is done! The act seemed so nearly innocent; the avoidance of its guilty consequence is so very hard.

Anyhow, Peter is there now among *the slaves and the officers*, that is, the Temple police; it is cold and they have made a fire; and Peter was there with them, *standing and warming himself*.

*

19–24. The high priest, therefore, asked Jesus about his disciples and his teaching. Jesus answered him 'I have spoken openly to the world; I always taught in synagogue and in the temple, where all the Jews come together, and in secret I spake nothing. Why dost thou ask me? Ask them who have heard what I spake to them; behold, they know the things which I said.' And when he had said these things, one who was standing by, one of the officers, struck Jesus with his open hand, saying 'Is that the way for thee to answer the high priest?' Jesus answered him, 'If I spake ill, bear witness of the ill; but if well, why dost thou smite me?' So Annas sent him bound to Caiaphas the high priest.

The purpose of this informal enquiry is to find evidence which can be presented at the formal session of the Sanhedrin a few hours later, so that a verdict and sentence can then be pronounced at once, and the case sent on to Pilate. The only charge that is likely to move Pilate to action is that of sedition; and it was a political argument to which he ultimately yielded (xix, 12). So the first point of enquiry concerns the disciples, and what was the teaching given to them: *the high priest asked Jesus about his disciples and his teaching*. Of course he hoped by cross-examination to elicit something which would show that the Lord was training a group of rebels. The Triumphal Entry had looked like a serious rising and had created consternation among the Pharisees (xii, 19). But the Lord's answer gives him no ground for encouragement. Instead of answering the question, He challenges the method of the enquiry. The proper course was to formulate a charge and call witnesses, when (incidentally) the Jewish custom would require witnesses for the defence to be called first. What Annas is attempting is to inveigle the Prisoner into giving evidence against Himself. This He will not do. In His answer the first pronoun is very emphatic: '*I* am not a secret conspirator'; *I have spoken openly to the world. I always taught in synagogue and in the temple* (as we might say, in Church or in the Cathedral), *where all the Jews come together, and in secret I spake nothing.* The teaching given in the Upper Room and in the Temple Court, contained in Chapters XIII to XVII, was in substance no more than an articulation of what He had often said in public. So there are no secrets to be disclosed. If Annas wishes for evidence about His teaching, he can obtain it in the usual way. *Ask them who have heard what* (it was that) *I spake to them; behold, they know the things which I said.*

That this enquiry was irregular and informal is proved by the next episode; it is incredible that one of the police should smack the Prisoner's face (for that is what the words mean) during a formal trial before the Sanhedrin. *When he had said these things, one who was standing by, one of the officers, struck Jesus with his open hand, saying 'Is that the way for thee to answer the high priest?'* The Lord remains perfectly calm, recalling the policeman, as He had recalled the High Priest, to the method appropriate to a legal enquiry: *If I spake ill, bear witness of the ill; but if well, why dost thou smite me?*

St. John does not recall the rest of the trial — neither the attempt to find witnesses who can prove that Jesus was preparing a riot aiming at the destruction of the Temple, which He would then replace with a miraculous structure of His own

(*St. Mark* xiv, 58), though he has told us of the saying of Jesus which was twisted into this (ii, 19); nor the direct question of the High Priest, though to this too he alludes, in so far as the Jews demand of Pilate the death-penalty because of the Lord's claim to be the Son of God (xix, 7). Though this latter is not what would be most welcome for submission to Pilate, it can be made to serve, for it can be twisted into a political charge (compare xix, 7, with xix, 12). *So Annas sent him bound to Caiaphas the high priest.* •

ST. PETER'S LATER DENIALS

25–27. And there was Simon Peter standing and warming himself. They said to him therefore 'Surely thou art not also one of his disciples?' That man denied it and said 'I am not'. There saith one of the slaves of the high priest, being a kinsman of him whose ear Peter cut off, 'Did not I see thee in the garden with him?' Again therefore Peter denied, and immediately a cock crew.

We are taken back to the courtyard where Peter is standing with the rest. One of these asks him the same question as the maid had put to him — again with the suggestion that he is not one of the disciples; and again he yields to the suggestion. But then one notices him who recalls his features; he had seen that face in the garden; but Peter again denies. *And immediately the cock crew.*

St. John has a double purpose in this narrative — first, to point out the contrast between the serene calm of the Lord, whose constancy was leading Him to torture and death, and the frightened inconstancy of the disciple, who had nothing worse to fear than mockery; secondly, to offer some excuse for Simon Peter by showing how easy it was for him to slip. With the first object in view he breaks the story of the denials into two parts, and takes us backwards and forwards between the room where the Lord stands with bound hands before Annas and the courtyard where Peter stretches out his free hands to the charcoal fire in the brazier. With the second object, he gives the actual tone of the first two questions to Peter, and passes rapidly over his actual fall; there is no word here of cursing and swearing, as there was in Peter's own story of his sháme (*St. Mark* xiv, 71). St. John does not want to exhibit St. Peter's shame, but to warn us by his example how very easily we slide towards denial of our Lord.

Everyone who has found himself 'in a tight place' and seized an unexpected opportunity of escape will recognise the difference in the force of temptation latent in the two forms of question, 'You aren't one of them, are you?' and 'You are one of them, aren't you?' To deny the second is to refuse a direct challenge; it was what Peter did the third time. To accept the suggestion of the first is scarcely more than a refusal to look for trouble. The suggestion is that he is not likely to be a disciple, and no one will suppose he is unless he says so; he had little more to do than to let well alone. But that little more is fatal. If the third question had come first, perhaps he could have met it with truth and loyalty. Peter was not one to be browbeaten into apostasy! But he was one to fear laughter, and to take a way of avoiding it when it was offered him.

Meanwhile the Lord was being sent from Annas to Caiaphas, that is, to the Sanhedrin where Caiaphas is president. He must pass through the courtyard, and on the way 'the Lord turned and looked on Peter'. At the same moment a cock crew (27; *St. Luke* xxii, 60).

Probably the cock's crow was not the cry of a bird but the trumpet sounding the 'cock-crow' which marked the transition from the third watch of the night, called 'Cock-crowing', to the fourth, called 'Early'; the four night watches were Late, Midnight, Cock-crowing and Early. This makes the Lord's prediction in xiii, 38, more natural; before 'cock-crowing' was a definite indication of time.

Time had been carefully calculated; it was important to secure Pilate's sentence early, so that the actual crucifixion should be carried through and finished before the day of the feast should begin at 6 p.m. (cf. xix, 31). The proceedings in the Sanhedrin would be very short — just the one question, 'Art thou the Christ?' which the Prisoner cannot refuse to answer, and by answering which He must involve Himself in the guilt of blasphemy. So at the moment of 'cock-crow', as the sound of the trumpet rings out, the enquiry before Annas is closed; the Sanhedrin meets — it is the earliest hour at which a condemnation to death would be technically legal; and at once the Prisoner is led to Pilate, in that phase of the night which the trumpet ushers in and which is called Early.

*

(3) THE TRIAL BEFORE PILATE (xviii, 28–xix, 16)

The trial before Pilate is divided into sections by the movements of Pilate in and out of the Praetorium. Westcott describes them as follows:

1. Without the Praetorium. The Jews claim the execution of their sentence (xviii, 28–32).
2. Within the Praetorium. 'The good confession.' Christ a King (33–38).
3. Without the Praetorium. First declaration of innocence. Barabbas (38–40).
4. Within the Praetorium. Scourging; mockery (xix, 1–3).
5. Without the Praetorium. Second and third declarations of innocence. 'Ecce Homo' 'Son of God' (4–7).
6. Within the Praetorium. The source of authority and from this the measure of guilt (8–11).
7. Without the Praetorium. Conviction overpowered: the King abjured: the last sentence (12–16).

*

1. Without the Praetorium. The Jews claim the execution of their sentence (xviii, 28–32):

They lead Jesus therefore from Caiaphas into the palace; and it was Early;
and themselves they did not enter into the palace, that they might not be
defiled but might eat the Passover. Pilate therefore went out to them
outside, and saith 'What accusation do ye bring against this man?'
They answered and said to him 'If this man were not doing evil, we
should not have delivered him to thee'. Pilate therefore saith to them
'Take him yourself, and according to your law judge him'. The Jews
said to him 'To us it is not allowed to put anyone to death' — that the
word of Jesus might be fulfilled which he said signifying by what manner
of death he was about to die.

They lead Jesus therefore from Caiaphas to the palace, that
is, from the Court of the Sanhedrin to the Praetorium, the
house of the Governor. *And it was Early*; it was, in fact, a
little after 3 a.m., at which hour the trumpet had sounded
Cock-crow. *And themselves they did not enter into the palace,
that they might not be defiled but might eat the Passover*. They
were demanding the crucifixion of the Lord of Glory, but of
course no one thought of that as defilement; to enter the
heathen ruler's house would be defilement! (A besetting sin
of all of us, who are concerned with the ordering of religious
life and worship, is the loss of proportion and perspective, and
the attribution of primary importance to secondary or even to
tertiary and quaternary concerns!) But as they would not go
in, Pilate must needs come out, and his frequent movements
backwards and forwards are due to their scrupulosity. It is
natural to suppose that this added to Pilate's contemptuous
irritation, and made him the more determined to impose
upon these tiresome priests a good deal of humiliation
before he granted their request. *Pilate therefore went out to
them outside, and saith 'What accusation do ye bring against
this man?'*

Pilate must have known that the chief priests were going to
bring before him a man whose execution would be demanded.
He had lent troops to assist in the arrest; and he is ready at this
early hour to hear the case. But he is now to act as judge; he
must hear the charge and the defence. Probably he expected
a charge of sedition already heard and decided by the

Sanhedrin; in that case his own enquiry need not take long; but a definite accusation must be made. There is no reason to suppose that Pilate begins with any other expectation than a speedy verdict of guilty and sentence of death — though it is possible that already he was uneasy as a result of his wife's message (*St. Matthew* xxvii, 19).

Unfortunately for them, the chief priests have no such charge to bring forward as will at all certainly lead Pilate to pronounce the death-sentence on which they are determined. So they try to avoid stating a definite charge at all. They have held a trial themselves and have found the Prisoner guilty of evil-doing; that is enough; Pilate has only to ratify their findings: *If this man were not doing evil we should not have delivered him to thee.*

(Doing evil!

> Why, what hath my Lord done?
> What makes this rage and spite?
> He made the lame to run,
> He gave the blind their sight.
> Sweet injuries!
> Yet they at these
> Themselves displease
> And 'gainst him rise.[1])

Pilate was cynical and cruel, but he was not stupid, and no Roman governor could be without some sense of the majesty of Roman law. That law entrusted the death penalty to no local or 'native' court, but reserved it to the representative of Rome. It was not unknown for a High Priest to be deposed for inflicting it. If so, it could not be consonant with the law that the Governor should inflict that penalty at the demand of the local court without any further trial held by himself. The reply of the chief priests was, in fact, a piece of impertinence with which Pilate was very competent to deal. He says in effect 'Very well; if you want the matter settled by the verdict of your court, let that court pronounce sentence', knowing, of

---

[1] Samuel Crossman: see *Songs of Praise*, 127.

N

course, that their court could not pronounce sentence of death: *Take him yourselves and according to your law judge him*. Now the Jews have to show their hand, for death alone will satisfy them: *To us it is not allowed to put any man to death*. This was itself a grievance, a constant reminder that they were a vassal state. But the result, as St. John points out, was that the Lord's death when it came fulfilled His own prediction — He was *lifted up from the earth* (xii, 32). If the Sanhedrin condemned any man to death the sentence was carried out by stoning, as in the case of St. Stephen (which was probably after Pilate's disgrace, and Vitellius, who succeeded him, went very far in concessions to the Jewish authorities). None but the Roman authority could crucify.

*

2. Within the Praetorium. 'The good confession.' Christ a King (33–38):

Pilate therefore went into the palace again and called Jesus and said to him 'Thou — art thou the King of the Jews?' Jesus answered 'Of thyself dost thou say this or did others say it to thee concerning me?' Pilate answered 'Am I a Jew? The nation which is thine and the chief priests delivered thee to me. What didst thou do?' Jesus answered 'The kingdom which is mine is not from this world; if from this world were the kingdom which is mine, the officers who are mine would be fighting that I should not be delivered to the Jews; but as it is the kingdom which is mine is not from hence'. Pilate therefore saith to him 'Then art thou — thou — a king?' Jesus answered 'Thou sayest that I am a king. I to this end have been born and to this end am come into the world, that I may bear witness to the truth. Everyone who is from the truth heareth my voice.' Pilate saith to him 'What is truth?'

Pilate goes back into the palace; no doubt the soldiers have by now taken charge of the Prisoner, and they bring Him too. Pilate is puzzled. He knew that the charge was to be one of sedition; but it has not been made; and the Prisoner does not look like the leader of a serious revolution. Pilate does not constitute his court, but questions the Prisoner himself. The Jews had looked dangerous and if he insisted on sending the case back for such action as the Sandehrin could take, the consequences might be grave. He had better keep the matter in his own hands now that it has reached them. So he goes behind the general charge of 'doing evil', which was all that was formally presented, to that which he had been led to expect. Only now it seems preposterous: *Thou — art thou the King of the Jews?* The Prisoner does not look the sort of person to usurp a throne. *Thou — the* pronoun is so placed as to be most emphatic. It is evident that Pilate is already convinced that he is not dealing with a rebel whom Rome need fear. At first the Lord does not answer the question, but asks another. He has heard what the chief priests and Jews had said outside, and it contained no reference to any claim to Kingship. Has Pilate any information of his own to suggest that this claim had been made, or was the statement brought to him from other (that is, Jewish) quarters? If the former, the information can be tested; if the latter, the charge should be presented in proper form, and this the Jews have not done, for the very good reason that they had not been able to establish it. *Of thyself dost thou say this? or did others say it to thee concerning me?* No doubt the High Priest or his representative had said it when arrangements were made for the loan of the troops. But that was a private conversation, of which the course could not be conveniently made public. Pilate has recourse to contemptuous indignation: how should he hear of such things? He is not a Jew or interested in Jewish concerns, except so far as he had to keep that turbulent tribe in order. *Am I a Jew?* Again the pronoun is emphatic, He was a Roman, not one of this despised race. *The nation which is thine and the chief priests delivered thee to me. What didst thou do?* It was the Lord's own people who had brought Him, not a private group of citizens but the nation as represented by its own leaders. If He were a champion of national independence they would be supporting Him; but somehow He has provoked them to fury: *What didst thou do?* If He is to be found guilty there must be an offence of which He is guilty.

The Lord's reply takes up what is the real charge — that He claims to be the Son of God, the Messiah (xix, 7; cf. *St. Mark* xiv, 61, 62). In that sense He does claim to be the *King of Israel* (i, 49); but He has transformed the conception of that Messianic Kingship. He has royalty, but not what the world means by royalty, for it neither proceeds from the world nor is recognisable by the world: *The kingdom which is mine is not from this world.* He does not claim a kingdom, but, so to speak, acquiesces in that description of His realm; it is a special kind of kingdom — *the kingdom which is mine* — and it is *not from this world.* He had claimed to be the Messiah; and the Messiah was a King — but not the sort of King whose dominion constituted a challenge to the political authority of Rome. *Not from this world*; the phrase represents both origin and character due to origin. An earthly king depends for any effective authority upon the loyal support of his people and the force that they can offer in his support. The Messiah derives His authority from God alone. The quality of an earthly kingdom is, partly at least, the maintenance of order by the forcible coercion of malcontents; in the political sphere this is right, and the earthly State is rightly entrusted with force wherewith to uphold the law and prevent the lawless use of force. But the divine kingdom cannot be content with this; it must control not only outward conduct but hearts and wills; its authority is from God, who is Love; its actuality is in the willing obedience of those whose love has been called out in response to the manifested love of God. Consequently it can never fight for its 'vital interests', because by fighting it betrays them. The State may rightly fight in national self-defence or for the maintenance of the law of nations; the Church may not fight, nor use for its defence or extension any other method than the lifting up of its King that He may draw all men unto Him: *If from this world were the Kingdom which is mine, the officers who are mine would be fighting that I should not be delivered to the Jews; but as it is the kingdom which is mine is not from hence.*

Who are His *officers*? (The word is that used elsewhere in this narrative for the Temple police. Wherever it occurs it represents the agents of a king or other public authority.) Can He mean the eleven disciples? One of them had begun to fight with precisely the object here mentioned. But they are evidently helpless against the Temple police and the Roman legionaries. Had He then other *officers* on whom He might call? Yes; 'more than twelve legions' of them (*St. Matthew* xxvi, 53). But to call in the heavenly hosts, the 'officers' of the 'Kingdom of Heaven', to act coercively would be to turn that Kingdom into a Kingdom 'from this world'. For it is not the difference of the supernatural from the natural that distinguishes Christ's Kingdom; it is the difference between control of conduct by force and control of heart and mind and will by love and truth. His *Kingdom is not from hence.*

Pilate is baffled. It seems the Prisoner does claim kingship after all. *Then art thou — thou — a king?* Once more there is great emphasis on the pronoun. Before the Roman Governor stands a man with hands bound behind His back; He was arrested without difficulty — no more than a scuffle in which one slave was cut on the side of the head; He has no air of pomp or domination; He is, indeed, fearless, and answers the Governor without a trace of subservience; but there is nothing regal about Him: *Then art thou — thou — a king?*

Thou sayest that I am a king; the use of the term 'king' was introduced by Pilate. It is his word, not the Prisoner's. It could not be accurately accepted or rejected; to say No would convey one false impression, to say Yes would convey another. So the Lord says in effect 'That is your expression, not mine; but here is an exact statement of the facts: *I to this end have been born and to this end am come into the world, that I may bear witness to the truth. Everyone that is from the truth heareth my voice.*'

(The expression 'Thou sayest' or 'Thou hast said' is not a
direct affirmative. To interpret it so in *St. Matthew* xxvi, 64
is to lose part of the meaning of that scene. It is neither Yes
nor No, but indicates that while the phrase used may be quite
misleading, yet there is a sense in which it must be accepted.
The Lord refuses to say that He is or that He is not the
Messiah; for that required a definition of the Messianic
office. But He goes on to say that Daniel's prophecy is now
fulfilled.)

The kingdoms which are *from this world* rest in part upon
falsehood — most conspicuously upon the necessary but
false, false but necessary, supposition that the State really acts
in the interest of the whole community, whereas in fact it
always acts primarily in the interest of that section of the
community which is able in practice to work its machinery.
It is a pretended community; this is far better than no community at all, which is the only actual alternative until the
Kingdom of God is come. But that Kingdom rests on truth
— on the real constitution of the universe wherein God the
righteous Father is supreme. To that *truth*, the real constitution of the universe, Christ came to *bear witness*; not to beautiful dreams but to bed-rock reality (cf. *St. Matthew* vii, 24, 25).
*Everyone who is from the truth heareth my voice. From the
truth;* the phrase answers *from this world*; again the suggestion
is of origin and character due to origin. It is those who are
born from above who may hope to *see the kingdom of God* (iii,
3). Those whose outlook is directed by the truth, whose
judgement springs from the truth, hear the voice of Christ,
the truth (xiv, 6). So He had said that *the sheep that are mine
hear my voice* (x, 27); but of others — *Why do ye not recognise
my manner of speech?* — *because ye cannot hear the word that
is mine* (viii, 43). *Everyone who is from the truth heareth my
voice.*

This makes Pilate impatient, but also convinces him that
the Prisoner is harmless. Abstractions like Truth have nothing
to do with a trial for sedition; it is absurd to introduce such

a topic; '"*What is truth?*" said jesting Pilate and would not stay for an answer.'[1]

But it is better to stay and wait for the answer. We know that answer quite well: *I am the truth* (xiv, 6). Can we say that we are *of* or *from the truth*?

*

3. Without the Praetorium. First declaration of innocence. Barabbas (38–40):

And having said this again he went forth to the Jews and saith to them 'I find no crime in him. But there is a custom with you that I should release one prisoner to you at the Passover. Do ye wish then that I release to you the King of the Jews?' So they shouted aloud again saying, 'Not this man but Barabbas'; and Barabbas was a robber.

Pilate is sure the Prisoner is no criminal. He hopes to deal with the matter by using the custom of releasing one prisoner at the Passover — a strictly limited amnesty. It is a cynical proposal, because if Jesus is innocent He should be acquitted and some other released; the crowd is entitled to claim both Jesus and Barabbas. Perhaps they are irritated at this attempt to get out of granting the amnesty to a real rebel by releasing one who, Pilate says, is no rebel at all. They are bound to be irritated by the scorn implied in the use of the title which the Lord was accused of claiming — *the King of the Jews*. Pilate's device is self-defeating; certainly it fails. The crowd will have its real rebel released: *Not this man but Barabbas*.

Barabbas was guilty of sedition and of murder (*St. Luke* xxiii, 19); he was an undoubted criminal. But he had defied Rome, and it would be easy for the chief priests to persuade the crowd to demand the release of a bandit-patriot rather than that of One who has only disappointed their nationalist aspirations. Pilate is foiled.

---

[1] Bacon. *Essay on Truth.*

But the choice of Barabbas is more than an episode. It is a symbol. The world has its choice between the real King and the bandit chief; it chooses Barabbas — *and Barabbas was a robber.*

CHAPTER XIX

The Civil Trial Continues

4. Within the Praetorium. Scourging; mockery (1–3):

Then Pilate took Jesus and scourged him. And the soldiers, having plaited a crown out of thorns put it on his head, and cast a purple cloak about him, and were making approach to him and saying 'Hail, King of the Jews!' and they smote him with their open hands.

Pilate goes back into his palace and orders Jesus to be scourged, in the hope that this fearful punishment will satisfy the Jews; for a Roman scourging was a thing of terror. The soldiers who administer the torture enter with zest into a situation which enables them to show their scorn of the Jews. They take the supposed accusation in mock seriousness; they plait a crown or wreath of thorn-twigs to represent the laurel-wreath of a victor; they cast about the lacerated body a coarse scarlet cloak in place of the regal purple; they advance towards Him, one as though to offer homage, another as though to present a petition, saying *'Hail, King of the Jews!'* — fit king (they suggest) for such a people. Then rising from the bended knee they slap Him on the face.

St. John records enough to emphasise the humiliation and the pain; but he does not dwell on it. No record is so little directed towards the harrowing of feelings. All attention is directed towards the bearing of the Sufferer.

*

5. Without the Praetorium. Second and third declarations of innocence. 'Ecce Homo'; 'Son of God' (4–7):

And Pilate came forth again outside and saith to them 'Behold, I bring him to you outside that ye may recognise that I find no crime in him'. Jesus therefore came forth outside, wearing the crown of thorns and the purple cloak. And he saith to them 'Behold, the man'. When therefore the chief priests and the officers saw him they shouted aloud, saying

'Crucify, crucify'. Pilate saith to them 'Take him yourselves and crucify him; for I do not find crime in him'. The Jews answered him 'We have a law, and according to the law he ought to die, because he made himself Son of God'.

Pilate now comes out to make his appeal for sympathy. He hopes that his declaration of the Prisoner's innocence, coupled with the sight of His tortured form, may satisfy the rage of the accusers. (But if He was innocent, why was He scourged? Even in the method by which Pilate seeks to release Him there is an outrage upon justice.) So *Jesus came forth outside, wearing the crown of thorns and the purple cloak*; He is exhibited in the trappings put on Him for mockery; and Pilate says *Behold, the Man*.

It is one of those pregnant phrases which cannot be translated adequately. On Pilate's lips — and so the Jews would understand it — the words meant 'Look at the poor fellow'. But as we hear them across the centuries they come charged with another meaning. Here, in this life of perfect obedience and love; here, in this courage that bears the worst that hate can do and is still unfalteringly calm; here, in this love that is unquenched and undiminished by the desertion of friends, by the blows and jeers of enemies — here we see Man fulfilling his true destiny and manifested as superior to circumstance. 'We see not yet all things subject to man. But we behold him who hath been made a little lower than the angels, garlanded for the suffering of death with glory and honour' (*Hebrews* ii, 8, 9). As the victim was garlanded for the sacrifice, so Jesus for the Cross — with thorns of glory and honour.

But the sight of their enemy, as they account Him, rouses the chief priests and their satellites to frenzy. They *shout aloud* . . . '*Crucify, crucify*'. Pilate answers with a sneer: 'Do it yourselves'; for he knows that they cannot. They hold Him guilty, but will not inflict the only penalty in their power; they demand the death-penalty, which can only be inflicted by the judge who has pronounced Him innocent! '*Take him yourselves and crucify him; for I do not find crime in him.*'

This drives the Jews to state what it is that they have really established against Him. In itself it is blasphemy, and for this He was sentenced to death by the Sanhedrin (*St. Mark* xiv, 61–64); and Pilate may not be prepared to execute for blasphemy; still, the claim of the Lord can be presented as constructive treason (12),[1] and in any case the Jewish law required death as the penalty for such blasphemy as was certainly involved in the claim of Jesus — if it were not the truth! *We have a law, and according to the law he ought to die, because he made himself Son of God.* Yes; when adjured by the High Priest in the name of the living God, He had made the claim that He was 'the Christ, the Son of the Blessed' (*St. Mark* xiv, 61, 62). And with the title Son of God goes the title King of Israel (i, 49). The Jews have at any rate stated their full case now.

*

6. Within the Praetorium. The source of authority and from this the measure of guilt (8–11):

When Pilate therefore heard this word he was more afraid, and went into the palace again and saith to Jesus 'Whence art thou?' But Jesus did not give him an answer. Pilate therefore saith to him 'To me dost thou not speak? Knowest thou not that I have authority to release thee and I have authority to crucify thee?' Jesus answered him 'Thou hadst not any authority against me unless it had been given thee from above: for this reason he that delivered me to thee hath greater sin'.

Pilate has little or no respect for the Jewish law, which he regarded, no doubt, as the barbarous code of a contemptible tribe. But, like most heathen cynics, he has a superstitious dread of the supernatural. This Prisoner with His unruffled calm and His talk about a Kingdom of Truth is, no doubt, a fanatic; but there might be something abnormal and supernatural about Him. The title *Son of God* would not for Pilate bear the august meaning which it had for the chief priests, and which made the claim to it blasphemous if it was not true.

[1] St. Luke represents it as so interpreted from the first: xxiii, 2.

But this Prisoner might be a son of a god — and the phrase used by the chief priests, where no definite articles are employed, can mean this; Pilate would not want to incur the hostility of a local deity. So he was *more afraid* than he had been till now; he goes inside the palace again, and asks the Prisoner *Whence art thou?*

To that Jesus gives no answer. How could He give one? What is the use of saying to Pilate *I came forth from the Father and am come into the world*? (xvi, 28). With his mind full of stories about gods who married women, and of the offspring of such unions, how can he begin to understand the relation of Jesus, Son of God, to the Father?

Pilate is vexed by His silence; it is in effect contempt of court. *To me dost thou not speak?* It is foolish to despise a judge who has power of life and death: *Knowest thou not that I have authority to release thee and I have authority to crucify thee?* Pilate rightly uses the word which means delegated authority; he thinks of its source as Caesar. But Caesar's authority too is delegated. *Thou hadst not any authority against me unless it had been given thee from above.* Pilate's authority comes, like all real authority, from God. The State has the authority of God in its own sphere; but this is a check as well as a sanction; for the State is confined within its own sphere by the very source of its authority; and even inside that sphere its authority is to execute justice, not to serve the interest of the rulers. If it steps outside its sphere, or uses its power to commit injustice, it becomes at once a usurper. Pilate has authority from God over the Jews and over Jesus as a Jew; he holds it in order to do justice with it; if he uses it for injustice the authority will evaporate. *Therefore he that delivered me to thee hath greater sin.* The sin of Caiaphas is greater because Pilate's authority is from God; and it was the duty of Caiaphas to know and teach as well as do the will of God. But he, the official representative of Israel, the People of God, has had recourse to this heathen, who holds certain authority from God, in order that power conferred by God for the execution of justice may be employed for the perpetration of injustice. That the High Priest, of all men, should say 'Though you have found the Prisoner innocent, yet condemn Him to death to gratify our concern for our law', is far worse than it is for that heathen to execute one apparently deluded fanatic in order to avoid an insurrection.

•

7. Without the Praetorium. Conviction overpowered; the King abjured; the last sentence (12–16):

From that time Pilate was seeking to release him; but the Jews shouted aloud saying 'If thou release this man, thou art not a friend of Caesar; everyone who maketh himself a King speaks against Caesar'. Pilate therefore, having heard these words, led Jesus forth outside and sat upon a judgment seat in the place called Pavement but in Hebrew Gabbatha. And it was Preparation Day of the Passover, and it was about the sixth hour. And he saith to the Jews 'Behold, your king'. They shouted therefore 'Away with him, away with him, crucify him'. Pilate saith to them 'Your king — shall I crucify him?' The chief priests answered 'We have not a king except Caesar'. So then he delivered him to them to be crucified.

Pilate is now more than ever convinced that the Prisoner is harmless; no one who recognised the Roman rule as having authority *from above* could be engaged in a serious rebellion; so *from that time Pilate was seeking to release him.* But the Jews are implacable. The word which is here translated *shouted aloud* means 'yelled' or 'screamed'; but in English this seems to be out of harmony with the dignity of the narrative. (It is the same word in verse 6 and in xviii, 40.) Their shout this time is to terrify: *If thou release this man, thou art not a friend of Caesar.* Pilate's office entirely depended on the favour of Tiberius; a report sent to Rome that he had released a claimant to the throne of Judaea would be very dangerous to him; and he could not deny either that *everyone who maketh himself a king speaketh against Caesar* or that the Prisoner had admitted that in some sense He claimed to be a king (xviii,

36, 37). If he reported on his own behalf what the Prisoner had actually said to him, this would seem too preposterous to be even plausible.

So Pilate, *having heard these words*, establishes his court for the first time. Everything hitherto has been preliminary. He takes his seat upon a chair placed for him on the dais of mosaic pavement, according to custom; Julius Caesar is said to have carried about a tessellated pavement to be set down wherever he encamped, so that from it he could deliver judgements. At this moment, when the formal trial before the Governor takes place, St. John gives a note of date and hour: the day was that of Preparation, or as we might say 'Friday of Passover week'. Preparation is the name of the day before the Sabbath, that is, Friday; *and it was about the sixth hour*. Does this mean 6 A.M. or noon? Westcott gives sufficient reason for thinking that St. John is following the use of Asia Minor, where he was writing, in reckoning the hours from midnight, not (as was the Jewish custom) from 6 A.M. If so, the formal trial and sentence took place at 6 A.M. and it was possible for the Crucifixion itself to begin, as St. Mark tells us (xv, 25) at 9 A.M. ('the third hour'). As it was about 3 A.M. when the chief priests brought Jesus from the Sanhedrin to Pilate, there was plenty of time for the preliminary enquiry and Pilate's movements in and out of his palace before 6 A.M.

Pilate is yielding to the clamour of the Jews; but he will show his scorn of them, and he will extract their profession of loyalty. He presents Jesus again to them: *Behold, your king*. Here is the man they present as a leader of revolt; well, perhaps He is a fitting king for such folk! The sight of the Lord calls forth a fresh outcry: *Away with him, away with him, crucify him*. Pilate presses his sarcasm home upon them: *Your king — shall I crucify him?* Now he hears what he has been waiting for. *The chief priests* — the official representatives of the Jewish theocracy — *answered 'We have not a king except Caesar'*.

He has humiliated these priests by forcing them to proclaim their loyalty to Caesar; so now he yields his Prisoner to them, so that the fury of the mob may be appeased and he himself escape the danger of a damaging report to Tiberius: *So then he delivered him to them to be crucified.*

*

(4) THE CRUCIFIXION (17–37)

(a) The Title (17–22)

So they received Jesus; and bearing the cross for himself he went forth
   to the place called the place of a Skull, which is called in Hebrew
   Golgotha, where they crucified him and with him two others on this
   side and on that, and in the midst Jesus. And Pilate wrote a title also
   and put it on the cross; and it was written 'Jesus of Nazareth the King
   of the Jews'. This title therefore read many of the Jews, because the
   place where Jesus was crucified was nigh to the city; and it was written
   in Hebrew, in Latin, and in Greek. The chief priests of the Jews therefore began to say to Pilate 'Do not write "The King of the Jews" but
   that he said "I am King of the Jews"'. Pilate answered 'What I have
   written, I have written'.

They received Jesus from the hands of Pilate, who has given the sentence, but leaves them to see to its execution. The Lord goes forth *bearing the cross for himself*. Later He would sink under its weight and they would make Simon of Cyrene bear it after Him (*St. Mark* xv, 21). He bore it for Himself; when we turn to the spiritual load which it represents, we know that none other can bear this; only God can bear it. And even for Him it seems too great. We must ever keep in mind the two thoughts — God the Creator of the universe, which came into being at His word; God the Redeemer staggering beneath a load that crushes Him as He goes from Jerusalem to Calvary: so far harder is it to redeem men from selfishness to love than to create the wheeling systems of the stars. (And Simon of Cyrene — the one African figure in the Gospels: how true it is that Africa has been compelled to carry the burden of a whole world's sin!)

And with him two others. Three crosses were set up that day, and one or other we must accept for ourselves. One is the cross of the sinless Redeemer, which cannot be ours. The others are the crosses of impenitence and penitence; between those two we may, indeed we must, make our choice.

St. John does not tell us that the *two others* were thieves; we know, of course, that they must be condemned criminals; it is at least likely that they were followers of Barabbas and that one of them brooded on the difference between the leader whom he had followed in a worldly insurrection and this other leader who also is condemned because He claims a Kingdom (*St. Luke* xxiii, 42).

That He was condemned on that ground is made plain by the title which Pilate wrote and put on the cross. Pilate did not miss this further opportunity to show his contempt for the Jews. He now treats Jesus as having been what alone would justify the Jews in demanding, or himself in pronouncing, the death-sentence. If He was a merely idle claimant there was no need to kill Him; let the chief priests suffer the shame of the implication that there had been an ineffectual rising against the hated but irresistible power of Rome. When they begin to protest Pilate cuts them short with a snub; he will not change what he has written to please them.

So the Lord was *lifted up* (xii, 32) and began to 'draw the nations nigh'. His reign is inaugurated. He is mounted on His throne of shame and power, the crown of glory and thorns is on His brow; and over His head is His title — the King of Israel, the King in the Kingdom of God. For so it was necessary that the Kingdom should be founded, since it must control the hearts and wills of men. 'The Son of Man must suffer.' He reigns from the Tree.

(*b*) The Distribution of Garments (23-24)

The soldiers therefore, when they crucified Jesus, took his garments and
made four parts, to each soldier a part — and his coat. But the coat was
seamless, woven from the top throughout. They said therefore to one
another 'Let us not tear it but cast lots for it, whose it shall be'; that the
scripture might be fulfilled 'They parted my garments among themselves and upon my vesture they cast lots'. The soldiers therefore did
these things.

It was a recognised custom that the soldiers who carried out
an execution should take the clothes of the condemned prisoner
as perquisites. As usual, a quaternion was charged with the
duty of execution, so they make four piles of the other garments, but decide to cast lots for the seamless coat. That the
coat is such is an illustration of the simplicity of the Lord's
attire; His 'coat' was a one-piece garment. But to the Evangelist it probably recalled the seamless coat of the High Priest,
and was felt to be appropriate to Him who offered Himself
as the one perfect sacrifice and atonement. Certainly he sees
in the behaviour of the soldiers a fulfilment of *Psalm* xxii, 18,
so that even the conduct of the soldiers is part of the divine
purpose which is being at once revealed and accomplished.

∗

(*c*) Three Words of the Crucified (25-30)

25-27. And there were standing by the Cross of Jesus his mother and the
sister of his mother, Mary the wife of Clopas and Mary Magdalene.
Jesus therefore seeing his mother and the disciple standing by whom he
loved, saith to his mother 'Woman; behold, thy son!' Then saith he to
the disciple 'Behold, thy mother'. And from that hour the disciple took
her to his own home.

There were four women by the Cross — Mary the Mother
of the Lord and her sister, Salome, the mother of the Beloved

Disciple; also Mary the wife of Clopas (brother, according to
Hegesippus, of St. Joseph) and Mary Magdalene; and among
them was the Beloved Disciple, the son of Salome, the nephew
of the Blessed Virgin and cousin of the Lord.

As the Lord looks down from the Cross He sees this group
of intimately dear friends. Especially He sees His mother and
knows how truly the prophecy of Simeon is finding fulfilment
— 'a sword shall pierce through thine own soul' (*St. Luke*
ii, 35). Also He knows that His own deepest agony is approaching — the agony which, as it passes away to be succeeded by
the calm of achievement and trust, will find expression in the
words of the Psalmist 'My God, my God, why didst thou forsake me?' (*St. Mark* xv, 34). He would not have His mother
witness that agony. He commends her to the care of her own
nephew who is His closest friend. And that disciple at once
leads her away from the scene of suffering. While he is absent
the period of darkness comes and passes; he returns to hear
the last words and to see the wondrous end.

•

28-30. After this Jesus knowing that all things are now finished, that the
scripture might be accomplished, saith 'I thirst'. A vessel was set there
full of vinegar; so they filled a sponge with the vinegar and, putting it
on a javelin, lifted it to his mouth. When therefore he received the
vinegar Jesus said 'It is finished' and having bowed his head he gave up
his spirit.

After this; the phrase does not mean that the later episode
followed the earlier immediately, but only that it was later.
In fact it was, no doubt, after the return of the Beloved Disciple,
and therefore at least three hours later than the previous Word.
The Lord knows that *all things are now finished*, as He will
Himself proclaim very shortly (30). But He cannot make that
proclamation till His parched throat is cooled and moistened.
So He says '*I thirst*', and in this again the Evangelist sees a
fulfilment — indeed he calls it an accomplishment — of
scripture, for the Psalmist had written 'When I was thirsty

they gave me vinegar to drink' (*Psalm* lxix, 21): but this reference is in the mind of the Evangelist rather than of the Lord Himself.

This Word *I thirst* is the only one of the seven which refers to the physical pain, and this is mentioned only to prepare for the great cry that follows. How impressive that though the pain of body was so great there was only this incidental allusion to it! Nor can we doubt that the very words *I thirst* carried with them for the Lord a recollection of the Cup that He had once prayed might pass from Him. He has accepted it with calm resolve; *the cup which my Father has given me, am I not to drink it?* (xviii, 11). Now He is eager to drink it to the dregs that all may be finished — *I thirst*.

Some kindly soldiers act in response; the *vinegar* or sour wine was there for the soldiers who had to keep watch. One or more of them *filled a sponge and, putting it on a javelin, lifted it to his mouth*. The true reading here is preserved in an ordinarily unimportant manuscript (the eleventh-century cursive, 476); if the sponge were attached to 'hyssop',[1] some rod or pole would still be needed to lift it. But the corruption which led to this reading is easily understood, and we need not hesitate to follow the one manuscript which tells us that a javelin was used (see Bernard *ad loc.*).

When therefore he had received the vinegar — as soon as the parching thirst of His throat was allayed — *Jesus said 'It is finished'*.

He knew *that all things were now finished* and He proclaims it to the world. This word was spoken 'with a loud voice' (*St. Mark* xv, 37; *St. Matthew* xxvii, 50; *St. Luke* xxiii, 46). Each of the three Synoptists records that mighty cry; only St. John tells us what word was uttered. *It is finished.* All that prophets had foretold; all that the Father had sent Him to do (xvii, 4); the power of sin broken; the world overcome (xvi, 33); '*It is finished*'.

---

[1] Hyssop is a plant which does not supply a strong stem, but does supply a bunch of leaves suitable for use as a ' sprinkler ': cf. Exodus xii, 22..

And having bowed his head, he gave up his spirit. So St. John refers to the words whispered with bowed head: 'Father, into thy hands I commend my spirit' (*St. Luke* xxiii, 46). His death was a voluntary act; He had *authority to lay down* His life (x, 18), and He exercises that authority. His final act is to 'give up' — of course to the Father — that spirit which was always *in the bosom of the Father* (i, 18). He goes His way to the Father (xvi, 10).

*

(d) The Spear-thrust (31–37)

The Jews therefore, since it was Preparation, that the bodies might not remain upon the cross on the sabbath, for the day of that sabbath was a great day, asked Pilate that their legs might be broken and that they might be taken away. The soldiers therefore came and brake the legs of the first and of the other who was crucified with him. But having come to Jesus, when they saw that he was already dead, they did not break his legs, but one of the soldiers with a spear pierced his side and forthwith came there out blood and water. And he who hath seen hath borne witness, and true is his witness and he knoweth that he saith things that are true that ye also may believe. For these things came to pass that the scripture might be fulfilled 'A bone of him shall not be broken'; and again another scripture saith 'They shall look on him whom they pierced'.

The law forbids that criminals should remain on the cross after sunset (*Deuteronomy* xxi, 23); and this was specially urgent if at that sunset the Sabbath began so that another twenty-four hours must elapse before they could be buried; if the Sabbath were the *great day* of a feast the urgency was all the greater. But the Roman custom, while burial on the same day was not forbidden, was to leave the corpse on the cross as a deterrent to others. So Pilate's leave was necessary. He had not wanted to condemn Jesus to death; nor can he want trouble when the pilgrims flock into the city for the feast; so his consent is readily given. The customary way of ending the life of crucified criminals was the cruel one of breaking their legs with a heavy mallet, when the shock would cause the death which exhaustion had brought near. The soldiers break the legs of the other two, whom we must therefore suppose to be still alive at the time; but they find Jesus already dead. One of them, perhaps to make doubly sure, thrusts a spear into His side. *And forthwith came there out blood and water.*

The Evangelist attaches great importance to this strange event. He seems to regard it as in some way a sign that the Lord, though truly dead, is yet also alive. Probably also he thinks of the blood as the Blood of the New Covenant, shed upon the Cross but also given and received in the Eucharist, and of the water as the symbol of spiritual life (iv, 14; vii, 37–39) and the cleansing element of Baptism; so that from the sacrifice of the Cross flows the grace of the two great sacraments.

The Evangelist is careful to insist that his record rests on the testimony of an eyewitness — *he who hath seen hath borne witness*; that this testimony is reliable — *and true is his witness*; and that the eyewitness himself, the Beloved Disciple (who must therefore have been still alive when the Elder wrote the Gospel), *knoweth that he saith things that are true; that ye also* — like that apostle — *may believe.*

Then the Evangelist adds his own tracing in these events of the fulfilment of scripture, and consequent new understanding of the events themselves. As the seamless coat suggested the High Priest, so the unbroken bones suggest the Paschal Lamb (*Exodus* xii, 46); He is Himself both Priest and Victim. The other reference carries us forward; for the words of Zechariah xii, 10, 'they shall look unto Him whom they have pierced', speak of a repentance of Jerusalem for the killing of that 'good shepherd whom her people have rejected and slain'.[1] Thus the present episode points to the time when the Lord on His Cross shall indeed draw all men unto Him, even those who nailed Him there — even us who crucify Him afresh.

*

[1] George Adam Smith, *The Book of the Twelve Prophets*, p. 482.

(5) The Burial (38–42)

And after these things Joseph of Arimathea, being a disciple of Jesus, but
secretly for fear of the Jews, asked Pilate that he might take away the
body of Jesus. And Pilate gave leave. He came therefore and took his
body. And there came also Nicodemus, who came to him by night at
the first, bringing a mixture of myrrh and aloes, about a hundred pounds.
So they took the body of Jesus and wound it in linen clothes with the
spices, as is the custom for the Jews to bury. And there was, in the place
where he was crucified, a garden, and in the garden a new tomb, in
which no one had yet been laid. There, therefore, because of the Jews'
Preparation, because the tomb was near, they laid Jesus.

Joseph of Arimathea was a timid disciple, like most of us.
But he could not bear that the body of the Lord should be
dishonoured. As with many timid natures, a strong and deep
sentiment prevailed where the call of truth was insufficient.
He 'plucked up his courage' (*St. Mark* xv, 43) and begged
Pilate for the charge of the body. His request was granted,
and he superintended the taking down of the body from the
Cross (*St. Mark* xv, 46). His courage gave courage to another
similarly placed, so that the last rites were rendered by two
men who had never dared to avow themselves disciples. Yet
perhaps it was for that very reason that they were able now
to show the care and reverence for which all Christians thank
them. It would seem that this burial was regarded as pro-
visional, as it was certainly hurried. It was the impending
Sabbath which caused the haste. So that Sabbath law which
was the first occasion of a conspiracy to kill the Lord (v, 18)
determined the manner of His burial.

Had the old system and the power of darkness triumphed?

ACT V

THE DAWN

CHAPTER XX

THE conflict of Light with Darkness is finished. For a moment Darkness seemed to prevail: 'this is your hour and the power of darkness' (*St. Luke* xxii, 53). But the fight was fought out and the victory won: *It is finished* (xix, 30). The date of the triumph of love is Good Friday, not Easter Day. Yet if the story had ended there, the victory would have been barren. What remains is not to win it, but to gather in its fruits. Consequently St. John does not present the Resurrection as a mighty act by which the hosts of evil are routed, but rather as the quiet rising of the sun which has already vanquished night. The atmosphere of the story has all the sweet freshness of dawn on a spring day. Fra Angelico, in his delicious *fresco* of the appearance of the Lord to Mary Magdalene, has perfectly caught its tone and feeling.

The story is told, and the Appearances selected, so as to illustrate, as Westcott says, 'the passage from sight to faith'. The Beloved Disciple believes when he sees the grave-clothes; Mary Magdalene when she hears a well-known voice pronounce her name; the ten apostles when they see the Lord's wounds; St. Thomas when he sees those same wounds and is invited to handle them. But better than all of these is a faith that needs no such support from experiences of the senses (29). All the Appearances, as we shall see, give emphasis to what had been said: '*It is expedient for you that I go away. For if I go not away, the Comforter will not come to you, but if I depart I will send him to you* (xvi, 7). Mary is to cling to the ascended Lord, not to the Master who addresses her with physical speech; the Apostles are to receive Christ's own life-breath or spirit to be their spirit and the breath of their lives; Thomas, who reaches the first confession of full Christian faith, is pointed to an apprehension of divine truth which is independent of all external evidence. The Lord is calling His followers to enter on the transition 'from sight to faith' — from outward companionship to inward communion, from the discipleship which rests on a bodily Presence to one which is perfected in spiritual union — '*I in them, and thou in me*' (xvii, 23; cf. xiv, 20).

•

(1) THE EMPTY TOMB

1–10. But on the first day of the week Mary Magdalene cometh early, while it was still dark, to the tomb, and seeth the stone taken away out of the tomb. So she runneth and cometh to Simon Peter, and to the other disciple whom Jesus loved, and saith to them 'They took the Lord out of the tomb and we do not know where they put him'. So Peter set out and the other disciples; and they were coming to the tomb; and they began to run, the two of them together; and the other disciple ran on in front, quicker than Peter, and came first to the tomb and, peeping in, seeth lying there the linen clothes, yet he did not go in. So Simon Peter cometh also, following him, and went into the tomb; and he taketh note of the linen clothes lying, and the napkin, which was on his head, not lying with the linen clothes but apart, wrapped into one place. So then the other disciple also went in — he who came first to the tomb — and saw and believed. For not yet did they know the scripture, that he must rise from the dead. So the disciples went away again to their own homes.

It is most manifestly the record of a personal memory. Nothing else can account for the little details, so vivid, so little like the kind of thing that comes from invention or imagination.

On the first day of the week Mary Magdalene cometh early. She who is supremely the forgiven sinner, whose heart is utterly given to her Saviour, is the first to go, when the Sabbath is over, to be near by that Body of which she has twice already anointed the feet, and to which she would now aid in giving the last care of love (*St. Luke* vii, 36–50; *St. John* xii, 1–8; *St. Mark* xvi, 1). Perhaps she came with the other devoted women; but if so St. John's narrative suggests that she was before them. She comes *early* — that is to say, soon after 3 A.M. (see xviii,

28) — *while it was still dark*. But the dawn is already breaking, and she can see that something has happened; the mouth of the tomb, which had been closed by a great stone, is open; *she seeth the stone taken away out of the tomb*. She does not look further; she jumps to two conclusions — first that the Body of the Lord is no longer in the tomb, and secondly that this is because His enemies have stolen it. At once she turns and *runneth and cometh to Simon Peter, and to the other disciple whom Jesus loves, and saith to them 'They took the Lord out of the tomb and we do not know where they put him'*. She runs first to Peter, who, in spite of his denials, is still thought of as the leader, and to that other disciple who was known as the most intimate; the Greek phrasing makes it clear that they were not together and she had to run on a separate errand to each. Her message is not what she had seen, but the inference she had drawn; in her dismay she is so sure that she states it as a definite fact: *they took* — in English it would be *they came and took the Lord out of the tomb and we do not know where they put him*. This loving woman, who had anointed and kissed the feet of the Lord, identifies Him with His Body. To remove that is to remove Him; and she does not know how to show Him reverence.

There follows a very vivid description of the two disciples hurrying to the tomb. They set forth at once; as they approach the tomb they begin to run; the younger, John, gains on his comrade and reaches the tomb first. *So Peter set out, and the other disciple; and they were coming to the tomb; and they began to run, the two of them together; and the other disciple ran on in front quicker than Peter, and came first to the tomb, and, peeping in, seeth lying there the linen clothes; yet he did not go in*. The Beloved Disciple is the first to reach the tomb; but he can at first do no more than *peep in* — for this was at the date of the Gospel's writing the common meaning of the Greek word here used; a sacred awe of the Lord's burial-place holds him outside. But he sees what later he will recognise as most significant — *lying there the linen clothes*. The eager and

impulsive Simon Peter is not content to stand outside. *So
Simon Peter cometh also, following him, and went into the tomb.*
He not only *seeth* the linen clothes, but carefully observes
them: *he taketh note of the linen clothes lying, and the napkin,
which was on his head, not lying with the linen clothes, but apart,
wrapped into one place.* The Body of the Lord had, as it
would seem, passed through the winding-sheets that were
about it, so that these lay there, the upper layer having fallen
upon the lower; more significant still, *the napkin which was
on his head* had similarly fallen in upon itself and lay there,
apart — separated by the brief space where the neck had been
— *wrapped* or *heaped into one place.* It is extraordinarily
vivid, and such as no invention would devise, no freak of
imagination conjure up. Peter does not see the significance.
'Peter . . . seeth the linen clothes by themselves; and went away
to his home wondering at that which was come to pass'
(*St. Luke* xxiv, 12).

Then the Beloved Disciple, taking courage from Peter, goes
into the tomb; he saw what Peter had seen; but he grasps its
meaning. *So then the other disciple also went in — he who came
first to the tomb — and saw and believed.* Perhaps he who was
in heart nearest to the Lord had some instinct of understanding which enabled him to interpret what he saw and grasp
the truth; anyhow, the 'disciple whom Jesus loved' was the
first to believe in His resurrection.

The Evangelist adds a note to explain how it was that the
apostles needed to reach that belief by gradual stages. *For not
yet did they know the scripture, that he must rise from the dead.*
They had not learnt to apply to their Lord, as Peter would a few
weeks later, the great declaration of the Psalmist: 'Thou wilt not
leave my soul to Sheol; neither wilt thou suffer thy holy one to
see corruption' (*Psalm* xvi, 10; *Acts* ii, 27). But for the disciple
whose heart was uplifted by faith there was no more to see or to
do at the tomb than for the disciple whose heart was full of bewilderment. *So the disciples went away again to their own homes.*

∗

(2) The Appearance to Mary Magdalene

But there was one who could not leave the tomb. Mary Magdalene, having taken her despairing message to Peter and John, had returned to the tomb, and lingered there. Even though the Lord had been taken away, it was here that He had been laid; this is the place of latest association with Him.

11–18. But Mary stood by the tomb without, weeping. So as she wept, she peeped into the tomb; and she noticeth two angels in white sitting one by the head and one by the feet where had lain the body of Jesus. And they say to her 'Woman, why art thou weeping?' She saith to them 'They took my Lord and I do not know where they put him'. Having said this she turned backwards and noticeth Jesus standing, and did not know that it was Jesus. Jesus saith to her 'Woman, why art thou weeping? For whom art thou looking?' She, thinking that it is the gardener, saith to him, 'Sir, if it was thou that carried him away, tell me where thou didst put him and I will take him'. Jesus saith to her 'Mary'. She turned and saith to him in Hebrew 'Rabboni' (which means Master). Jesus saith to her 'Cling not to me, for not yet am I gone up to the Father. But go to my brethren and say to them — I go up to my Father and your Father, and my God and your God.' Mary Magdalene cometh announcing to the disciples 'I have seen the Lord' and that he said these things to her.

Mary remains at the tomb in tears; so she had wept at the tomb of her brother, Lazarus (xi, 31). Gradually her sorrow becomes tinged with wonder of what it was that the two apostles had seen when they went into the tomb; so she too looks in, peeping as John had peeped at first. What catches her attention is not the linen clothes, but *two angels in white sitting one by the head and one by the feet where had lain the body of Jesus*. The place of His Death was between two thieves; 'He was numbered with the transgressors' (*Isaiah* liii, 12; *St. Luke* xxii, 37). The place of His burial was between two angels; for God had set Him forth in His blood to be a mercy-seat — the place where God's forgiveness meets man's sin (*Romans* iii, 25).

We do ill to ask whether there was one angel (*St. Mark* xvi, 5) or two (*St. Luke* xxiv, 4). It is not to be presumed that

angels are physical objects reflecting rays of light upon the
retina of the eye. When men 'see' or 'hear' angels, it is rather
to be supposed that an intense interior awareness of a divine
message leads to the projection of an image which is then
experienced as an occasion of something seen and heard. That
divine messengers were sent and divine messages received we
need not doubt; that they took physical form so that all who
'saw' anything must 'see' the same thing we need not suppose.
Here they are the manifestation to Mary that God was intimately
active in this strange matter of the empty tomb, and was active
also to comfort the sorrow of her heart. The divine consolation
approaches her tenderly; the angels ask only why she is weeping. Her answer is to repeat the message of dismay which she
had brought to the two disciples; but she repeats it with two
little variations; now it is not 'the Lord' but 'my Lord' — not
'we do not know' but 'I do not know'. For when she first
came and found the stone removed (1) she came in company
with the other women or had been joined by them (*St. Mark*
xvi, 1). But now she is alone: *They took my Lord and I do not
know where they put him.*

As she says this, the sorrow comes upon her again in its first
fulness, and she turns away from the tomb and its angels. She
notices someone standing there; but she does not recognise Him;
probably she does not look up at Him; no doubt it is someone
who has his own business there. *She turned backward and
noticeth Jesus standing, and did not know that it was Jesus.*
He too begins, as the angels had begun, by asking the cause
of her grief — the first step towards ordinary sympathy:
Woman, why art thou weeping? But He knows the real answer,
so He adds words which show His understanding. *For whom
art thou looking?* She still does not look up or straight towards
Him; speaking with downcast face and looking away to hide
her tears, supposing that He is the gardener she says, *Sir, if
it was thou that carried him away, tell me where thou didst put
him and I will take him.* The word for 'carried away' has a
suggestion of stealing (xii, 6), but here contains no more than

a sad complaint, not a charge. Mary does not answer the question, nor indicate in any way of whom she speaks. That, in her absorption in her grief, seems to her manifest. Her one desire is to find the Lord's Body and take it where friends will pay to it the last tribute of love and honour.

Mary: the answer is her own name, spoken by a voice she knew. The earlier questions, though spoken by that voice, could not recall the old association. Her name, so spoken, reaches her heart. She turns to face the Speaker. *Rabboni:* the cry of devotion accompanies a movement as she hastens to clasp those feet which once she had bathed with tears. So she draws the first declaration of the Risen Christ. *Cling not to me, for not yet am I gone up to the Father.* The weakness to which such love as Mary's is liable is that it clings too closely to the physical form, of which the whole purpose is to express and serve the spiritual self. To her therefore this warning is appropriately given, but its meaning is for all. She must learn to love and trust and serve, even though she can no longer caress His feet or hear His voice pronounce her name. Not to the Lord as He tabernacled in the flesh, subject to all limitations of the body, is she to cling; but to the Lord in His perfect union with the Father.

So He taught her the meaning of that last appearance, the final withdrawal of His physical presence, which we call the Ascension. It was separation in one sense, for it closed the period of the first form of intercourse. But in a profounder sense it was the inauguration of a fuller union. In the days of His earthly ministry, only those could speak to Him who came where He was. If He was in Galilee, men could not find Him in Jerusalem; if He was in Jerusalem, men could not find Him in Galilee. But His Ascension means that He is perfectly united with God; we are with Him wherever we are present to God; and that is everywhere and always. Because He is 'in Heaven' He is everywhere on earth; because He is ascended, He is here now. Our devotion is not to hold us by the empty tomb; it must lift up our hearts to Heaven so that we too 'in heart and

mind thither ascend and with Him continually dwell'; it must
also send us forth into the world to do His will; and these are
not two things, but one.

Not yet am I gone up to the Father. To use the word 'ascended'
is to introduce a specialised term where a quite general one is
found in the Greek. He had spoken of Himself as *coming down
out of heaven* (vi, 38), and had balanced this by speaking of His
going up where he was before (vi, 62). He has repeatedly spoken
of 'going to the Father'. All this is here in mind. The essential
moment of His going to the Father is the consummation of
Love upon the Cross: *It is finished.* But He still subjects Himself to some measure of physical limitation that He may appear
in His Risen Body to the disciples and send them out to gather
the fruits of His triumph. *Not yet* therefore is complete that
'going' or 'going up' to the Father, which is at once the climax
of His earthly life, and the source of His disciples' power to do
wonders in His Name (xiv, 12). Alike for fulness of our love
to Him, and for fulness of His power working in us, we are to
cling, not to the Lord known after the flesh (*II Corinthians* v,
16) but to the Lord enthroned at the right hand of the Father
and active within us by the energy of His Holy Spirit.

Mary is to carry to the disciples the news of the imminent
consummation; the message is expressed in language which
emphasises communion rather than separation. *Go to my
brethren* — a new title for the disciples due to the prominence
of the thought that the Father is both His Father and ours; it
is characteristic of the days after the Resurrection; see *St.
Matthew* xxviii, 10, where also it is associated with direction
to await the Ascension — *and say to them* — *I go up to my
Father and your Father, and my God and your God.*

The command is at once obeyed. This forgiven sinner
becomes the messenger of Christ to the Apostles themselves,
declaring the Resurrection of her Lord and theirs. *Mary Mag-
delene cometh announcing to the disciples 'I have seen the Lord'
and that he said these things to her.*

*

First Appearance to the Disciples

19–23. When therefore it was evening on that day, the first day of the week, and the doors having been shut where the disciples were on account of their fear of the Jews, came Jesus and stood in the midst, and saith to them 'Peace to you'. And having said this he showed both his hands and his side to them. Filled with joy therefore were the disciples on seeing the Lord. So Jesus said to them again 'Peace to you. As the Father hath sent me, I also send you.' And having said this he breathed upon them and saith to them 'Receive holy spirit (or breath). If of any ye forgive the sins, they are forgiven them; if of any ye hold them fast, they are held.'

When therefore it was evening on that day, — late in the evening, for the two disciples who had walked to Emmaus were returned (*St. Luke* xxiv, 29, 33–36) — *and the doors having been shut where the disciples were on account of the fear of the Jews,* for no doubt the story of the empty tomb was known and the disciples might well be charged with stealing the Body — *came Jesus and stood in the midst.* We need not say that He came through the closed doors; the Evangelist does not say that; the word *came* implies no more than that at one time He was not there and at a later time He was there. But the story does imply that the Risen Body was free from some of its former limitations. He stood there among them, and spoke the familiar greeting *Peace to you.* It was a common salutation. But the disciples would recall the words: *Peace I leave to you, the peace that is mine I give to you. Not as the world gives do I give to you. Let not your hearts be troubled or dismayed* (xiv, 27). To confirm their conviction that it is He Himself, *having said this he showed both his hands and his side to them.* It was proof of identity; this, however transmuted, was the Body which had hung on the Cross and was laid in the tomb. But the scars are more than this; they are the evidence not only that what they see is the Body of Jesus, but what is the quality for ever of the Body of Him whom they know with ever-deeper understanding as the Christ: 'the Son of Man must suffer'.

The wounds of Christ are His credentials to the suffering race of men. Shortly after the end of the Great War, when its memories and its pains were fresh in mind, a volume was published under the title *Jesus of the Scars, and Other Poems* by Edward Shillito. The poem from which the title was taken stands first in the book and is headed by the text, 'He showed them His hands and His side':

> If we have never sought, we seek Thee now;
>   Thine eyes burn through the dark, our only stars;
> We must have sight of thorn-pricks on Thy brow,
>   We must have Thee, O Jesus of the Scars.
>
> The heavens frighten us; they are too calm;
>   In all the universe we have no place.
> Our wounds are hurting us; where is the balm?
>   Lord Jesus, by Thy Scars, we claim Thy grace.
>
> If, when the doors are shut, Thou drawest near,
>   Only reveal those hands, that side of Thine;
> We know to-day what wounds are, have no fear,
>   Show us Thy Scars, we know the countersign.
>
> The other gods were strong; but Thou wast weak;
>   They rode, but Thou didst stumble to a throne;
> But to our wounds only God's wounds can speak,
>   And not a god has wounds, but Thou alone.

Only a God in whose perfect Being pain has its place can win and hold our worship; for otherwise the creature would in fortitude surpass the Creator.

Filled with joy therefore were the disciples on seeing the Lord. His promise was fulfilled: *I shall see you again, and your joy no man taketh from you* (xvi, 22). We imagine a few moments of silent rapture at this proof that their Lord is alive and that their fellowship with Him is renewed. Then He repeats His greeting and goes on to give the apostolic commission and at the same time to suggest the new form which must now be taken by the fellowship of the disciples with Himself: *Peace to*

you. As the Father hath sent me, I also send you. Still the
position of Mediator is asserted; the Father : the Son : : the
Son : the Apostles. We are called to share His apostolic
ministry; but no other among men, however inspired, becomes
the equal of Christ; for His mission is from the Father without
intermediary, and ours is from the Father through Him. But
as there is need at times to check our sense of the dignity of
our status, so it is impossible to exaggerate the greatness of our
calling. It is to continue in the world that divine Mission of
which the inauguration was the sending of the Son by the
Father to be the Redeemer of the world. We are members of
the Body of Christ, through whom He would accomplish His
purpose. All accounts of the charge given to the disciples by
the Risen Lord agree in its content; they were to go forth to
be His witnesses (*St. Luke* xxiv, 47, 48; *Acts* i, 8), to proclaim
the Gospel (*St. Mark* xvi, 15), to make disciples of all the
nations (*St. Matthew* xxviii, 19), to continue the Mission of the
Incarnation (*St. John* xx, 21). For this purpose they could
rely on His presence (*St. Matthew* xxviii, 20) — the power of
the Holy Spirit (*Acts* i, 8; *St. Luke* xxiv, 49; *St. John* xx,
21).

This is the primary purpose for which the Spirit is given:
that we may bear witness to Christ. We must not expect the
gift while we ignore the purpose. A Church which ceases to
be missionary will not be, and cannot rightly expect to be,
'spiritual'.

And having said this he breathed upon them and saith to them
'*Receive holy spirit* (or *breath*). *If of any ye forgive the sins,
they are forgiven them; if of any ye hold them fast, they are held.*'
The fellowship of the old days has for a moment been renewed,
but only that it may give place to the new and still closer
fellowship which is to last for ever. He imparts to them His
own life-breath; the outward sign, helped by the play on
words, suggests that henceforth His own spiritual energy will
be within them. *Receive holy spirit.* The gift is freely offered,
but it can be refused; there is a definite act of reception. The

Lord now fulfils the promise of the Baptist concerning Him
(i, 33); He baptises His disciples, not in water which washes
away stains, but in holy spirit — the energy of a holy life in
obedience to God.

Receive holy spirit — not 'the Holy Spirit'. What is bestowed
is not the Divine Person Himself but the power and energy of
which He is the source. Earlier it had been said *not yet was
there spirit, because Jesus was not yet glorified* (vii, 39). But
now that glorification is complete, and it is possible for the
new divine energy, which operates through man's response to
the manifested love of God, to begin its activity. Of this the
outstanding manifestation will be the continuance of that
divine offer of life which always (incidentally) involves judgement (iii, 17–19). *If of any ye forgive the sins, they are forgiven
them; and if of any ye hold them fast, they are held.* The body
of disciples, being the Body of Christ, and being filled with that
holy spirit which Christ has breathed into them, carries forward
His work of pronouncing God's forgiveness of sin. The
authority here bestowed is given to the body, not, or at least
not necessarily or certainly, to any one member of that body;
and it is given in connexion with the bestowal of holy spirit —
the energy and power of God the Holy Spirit in the fellowship
and in the heart. The principle is clear. To the Church as the
fellowship of the Spirit is given the authority of Christ Himself
as Pardoner and Judge. But only so far as the Church in and
through its members fulfils the condition — *Receive holy spirit*
— can it discharge this function.

In practice the Church must do this through appropriate
organs, and the parallel charge to St. Peter included in the
Matthaean account of his confession at Caesarea Philippi (*St.
Matthew* xvi, 19) supports the practice of the Church in trans-
lating this commission from the plural to the singular in the
Ordination of Priests. But

the fundamental Christian Ministry is the Ministry of Christ.
There is no Christian Priesthood or Ministry apart from His.
His priestly and ministerial function is to reconcile the world to

God in and through Himself, by His Incarnation and by His 'one sacrifice once offered', delivering men from the power of sin and death.

The Church as the Body of Christ, sharing His life, has a ministerial function derived from that of Christ. In this function every member has his place and share according to his different capabilities and calling. The work of the Church is to bring all the various activities and relationships of men under the control of the Holy Spirit, and in this work each member has his part. The particular function of the official Ministry can only be rightly understood as seen against the background of this universal ministry.[1]

Every Christian has a responsibility for drawing others to Christ, and for declaring, if occasion so require, the forgiveness which the divine love offers to all who come in penitence. It is evidently appropriate that this, like other functions, should be representatively exercised by those appointed for the purpose; none the less the minister so appointed, when he pronounces absolution, does it, not in the name of his fellow-Christians, but in the name of Christ; for it is only in His name and by His commission that it can be pronounced at all.

If the gift of holy spirit has been fully and perfectly 'received', the individual Christian so endowed would have perfect discernment and his judgement in forgiving sins or 'retaining' them would be that of God Himself. But only the Lord Himself was able to receive the gift of the Spirit in that fulness. The individual priest, who has been bidden at his Ordination to receive that gift, must do his best according to the measure in which he has in fact received it. The Church, for its temporal purposes, must act as though the judgement of the priest were that of God, and must warn a sinner who has been judged impenitent and to whom absolution has been refused, not to share in the Holy Communion. But the Church does not suppose that its ministers are infallible, or declare

[1] *Doctrine in the Church of England* (The Report of the Archbishops' Commission on Doctrine), p. 114.

that one who is excluded from the Christian fellowship on earth is certainly excluded from the fellowship of Christ in Heaven. And the priest, though he rightly warns those who approach him that they need to 'receive' the benefit of absolution, and that this is only possible so far as their penitence is real, will not so far trust his own 'reception' of the gift of the Spirit as to refuse to pronounce absolution unless the lack of penitence is very evident. For the ministry which he has received is not essentially a ministry of judgement; it is essentially a ministry of reconciliation, and of judgement only incidentally, to those who refuse to be reconciled.

*

THE APPEARANCE TO THOMAS

24–29. But Thomas, one of the Twelve, called Didymus, was not with them when Jesus came. So the other disciples began to say to him 'We have seen the Lord'. But he said to them, 'Unless I see in his hands the print of the nails and put my finger into the print of the nails, and put my hand into his side, I shall in nowise believe'. And after eight days again his disciples were within and Thomas with them. Jesus cometh, the doors having been shut, and stood in the midst and said 'Peace to you'. Then he saith to Thomas 'Bring hither thy finger and see my hands; and bring thy hand and put it into my side, and do not become unbelieving but believing'. Thomas answered and said to him 'My Lord and my God'. Jesus saith to him 'Is it because thou hast seen me that thou hast believed? Blessed are they who saw not and have believed.'

So doubting Thomas receives the 'sign' which was refused to enquiring Pharisees — e.g. *St. Mark* viii, 11, 12. Why are they differently treated? Of course it is because the Pharisees did not want to believe, and if they had been convinced by a 'sign from heaven' they would have been unwilling adherents, not truly disciples at all. To give them the sign would be to yield to the temptation typified by the throwing of Himself down from the pinnacle of the Temple. Their demand proceeded from ill-will; it was necessary first to cure that ill-will. Nothing can be more remote from discipleship than a man who should suppose the Gospel to be true while wishing that it were not.

The doubt of Thomas, on the other hand, proceeded from loyalty and good-will. He was utterly devoted. It was he who had said *let us also go that we may die with him* (xi, 16). But he was rather literal-minded; it was he who said *We know not whither thou goest: how know we the way?* (xiv, 5). He could not dare to believe the tremendous news; and, after all, the other disciples were equally unable to believe at first (*St. Luke* xxiv, 11). He was not present when on the evening of the first Easter Day the Lord appeared to the ten apostles and, perhaps, to other disciples assembled with them; and when they tell him, he still refuses to believe. It is natural to the prosaic temperament to demand certainty as a condition of self-committal. His negative is very strong: *unless I see in his hands the print of the nails and put my finger into the print of the nails, and put my hand into his side, I shall in nowise believe* — or — *there is no chance of my believing.* Such vigour of disbelief plainly represents a strong urge to believe, held down by common sense and its habitual dread of disillusionment.

The Lord waits till all the associations of the earlier scene can again be present. Again it is the first day of the week — the resurrection-day. Again the disciples are assembled behind closed doors. Again the Lord suddenly stands in the midst with His salutation *Peace to you.* Then at once He turns to Thomas and shows His knowledge of His disciple's heart. Thomas is offered precisely the test which he had demanded; but he does not avail himself of it. He does not touch the marks of the wounds; but at once he leaps to the first confession of true Christian faith: *My Lord and my God.*

The disciples could not maintain themselves at that level. The full doctrine of the Deity of Jesus is not apparent in the speeches recorded in Acts. But St. Stephen grasped this truth devotionally, when he commended his spirit to the Lord Jesus as to God (*Acts* vii, 59); and there was, apparently, no sense that St. Paul was departing from the original Gospel as he developed his Christology. The Church of Jerusalem was perplexed and troubled about him in many ways, but not in this. Gradually we watch the Church moving towards a well-grounded assurance of that truth which St. Thomas reached in the exaltation of his sudden deliverance from obstinate gloom to radiant faith.

Do not become unbelieving but believing. He was not an unbeliever, in the sense of distrusting the Lord who had been his Master. But he was on the way to this through his fixed refusal to believe the new revelation of that Lord. Let him reverse the process of his mind, and instead of moving towards unbelief, move towards full belief.

And so he did. But he must not be left to suppose that the real cause of his new and full belief is the granting of his desire for a test, even to the limited extent to which he had availed himself of what was offered. He had demanded sight and touch; the Lord has offered Himself to both; Thomas does not seek to touch. He has seen; that is enough. But that is not the real cause of his belief, any more than a similar wonder had been the cause of Nathanael's belief long ago (i, 50): *Is it because thou hast seen me that thou hast believed?* Do you really suppose that the ground of your faith is your experience in this moment? No; of course not; it is grounded in that loyalty which made you ready to share your Master's journey to death. This moment has done no more than release a faith which was ready, if it could find an occasion, to burst its inhibitions.

Yet it is true that the most blessed state is that of a faith which has no inhibitions to burst through. Just as it is best to believe that Christ is in the Father and the Father in Him by a direct apprehension of the Deity manifest in Him, whereas to believe *for the works' sake* is a second-best (xiv, 11), so it is most blessed to be able to believe in His Deity and triumph over death by direct apprehension, because as we dwell with Him we behold His glory: *blessed are they who saw not and have believed.*

St. Peter wrote to Christians who, like ourselves, had had no opportunity to see the Lord, and used the expression 'Whom, not having seen, ye love; on whom, though now ye see him not, yet believing, ye rejoice greatly with joy unspeakable and full of glory' (*I Peter* i. 8). We have not seen. Do we believe? Do we love? Can we claim the blessing — the 'joy unspeakable and full of glory'?

•

THE CONCLUSION

30-31. Many other signs truly did Jesus in the presence of the disciples, which have not been written in this book. But these have been written that ye may believe that Jesus is the Christ, the Son of God, and that believing ye may have Life in his name.

St. John has not attempted to give a complete account of the Lord's life. There was much that He did which His disciples saw, and much of this had been already recorded. (The Fourth Evangelist was certainly familiar with our Second and Third Gospels.) And nearly everything He did was a 'sign'; that is to say, it was an expression of a spiritual truth or power, to which it pointed. Among all the acts that might be recorded, St. John has chosen those which are written in his book, in order that we may find in them what he has found: *that ye may believe that Jesus is the Christ, the Son of God, and that believing ye may have Life in his name.*

That Jesus is the Christ, the Son of God. Peter reached this belief at Caesarea Philippi; Martha confesses it before the restoration of Lazarus to life (xi, 27). But the words mean more now; for men have 'crucified the Lord of glory', and if we preach Christ Jesus as Lord, we preach a Christ on a cross (*I Corinthians* ii, 8; *II Corinthians* iv, 5; *I Corinthians* i, 23). We are to believe that the Kingdom of God was inaugurated — for this is the function of the Christ — by the Life and

Death and Resurrection of Jesus; we are to believe that He is the Son of God, in whom we see the Father.

Believe and have life. The two go together. 'He that hath the Son hath the Life; he that hath not the Son of God hath not the Life. These things have I written unto you, that ye may know that ye have eternal Life, even unto you that believe on the name of the Son of God' (*I John* v, 12, 13). Indeed Life does not so much result from, but rather consists in the knowledge of God in His Son: *this is the eternal Life, to know thee the only true God, and whom thou sendedst — Jesus Christ* (xvii, 3).

We are to have this Life *in his name* — in His manifested nature and character. There we find it; abiding there we enjoy it.

'This is the true God and eternal Life. Little children, guard yourselves from idols' (*I John* v, 20, 21).

EPILOGUE

CHAPTER XXI

THE Gospel as originally planned is now ended, and the motive of its composition has been stated: *that ye may believe that Jesus is the Christ, the Son of God, and that believing ye may have Life in his name* (xx, 31).

Yet to end there would be in a very real sense misleading. For the work of the Lord, which is at once the ground of faith in Him and the vindication of that faith, was in one sense incomplete. The victory was won; but its fruits had still to be gathered. In respect of what the Lord actually accomplishes in the souls of men, the narrative of His earthly ministry can be no more than the record of 'all that Jesus *began* both to do and to teach, until the day in which he was received up' (*Acts* i, 1, 2). The *Book of the Acts of the Apostles* and the subsequent history of the Church tell us what Jesus went on, and goes on, both to do and to teach after the day in which He was received up. To complete the Gospel itself there is need of an indication of the principles of the Lord's activity in His Body, the Church; this is now given in two narratives, of which the former speaks of the condition on which alone the work of disciples is effectual (1–14), while the latter speaks of the condition on which alone the commission to work for Christ is given (15–22).

At the same time the opportunity is taken to answer two questions which were causing perplexity to that generation for which the Gospel was originally written. The first of these concerned the position in the Church occupied by St. Peter from the earliest days after the Ascension (*Acts* i, 15, etc.); the other concerned the apparent probability that the Lord's Coming would not take place until the last of the Apostolic band was already dead, though He Himself had said, 'There be some here of them that stand by, which shall in no wise taste of death, till they see the kingdom of God come with power' (*St. Mark* ix, 1). The Kingdom of God did come with power in and through the Crucifixion (see Introduction, pp. xxxi–xxxiii). But this had not been understood. When all the Apostles were dead except the Beloved Disciple, it was natural to connect this saying with him, and to suppose that to him it had been promised that he should not die till the final consummation; and the words used to St. Peter with a very different purpose were misinterpreted in this sense. It was important to fend off the disappointment that would arise when the Beloved Disciple died and the end was not yet.

*

(1) THE LORD AND THE BODY OF DISCIPLES (1–14)
(*a*) The Work of the Disciples (1–11)

(i) *At their own Pleasure*

1–3. After these things Jesus manifested himself again to the disciples by the sea of Tiberias; and he did it in this way. There were together Simon Peter, and Thomas who is called the Twin, Nathanael from Cana of Galilee, and the sons of Zebedee and other of his disciples two. Then saith to them Simon Peter 'I am going off to fish'. They say to him 'We too are coming with thee'. So they went out and got into the boat; and in that night they caught nothing.

In spite of the great experiences recorded in Chapter XX the disciples have not yet found the new direction for their lives. They are returned to Galilee. The only change from the old days, before ever they heard the Baptist say, 'Behold, the Lamb of God' (i, 29, 36), is that they are a company united by the fact of their discipleship. Here are Peter and the sons of Zebedee, as of old; one of the two unnamed is likely to have been Andrew; that makes the old quartet (*St. Mark* i, 16–19). But now there are also Thomas and Nathanael. There is nothing to do but return to the old occupations. Simon Peter, as so often, takes the lead. The word he uses is that which we have often translated 'go his way'. It expresses a completely voluntary and self-chosen action; it may be used of wilful choice or the fulfilment of a destiny, but it suggests that the 'going' is an individual act; *I am going off to fish.* The others at once decide to join: *We too are coming with thee.* So they go on their self-chosen occupation — innocent, but self-chosen. Night was the best time for fishing; but *in that night they caught nothing.* The work which we do at the impulse of our own wills is futile.

*

(ii) *At the Lord's Command*

4–11. But when dawn was now breaking, there stood Jesus on the beach howbeit the disciples did not know that it was Jesus. So Jesus saith to them, 'Children, have ye any meat?' They answered him 'No'. But he said to them 'Cast the net on the right side of the ship and ye will find'. So they cast, and no longer had they strength to draw it for the multitude of the fishes. So that disciple whom Jesus loved saith to Peter 'It is the Lord'. So Simon Peter, having heard that it was the Lord, girt on his coat, for he was naked, and cast himself into the sea. But the other disciples came in the dinghy (for they were not far from the land but about two hundred cubits) towing the net full of fishes. As soon then as they disembarked on to the land, they see a charcoal-fire laid and fish laid thereon and bread. Jesus saith to them 'Bring of the fish which ye caught just now'. So Peter went aboard and drew the net to the land full of great fishes, a hundred and fifty three. And though there were so many, the net did not break.

All *that night* they had toiled in vain. But when the early glimmer of dawn appears, they see a figure standing on the beach. It is still too dark for recognition. He hails them as any casual passer-by might do. I have kept in the translation the words of the Revised Version, *Children, have ye any meat?* But I have done this only because I cannot find a phrase which really gives the sense without falling below the dignity of the whole narrative. Bernard offers, 'Boys, you have not had any catch, have you?' which is exactly right in content but jars somewhat in tone. Anyhow, it is no more than a casual, friendly greeting, which does not in the least disclose the identity of the Speaker.

So often the message of the Lord reaches us through some experience or acquaintance reckoned at the time as ordinary and commonplace. Only afterwards, and in the light of results, do we realise what or who was really in touch with us through the apparently commonplace event or person.

When the disciples answer *No*, the Stranger's voice is heard giving a command or direction: *Cast the net on the right side of the ship and ye will find.* Advice so definite must represent knowledge, whencesoever derived; *so they cast, and no longer had they strength to draw it for the multitude of the fishes.* What is done in obedience to the Lord's command, even though He who gives the command is not recognised, results in overwhelming success.

Something convinces the Beloved Disciple, one of *the sons of Zebedee* (2), that the Stranger is the Lord. It is idle to speculate how he reached his conviction, but we notice that he who first believed the evidence of the Resurrection at the tomb (xx, 8) is he who first recognises the Lord in the figure dimly seen upon the beach. Simon Peter with characteristic impetuosity, seizes his coat and fastens it around his body, which he had stripped for working the boat and the nets, and casts himself into the sea to hurry to the shore. The other disciples, abandoning the effort to draw up their teeming net into the boat, get into the dinghy and tow the net to shore.

On arriving they find that somehow provision has been made already (9). But Jesus bids them bring of the newly caught fish; so Peter gets into the dinghy where it is beached and drags the net, now attached to its stern, to dry land. They count the fish according to custom — *a hundred and fifty three*. It is perverse to seek a hidden meaning in the number; it is recorded because it was found to be the number when the count was made. Yet *the net did not break.* The gift of God is always more than we can receive yet it never bursts the vessel which we can offer for its reception.

(b) The Lord's Gift of Sustenance

12–14. Jesus saith to them 'Come and break your fast'. None of the disciples was bold to examine him 'Thou — who art thou?' knowing that it was the Lord. Jesus cometh and taketh the bread and giveth to them, and the fish likewise. This is already the third manifestation of Jesus to the disciples after he was raised from the dead.

When His disciples have obeyed His command, the Lord Himself offers them refreshment and sustenance. By this time none is eager to ask the Stranger who He is or to demand His authority for giving them orders. (The word for 'ask' or 'examine' implies cross-examination or searching enquiry.) They know it is their Lord, and awe in His presence keeps them silent. The Lord again, as of old, is their host. It is strongly suggested that the meal He offers consists partly of what He had himself prepared and partly of what the disciples have brought to land. If so, the symbolism is true. The Lord refreshes us for His service by a gift which is in part derived from Him, in part the fruit of our own labour under His direction; but it is all His gift, for the whole fruit of our labour is His, not our own, and we only enjoy it rightly or fully when we accept it as from Him.

This is *the third manifestation*, that is, the third occasion on which the Lord was manifested; the first was Easter Day when He was manifested at the tomb (xx, 14–17), at Emmaus (*St. Luke* xxiv. 13–31), to Simon Peter (*St. Luke* xxiv, 34), to the assembled disciples (xx, 19–23). The second was a week later (xx, 24–29). This is the third. And this time St. Peter's failure will be recalled and his commission renewed.

●

(2) THE LORD AND INDIVIDUAL DISCIPLES (15–23)

(a) The Restoration of St. Peter

Before we consider the scene of St. Peter's restoration, let us recall his history as a disciple up to this point as the Evangelists, and especially St. John, bring it before us.

He did not find his own way to the Lord, nor did the Lord directly call him. He was brought by his brother Andrew. The Lord greeted him with the words *Thou art Simon son of John; thou shalt be called Rock-man* (i, 42). Rock-man was the most unsuitable name for Simon as he was at that time. *Thou art Simon;* you are our friend called Simon, whom we all know as a loyal, generous, impulsive and unreliable man. *Thou shalt be called Rock-man;* one day — not at once, but in the future — he will earn a title which speaks of strength exactly at what was his weakest point.

From that day, no doubt, Peter was a disciple, but had not yet been called to leave his livelihood to follow his Master. That came later, and the readiness with which he and others responded to the call, 'Come ye after me, and I will make you to become fishers of men' (*St. Mark* i, 17, 18) is accounted for by the earlier call and the phase of discipleship which it inaugurated.

After the difficult discourse on the Bread of Life, when *many of the disciples went back and walked no more with him,* and the Lord said to the Twelve *Do ye also want to go?* it was Peter who rallied them with the declaration, *Lord, to whom shall we go? Words of eternal Life hast thou* (vi, 67, 68).

Then there is the scene at Caesarea Philippi. In answer to the question 'Who say ye that I am?' Peter answers 'Thou art the Christ' (*St. Mark* viii, 29). This draws the declaration from the Lord that he has earned his new name: 'Thou art Rock-man, and on this rock I will build my Church' (*St. Matthew* xvi, 18). The quality which will turn Peter's weakness into strength is that on which the Church is to rest — the faith that

Jesus is the Christ of God. But when the Lord goes on to say what manner of Christ He will be — 'the Son of Man must suffer' — 'Peter took him and began to rebuke him' (*St. Mark* viii, 32). It seems incredible. He has just hailed his Master as the Christ of God; and he 'took him and began to rebuke him'. Peter acknowledges his Master as Christ, but the very quality of his loyalty leads him to protest against this notion of 'a Messiah on a cross' (*I Corinthians* i, 23). He will honour and follow his Lord; but that Lord must so behave as to deserve his honour! Deep in Peter's loyalty is a vein of self-will.

It is sadly easy for passionate loyalty to have this defect — a mortal defect, for it earns from the Lord the name of Satan (*St. Mark* viii, 33). Our passions are mostly egoistic if they rise to the fully personal level at all; the greater part of them are uncontrolled animality. But love and loyalty are personal; and when these are passionate they are as a rule possessive or self-assertive in some degree. We all need urgently the warning of Peter's failure at this point.

We find the same quality at the scene of the Feet-washing (xiii, 1-10). At first Peter wishes to refuse the service which the Lord offers. His loyalty protests. Then when he is told *If I wash thee not, thou hast no part with me* he wants more than was offered: *not my feet only, but also my hands and my head.* Loyal, yes; generous, yes; but submissive, no. The one thing he cannot do is leave the Lord alone to do what He wants. It is this same self-will at the heart of his loyalty that will lead to his great failure.

Then comes the prediction of the desertion of all the disciples. Peter is vehement; whatever others may do, he will not fail. 'Although all shall be offended, yet will not I' (*St. Mark* xiv, 29). *My life for thee I will lay down* (xiii, 37). It was true. He was ready to fight for his Master when fighting meant certain death (xviii, 10). But another test awaited him, when there would be no thrill of adventure, no hot blood, but a chill atmosphere, a mocking maid-servant, a jeering crowd — at

the hour of cock-crowing. What happened then has not yet
been wiped out.

*

15–19. So when the breakfast was over, Jesus saith to Simon Peter, 'Simon,
son of John, lovest thou me more than these?' He saith to him 'Yea,
Lord, thou knowest that I am thy friend'. He saith to him 'Feed my
lambs'. He saith to him again, a second time, 'Simon, son of John,
lovest thou me?' He saith to him 'Yea, Lord, thou knowest that I am
thy friend'. He saith to him 'Tend my sheep'. He saith to him the third
time 'Simon, son of John, art thou my friend?' Grieved was Peter
because he said to him the third time 'Art thou my friend?' And he said
to him 'Lord, all things thou knowest; thou seest that I am thy friend'.
Jesus saith to him 'Feed my sheep. Amen, Amen I say to thee, when
thou wast younger, thou girdedst thyself and walkedst where thou
wouldest; but when thou art grown old, thou shalt stretch forth thy hands,
and another will gird thee and carry thee where thou wouldest not.'
— (And this he said signifying by what manner of death he should
glorify God; and having said this he saith to him) — 'Follow me'.[1]

The Lord has by a 'sign' illustrated the blessing which rests
on work done in obedience to His command. He has refreshed
His friends with sustenance which is, in part, the product of
their own labour. Then He turns to the eager-hearted follower
whose loyalty so sadly failed as a result of the self-will that was
intermingled with it. He had once said, 'Although all shall be
offended, yet will not I'; he had claimed a devotion more
sure than that of his fellow-disciples. Does he claim that still?
Simon, son of John, lovest thou me more than these? Peter says
nothing of the comparison with others; on that score he can

---

[1]Some scholars have urged that there is no distinction to be drawn between the two
words for 'love'. Thus Bernard gives a whole list of passages where they are inter-
changeable. For myself I do not believe that any two words ever have precisely the same
meaning; there is always some difference of tone or suggestion. But, whether that is so
or not, in the passages quoted by Bernard one or the other of the two words occurs alone,
not both together. It is not reasonably conceivable that both should be used together,
and that with an alternation which challenges attention, if their meaning is quite the same.
Andrew Bradley remarks that for many purposes the two words 'steed' and 'horse'
mean the same thing; but if they are used together, their difference becomes evident, and
to transpose them may have a ludicrous result: e.g.

'Bring forth the steed.' The steed was brought.
In truth he was a noble horse.

So it may be with the two words used here. I have alluded to the distinction in com-
menting on xvi, 27. But while I think the distinction is relevant there, where only one
word is used, I have no doubt about it here where both are used.

make no claim. Nor does he claim to love his Lord with that
self-forgetful love which Christ had made known to men and
to stand for which the Greek word — Agapē — had been
drawn out of its commonplace obscurity. Human love is a
tainted thing, tinged with lust or with the possessiveness which
is self-will and is the spring of jealousy. The words commonly
used for love are not free from those associations. So this
word which had no bad suggestiveness because it had none at
all was used to stand for the pure and the holy love of God as
Christ disclosed it, to gather from that disclosure its associations and suggestions. Peter will not use this word of himself;
he uses the word of simple friendship; *Yea, Lord, thou knowest
that I am thy friend.* That at least, in spite of everything, he
can claim. Because he can make that claim, the commission
can be given: *Feed my lambs.*

Then the Lord repeats the question, but this time without
any addition of comparisons. Whether more or less than
others, does Peter love his Lord? *Simon, son of John, lovest
thou me?* Peter still gives the same answer: *Yea, Lord, thou
knowest that I am thy friend.* And again the commission is
given: *Tend my sheep.*

Once more the Lord questions Peter, and this time he
changes the form of question and adopts Peter's own word:
Simon, son of John, art thou my friend? Is even that true?
Peter was grieved, not only because, recalling the threefold
denial, the Lord puts His question for the third time, but also
because this time He questions even that lesser claim which
Peter had made. He pleads not only the Lord's unerring knowledge of what is in him, but his own manifest sincerity: *Lord,
thou knowest all things; thou seest that I am thy friend.*

Thou seest; elsewhere I have translated this Greek word
'recognise'. In the other two answers, and here in the first
phrase, Peter uses the word that stands for knowledge of facts
or truths; here he uses the word for acquaintance and appreciation. Before the Lord is His devoted, loyal and deeply penitent
disciple: *thou seest that I am thy friend.*

We too have often failed our Lord; we stand before Him ashamed and penitent. Can we say with Peter's confidence *Thou seest that I am thy friend*? If we can, the commission to do the Lord's work may be given to us. We may not be able to say that we love Him with love like that which He has shown to us; but we must be able to say 'I am thy friend'. We must have taken our stand on His side, with full intention to be constant in our devotion. We may fail through weakness; but if that be all we shall hear Him saying, *Let not your hearts be troubled. Trust God and trust me* (xiv, 1). If we can sincerely say we are His friends, He is ready to let us serve Him by serving His people.

The Lord's questions follow a declining scale: *Lovest thou me more than these? — Lovest thou me? — Art thou my friend?* But the commissions follow an ascending scale: *Feed my lambs — Tend my sheep — Feed my sheep.* The change of expression shows that some change of meaning is intended. *Feed my lambs:* the first charge is to supply the needs of the young of the flock — a task of infinite responsibility, but not, as spiritual work is reckoned, conspicuously difficult, for the lambs are ready to accept the sustenance offered to them. *Tend my sheep:* the second charge is to exercise general guidance of the flock, including its mature members, a task for one of greater experience than the first. *Feed my sheep:* the third charge is the hardest — to supply the needs of the mature members of the flock; for it is less easy to discern their needs than those of the 'lambs', and they often have no knowledge of what their own needs are, or, still worse, suppose that they know when in fact they do not.

My sheep. The words come back to mind: — *The sheep hear his voice, and his own sheep he calleth by name and leadeth them out . . . the sheep follow him because they know his voice. But a stranger will they not follow, but will flee from him, because they do not know the voice of strangers . . . the sheep that are mine hear my voice, and I know them, and they follow me* (x, 3, 4, 5, 27). Whether we seem to His sheep their shepherds or

strangers will depend on whether they can recognise our voice
as His; and this in turn will depend on the reality of our claim
— *thou knowest that I am thy friend*.

Once more the familiar and solemn words are used *Amen,
Amen I say to thee*. When they were last spoken to Peter they
heralded the prediction of his denial (xiii, 38). Now they
herald the prediction of his martyrdom. Once Peter had been
wilful and head-strong. His impulses were generous, but he
followed them as much because they were his as because they
were generous. He chose his own path and walked where he
would. As the ardour of youth cools and the feebleness of age
comes on, all this will change. He will stretch forth his hands
as he gropes along unknown ways, and others will carry him
against his choice. The words as spoken foreshadow a compulsion laid upon him, but not necessarily more than this. The
Evangelist, writing with St. Peter's martyrdom in mind, sees in
them a direct reference to it. For St. Peter's hands, like those
of his Lord, were stretched out upon a cross. *When thou
shalt be old, thou shalt stretch forth thy hands, and another
will gird thee and carry thee where thou wouldest not. Follow
me*.

Follow me. A few days before the Lord had said *Whither I go
thou canst not follow me now, but thou shalt follow afterwards*
(xiii, 36). Now He says *Follow me*. For it is possible now. The
outward presence of the Lord is being withdrawn; the power
of the Holy Spirit is given and will soon take possession;
Peter, reckless and cowardly by turns, fighting in the garden
but denying in the High Priest's court, will stand forth before
the rulers of his people in the serenity of imperturbable
courage — Rock-man indeed.

Yet it is with reference, not to what he will do, but to what
others will do to him, that the Lord says with so solemn and
emphasis *Follow me*. (Is it not true that in a certain deep sense
nothing which the Lord did was so important as what others
did to Him? No doubt His endurance is what gave its quality
to the event; but His passivity is more powerful than His

acts. He reigns from the Tree.) Will Peter follow to the end?

Yes, to the very bitter end; yet even so, if the legend is trustworthy, there lingered to the end some of the old weakness which makes Peter so unfailing a spring of encouragement to most of us. The example of Paul is of little use to me; I am not a hero. The example of John is of but little more use; my love is so feeble. But Peter is a source of constant encouragement, for his weakness is so manifest, yet because he was truly the friend of his Lord he became the Prince of the Apostles and glorified God by his death.

The story tells how Peter escaped from his Roman prison the night before his martyrdom and was fleeing along the Appian Way when he met a familiar Figure bearing a cross. '*Domine, quo vadis?*' — 'Lord, whither goest thou?' 'I am going to Rome to be crucified afresh.' Peter turned and was found in his prison when the guards came for him in the morning. History or legend? We do not know. If history, then fact or dream? We do not know. The story shows that the early Church thought of Peter as still showing to the end some of the weakness of Simon, son of John; but the love of the Lord led him captive at the last.

*

(b) The Vocation of St. John

St. Peter has received his commission and his call; it is a call to follow by difficult stages to the complete offering of the will that was by nature so self-assertive. Close beside the Lord is the Beloved Disciple. Is there any call for him? The Lord, it would seem, has illustrated the command *Follow me* by the gesture of moving away from the main body of the disciples, and as Peter followed, the Beloved Disciple moved with him. So Peter turns to 'follow', and his attention is caught by the presence of this one of all their company whom they knew to be the most intimate.

20–23. Turning about, Peter seeth the disciple whom Jesus loved following — who also leaned back on his breast at the supper and said 'Lord, who is it that is betraying thee?' So having seen him Peter saith to Jesus 'Lord, this man, what of him?' Jesus saith to him 'If I will that he abide while I am coming, what is that to thee? Do thou follow me.' So this saying went forth among the brethren that that disciple would not die. Yet Jesus did not say to him that he would not die, but 'If I will that he abide while I am coming, what is that to thee?'

As the Lord moves, the Beloved Disciple has moved too; it was natural that one so intimate as the incident at the Last Supper proves him to have been, should keep close to his Master without any special command. But Peter's curiosity is aroused. His own future has been declared; what of John's?

The Lord does not answer speculative questions or satisfy curiosity. To the question 'Are they few that be saved?' His answer was 'Strive to enter it by the narrow door' (*St. Luke* xiii, 24). So when St. Peter asks about the future in store for his fellow-disciple, the reply is *If I will that he abide while I am coming, what is that to thee? Do thou follow me.* Our duty is to obey, without waiting to know what orders or promises may be given to others.

Incidentally the recalling of this episode makes it possible to explain and dissipate the rumour that St. John would survive till the expected Second Coming. Nothing of the kind had been promised. All that was said was that even if this were the Lord's intention for St. John, this was no business of St. Peter's; his business was plain: *Do thou follow me.*

Abide while I am coming. This translation exaggerates the suggestion of the original, but the suggestion is there. The Coming of the Lord is, from the time of the Passion, permanent present fact. 'He cometh with the clouds'; that is present. 'Every eye shall see him'; that is future.

So the story of this Gospel ends with a little group standing apart from the company of the disciples. It consists of three: the Lord of love; the disciple in whom self would be offered; and the disciple in whom self would be forgotten.

If we are to enter into the Life to which the Lord Jesus invites us, the self in us must be eliminated as a factor in the determination of conduct; if possible let it be so effaced by love that it is forgotten; if that may not be, let it be offered. For if we are to *come to the Father*, self must be either offered or forgotten.

•

POSTSCRIPT

(3) THE FINAL TESTIMONY

The Gospel proper is ended. The Evangelist, whom we take to be John the Elder, an intimate disciple of John the Apostle, adds a brief note of testimony to the reliability of John the Apostle's witness, which lies behind this Gospel.

24–25. This is the disciple who bears witness of these things and who wrote these things, and we know that his witness is true. And there are also other things which Jesus did, the which, if they should be written every one, I suppose that even the world itself would not contain the books written.

This is the disciple who bears witness of these things: so the Beloved Disciple is still living when the Elder composes the Gospel. *And who wrote these things;* he is the real author; and very likely himself wrote or dictated parts of what is presented in the Gospel. *We know that his witness is true.* The Elder could say this because he knew his teacher, and because he had tested and proved his witness, probably by comparison with the witness of others, certainly by the test of life and of spiritual communion with the crucified and risen Lord.

It is only part of the story that is here set forth, as was said at the close of the Gospel as first planned (see xx, 30, 31). Now the Elder, who has written till these closing sentences under the direct influence of the Apostle and has handled the sublimest themes with severe and unbroken restraint, permits himself

one touch of hyperbole: for to tell the whole story of Jesus'
love and power would exhaust the capacities of the universe.

O Lord Jesus Christ, thou Word and Revelation of the
Eternal Father, come, we pray thee, take possession of
our hearts and reign where thou hast right to reign. So
fill our minds with the thought and our imaginations with
the picture of thy love, that there may be in us no room
for any desire that is discordant with thy holy will.
Cleanse us, we pray thee, from all that may make us deaf
to thy call or slow to obey it, who, with the Father and
the Holy Spirit art one God, blessed for ever. Amen.

THE END